INDUSTRIAL
STERILIZATION

B-D TECHNICAL SERIES

Lectures on Sterilization

JOHN H. BREWER, Editor

*Industrial Sterilization: International Symposium,
     Amsterdam 1972*

G. BRIGGS PHILLIPS and WILLIAM S. MILLER, Editors

Additional titles will be announced as published.

INDUSTRIAL STERILIZATION

INTERNATIONAL SYMPOSIUM, AMSTERDAM 1972

G. Briggs Phillips and William S. Miller, editors

DUKE UNIVERSITY PRESS

DURHAM NORTH CAROLINA 27708

FOREWORD

FAIRLEIGH S. DICKINSON, JR.

President, Becton, Dickinson and Company
Rutherford, New Jersey
April, 1973

INDUSTRIAL STERILIZATION of medical materials has assumed a position of significant importance in the health care field. Not only has much of the responsibility for sterilizing medical materials been transferred to industrial organizations, but the variety and amounts of sterile materials required for health care have increased in significant proportions. In addition, we have witnessed the development of many improvements and new techniques in sterilization. Thus the field of industrial sterilization is not static but rather a continuing spectrum of improvements and modifications intended to advance the state-of-the-art and to provide more reliable, high-quality medical products.

The B-D Lectures on Sterilization, a volume issued more than a decade ago, represented at that time a good summary of the state-of-the-art of sterilization in a number of areas. Many have found this small book (recently reprinted) to be of much value. Obviously, however, new research and new technologies have advanced the state-of-the-art to the point where an up-dating is needed.

The B-D International Industrial Sterilization Symposium held in Amsterdam, The Netherlands, in September 1972, provided a forum upon which to base an up-dated book on this subject. The purpose of this Symposium was to bring together an international body of experts representing industry, governments, and health care personnel to discuss and summarize the field of industrial sterilization.

The present volume is based on the scientific papers and discussions that took place at this most important Symposium.

There can be no doubt of the responsibility falling on industrial firms, regulatory agencies, and those providing medical patient care for using every means possible for assuring the sterility of the billions of such products used annually. Particularly for the use of disposable or one-use items, total dedication is needed to the proposition that every possible measure should be taken to assure the sterility of such products. This is accomplished, I believe, in the best possible fashion when industry, government, and the users of sterile medical materials have a good understanding of common goals and objectives and when there is a good mechanism at the scientific level for the exchange of scientific information and research results.

It is my sincere hope that this book will contribute to these common goals.

PREFACE

G. BRIGGS PHILLIPS, Ph.D.

Director, Becton, Dickinson Research Center
Research Triangle Park, North Carolina

PREPREPARED MEDICINALS and devices and the use of disposables have revolutionized the practice of medicine and ushered in a new age in medical care throughout the world. The responsibility for sterilization has largely shifted from the users of medical materials to the manufacturers who sell and distribute them. Concomitantly, government bodies are meeting the need to set standards and to regulate the manufacture and distribution of sterile medical materials. The users of these materials, in addition, have assumed a responsibility not only to transmit criteria and requirements to the manufacturer but also to use these materials and devices in a useful and correct manner. This triad—industrial firms, regulatory agencies, and the community—working in cooperation assures that sterile products at the moment of their use will remain sterile and safe for the ultimate beneficiary—the medical patient.

This volume on industrial sterilization includes representative contributions from those involved in the production, regulation, and use of sterile medical materials. Although all sterilization methods are not reviewed, the subjects covered are considered to be among those of the greatest interest to persons involved in the industrial sterilization of medical devices and their use or the control of these processes.

Presented in this volume are dissertations on selected aspects of both classical and newer methods of achieving sterility, including heat, radiation, ethylene oxide, and formaldehyde. Newer concepts for sterilization such as those represented by the combination of heat with radiation and the use of formaldehyde liberating substances in carrier materials are also presented. This volume pays particular attention to modern-day methods of controlling sterilization processes and to methods of testing for contamination prior to sterilization. The impact of the pre-sterilization contamination loading and its effects on the sterilization process are discussed, as well as modern methods of qualifying and internally controlling routine sterilization procedures in the manufacturing situation. Included also is information on methods of validating sterility, particularly on the use of microbial spores as indicators of sterility. While this volume is not a handbook of regulatory requirements and government guidelines, the view of regulatory representatives from several countries provide the reader with a sampling of the thinking of various governments on regulatory matters. Taken as a whole, these papers illustrate the need for international cooperation and standardization in this area.

An important segment of this book is the information contributing to our general knowledge on sterilization made by the United States Aerospace Program. The research and developments reported by the National Aeronautics and Space Administration has provided a valuable catalog of information useful to those interested in industrial sterilization.

This volume, as well, provides a storehouse of information on the effects of sterilization procedures on certain items being sterilized. The effects of ionizing radiation on various plastics are discussed, as well as the residuals left in plastics after sterilization with ethylene oxide. Included also is the important subject of packaging materials used for medical devices covering information on the types of materials available, their basic characteristics, and potential uses.

From the point of view of the users of sterile medical materials, the book provides important information as to how sterile goods should be handled in the hospital and provides helpful information for industry concerning the hospital's requirements for such goods.

It is clear, as illustrated by the content of this book, that a common philosophy of excellence by all concerned is needed for adequate quality sterile medical materials. This depends in no small measure upon the development of good channels of communication and understanding. It is not merely a question of the conduct and application of new knowledge gained through research or of the blind application of regulations. Rather, when communication and understanding exist, the common goal of better serving the health care needs of the nations is more easily accomplished.

The technology of sterilization is obviously moving fast, and new discoveries and methods needed to improve the end products should be put to use where feasible. This book, as well as many other activities and developments promulgated by industrial firms, illustrates the medical industry's realization and acceptance of the fact that responsibility goes together with involvement in the provision of health care products. Industry's obligation not only to assure the sterility of its products, but to encourage communication and cooperation among all elements concerned with the products is clear.

CONTENTS

INDUSTRIAL
STERILIZATION

PART ONE

Biological Control

1

Industrial Sterilization Control

WILLIAM S. MILLER, PH.D.

Director
Biological Safety and Control Department
Becton, Dickinson Research Center

INTRODUCTION

THE INDUSTRIAL manager faced with sterilization of a quarter million medical devices has a totally different problem from the hospital nurse who must sterilize a dozen instruments. The difference is not entirely due to numbers of items or size of the respective sterilizers. The industrialist has the advantage of great uniformity in his items. Each is of identical materials and design. Each item is as identical as manufacturing technology allows and is correctly packaged. His sterilizer has been used repeatedly with a similar product load and is operated by experienced people who may have no other major duties to detract their attention in the correct operation of the vessel.

Many times, however, the opposite is true in, for example, the hospital operation. The sterilizers may be new, or modified without recertification, personnel may be relatively inexperienced, and loads may be unique. Further, there probably has not been an extensive investment in total sterility control. The net result is that the manufacturer has a far better assurance of sterility than the hospital or clinic. Nevertheless, it is primarily to the former that inquiries and probing questions regarding assurance of sterility are directed. This is as it should be for several valid reasons. First, an error in sterilization processes at the industrial level can affect large numbers of patients. Second, the industrial producer is often unknown to the buyer, at least so far as his processes, controls, facilities, and personnel are concerned.

Listed below are some typical questions presented to us by hospital experts relative to industrial experience and practices. Each manufac-

turer can add significantly to this list from inquiries by his own marketing contacts.

1. What steps are taken to assure the adequacy of sterilization cycles
    as related to resistance of organisms found on products?
2. What policies govern proper use of biological indicators in your
    sterilization cycles?
3. Do you allow for slow growers on products after ETO-exposure?
4. What do you know about duration of sterility of items during shelf
    storage?
5. What work assures adequacy of culture media used to verify product
    sterility?
6. What is the likelihood for development of package impermeability
    due to desiccation before sterilization?
7. What possibilities are there for the occurrence of desiccation and,
    therefore, enhanced resistance of organisms on medical products
    before you sterilize them?
8. What can you do to alleviate the hospital's concern over the actual
    practices, policies, and problems of the medical device industry?

It is the purpose of this article to indicate the microbiological control
policies and procedures that are followed by Becton, Dickinson. It is
hoped that the description and analysis will not only be informative in
answering some of the questions of users of sterile disposable medical
products, but also provide guidelines useful to others.

GOALS AND ORGANIZATION

The general goal of our control program is to market no products
labeled sterile that are contaminated with viable organisms. This we all
recognize is an absolute, and we can expect only an asymptotic approach
to this goal. If one deals with literally billions of items per year, there
is a possibility for some minute number to be contaminated. Judging
by recent discussions among sterilization experts, there is a desire to
assure that the probability of sterility for medical devices is at least
one million to one. Nevertheless, the goal remains absolute sterility and,
therefore, virtually no control is disregarded that can move us closer,
without unreasonable cost impact.

Sterilization control begins with a corporate organization that is
independent of divisions or profit centers. The organization in Becton,
Dickinson is called Microbiological Quality Control (MQC) and is one

organizational element of Corporate Quality Assurance (see Figure 1). Other elements are concerned with control of electrical, chemical, or physical characteristics of products. The MQC has authority over sterilization, sterility tests, and all related areas in manufacturing plants. In addition, MQC also oversees all other microbiological quality of products, but these will not be discussed here.

For sterility control, the department operates through a plant bacteriologist who has laboratory and personnel resources for all control

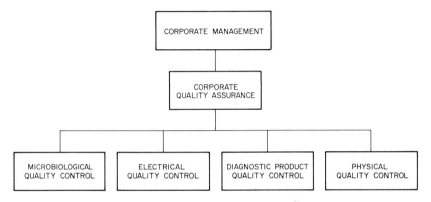

Figure 1   Organization of Corporate Quality Assurance.

work required in his particular environment. The chief of this unit reports only administratively to his plant manager. He is subordinate to Corporate MQC with respect to the microbial control policies and general procedures which he follows (Figure 2). On the other hand, he is obligated to his plant manager with respect to resources allocation, control status, reports of significant problems, and activity reports. In this way, both the corporate line of technical authority, providing autonomy from production pressures, and the plant line of communication, providing management with technical status, advice, and costs, are satisfied. Obviously, differences of opinion between plant control and plant management occur relative to the control programs. When this occurs, the profit center has recourse to the Corporate Director of Quality Assurance. Normally, differences are resolved at this level. In the rare occasion when the solution is debatable, there is not an arbitrary ruling by the Director of QA, but final judgment is sought from an executive board composed of top management officials in the company.

The MQC Department of Corporate Quality Assurance is the nerve center of the company sterility control program. It is from this center

that policies, decisions, consulting services, and training activities issue.
In addition to the technical communications with the division and plant
personnel, a laboratory capability is maintained at the corporate level.
This resource is committed to direct support of profit center needs.
These include:

1. Technology development for plant laboratory use.
2. Production and quality control for all biological indicators used
   throughout the company.
3. Plant bacteriologist training programs.
4. Services for divisions on product development or production problems related to biological control.
5. Control testing services for divisions where unique knowledge,
   equipment, or procedures exist only in the corporate laboratories.

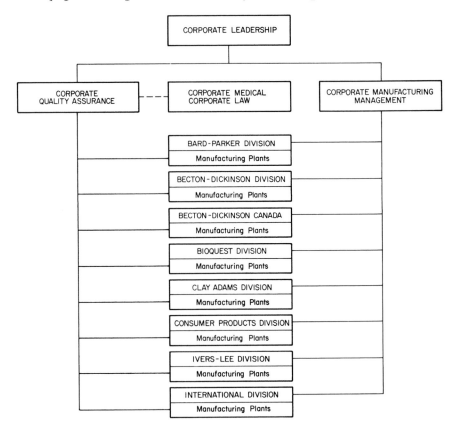

Figure 2 Authority relationship of corporate quality assurance to manufacturing
elements.

In addition to these functions, the MQC labs are continually involved in a product audit program. Samples of products are obtained from plant warehouses. These are subjected to laboratory evaluations for verification of sterility or other microbiologic claims. A number of other functions of the corporate laboratory staff of MQC are as follows:

1. Complaint investigations.
2. Review and approval of plant control specifications.
3. Preparation of manuals and other guidelines.
4. Collaborative control studies with regulatory agencies (FDA, EPA, USP) or industrial associations.

Essentially, then, the corporate laboratories carry out responsibilities related to the basic control programs for products in the plants. In addition, however, the microbiologic talents gathered for this purpose are applied also to new plant or new process concepts from the standpoint of biological control. Also, the corporate talents are applied as available on a lower priority to divisional problems when there is no other immediate capability available. Examples would be in the development or selection process for a new germicide product or a bacterial filter component of a product. The latter function reduces the overall company investment in separate divisional laboratories and personnel for certain product development activities and also reduces the need to seek laboratory contracts. It also results in dissemination of findings among all interested divisions because of a broad knowledge by MQC of the total company needs.

One means of economizing on microbiological control is by establishing the more elaborate and expensive test systems only in the corporate laboratories, thus eliminating duplication in several divisions. For example, aerosol challenge equipment and procedures have been developed by the MQC laboratories to test candidate packaging materials, or complete packages (2). The operation of this system requires capabilities for producing standardized bacterial cultures, aerosol technology, including disseminations and sampling, containment facilities to prevent laboratory contamination, and, of course, personnel who have the training and time to engage in these investigations. This apparatus is employed only by the Corporate MQC laboratories and is utilized as a standard for determining microbial penetration of packaging. In the plants, in-process tests are restricted to a charcoal recontamination system which is a noncontaminating, visual test procedure that is highly reproducible. It can be calibrated by the microbial aerosol method, but it is more easily and economically adapted to the manufacturing situation.

Another example of unique capabilities in the corporate laboratories is concerned with germicide evaluations. In the United States, the government tests required for commercial germicides are dependent upon the intended use of the material and on the label claims. For example, the Environmental Protection Agency requires specific tests for hospital germicides used on devices. A manufacturer's claims for activity against certain microorganisms often result in additional specific tests. The Food and Drug Administration, which controls germicides used on the body, may have other control requirements. The Corporate MQC labs, therefore, are the logical center for knowledge and materials for the conduct of all tests for which the corporation is responsible. Only selected procedures are taught to plant microbiologists as needed in their busy, complex specific programs.

NEW PRODUCT DESIGN REVIEW

The control of new products begins with a discussion of the product concept by the responsible division engineer and corporate level personnel. This discussion follows the transmittal of a notification form to the joint attention of the Director, Quality Assurance and the Corporate Medical Department. This form, required by corporate policy, provides a brief description of the proposed product from the standpoint of medical or quality assurance interests. The forms are routed through the organizational elements controlled by each director in order to determine the necessary control requirements.

The Medical Department interests include consideration of evidence for safety, efficacy, and reliability of the product in the planned medical environment. Accordingly, the Corporate Medical Office will review available data, establish new requirements, and monitor any necessary clinical trials.

For the microbial control interest, there is consideration of the following:

1. Proposed materials.
2. Product configuration.
3. Sterilization possibilities.
4. Pyrogenic potential due to microbial flora.
5. Proposed packaging materials, seals, printing modes.

6. Regulatory requirements.
7. Related product history.

The results of the review by the Microbiological QC function will result in the following:

1. Review of records for compatibility of materials in previous applications with the proposed method of sterilization.
2. Conduct of laboratory experiments to determine effects of sterilization on materials.
3. Laboratory scale experiments to evaluate sterilizability and sterility test procedures if materials, or configuration, differ from previous experience.
4. Review of manufacturing plans to pinpoint potential trouble areas where large contamination levels would be imposed.
5. Review of planned packaging material for previous experience related to penetrability of sterilizing gases, reliability of seals, tamper-proof protection, and protection against microbial penetration during storage under normal conditions by the user.

Many of the questions are actually resolved by the product engineer before presenting his plans to the corporate control groups. The degree of resolution depends, of course, on his experience as well as on the novelty of his product and its materials. It is our goal, however, to make use of all available information in order to maximize product safety at minimum cost. This can be done by the earliest possible definition of control problems or requirements.

During the initial new product review process, the physical quality control staff enters into the sterility control analysis. The requirements in terms of physical or chemical characteristics necessary to assure the biological property of the product are noted for future manufacturing specifications. This would include, for example, the weight, type, and porosity of paper packaging; or the specifications of materials subjected to experimental sterilization programs in order to assure that results are applicable in later manufacturing. The physical QC staff also provides competent and authoritative opinions as to the effects of the proposed sterilization alternatives on the product or on package materials or on critical properties such as seals.

It is important to bear in mind that the requirements developed in these interactions between divisional product development groups and the corporate control personnel become mandatory. The authority of the latter is established by corporate policy directives. Therefore, the system not only provides for impartial recommendations to produce products consistent with design characteristics, but also assures authority to implement those recommendations.

INCORPORATION OF PRODUCTS INTO MANUFACTURING

Following a decision of management to initiate manufacturing of a new product, the process of control implementation begins. A most important component involves specifications for raw materials. Those related to biological control of the future products include: (1) physical property specifications; (2) toxicity criteria; and (3) microbial contamination. The physical properties of raw materials can be of great importance to biological control. For example, establishment of acceptance criteria for porosity of packaging materials provides assurance of gas penetrability for products to be sterilized by ethylene oxide, but also for protection against bacterial penetration. Because of the critical nature of this determination, therefore, it is necessary to assure the correct properties of each lot of material. The same is true in many instances with respect to toxicity. The major cause of final product toxicity is often due to inherent properties of the bulk raw materials. Therefore, toxicology is often an integral part of the acceptance process. In fact, if there is evidence that this is the only source of product toxicity, it may not be necessary to test the final products for this property.

Microbial contamination of raw materials may be of great importance to acceptance, although normal levels are easily neutralized by subsequent product sterilization. As we become more sophisticated in the estimation and control of presterilization load and base our sterilization cycles more precisely on these estimates, however, it becomes increasingly important to consider this property. As discussed below, presterilization loads in a quantitative sense play an important role in planning for ethylene oxide cycles. They also are important to radiation dosage as recommended by the IAEA (1). Indeed, the cycle employed for ^{60}Co is to some extent dependent upon the microbial viable count. It is quite conceivable, therefore, that a high count from a vendor's delivery could call for rejection on the basis of not meeting a written specification. It is expected that increasing application of count limits will be seen in the future.

In addition to raw material specifications, biological control must be applied to in-process manufacturing. Therefore, serious consideration must be given to the following:

1. Machine cleaning materials and procedures.
2. Control of atmospheric contamination in manufacturing.
3. Control of contamination by personnel in manufacturing.
4. Personnel training, abilities, and practices.
5. Sterilizer operations.

All of these requirements must be documented in detail. At Becton, Dickinson, it is normally the responsibility of the chief bacteriologist in the plant to ensure that procedures are properly recorded and implemented. The Corporate MQC Department, in addition, provides surveillance of proper attention to these matters in a periodic on-site audit.

The sterilizer operations are controlled, however, to an additional degree. Every product must be accompanied by a specification describing the detailed sterilization cycle. This document is not only internally circulated, but must be reviewed and approved by a sterilization engineer assigned to Corporate MQC. This review and authority assure consistent company practices from the standpoint of adequate sterilization dosage, physical monitoring, load density, and use of biological indicators.

Additional requirements exist in the plant for the sterility test procedures. In this case, each product has an associated specification, prepared by the plant chief bacteriologist, but reviewed and approved by the Corporate MQC staff. Again, although the conduct of tests and the supervision of the biological control activities are plant matters, the procedures related to test sample numbers, media, incubation conditions, product quarantine, product release, and so forth are part of company policies and, therefore, must be in compliance. The bacteriologist, of course, has responsibility to assure that all requirements for control of the biological products have been met and, as a result, can sign the release allowing shipment of products to occur. He also is responsible for reporting to Corporate QA any instances where the corporate requirements are not met.

Several additional areas of control exercised by MQC at the corporate level are discussed below.

PROCESS AND EQUIPMENT
CALIBRATION PROGRAMS

STERILIZER CERTIFICATION

The installation of a new gas sterilizer or significant alterations to an older unit in a plant require a test program to verify adequacy of operation both physically and biologically. This program is approved at the Corporate MQC level. The tests are conducted as much as possible under actual use conditions. Accordingly, a typical product for future operations is selected and palleted in a representative way. It is the objective then to conduct sterilization cycles with this product and concurrently to measure physical cycle parameters such as temperatures, gas concentrations, relative humidity, and pressures. Biological indicators are placed throughout the load at concentrations including one planned for normal operations and others at a concentration 100 times higher. These are recovered after sterilization, in addition to a large number of products. All are inoculated into prescribed media and incubated for 30 days. Consistency is estimated by a normal certification series of five such runs. Overall, it is the objective of these tests to certify physically and biologically that each unit of volume in the chamber will consistently sterilize the anticipated product load.

The same type of program is followed for a new autoclave, dry heat unit, or irradiation facility. Normal loads of typical products are cycled with precise physical measurements being taken throughout the facility. Sterilization is measured by tests of indicators and products for viable organisms.

CERTIFICATION OF A PRODUCT–STERILIZER
COMBINATION

It is possible to have evaluated a sterilizer with one product, yet still have inadequate conditions for sterilization of another product; that is, to have a properly operating chamber but not achieve sterilization. This is particularly true with a method such as ethylene oxide, as pointed out by R. R. Ernst elsewhere in this book. The introduction of a product having areas resistant to gas penetration will require alterations in gas concentration, exposure time, or vacuum pressures. Accordingly, the practice is followed of conducting an additional certification program for each product introduced into sterilization programs. These investigations are well designed experimental efforts, conducted along general guidelines prescribed by Corporate MQC.

These are concerned with detection of slow growers by incubation of product and biological indicator samples for 30 days in multiple media at a range of incubation conditions. A typical test requirement for product loads of > 50,000 units is as follows:

1. 20 units: Fluid Thioglycollate Medium
2. 20 units: Thioglycollate Medium
3. 20 units: U.S. Alternate Thioglycollate Medium
4. 40 units: Trypticase Soy Broth* (2 temperatures)
5. Exposed biological indicators for the particular load combination incubated at the appropriate temperatures for 30 days in Trypticase Soy Broth.

The test media are prepared as directed by the manufacturer. All containers are incubated for a minimum of 30 days and are critically examined for visible evidence of microbial growth on days 2, 4, 7, 10, 15, 20, 25, and 30 (or nearest working day). Test data are forwarded to MQC upon completion of the test for each individual run. The results of these tests determine the final approval of a cycle-product combination for routine release purposes.

STERILIZATION CYCLE ESTABLISHMENT

Becton, Dickinson has given a great deal of attention to systematic establishment of ethylene oxide cycles in order to achieve maximum product safety with minimum product cost. The procedures followed are given in some detail in the following paragraphs.

It is readily apparent to anyone who carefully studies the unknowns in establishing a sterilization cycle that some biological factors are susceptible to determination, while others must remain assumptions. Those factors susceptible to reasonable definition on the basis of laboratory tests are as follows:

1. Estimates of presterilization contamination load.
2. Estimates of maximum resistance characteristics of product contaminants.
3. Estimates of relationship of resistance of organisms on products compared to that of the biological indicator of choice.
4. Time required to kill the indicator in proposed sterilizer at the selected gas concentration and temperature.

Our approach to estimating and applying the parameters listed here

---

* BBL, BioQuest, Division of Becton, Dickinson and Company.

was presented in a paper in 1972 (3). That report presents results of sample assays for total numbers of viable microorganisms on a group of products before sterilization. The products evaluated were plastic disposable syringes in paper envelopes. The procedures and results from that study are summarized below. However, the same protocols are being followed in a number of plants with a variety of products.

Counts on devices before sterilization were determined as follows. Sixty product samples were collected from a production lot. Twenty were assayed for aerobes, 20 for strict anaerobes, and 20 for exclusive growth on Sabouraud's Dextrose Agar (SDA). All microbial testing was conducted in filtered laminar flow air by testing teams wearing sterilized clean room garments and latex gloves. Aseptic technique identical to that applied to product sterility testing was employed. Syringes were disassembled individually and immersed in 100 ml of sterile APHA phosphate buffer-Tween 80 solution in screw cap jars. Jars were placed on a reciprocating shaker and eluates were then filtered. Filters were planted and incubated for seven days as shown in Table 1. Ground rules were adopted to prevent duplication of counts. At the end of the incubation period, all colonies appearing on Eugonagar under aerobic conditions were counted. Those appearing after incubation under anaerobic conditions were subcultured aerobically. Only those confirmed as strict anaerobes were added to the product total count. In the case of SDA growth, colonies not detected or not counted on Eugonagar were counted.

Table 1 Protocol for estimating counts

Medium	Incubation condition	Temperature
Eugonagar	Aerobic	30–35 C
Eugonagar	Anaerobic	30–35 C
SDA	Aerobic	20–25 C

Package interiors were assayed by application of RODAC plates utilizing the three media and incubation conditions noted before. Results are shown in Table 2. The assays were conducted on samples from a lot that had received a minimum of 12 hr of presterilization conditioning at 50 % relative humidity and 135 F. It was found that one syringe subjected to aerobic assay had one contaminating organism. None of the 20 syringes subjected to anaerobic assay exhibited growth, nor did

Table 2 Presterilization contamination levels

SYRINGES

Organisms recovered	No. of syringes		
	Aerobic assay	Anaerobic assay	SDA assay
None	19	20	20
1	1	0	0

SYRINGE PACKAGES

Organisms recovered	No. of packages		
	Aerobic assay	Anaerobic assay	SDA assay
None	19	20	20
1	0	0	0
2	1	0	0

any of the 20 assayed for fungi exhibit growth. Assays of the interior surfaces of packages indicated one of 20 with two aerobic organisms. No recoveries were found on anaerobic or fungal media. We have found in these assays that there are no apparent relationships in the occurrence of the three classes of organisms. Thus, aerobes, anaerobes, and molds when found occur randomly.

The study has subsequently been extended over one year with assays being conducted at monthly intervals. The recoveries have remained extremely consistent for the product–plant combination. These data clearly indicate a rather reproducible maximum contamination load on preconditioned products that offers a great deal of assurance of safety if these numbers are the basis for choice of biological indicator concentration.

One approach to determination of indicator numbers is a statistical analysis of the data, to arrive at an estimate of the microbial load in a sterilization lot. Considering a sterilizer lot size of $\frac{1}{4}$ million units, it was estimated on the basis of a γ-distribution that the total microbial load would be 85,000 organisms with only one chance in one million that this number would be exceeded in a sterilizer load. If we accept these reasonable odds, our indicator numbers for a load would be about 1×10^5 spores. If, for example, 100 indicator strips were distributed throughout the load, then each should contain 1×10^3 organisms. Obviously, it is necessary to confirm the representativeness of the indicator resistance to ETO by comparison to the resistance of organisms found on products. This can be accomplished by direct comparisons of product sterility to indicator strip sterility following simultaneous exposure to an ETO cycle. For maximum information, the exposure time in the cycle should be the minimum required to kill the indicator. Then, sterility of the product indicates flora resistance equal to or less than that of the indicator organism. Obviously, careful consideration of product contamination rates must be made in selecting the number of products for the test, in order that one is assured of a valid comparison. With inadequate product numbers combined with a low natural contamination rate, one could fail to include contaminated product. There is unquestionably a need to repeat these resistance comparisons over a number of lots since there may be a resistance variation by virtue of physical protective factors. Further, it is good practice to extend these tests over seasons to detect any abnormal or seasonally unique microbial populations. It is our practice to collect product data monthly for one year. Therefore, only occasional monitoring is necessary.

The same recommendations apply, of course, to estimating total viable counts. Monthly sampling over the period of one year offers a solid data base to establish ETO cycles. This schedule would require a revision for products only infrequently produced or where wide variation in manufacturing conditions exists.

Following the confirmation of indicator resistance adequacy, it is still necessary to determine the exposure time in the manufacturing plant sterilizers that will kill the organisms on the indicator strips. In this determination, the indicators are placed in the least accessible location in the product. In a syringe, this would be between the stopper ribs. Once obtained, this information leads directly to establishment of the final cycle.

There are, of course, unknowns that work against confidence in cycles established in the way described here. These include temperature, relative humidity, gas quality and quantity, and other similar conditions that might be out of normal control. However, careful monitoring of plant conditions can eliminate gross deviations from the desired values. One obvious approach is careful control of raw materials and the automation of manufacturing procedures. Under the right conditions, products are remarkably clean before sterilization. For example, in one Becton, Dickinson plant where plastic disposable syringes are manufactured virtually automatically, it has been found that odds are 100 : 1 that only $\frac{1}{3}$ of the products or their packages bear any microbial contamination before sterilization and after preconditioning.

SUMMARY

It is apparent from the foregoing that release of sterile products is based on far more than a sterility test or, in fact, than on tests of the much more significant biological indicators. Certification and release of products as sterile are a function of satisfactory results by these criteria, but in addition, are a function of a number of other factors including:

1. A suitable product design.
2. Component control.
3. Precise manufacturing specifications.
4. Properly operating sterilizers.
5. In-process quality control.
6. Biological certification of the product cycle.
7. Presterilization load control.

The implementation of this program has provided a high degree of confidence in the biological properties of Becton, Dickinson products. While the cost is significant, it is well to weigh this against health costs to the unprotected customer.

References

1. Berry, R. J. 1967. International Atomic Energy Agency recommended code of practice for radiosterilization of medical products. I.A.E.A. (Vienna), Proc., pp. 423–431.
2. Miller, W. S. 1972. A system for testing integrity of sterile product with aerosols. Presented at the IVth International Symposium on Aerobiology, Technological University of Twente, Enschede, The Netherlands, Sept. 4–7, 1972.
3. Miller, W. S. 1972. Establishment of ethylene oxide sterilization cycles. Bull. of the Parenteral Drug Association **26**(1): 34–40.

2

Biological Indicators and the Effectiveness of Sterilization Procedures

THOMAS J. MACEK, PH.D.

Director of Revision
The United States Pharmacopeia

INTRODUCTION

THE PROCEDURE for sterilizing a drug product, a surgical aid, or a medical device is determined largely by the nature of the product. The objective for sterilization of any article is to bring about the removal or the destruction of all microorganisms. There is no distinction as to the kinds of microorganisms destroyed, whether pathogenic or nonpathogenic, vegetative or spore forms. Sterilization includes also the inactivation of viruses. Proper usage of the terms *sterile*, *sterilize*, and *sterilization* signifies the absence of all microorganisms. This is the accepted standard.

Yet, in practice, absolute sterility may not be achievable. Random sampling of the sterilized product, and compliance with official sterility test requirements, while necessary as a standard, cannot avoid the risk of encountering nonsterile items. The nature and viability of the residual, surviving microorganisms, although randomly few in number, determine the *effective* sterility of the product. Therefore today sterility is viewed in terms of the probability of encountering a contaminated article. For effective sterilization the conditions need to be so arranged that the probability for the occurrence of actual contamination in articles claimed to be sterile is extremely small. One criterion that has been proposed is that no more than one organism shall survive on one million items sterilized. According to this proposal, an industrial operation involving the sterilization of one million items a year and an inactivation factor of 10^6 is likely to produce one positive each year even if the initial rate of contamination is equivalent to only one resistant organism per object. To achieve such performance, marginal ingredients and practices in producing sterile drugs and medical articles cannot be accepted on the grounds that the final sterilization procedure will eliminate all contamination. Emphasis must be placed instead on the microbiological purity of the starting materials and on strict production hygiene in order to achieve low microbial counts before sterilization. An appropriate procedure for sterilization can then be selected to give a very high degree of assurance of sterility. In general, the sterilization procedure should be the most stringent method that is compatible with the material being treated. The measurement of the effectiveness of that procedure can then be accomplished by a determination of the kinetics of microbial destruction, which allows for the calculation of the probabilities for survivors, and by challenge of the system with suitable biological indicators of appropriately resistant organisms.

The selection of a biological indicator is critical, and due weight must be given to the resistance of the organism to the specific sterilization procedure employed. The control of indicators includes a determination that a sufficient number of viable cells are present at the time of their use and that the performance characteristics of the indicator are known with respect to survival and kill. Biological indicators generally comprise spores rather than vegetative forms because of the known higher resistance of spores to various processes. It has been necessary to take this into account in examining methods for achieving sterilization. More comprehensive investigation into the biochemistry of the resistance of spores is needed, even though the accumulated knowledge on the destruction of the microbial cell and on the survival of spores already is substantial. This information is of considerable practical value, and is applicable directly to the assessment of sterilization processes. Some observations on cell destruction, therefore, will serve to place in perspective certain qualifications on the methods for testing for the detection of surviving microorganisms.

Just as absolute sterility may not be achievable, so also the absolute measurement of the destruction of microorganisms has its limitations. Tests for sterility may reveal only that living organisms have been removed or destroyed to the extent where they no longer multiply in appropriate culture media under favorable conditions. Confidence in the results of the tests is based upon the knowledge that the material has been subjected to a sterilization procedure of proven effectiveness. The assessment of the efficiency and the control of sterilization processes with biological indicators is far more beneficial than any other method now at our disposal. By current knowledge, the only single practical criterion of the death of microorganisms is their failure to reproduce when suitable conditions for growth are provided.

The factors that cause death of microorganisms may be divided into physical and chemical. Physical factors include moist heat, dry heat, and irradiation. The resistance to heat of many microorganisms, especially spores, exceeds that of most other forms of life. Chemical influences include gaseous sterilization and sterilization by means of germicidal and sporicidal agents of various kinds. Sterile filtration is a physical process that removes microorganisms, but does not destroy them. Unfortunately, it is therefore not amenable to evaluation by means of biological indicators since they depend upon kill.

MEASUREMENT OF DEATH AND SURVIVAL

Much of the early work on the resistance of microorganisms was conducted with heat employing a determination of the *thermal death point* (26). In this procedure samples of a culture were exposed for 10 min to various, carefully controlled temperatures. The survival or death of the microorganisms was determined by direct incubation if the suspending medium was appropriate, or by subculture into another suitable growth medium. The *thermal death point* was the lowest temperature that resulted in no survival after the given period of exposure. Few attempts were made in this early work to define the concentration of viable cells, their age, their physiological condition, and the nature of the suspending medium. It is significant, too, that our knowledge of what constitutes optimum conditions for microbial growth and recovery has changed as new information and new media were developed. Since spores survived much longer at temperatures that killed vegetative cells, subsequently a determination of the *time* to kill the spores was made following exposure to various temperatures. The values so obtained were referred to as *thermal death time*.

The first attempt to control the conditions for these determinations was by Bigelow and Esty (1) who determined thermal death time by exposing a known number of spores in a specified medium of known hydrogen ion concentration in sealed glass tubes to precise temperatures in an accurately controlled oil bath. The sample tubes, and later, multiples of such sample tubes, were removed from the temperature bath after different times of exposure and the contents were transferred to a nutrient medium to determine if the spores had survived or been killed. Under these conditions, thermal death time was extrapolated to be between the longest time showing survival and the shortest time showing no survival. The principles established by this early work have become fundamental in almost all modern studies on the thermal resistance of microorganisms. Using their technique, these authors demonstrated that with any given spore suspension, thermal death time was a function of the spore concentration, and that the thermal death time decreased with increasing temperature. Bigelow (6) pointed out the linear relationship for these data when the survival and destruction points for any given preparation were plotted on a log scale against the corresponding temperatures on a linear scale. Subsequently, Ball (4, 5) characterized Bigelow's thermal death time curves by a point and a slope. The point, designated by F, was selected to indicate the time required to destroy the organism at 250 F. The slope, symbolized by z, was defined as the number of degrees required for the curve to traverse one log cycle. Alternatively, this value was the equivalent of the number of degrees that the temperature had to be raised or lowered from a given reference temperature to produce a tenfold decrease or increase in destruction time. The slope of the survival curve, or the z value (usually 18 F, or 10 C), can be useful for estimating the time required for effective sterilization at temperatures below or above a given reference temperature. In these cases, however, the effectiveness of such extrapolations is best evaluated with biological indicators.

The description of thermal resistance gave way to an estimation of the numbers of survivors remaining in relation to time (21, 22, 23, 46). The destruction rates of suspensions by heat were measured using plate count techniques after exposure of the suspensions to various intervals of time. In many cases, the logarithm of the number of survivors plotted against exposure time gave a straight line (42, 39). The slope of the line could be used as a quantitative expression of the resistance of the population. The linearity of this relationship was typical of first-order kinetics and implied that in any given time interval a constant proportion of the survivors lost viability, or were killed. The slope of the line determined the constant, K. Based on the same straight line, the time required to reduce the surviving population by a factor of ten was designated the D value (30). The decimal reduction time, D, was thus the reciprocal of the constant, K. Tables of D values for moist heat, dry heat and ionizing radiation have been published (10). D values for ethylene oxide sterilization and for chemical sterilization are much less reliable. These relationships have been used, however, to measure and to predict the effectiveness of various sterilization procedures.

Death-rate or survivor curves can be constructed for each method of sterilization by plotting the number of organisms in logarithms on the y axis against the length of heating time, the time of exposure to a given gas or chemical concentration, or to a radiation dose, on the linear x axis. Such curves serve also as a means of comparison for the resistance of various biological indicators to given sterilizing conditions.

Sometimes the shape of survivor curves may vary from the straight line to a curvilinear plot or to a biphasic curve. The evidence in favor of a logarithmic order of death is considerable, however, and justifies the general application of first-order kinetics to experimental data. The advantages to assuming a logarithmic order generally outweigh possible errors that may be encountered experimentally. On the other hand, it is important to keep in mind that survivor curves apply to and describe populations of microorganisms and not individuals. While we speak of the resistance of a cell or of a spore all that can ever be studied is the behavior of a population of cells or spores. The determination of survivors or the endpoint of survival obviously depends also to a large degree upon the particular substrates and conditions, such as time and temperature, that are used for determining survival. In this connection, experience indicates that the definition and standardization of the components as well as the finished culture media that are employed for sterility and growth testing, as noted, is a task that commands urgent attention. A more precise determination of the time of incubation of inoculated specimens likewise bears further scrutiny.

STEAM STERILIZATION

The most dependable and universally standard procedure for the destruction of all forms of microbial life is the application of moist heat. Where specified in the *U.S. Pharmacopeia* (50), steam sterilization denotes heating in an autoclave employing saturated steam under pressure at a minimum of 121 C for a minimum of 15 min (20). The time is measured after the temperature of the material being sterilized reaches 121 C. The *Pharmacopeia* does not prohibit the use of moist heat for

sterilizing purposes at temperatures other than 121 C, for example at
115 C, but draws a distinction by definition between such conditions and
steam sterilization. Furthermore, it clearly recommends the use of a
suitable biological indicator where the moist heat process involves sterilization at a temperature other than at 121 C.

Under normal circumstances, one might expect that a process as
rigorous and widely used as steam sterilization would not regularly
require monitoring with biological indicators. This may be generally true
since physical controls consisting of pressure gauges, thermometers and
thermocouples, and various other devices that are capable of indicating
minimum and maximum variations in the physical parameters, serve
useful purposes. On the other hand, tragic accidents from inadequate
sterilization of articles stand as evidence to the failure of these controls
alone for efficiently monitoring steam sterilization on a consistently
positive basis. Sterilization is performed to terminate a biological process, hence a biological rather than a mechanical system is required to
assure that sterilization has taken place. The use of biological indicators
has been recommended for the purpose; all other methods are secondary.
These indicators, which generally incorporate a single species of a thermophilic aerobe or mesophilic anaerobe, as for example *B. stearothermophilus* spores or *Clostridium sporogenes*, respectively, can be of two forms.
In one form, the culture is added to representative units or articles of
the lot to be sterilized. If the use of this form is not practical, as in the
case of solids, an alternative adventitious indicator is required in which
the culture is added to discs of filter paper or metal, glass, or plastic. It
is preferable that the carrier of the biological indicator be as similar as
possible in composition to the package or item being sterilized. The substrate is extremely important; the best substrate is the product itself.
If the material to be sterilized is a liquid, and if it is not practicable to
add a biological indicator to selected units of the lot, the viable culture
may be added to a simulated product that offers no less resistance to
sterilization than the product itself. When such inoculation is not possible, the alternative is to use the biological indicator on some other
carrier. The inoculum of spores incorporated in the indicator should
exceed the level of total contamination normally present in the product
being sterilized. The destruction of resistant indicators during monitoring of steam sterilization cycles provides the assurance that viruses,
vegetative bacterial cells, fungi, yeasts and molds, and spores of lesser
resistance have not survived the process.

Recently, a USP Advisory Panel examined the performance characteristics of five adventitious indicators, obtained from commercial sources, in a collaborative study using steam autoclaves in ten different laboratories (38). The performance of the five indicators, as measured by their survival and kill in autoclaves without load at 121 C, was found to be significantly different. The bacterial counts among the biological indicators studied also were significantly different, ranging from 2×10^2 to 1×10^6. These indicators, nonetheless, revealed greater variability in the performance of the ten autoclaves than expected. In view of these findings, it was concluded that commercial biological indicators need to be improved and standardized. The study also demonstrated the need to improve the reliability of autoclaves, and that this might be accomplished by the use of standardized biological indicators. A previous call for the standardization of spore indicators for heat resistance, or their preparation by a reference laboratory, was made in 1958 by Kelsey (33), who also cautioned against the use of thermophiles that were too heat resistant and would thus lead to unnecessary rejection of a sterilization procedure. In 1961, Kelsey (34) described the preparation of thermophilic spore papers for testing hospital sterilizers using *B. stearothermophilus*, and calibrated these by plotting dose–response curves for exposure to steam, at 121 C. Recommendations to develop *reference biological indicators* for use in both the calibration of sterilization procedures, as well as other indicators, were made at the time of the USP Open Conference on Biological Indicators in 1970 (1). These matters, particularly the problem of developing reliable testing methods, are tasks now before the USP Advisory Panel. It is expected that this activity will lead to the definition of meaningful specifications and the recommendation of USP standards for biological indicators in due course.

DRY HEAT STERILIZATION

Dry heat usually is regarded as less efficient than moist heat for sterilization. Consequently, longer periods of exposure and higher temperatures generally are required. Specific times and temperatures must be determined for each type of material treated. When the nature of the material permits, a generous safety factor frequently is included in the exposure conditions to compensate for variables that can affect the sterilizing cycle. In the pharmaceutical industry, it is common to sterilize glass containers for injections at 275 C for 3 or more hr, for example, in order to assure sterility and freedom from pyrogenic substances. For foods and drugs, dry heat sterilization is applied infrequently. As a consequence, very little fundamental data about this form of sterilization were developed until recently when there was renewed interest in connection with the sterilization of craft for use in space explorations.

In reviewing the requirements of various pharmacopeias for dry heat sterilization, Bruch (8) called attention to the lack of the standardization of humidity in this process. Since water contained in a microbial cell is in equilibrium with that in the external environment, the amount of water present externally is of potential crucial importance to the moisture within the cell and its physical state. Increased resistance of cells in the absence of water had been generally accepted for years. Indeed, even super-heated steam was observed to function as dry air, and at 140 to 150 C it had less killing effect than wet steam at 100 C (45). Controlled studies on heat resistance at low external relative humidities were significantly absent for a long time, however, partly because of the lack of sensitive techniques for measurement. More recent research by a number of authors (29, 41, 40, 3, 27) has demonstrated the importance of moisture on the destruction of microorganisms by dry heat. The amount of moisture associated with spores prior to heating also influences the rate of their destruction during exposure. When spores are trapped in solids their increased heat resistance may be due to the moisture relationships within this environment rather than to slower thermal penetration through the solid mass, as once suspected. In this regard, Bruch (9) has summarized data showing approximately 50 % greater resistance to dry heat sterilization of spores of *B. subtilis* var. *niger* trapped in dental plastics than when exposed as dried spores on paper or glass. Drummond and Pflug (16) found that the dry heat resistance of spores of *B. subtilis* var. *niger* was dependent on the relative humidity both before and during treatment, which in turn affected the water content of the spores. In their studies, higher humidities increased the resistance of the spores.

In attempting to establish a biological indicator for dry heat sterilization, the water condition of the spores to be inactivated therefore must be taken into account. The *D* value of a microbial contamination to dry heat could possibly vary by a factor of 100 from a very dry to a very high humidity condition. The question then is for what condition must the biological indicator be designed? Very dry spores in a very dry atmosphere might be killed more readily than wet spores at high humidity. Similarly, spores on a spore strip being dry, could be destroyed more readily than the contamination in the product itself.

A number of different organisms have been evaluated for use in monitoring dry heat sterilization. Two stand out as being most used, the spores of *B. subtilis* var. *niger*, and the spores of *B. stearothermophilus*. The standard test organism in the early NASA programs was *B. subtilis* var. *niger*, which was used to monitor dry heat sterilization at 125 C for 24 hr. To minimize destruction to spacecraft equipment, these temperatures have gradually been decreased with a corresponding extension in sterilization time. A wide range in kill time value can be obtained even with these indicators, however, depending upon the humidity conditions, the form of substrate, carrier, etc. An interesting extension of the use of *B. subtilis* var. *niger* indicator, incorporated into a thin sheet polymer of methylmethacrylate has been described for monitoring sterilization by thermoradiation methods (47).

In considering the problems of standardization of dry heat indicators, the USP Advisory Panel has concluded that the test conditions under which these indicators are evaluated must include provisions to control humidity, and that the indicators themselves must be preconditioned to that humidity before use. In addition, the dry heat sterilizer in which the biological indicators are tested should be constructed to provide for virtually instantaneous entry or removal of the indicator samples from the heated environment. Plans are being developed for a collaborative evaluation of commercial indicators for dry heat sterilization.

GAS STERILIZATION

Gases such as ethylene oxide, propylene oxide, and formaldehyde have been recommended for sterilization but only where other methods, such as heat, cannot be used. Even radiation sterilization generally is considered more reliable than gas, where applicable. Nonetheless, ethylene oxide has found far-reaching applications particularly for the sterilization of many disposable medical devices of plastic, textile, glass, rubber, and metal construction. Much of this use is based upon the early work of Phillips and Kaye (44, 43, 31, 32) who published a series of reports confirming the lethality of ethylene oxide for microorganisms and establishing the conditions under which the gas was most effective. In this book an extensive review of the use of ethylene oxide for sterilization is provided by Ernst (pp. 181–208).

Sterilization with ethylene oxide requires proper control of temperature, humidity, gas concentration, time of exposure, and a significant knowledge of the physical and chemical characteristics of the material being sterilized, including the packaging. All of these variables influence the rate of destruction of the microorganisms. Under experimental conditions of use, ethylene oxide has been shown to be effective in killing all microorganisms for which it has been tested. The problems that arise in large-scale sterilization with ethylene oxide are concerned with the consistent control of these important variables, and the reliability of the penetration of gas and water vapor into remote segments of the articles being treated. On this basis, sterilization with ethylene oxide is a complex process and may unknowingly cause difficulties even in the best facilities. A correspondent (49) recently stated the problem succinctly when he observed that ethylene oxide has so many possibilities for failure that control measures need to be stringent and extensive if we are to achieve sterility rather than decontamination. Of major importance then are the criteria by which the performance of this process can be measured regularly and controlled.

Complete monitoring and integration of all physical variables is essential, but the routine use of appropriate biological indicators perhaps is more critical in this case than with any other process. Although spores of *B. subtilis* var. *niger* are commonly employed, several factors enter into consideration in the selection of the indicator. The killing action of ethylene oxide depends upon the gas getting into the cell of the microorganism; moisture is a carrier for the gas. If the process is performed with insufficient moisture, such as at a high vacuum, high temperature, or low humidity, the inactivation of the desiccated spores can be reduced substantially. Highly desiccated spores, in fact, even acquire a resistance to the gas as a result of desiccation. In this connection, Kereluk (35) provided results illustrating the relative variation among organisms when exposed to ethylene oxide; his data disclosed significant differences when the organisms were dried on nonhygroscopic and on hygroscopic surfaces. Of even greater concern was the report that the vegetative cells of some nonsporeformers were almost as resistant to the gas as were the spores of several resistant organisms (*Cl. sporogenes*, *B. stearothermophilus* and *B. pumilus*). Doyle (15) separately reported that desiccated spores of *B. subtilis* sealed in various polymeric films were much more resistant to ethylene oxide sterilization than were nondesiccated spores. This finding demonstrated, once again, the importance of moisture in close proximity to the bacterial spores in ethylene oxide processes. To increase the resistance of microorganisms and thus provide a safety factor for ethylene oxide sterilization, biological indicators comprising unwashed *B. subtilis* spores incorporated into sand have been recommended by Christensen (13, 36). Doyle (14) has described a spore preparation of *B. subtilis* enclosed within a plasticized water-soluble resin.

In view of these factors, there is a greater concern about the monitors for ethylene oxide sterilization on the part of the USP Advisory Panel than there is for any other process. The panel currently is addressing itself to questions of how good the available indicators are, how they compare with each other, and how they compare with criteria which the panel and its advisors consider necessary for valid assessment of this sterilization process. Preliminary labeling requirements for biological indicators, published in the First *USP* XVIII Supplement (20), called for the identification of the organism by species, the form of the vehicle (e.g. strip, beads, or liquid), lot number, expiration date, storage conditions, directions for use including recovery medium and incubation conditions to be employed, performance characteristics (for survival and kill) for different types of sterilization procedures, and recommendations for disposal. Panel activity now is directed to the development of reproducible test procedures for the determination of survivor curves for biological indicators under standardized conditions, ultimately leading to specifications for these monitors for ethylene oxide sterilization.

RADIATION STERILIZATION

Radiation sterilization involves the application of sufficient ionizing energy to render an article free of viable microorganisms. Other papers at this symposium deal with various aspects of radiation sterilization. When protected from recontamination, the irradiated article remains free of organisms regardless of the duration or conditions of storage (24). This definition takes cognizance of the much discussed possibility of radiation damage to organisms that may slowly recover and grow out given the proper conditions and length of time in sterility testing.

Ionizing energy exerts its lethal effects on microorganisms both directly and indirectly. Direct action is based on the target organism being hit by an ionizing particle or ray. When microorganisms are destroyed by direct hits, this involves a probability concept that depends only on the number of particles or rays (i.e., the dose) and the number of targets. According to Lea (37), for the target theory to be operable the rate of destruction of the microorganisms can be influenced only by the dose or the number of ionizing particles. The concentration of organisms, the medium, temperature, or the dose rate are not important factors.

Ionizing energy also exerts its lethal effects by indirect action, however, and these effects are very important in the destruction of microorganisms. Free radicals and reactive compounds formed as a result of the radiolysis of water, for example, can have a profound effect on sterilization. The medium, temperature, concentration of solutes, pH, and the gaseous environment all have an important effect on indirect action. Different species of organisms are affected in varying degree by the direct and indirect action of radiation. This results in varying radiosensitivities of microorganisms. In general, bacterial spores and viruses are most resistant to radiation, and gram-negative rods are the most sensitive; the yeasts, the fungi and gram-positive bacteria range between. Unfortunately, there are several notable exceptions including *M. radiodurans*, a highly radiation resistant, gram-positive coccus. The radiation resistivities of various organisms have been tabulated by Silverman and Sinskey (48).

The destruction of microorganisms by irradiation is first order. Hence any logarithmic increase in the initial concentration of organisms will result in a linear increase in the dose required for their destruction (25). Conversely, initial low levels of contaminants on articles require a smaller radiation dose for their sterilization. In addition, the probability for encountering pathogens or resistant forms is reduced substantially as the initial count is kept low on articles to be sterilized. This is an important concept both from the standpoint of effective sterilization and for selecting suitable biological indicators for monitoring radiation sterilization processes.

Radiation sterilization is most often employed as a continuous process during which the materials to be sterilized are exposed to a radiation source, such as an electron accelerator or to radioisotopes, sufficient to absorb a predetermined dose of ionizing energy, usually 2.5 Mrad or more. The positive effect of radiation in sterilizing medical devices and other articles in their final sealed packages, or even in shipping cartons, is direct and uncomplicated. Of necessity, radiation sterilization procedures have been more intensively controlled and monitored than other processes, especially through the use of physical and chemical dosimetry. The biological indicator most frequently employed for radiation sterilization at the 2.5 Mrad dose consists of the spores *B. pumilus E 601*. The vegetative form of *S. faecium*, strain $A_2 1$, and the spores of *B. sphaericus*, strain $C_1 A$, have been employed for monitoring sterilization in the range of 3.0 to 4.5 Mrad (12, 17). The radiation-resistant *M. radiodurans* has been studied experimentally for radiation doses in excess of 4.5 Mrad (2).

Mutants of *M. radiodurans* have been produced by cyclic irradiation with even higher resistance than the original strain (19). Several other organisms highly resistant to radiation have been identified (11, 18).

The *USP* XVIII currently recognizes a radiation dose of minimum 2.5 Mrad, delivered as uniformly as possible, to all parts of the product being sterilized. This does not rule out the application of higher radiation doses when considered necessary by the complexity of the article being treated, by the manipulations that may be involved in its preparation or assembly, or for other good reason. However, as with any other sterilization process, the presterilization levels of microbial contamination on the articles to be sterilized generally will dictate the dose to be used. These levels need to be known and controlled with care in order to justify the use of radiation sterilization under conditions that are effective, yet practical from the standpoint of economics and with a minimum destructive effect on the product due to excessive irradiation. The International Atomic Energy Agency (IAEA) has recommended a code of practice for the radiation sterilization of medical products (28, which only recently was revised.

The USP Advisory Panel is embarked on a collaborative study of the effectiveness of biological indicators for radiation sterilization at the 2.5 Mrad dose. Two indicators will be employed in this study consisting of *B. pumilus 601* at two different spore concentrations, together with concurrent dosimetry. It is expected that about a dozen laboratories will participate in the study.

CONCLUSION

The destruction of microorganisms employing steam, dry-heat, gas, or irradiation sterilization for drugs, medical devices, and biomedical products involves a biological process. The efficiency of that process is determined and controlled most effectively through the systematic use of properly standardized biological indicators.

References

1. *Abstract of Proceedings*, USP Open Conference on Biological Indicators for Sterility Assurance. 1970. The United States Pharmacopeia, Rockville, Md.
2. Anderson, A. W., H. C. Nordan, R. F. Cain, G. Parrish, and D. Duggan. 1956. Studies on a radio-resistant micrococcus. I. The isolation, morphology, cultural characteristics and resistance to gamma radiation. Food Technology **10**: 575–577.

3. Angelotti, R., J. H. Maryanski, T. F. Butler, J. T. Peeler, and J. E. Campbell. 1968. Influence of spore moisture content on the dry-heat resistance of *Bacillus subtilis* var. *niger*. Appl. Microbiol. **16**: 735–745.

4. Ball, C. O. 1923. Thermal processes for canned foods. Natl. Research Council Bull., Pt. 1, No. 37, 76 pp.

5. Ball, C. O. 1928. Mathematical solution of problems on thermal processing of canned food. Univ. Calif. (Berkeley) Publ. Public Health, **1**: 15–245.

6. Bigelow, W. D. 1921. The logarithmic nature of thermal death time curves. J. Infectious Diseases **29**: 528–536.

7. Bigelow, W. D., and J. R. Esty. 1920. Thermal death point in relation to time of typical thermophilic organisms. J. Infectious Diseases, **27**: 602–617.

8. Bruch, C. W. 1965. Dry heat sterilization for planetary-impacting spacecraft. pp. 207–229. In *Proceedings of the First National Conference on Spacecraft Sterilization Technology*. Publ. SP-108. National Aeronautics and Space Administration. Washington, D.C.

9. Bruch, C. W. 1968. Spacecraft sterilization. pp. 686–702. In C. A. Lawrence and S. S. Block [Eds.], *Disinfection, sterilization and preservation*. Lea and Febiger. Philadelphia.

10. Bruch, C. W., and M. K. Bruch. 1971. Sterilization. pp. 592–623. In Eric W. Martin [Ed.], *Dispensing of medication*. Mack Publishing Co. Easton, Pa.

11. Christensen, E. A. 1972. Radiation induced mutants with increased resistance against ionizing radiation. IAEA Working Group Meeting on the Recommended Code of Practice for the Radiation Sterilization of Biomedical Products. June 5–9. Risö, Denmark.

12. Christensen, E. A., L. O. Kallings, and D. Fystro. 1969. Microbiological control of sterilization procedures and standards for the sterilization of medical equipment. Ugeskr. Laeg. **131**: 2123. In Danish.

13. Christensen, E. A., H. Kristensen, and C. Borg-Petersen. 1967. Kontrol med. sterilisationsprocedurer. Ugeskr. Laeg. **129**: 707. In Danish.

14. Doyle, J. E. 1971. Sterility indicator with artificial resistance to ethylene oxide. Bull. Parenteral Drug Association **25**: 98.

15. Doyle, J. E., A. W. McDaniel, K. L. West, J. E. Whitbourne, and R. R. Ernst. 1970. Ethylene oxide resistance of nondesiccated and desiccated spores of *Bacillus subtilis* var. *niger* hermetically sealed in various polymeric films. Appl. Microbiol. **20**: 793–797.

16. Drummond, D. W., and I. J. Pflug. 1970. Dry-heat destruction of *Bacillus subtilis* spores on surfaces: Effect of humidity in an open system. Appl. Microbiol. **20**: 805–809.

17. Emborg, C., E. A. Christensen, W. H. Eriksen, and N. W. Holm. 1971. Control of the microbiological efficiency of radiation sterilization plants by means of *B. Sphaericus*, strain C_1A, and *Str. faecium*, strain A_2l. Progress report, IAEA Research Contract No. 973/R1/RB. IAEA Contractors Coordination Meeting, November 18–19. Risö, Denmark.

18. Emborg, C., and W. H. Eriksen. 1972. Radiation inactivation of dried preparations with spores of various Bacillus strains and their possible use in control of radiation sterilization procedures. June 5–9, Risö, Denmark.

19. Emborg, C., and W. H. Eriksen. 1972. Radiation induced radiation resistance in *M. radiodurans*, strain R_1. IAEA Working Group Meeting on the Recommended Code of Practice for the Radiation Sterilization of Biomedical Products. June 5–9. Risö, Denmark.

20. *United States Pharmacopeia* XVIII First suppl. 1971. Mack Publishing Co. Easton, Pa., p. 32.

21. Gillespy, T. G. 1946. The heat resistance of the spores of thermophilic bacteria. I. Introductory. Ann. Rept. and Veg. Presvn. Stn., Campden, 68–75.

22. Gillespy, T. G. 1947. The heat resistance of the spores of thermophilic bacteria. II. Thermophilic anaerobes. Ann. Rept. and Veg. Presvn. Stn., Campden, 40–54.

23. Gillespy, T. G. 1948. The heat resistance of spores of the thermophilic bacteria. III. Thermophilic anaerobes (continued). Ann. Rept. and Veg. Presvn. Stn., Campden, 34–43.

24. Goldblith, S. A. 1967. General principles of radiosterilization. pp. 3–22. In *Radiosterilization of medical products*. IAEA. Vienna.

25. Goldblith, S: A. 1971. The Inhibition and Destruction of the Microbial Cell by Radiations. pp. 285–305. In W. B. Hugo [Ed.], *Inhibition and destruction of the microbial cell*. Academic Press. London.

26. Hampill, B. 1932. The influence of temperature on the life processes and death of bacteria. Quart. Rev. Biol. **7**: 172–196.

27. Hoffman, R. K., V. M. Gambill, and L. M. Buchanan. 1968. Effect of cell moisture on the thermal inactivation rate of bacterial spores. Appl. Microbiol. **16**: 1240–1244.

28. International Atomic Energy Agency, Recommended code of practice for the radiosterilization of medical products. 1967. pp. 423–431. In *Radiosterilization of medical products*. International Atomic Energy Agency. Vienna.

29. Jacobs, R. A., R. C. Nicholas, and I. J. Pflug. 1965. Heat resistance of *Bacillus subtilis* spores in atmospheres of different water contents. Mich. Agr. Expt. Sta. Quart. Bull. **48**: 238–246.

30. Katzin, L. I., L. A. Sandholzer, and M. E. Strong. 1943. Application of the decimal reduction time principle to a study of the resistance of coliform bacteria to pasteurization. J. Bact. **45**: 265–272.

31. Kaye, S. 1949. The sterilizing action of gaseous ethylene oxide. III. The effect of ethylene oxide and related compounds upon bacterial aerosols. Am. J. Hyg. **50**: 289–295.

32. Kaye, S., and C. R. Phillips. 1949. The sterilizing action of gaseous ethylene oxide. IV. The effect of moisture. Am. J. Hyg. **50**: 296–306.

33. Kelsey, J. C. 1958. The testing of sterilizers. Lancet, Feb. 8, 306–309.

34. Kelsey, J. C. 1961. The testing of sterilizers. 2. Thermophilic spore papers. J. Olin. Path. **14**: 313–319.

35. Kereluk, K., R. A. Gammon, and R. S. Lloyd. 1970. Microbiological aspects of ethylene oxide sterilization. II. Microbial resistance to ethylene oxide. Appl. Microbiol. **19**: 152–156.

36. Kristensen, H. 1970. Ethylene oxide resistance of microorganisms in dust compared with the resistance of *Bacillus subtilis* spores. Acta Pathologica et Microbiologica Scandinavica. **78B**: 1–7.

37. Lea, D. E. 1946. *Actions of radiations on living cells.* Cambridge University Press. London.
38. Mayernik, J. J. 1972. Biological indicators for steam sterilization—A U.S.P. collaborative study. Personal communication.
39. Murrell, W. G., A. M. Olsen, and W. S. Scott. 1950. The enumeration of heated bacterial spores. II. Experiments with Bacillus species. Australian J. Sci. Research **3**: 234–244.
40. Murrell, W. G. and W. J. Scott. 1966. The heat resistance of bacterial spores at various water activities. J. Gen. Microbiol. **43**: 411–425.
41. Murrell, W. G., and W. J. Scott. 1966. The heat resistance of bacterial spores at various water activities. Nature **179**: 481–482.
42. Olsen, A. M., and W. J. Scott. 1950. The enumeration of heated bacterial spores. I. Experiments with *Clostridium botulinum* and other species of Clostridium. Australian J. Sci. Research **3**: 219–233.
43. Phillips, C. R. 1949. The sterilizing action of gaseous ethylene oxide. II. Sterilization of contaminated objects with ethylene oxide and related compounds: Time, concentration and temperature relationships. Am. J. Hyg. **50**: 280–288.
44. Phillips, C. R., and S. Kaye. 1949. The sterilizing action of gaseous ethylene oxide. I. Review. Am. J. Hyg. **50**: 270–279.
45. Precht, J., J. Christeophersen, and H. Henzel. 1955. In *Temperatur und Leben.* Springer Verlag. Berlin.
46. Reynolds, H., and H. Lichtenstein. 1952. Symposium on the biology of bacterial spores. Part VIII. Evaluation of heat resistance data for bacterial spores. Bact Rev. **16**: 126–135.
47. Reynolds, M. C., and D. M. Garst. 1970. Optimizing thermal and radiation effects for bacterial inactivation. Space Life Sciences **2**: 394–399.
48. Silverman, G. J., and T. J. Sinskey. 1968. In C. A. Lawrence and S. S. Block [Eds.] *Disinfection, sterilization and preservation.* Lea and Febiger. Philadelphia, pp. 741–760.
49. Starkey, D. H., Personal communication.
50. *United States Pharmacopeia* XVIII. 1970. Mack Publishing Co. Easton, Pa., p. 830.

3

Sterility Testing

FRANCES WILLARD BOWMAN

Chief, Sterility Testing Branch
National Center for Antibiotic Analysis
Food and Drug Administration
Washington, D.C.

THE REQUIREMENT that certain drugs be sterile has necessitated the development of meaningful tests for use in regulatory quality control. All countries that exercise control over drugs manufactured or distributed within their boundaries require that "statutory" sterility tests be performed on injectable preparations. Pharmacopeias of the various countries that promulgate the standards for the legal control of drugs generally specify in the relevant monographs which drugs have a sterility requirement. The directions and methodology for performing the official sterility test are usually described in a separate chapter of the pharmacopeia.

In England the Therapeutic Substances Acts and the regulations promulgated there are concerned with the maintenance of sterility of all substances commonly known as vaccines, toxins, antitoxins, antigens, sera, human blood products, insulin, hormones, and certain antibiotics marketed for parenteral use (22). It was appreciated in the deliberations of the English advisory committees which were responsible for framing the first (1925) act that sterility must be built into a product and cannot be guaranteed by sterility testing. Emphasis was laid from those early days on the necessity for inspecting premises, plant, and personnel where the manufacturing of sterile products takes place. This same principle of inspection by a licensing or certifying authority is recognized in the United States by the Food and Drug Administration in its control of sterile biologicals, antibiotics, insulin, and to a considerable extent, other drug products.

Bryce (10) has described the limitations of the methods given in the various official compendia. These limitations derive from two practically insoluble problems. The first is that of adequate sampling, and the second is the inability to cultivate all viable microorganisms that may be present. Bryce stated that pharmacopeias imply that sterility is the state of being free from living organisms of all types. This concept is simple enough, but unfortunately it is unrealistic, because complete sterility cannot be verified experimentally. He concluded that the sterility test is, in fact, a test for detecting certain contaminant organisms. In addition, he said that since the test attempts to infer the state of the whole from the result of an examination of the part, it is essentially a statistical operation.

In both the 18th revision of the *United States Pharmacopeia* (*USP*) (36) and the first supplement to the 13th revision of the *National Formulary* (*NF*) (26) the difficulties of experimentally verifying the sterile state are recognized. Therefore, the objective of the sterility test as well as the limitations are explained as follows: The objective of the sterilization process is to make the article safe for use, but sterility tests may be expected to reflect only that living organisms have been removed or destroyed to the extent that they no longer multiply in appropriate culture media under favorable conditions. Interpretation of the results of sterility tests must allow for the possibility that the degree of contamination is of a low order of magnitude. Confidence in the results of the tests with respect to a given lot of articles is based upon knowledge that the lot has been subjected to a sterilization procedure of proven effectiveness.

Sterility tests were first introduced into the *USP* and the *NF* in 1936. Both the *USP* and the *NF* are recognized as official compendia by the federal Food, Drug, and Cosmetic Act and by comparable laws of the individual states of the United States. In addition to the official compendia, two federal agencies of the United States promulgate regulations governing the sterility testing of pharmaceuticals. The sterility test for serums, toxins, antitoxins, and blood products are described in Title 42, Part 73.73 of the *Code of Federal Regulations* (13). The standards of potency and purity of antibiotics are established under Title 21 of the *Code of Federal Regulations* which is issued by the commissioner of Food and Drugs, and changes in it are published in the *Federal Register* (15). The *Code of Federal Regulations* includes a sterility test procedure for each antibiotic that is required to be sterile. For both biologics and antibiotics, the compendial monographs of the *USP* and *NF* conform to the appropriate regulations of the regulatory agency.

METHODS FOR STERILITY TESTING

Current compendial regulations recognize two basic methods for performing sterility tests. One is the direct method (DM) which allows the test sample to be inoculated directly into the appropriate sterile culture medium. The other is the bacterial membrane filter method (MF) in which the sample is solubilized or dissolved, in a nontoxic sterile diluting fluid which is then filtered through a bacteria-retentive membrane usually composed of cellulose esters. The membrane is washed to remove inhibitory substances contained in the sample that might have been retained on the filter and is then transferred aseptically to an appropriate sterile culture medium. The original sterility test introduced into the pharmacopeias of various countries was invariably some version of the direct method. This test was generally satisfactory until the advent of the antibiotic era. Since there were no suitable inactivators for antibiotics other than penicillin, the direct method could detect only organisms that were highly resistant to the inhibitory action of the particular antibiotic. The membrane filtration sterility test method was introduced by Holdowsky (21) in 1957 to separate microorganisms from the antimicrobial effects of antibiotics in order to obtain reliable sterility tests of antibiotic drugs. Research on the application of the membrane filtration technique to the sterility testing of antibiotic drugs by Bowman (2) produced practical methods for solubilizing and filtering a number of antibiotic preparations. The *Antibiotic Regulations* (14) were amended in 1964 to incorporate the filtration procedures, which greatly increased the sensitivity of the antibiotic sterility tests. This method for sterility control of antibiotics was included in the *Austrian Pharmacopeia* in 1960, the *British Pharmacopoeia* in 1963, the *USP* and *NF* in 1964, the *Italian Pharmacopeia* in 1965, the *International Pharmacopeia* in 1967, and the *Nordic Pharmacopeia* in 1971.

After the soundness of the membrane filtration approach for the sterility testing of antimicrobial substances had been universally acclaimed, filtration techniques were successfully applied to the sterility testing of oils and ointments (28, 34). The *USP* XVIII and *NF* XIII (First Supplement), which became official September 1, 1970, provide for the use of the MF method when applicable for drugs or devices. Since the sterility test chapters of the *USP* and *NF* are identical, all future references to *USP* XVIII apply to *NF* XIII as well. The *USP* XVIII states that the procedure is particularly applicable where the substance under test is an oil, an ointment that can be put into solution, a nonbacteriostatic solid not readily soluble in culture media, or a soluble powder or solution that possesses inherent bacteriostatic or fungistatic properties. The methodology for performing the test was given in detail for the first time in the *USP* in its 18th revision. The revision makes it mandatory to test insulin solutions and suspensions by the MF method and provides an ascorbic acid diluting fluid to solubilize the suspensions prior to filtration. The Third Interim Revision of *USP* XVIII designates the MF test for large-volume intravenous solutions and gives detailed instructions for the test and its interpretation (37).

The improvement in sensitivity offered by the MF method is achieved at the cost of the difficulty of aseptically handling all the equipment necessary for its performance. The *USP* XVIII recognizes the problem by stating: "The successful use of this technique requires exceptional skill and expert knowledge. The frequent use of positive and negative controls is highly advisable. Good practices include the occasional use of known contaminated solutions containing very few (approximately 10 cells in the total volume concerned) of varying types of microorganisms to confirm the adequacy of the technique being used."

Streeter and Robertson (32) state that people using MF techniques require at least 3 months practice in order to achieve reproducible and accurate results. Taubert (33) said that his experience showed that this length of time was in no way too long. From personal experience in training microbiologists to perform the MF tests the author concurs with these opinions.

Since the adoption of the MF sterility tests for antibiotics in 1964, we have acquired vast experience with these procedures. Notwithstanding their important contribution to the effectiveness of antibiotic and insulin sterility testing, these techniques require a great deal of expertise on the part of all personnel connected with sterility testing. This includes the auxiliary personnel who sterilize the equipment as well as those who actually perform the test.

Laboratories performing a large number of tests daily generally use sterility test units such as the one shown in Figure 1 consisting of six separate Pyrex filtering devices on a manifold. This unit was expressly designed for the sterility testing of antibiotics and was produced to meet the specific requirements described in the *Antibiotic Regulations*. If such equipment is used, it is imperative that the manufacturer's directions for proper use (30) be carefully followed for best results.

Because of recent deaths and septicemias in Britain (31) and the

Figure 1 Sterility test unit assembled with diluting fluid for performing membrane filtration tests.

United States (12) following the administration of contaminated intravenous solutions, attention has been focused on the problem of sterility assurance of these preparations. In an effort to make the sterility tests more stringent, the Third Interim Revision Announcement of *USP* XVIII dated June 1, 1972, included detailed instructions for the performance and interpretation of MF sterility tests on these preparations. The test procedure requires that the entire contents of ten units from each sterilizer load be filtered through membrane filters designed for sterility testing. The equipment in Figure 2 was designed for performing the MF test on large-volume intravenous solutions. The entire contents of the bottles can be filtered through one membrane. The membrane is then halved; one-half is placed in fluid thioglycollate medium and the other half in soybean-casein digest medium.

The units shown in both Figure 1 and Figure 2 accommodate 47 mm diameter membrane filters specifically designed for sterility testing. Compendial specifications state that the 47 mm bacterial membrane filter should have a nominal porosity of 0.45 micron ± 0.02 micron. This puts some responsibility on the laboratory performing the test to assess the membranes selected for use. An Acceptance Test Procedure for these membranes was developed by Bowman et al. (5). This test determines whether the filter will retain particles larger than the nominal pore size of the membrane. *Serratia marcescens* ATCC 14756 is used in this passage test for accepting the membranes used for sterility testing.

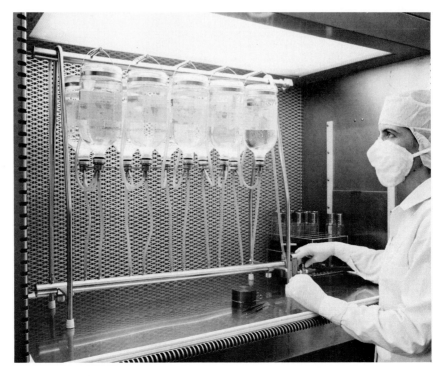

Figure 2   Commercial manifold for the membrane filtration sterility test for large volume intravenous solutions. (Courtesy of the Millipore Corporation, Bedford, Mass. USA.)

Pseudomonas dimunata ATCC 19146 is used for the Acceptance Test Procedure for 0.22 micron membrane filters which are required for sterile filtration of enzymes and isopropyl myristate used for sterility testing.

Voggel and Perl (38) state that membrane filters with a hydrophobic edge are particularly suited for testing antibiotics. They postulate that this hydrophobic edge eliminates the diffusion of the antibiotic to the portion of the membrane that is under the sealed area of the pyrex glass filter holder. Our studies on the residual antibiotics found in hydrophobic-edge membranes following a sterility test compared to the residual antibiotic retained in nonhydrophobic-edge membranes support their claim. Therefore, membrane filters with a hydrophobic edge should be used for non-penicillin antibiotics. Regular membranes are acceptable for the sterility test of the penicillin and cephalosporin classes of antibiotics, since in these products the residual antibiotic is hydrolyzed by penicillinase added to the diluting fluid.

CULTURE MEDIA

From the time of the first sterility tests until the present, the test results have been influenced by the types and sensitivity of the culture media. Since no single medium will support the growth of all bacteria, molds, and yeasts, more than one medium must be used. The question of which to use has been the subject of many conferences, study groups, and published reports.

Since there is no ideal or universal medium for sterility testing, *USP* XVIII recommends that in choosing conditions for testing a given product, trials should be made in a variety of media, over a range of incubation temperatures, and for longer periods of time than the minimum specified. The extent of such additional testing depends upon the nature of the article concerned, the manufacturing process, and the type(s) of microbial contamination most likely to be encountered.

Many media are being used for sterility testing, and the formulas for these appear in the pharmacopeias of many countries. In the report of a World Health Organization Study Group (39) formulas were listed for nine media for culturing bacteria and six for culturing fungi. The group could not recommend any one medium in preference to another because of lack of comparative data.

In 1949 Brewer (8) introduced the use of a fluid thioglycollate medium to provide aerobic and anaerobic conditions in one medium. It provided these conditions in one test tube and in addition, neutralized the bacteriostatic action of mercurial preservatives.

Bowman (4) and Doyle et al. (18) have cautioned that thioglycollate medium does not support growth of *Bacillus subtilis* spores when they are entrapped or held so that the organisms cannot be released into an environment of high oxygen tension. Macheak and Claus (24) found it necessary to reinforce this medium with 20% beef infusion broth for fastidious anaerobes, i.e., *Clostridium haemolyticum*, *C. novyi* and *C. chauvoei*.

Although liquid Sabouraud medium had been used for many years to recover molds and yeasts, many investigators opposed its use in sterility testing. Since the test is intended to detect as many microorganisms as possible, they thought it patently undesirable to use a medium, such as fluid Sabouraud at pH 5.7 ± 0.1, that inhibits certain bacteria. To eliminate the use of a selective medium for the sterility test, the *USP* XVIII replaced fluid Sabouraud *USP* XVII with a soybean-casein digest (SBCD) medium which has a pH of 7.3 ± 0.2. However, before implementing any change in the sterility tests for antibiotics as required in the *Antibiotic Regulations*, we performed a collaborative study to compare the growth-promoting qualities of SBCD medium to those of fluid Sabouraud (7). The study showed that the recovery of microorganisms was better in SBCD medium than in fluid Sabouraud medium. Accordingly, the *Antibiotic Regulations* were amended to change fluid Sabouraud to SBCD medium (20), thus assuring a high recovery of microorganisms and improving the sensitivity of the antibiotic sterility test.

TIME AND TEMPERATURE OF INCUBATION

For products tested in fluid thioglycollate medium *USP* XVIII requires an incubation temperature of 30 to 35 C, and for products tested in soybean-casein digest medium a temperature of 20–25 C. The minimum incubation time for tests performed by membrane filtration is 7 days. The time of incubation for the direct method varies from 7 to 14 days depending on the method of sterilization used to achieve sterility of the product. In 1967 Brewer and Keller (9) presented data to support the existence of slow-growing organisms that could not be detected until the 21st day of incubation. Recently, Borich and Borich (1) and Ernst et al. (19) refuted the "slow-grower" phenomenon. Each conducted studies in which the incubation time of samples under test was extended to 30 days. They concluded that delayed growths reported were artifacts produced by the insufficiency of the media used or to the inadvertent introduction of contamination of the media during incubation.

DILUTING FLUIDS

Diluting fluids are necessary to dissolve or solubilize samples prior to performing MF sterility tests. The *Antibiotic Regulations* specify four aqueous diluting fluids and the *USP* lists three. However, the *USP* states that any diluent that does not manifest bactericidal or fungicidal activity may be suitable for dissolving a preparation under test for sterility. Investigational studies performed on the diluting fluids given in the *Antibiotic Regulations* and the *USP* have shown them to be non-toxic to microorganisms (2, 6, 11). Therefore, when prepared and used as directed in the compendia they are safe.

Isopropyl myristate (IPM), a nonaqueous diluting fluid, is required to solubilize petrolatum-based ophthalmic ointments for the MF sterility tests. Early studies performed on this organic solvent proved that it is nontoxic to microorganisms (28, 29) when sterilized by filtration through a 0.22 micron membrane.

Recent reports of the microbial toxicity of IPM has been investigated by Tsuji (35) who found that the toxicity of some batches was attributed to the source. He studied the problem extensively and found that the toxicity cannot be predicted from an examination of the usual physical and chemical characteristics of IPM. Therefore, at the present time, a determination of the D value (time in minutes required to kill 90 % of the microorganisms) of IPM to *Pseudomonas aerurinosa*, ATCC 10145, gives information that best expresses the suitability of the solvent for use in sterility tests. If the D value is 60 or greater, the solvent is acceptable for the test.

BIOLOGICAL INDICATORS

One of the most significant changes in the sterility test in *USP* XVIII was the introduction of the use of biological indicators (BIs). Where applicable, they are the most effective means of demonstrating the adequacy of a sterilization process. Macek (23) reviewed the use of BIs for the determination of the effectiveness of a sterilization process. He concluded that, with proper use of BIs having adequate resistance, conventional sterility tests may be eliminated and the time for quarantine of sterilized goods prior to release may be shortened substantially. However, BIs cannot be employed when products are sterilized by filtration and aseptically filled into their final containers. Many therapeutically important drugs such as antibiotics, insulin, and hormones must be filter-sterilized. Tests for sterility performed on samples of the product are of vital importance for these drugs. The USP Advisory Panel on Sterilization recognized that this means of achieving sterility is difficult and therefore required a larger sampling plan for products not sterilized in their final containers.

SAMPLING PROCEDURES

The proper sample size and sampling procedure for the sterility test have been the subject of much debate and discussion among manufacturers and control authorities of sterile drugs and devices. The relative merits of sampling schemes based on constant sample size, regardless of lot size, versus those based on proportional samples were reviewed by Bryce (10). Control authorities demand that the manufacturers take all necessary precautions to ensure the production of a sterile product since sterility tests employing reasonable sampling detects only gross contamination. It is generally recognized that the lowest contamination rate which can be detected with at least 95 % probability are 28 %, 15 %, and 7 % when testing 10, 20, and 40 samples, respectively.

The 18th revision of the *USP* states that the adequacy and quantity of information provided by a sterility test are related to the number of articles in the sample tested and are independent of the size of the lot from which the sample was taken. In the "Procedural Details for Sterility Tests" given in this revision the minimum number of test units to be examined for various types of sterilization is specified. It also provides for testing a reduced number of products if biological indicators are used.

The *Antibiotic Regulations* require 20 immediate containers collected at approximately equal intervals from each filling operation. A filling operation is defined as that period of time not longer than 24 consecutive hours during which a homogeneous quantity of a drug is being filled continuously into market-size containers and during which no changes are made in equipment used for filling.

ENVIRONMENTAL CONDITIONS

It is axiomatic that if the results of sterility tests are to be reliable, they must be performed in a sterile environment. For this reason federal regulations and the compendia state that the tests should be performed in an area as free from microbial contamination as is possible to achieve. The *USP* XVIII states that ideally, the sterility test area should comply with the NASA standard for "Clean Rooms and Work Stations for Microbially Controlled Environment" and Class 100 conditions as described in Federal Standard No. 209A, entitled "Clean Room and Work Station Requirements, Controlled Environment" (25). Davies and Lamy (16), Parisi and Borich (27), Bowman (3), and others have described the advantages of laminar flow hoods or rooms over conventional clean rooms for sterility testing.

FUTURE TRENDS

The state of the art of sterility testing is changing rapidly and such changes are reflected in revisions and amendments to official requirements for sterility assurance. The "Procedural Details for Sterility

Tests" in *USP* XVIII describes three official procedures: (1) sterility tests on the product; (2) test on product-carried biological indicators; and (3) tests on biological indicators in or on some convenient form of carrier (e.g., paper strips or glass beads) plus sterility tests on the actual product.

Recently there have been some attempts to introduce automation procedures for product sterility testing. An instrument has been designed for the rapid detection of bacterial growth with ^{14}C-labeled glucose (17). It has been successfully used for automated radiometric detection of bacterial growth in blood cultures and its designers believe that it has promise in detecting bacteria in pharmaceuticals. Any automated procedure that can reliably detect microbial contamination in pharmaceuticals or biologicals in less time and with less effort than required for present official sterility tests will certainly be universally welcomed.

Since present official sterility tests are incapable of detecting viruses, protozoa, or mycoplasma, sterility tests of the future may correct these deficiencies by requiring additional procedures and media.

References

1. Borich, P. M., and J. A. Borich. 1972. Sterility testing of pharmaceuticals, cosmetics and medical devices. pp. 1–38. In M. S. Cooper [Ed.], *Quality control in the pharmaceutical industry.* Vol. 1. Academic Press. New York and London.
2. Bowman, F. W. 1966. Application of membrane filtration to antibiotic quality control sterility testing. J. Pharm. Sci. **55**: 818–821.
3. Bowman, F. W. 1968. Laminar air flow for environmental control and sterility testing. Bull. Parenteral Drug Ass. **22**: 57–65.
4. Bowman, F. W. 1969. The sterility testing of pharmaceuticals. J. Pharm. Sci. **58**: 1301–1308.
5. Bowman, F. W., M. P. Calhoun, and M. White. 1967. Microbiological methods for quality control of membrane filters. J. Pharm. Sci. **56**: 222–225.
6. Bowman, F. W., E. W. Knoll, and M. P. Calhoun. 1967. Solubilization of lecithin in antibiotic preparations by a non-ionic surfactant. J. Pharm. Sci. **56**: 1009–1010.
7. Bowman, F. W., M. White, and M. P. Calhoun. 1971. Collaborative study of aerobic media for sterility testing by membrane filtration. J. Pharm. Sci. **60**: 1087–1088.
8. Brewer, J. H. 1949. A clear liquid medium for the "aerobic" culture of anaerobes. J. Bacteriology, **39**: 10.
9. Brewer, J. H., and G. H. Keller. 1967. A comparative study of ethylene oxide and radiation sterilization of medical devices. pp. 311–337. In *Radiosterilization of medical products.* International Atomic Energy Agency. Vienna.

10. Bryce, D. M. 1956. Tests for the sterility of pharmaceutical preparations. J. Pharm. Pharmacol. **8**: 561–572.
11. Calhoun, M. P., M. White, and F. W. Bowman. 1970. Sterility testing of insulin by membrane filtration: A collaborative study. J. Pharm. Sci. **59**: 1022–1024.
12. Center for Disease Control. 1971. Nosocomial bacteremias associated with intravenous fluids. Morbid. Mortal. Weekly Report. **29**: 91–92.
13. *Code of Federal Regulations.* 1967. Title 42: Pt. 73.73, p. 14.
14. *Code of Federal Regulations.* 1964. Title 21: Sec. 141.2, Fed. Reg. **29**: 4119.
15. *Code of Federal Regulations.* Revised as of Jan. 1, 1972. Title 21: Pt. 130 to end.
16. Davies, W. L., and P. L. Lamy. 1968. Laminar flow. Hosp. Pharm. **3**: 7–10.
17. DeLand, F., and H. N. Wagner, Jr. 1970. Automated radiometric detection of bacterial growth in blood cultures. J. Lab. Clin. Med. **75**: 529–534.
18. Doyle, J. E., W. H. Mehrhof, and R. R. Ernst. 1968. Limitations of thioglycollate broth as a sterility test medium for materials exposed to gaseous ethylene oxide. Appl. Microbiol. **16**: 1742–1744.
19. Ernst, R. R., K. L. West, and J. E. Doyle. 1969. Problem areas in sterility testing. Bull. Parenteral Drug. Ass. **23**: 29–39.
20. *Federal Register.* 1970. **35**: No. 231. p. 18195.
21. Holdowsky, S. 1957. A new sterility test for antibiotics—An application of the membrane filter technique. Antibiot. Chemother. **2**: 49–54.
22. Holgate, J. A. 1968. The law and the sterile package. Proceedings of symposium on packaging for radiosterilization. pp. 1–3.
23. Macek, T. J. Biological indicators—A U.S.P. review. Bull. Parenteral Drug Ass. **26**: 18–25.
24. Macheak, M. E., and K. D. Claus. 1970. Effects of certain anticorrosives in steam on *Clostridia.* Amer. J. Vet. Res. **31**: 2301–2304.
25. NASA standards for clean rooms and work stations for the microbially controlled environment. NHB 5340.2. Aug., 1967 edition. Superintendent of Documents, U.S. Government Printing Office, Washington, D.C.; Federal Standard No. 209A. 1963. "Clean room and work station requirements, controlled environment." General Services Administration, Business Service Center. Washington, D.C.
26. *National Formulary.* 1970. XVII First Suppl. Amer. Pharm. Ass. p. 15.
27. Parisi, A. N., and P. M. Borich. 1968. The application of laminar flow to sterility testing. Proceedings of the 7th Annual Technical Meeting of the American Association for Contamination Control. Chicago, Ill.
28. Russomanno, R., and E. G. Wollish. 1964. Method for sterility testing of oils. J. Pharm. Sci. **53**: 1538–1539.
29. Sokolski, W. T., and C. G. Chidester. 1964. Improved viable counting method for petrolatum-based ointments. J. Pharm. Sci. **53**: 103–107.
30. *Sterility testing with the membrane filter.* 1971. Application manual AM 201. Millipore Corp. Bedford, Mass.
31. Sterne, M. 1972. Microbes in transfusion fluids. New Scientist, May 4: pp. 272–274.
32. Streeter, H. W., and D. A. Robertson. 1960. Evaluation of membrane filter

technique for appraising Ohio river water quality. J. Amer. Water Works Ass. **52**: 229–246.

33. Taubert, H. 1968. Can sterility tests for medicines be simplified? Pharmazie **23**: 544–551.
34. Tsuji, K., E. M. Stapert, J. H. Robertson, and P. M. Wanyaki. 1970. Sterility test method for petrolatum-based ophthalmic ointments. Appl. Microbiol. **20**: 798–801.
35. Tsuji, K. Personal communications.
36. Sterility tests. *United States Pharmacopeia*. 18th rev. 1970. Mack Publishing Co., Easton, Pa. pp. 851–857.
37. Ibid. 1972. Third Interim Revision Announcement, Pharmacopeia of the United States, 18th rev.
38. Voggel, K. H., and H. W. Perl. 1970. Sterile filtration and sterility testing of pharmaceutical products with membrane filters. Drugs Made in Germany **13**: 150–156.
39. World Health Organization Report Series No. 200. 1960. *General requirements for the sterility of biological substances*. WHO. Geneva.

4

Sterilization of Plastics: Toxicity of Ethylene Oxide Residues

CARL W. BRUCH, PH.D.

Chief, Drug-Device Microbiology Branch
Food and Drug Administration
Washington, D.C.

EVERY STERILIZATION PROCEDURE has a benefit: risk ratio for its use. The benefit is the decrease of infections or disease syndromes associated with viable microorganisms or their by-products (endotoxins). The major portion of the risk has been related to the probability of insterility (survivors), which ranges from 10^{-3} for filter-sterilized drugs to $< 10^{-6}$ for items exposed to steam sterilization under pressure. More recently, it has been realized that chemical toxicities from residues left or induced by a specific sterilant should also have a significant input to such risk determinations. The human damage from such toxicities should be less than the probability of insterility in a sterilized product. On this basis the radiation sterilization of liquid or semi-wet organic products and the sterilization of drugs or devices by liquid or gaseous ethylene oxide (ETO) or other chemicals have the greatest potential to generate such toxicities. No attempt will be made here to peg the current levels of human damage from such toxicities since this type of epidemiological data is not routinely collected or made publicly available. Because the thrust of this symposium is toward the sterilization of disposable devices, the potential of ETO sterilization procedures to generate chemical toxicities by way of the several reaction mechanisms available to this alkylating agent will be examined.

An important but less significant aspect of the risk equation is the *economic cost* resulting from chemical/physical damage to a sterilized

49

item. Such product damage can also be an indirect factor in human injuries. For example, steam sterilization of foods results in some vitamin destruction, and some labile drugs have their potency seriously reduced by exposure to this process. The oxidation phenomena from dry heat sterilization are recognized by any supervisor of hospital central material supply services where the browning of paper wraps and the decrease in sharpness of surgical instruments are commonly encountered. Even an inefficient sterilant such as ultraviolet radiation has side effects from the generation of ozone. While product damage is an economic consideration in the employment of radiation and gaseous sterilization procedures, still the most significant issue with both sterilants is the generation of chemical toxicities.

It should be understood that the toxicities produced by ionizing radiation are more prevalent in liquid (moist) systems where the absorption of high energy radiation causes ionization in the materials. The so-called oxidation effect in radiation sterilization appears to arise from the interaction of O_2 molecules with ionized H_2O to yield oxidized radicals such as OH, HO_2, and peroxides. These radicals can react with carbonyl derivatives from the irradiation of amino acids and sugars to form toxic hydroxyalkyl peroxides. Such reactions have been primarily associated with food materials and have held up the approval of ionizing radiation as an indirect food additive in the U.S.A. (31). Furthermore, because such toxicities can be generated in drugs treated by ionizing radiation, the Food and Drug Administration (FDA) requires an approved new drug application for all drug products, including injectables, ophthalmic solutions, surgical sutures, and surgical dressings, sterilized by this process (18).

The use of ionizing radiation on plastics or other solids is not at issue since the generation of free radicals and their reaction products in these items has not been related to toxicity in humans or animals. The sterilization of medical devices, particularly disposables, by irradiation or any other sterilant requires no preclearance from the FDA because the new drug provisions of the 1938 and 1962 amendments to the Food, Drug, and Cosmetic Act covered only drug items and not medical devices. Therefore, here we will concentrate primarily on the toxicities from residual ETO and its reaction products, ethylene chlorohydrin (ETC) and ethylene glycol (ETG), in sterilized devices and will not cover toxicity native to the plastic material (leaching of plasticizers).

CHEMICAL PROPERTIES AND GENERAL TOXICITY OF ETHYLENE OXIDE AND ITS REACTION PRODUCTS

ETHYLENE OXIDE (ETO)

All epoxides, which group includes ETO, are alkylating agents. During the past 25 years there has accumulated a vast amount of data which show that alkylating agents are mutagenic, that they damage the cytoplasm and nuclei of rapidly growing cells, and that they cause injury to the chromosomal mechanism of rapidly dividing cells. It is a general property of these agents that they can interact with biochemical moieties through the alkylation of sulfhydryl, carboxyl, hydroxyl, and amino groups. Because their biological effects closely simulate those which occur in microorganisms following exposure to ionizing radiations, alkylating agents have been referred to as "radiomimetic poisons." Bruch and Bruch (12) summarized that the following biochemical proclivities are most likely to account for the sterilizing activity of gaseous alkylating agents such as ETO: (a) a common characteristic of these agents is that they react with groups (organic and inorganic anions, and amino and sulfide groups) which are electron-rich (nucleophilic); (b) epoxides react extensively with amino but not with the carboxyl groups of amino acids; (c) the reaction of epoxides with amino acids and proteins involves the hydroxyalkylation of an atom with one or more lone pairs of electrons, either nitrogen or sulfur; (d) the moisture requirements for ETO sterilization can be explained on the basis that H_2O facilitates proton reactions, and protons are required by an alkylating agent such as ETO in its reactions with tertiary nitrogen compounds; and (e) ETO exerts its principal biochemical effect by alkylation of the nucleophilic groups of nucleic acids (the ring nitrogen atoms of the purine and pyrimidine bases are hydroxyethylated before the phosphate groups are esterified).

The radiomimetic properties of ETO are supported by numerous reports of its mutagenic activity against pollen and seeds (12). However, this mutagenic activity has never been correlated to any carcinogenic activity for this compound. Of the monoepoxides that have been considered as gaseous sterilants only epichlorohydrin (36) and propylene oxide (60) have been implicated as possibly oncogenic. Although no cases of human neoplasms have ever been related to the monoepoxides, the users and practitioners of gaseous sterilization must be concerned with this potential health hazard, as well as with the acute and chronic toxicity that can result from exposure to ETO and its reaction products.

The acute toxicity of ETO and its irritant action on the skin and eyes are well known to industrial toxicologists. Pure anhydrous liquid ETO does not cause primary injury to dry skin of workers, but solutions of this chemical have a vesicant action (53) and may cause conjunctivitis if splashed in the eye. Burns are particularly likely to occur when the solutions is held in contact with the skin by clothing, gloves, and shoes. In common with many other irritants, ETO can produce sensitization. Such topical toxicity will be discussed in a later section on safe levels of ETO and its residues in sterilized materials.

Studies by Hollingsworth et al. (29) demonstrated that guinea pigs, rabbits, and monkeys tolerated 113 ppm, and rats and mice 49 ppm during 7 hr vapor exposures (5 days per week) over a period of 6–7 months. A concurrent independent study (30) noted that dogs, rats, and mice exposed daily over a 6-month period to 100 ppm of gaseous ETO exhibited no clinical signs of toxicity, but a few significant hematological changes were noted in one animal. The case histories of 37 chemical operators who have worked in ETO production for a mean period of 10 years revealed that the health experience of this group exceeded that of a non-ETO-exposed group (34). As a result of these investigations it has been suggested that an industrial hygiene standard for ETO vapor exposure for an 8 hr working day be 50 ppm, which is somewhat lower than the 100 ppm standard listed by the Manufacturing Chemists Association.

Table 1 summarizes the data obtained by the Woodard Research Corporation (65) under a contract from the Sterile Disposable Device Committee of the Health Industries Association for the acute toxicity of ETO by different routes of administration in several animal species. A comparison of these data with the results for ethylene glycol (ETG) and ethylene chlorohydrin (ETCH), which were also assayed in this contract study, revealed that in general the LD_{50} (mg/kg) of ETO was at least two orders lower (more toxic) than that of ETG. However, as will be shown later, ETCH had a lower LD_{50} in general than that found for ETO.

ETHYLENE GLYCOL (ETG)

Whenever ETO is held in the presence of H_2O (liquid or vapor), the major degradation product is ETG ($C_2H_6O_2$). Our concern is primarily with the toxicity of the monomeric species of glycol that result from

Table 1   Acute toxicity[a] of ethylene oxide to mice[b], rats[b], and rabbits[b, c]

Animal	Sex	Oral	I.V.	I.P.	S.C.
			LD_{50} (mg/kg) Route of administration		
Mouse	M	365	261	178	192
	F	282	261	178	261
Rat	M	242	355	178	141
	F	282	383	153	127
Rabbit	M	631	178	251	200
	F	631	178	251	200

[a] Death within 24 hr in most instances. Signs of pharmacological action included ataxia, prostration, labored respiration, and occasional tonic convulsion.

[b] Five animals of each sex for mice and rats at each of six dose levels; one rabbit of each sex at each of six dose levels.

[c] From Woodard and Woodard (65).

such reactions. The data obtained by the Woodard Research Corporation (65) for the acute toxicity of ETG in several animal species (Table 2) show that the LD_{50} of this substance is much greater (less toxic) than that obtained for ETO or for ETCH to be reported later.

Ethylene glycol received much notoriety from the outbreak of deaths associated with the consumption of "Sulfanilamide Elixir" in the late 1930s. Actually, it was the dimer of ETG, di-ethylene glycol ($C_4H_{10}O_3$), which was the vehicle for the sulfanilamide (54). It was estimated that consumption of from 9–100 ml of the elixir led to fatalities. Laug et al.

Table 2   Acute toxicity[a] of ethylene glycol to mice[b], rats[b], and rabbits[b, c]

Animal	Sex	Oral	I.V.	I.P.	S.C.
			LD_{50} (mg/kg) Route of administration		
Mouse	M	17,000	4,460	2,610	6,550
	F	17,000	5,210	2,420	6,550
Rat	M	10,400	5,210	6,070	7,650
	F	15,300	5,210	4,460	7,650
Rabbit	M	6,310	7,940	6,310	10,000
	F	6,310	7,940	6,310	10,000

[a] Toxic signs were bloody urine, a number of instances of delayed deaths, and reduced weight gain in survivors.

[b] Five animals of each sex for mice and rats at each of six dose levels; one rabbit of each sex at each of seven dose levels.

[c] From Woodard and Woodard (65).

(38) have reported that the acute human LD_{50} for ETG is approximately 100 ml.

Animal studies showed that rats fed ETG at 1 and 2 % concentrations of the diet over a period of 2 years had a somewhat higher mortality than the untreated controls (44). These latter data were supported by the results of Blood (7) who noted no adverse effects in rats fed a diet containing 0.2 % ETG for 2 years. An earlier study by the same group (8) showed no adverse effects in monkeys fed a diet containing 0.5 % ETG for 3 years. Latven and Molitor (37) reported a subcutaneous LD_{50} of 5008 mg/kg and an oral LD_{50} of 8348 mg/kg for mice. The data of Allen et al. (2) implicated ETG and higher polymeric forms of this glycol as the factors responsible for the development of hemorrhagic diathesis in male mice held on ETO-sterilized pine shavings. Draize et al. (21) found that 15 % solutions of ETG were nonirritating to rabbit eyes or penile mucosa. From these findings it appears that the amounts of ETG that would be anticipated in a sterilized item would be far below the levels that would cause acute toxicity.

ETHYLENE CHLOROHYDRIN (ETCH)

Up until the early 1960s it had been believed that ETG was the only residue of concern (other than ETO per se) from gaseous ETO sterilization. The report in 1965 by Wesley et al. (62) that ETO decontamination of foods resulted in detectable residues of ETCH led to a reevaluation of the types of residues and potential hazards from the use of ETO on foods, drugs, and medical devices. ETCH (C_2H_5OCl) is formed when ETO reacts with chloride ions in the presence of moisture in foods and polymeric materials.

Ethylene chlorohydrin has a number of industrial uses, e.g., as a solvent for certain types of polymers and lacquers and as a starting material for synthesis of a host of organic compounds. Such industrial production led to investigations that revealed the serious systemic toxic effects that can result from exposures to this chemical. It can cause human poisonings by being swallowed, inhaled, or absorbed through the intact skin. The recommended vapor limit for continuous 8 hr exposures is 5 ppm (59).

The acute toxicity (LD_{50}) values for ETCH in various animal species are summarized in Table 3. The results of these studies point to LD_{50} values in a limited range (56–178 mg/kg) when ETCH was administered to mice, rats, rabbits, and dogs. The route of administration appeared to have little influence on the acute toxicity values. The compound is

Table 3 Acute toxicity of ethylene chlorohydrin to mice, rats, rabbits, and dogs

Animal	Sex	Oral	I.V.	I.P.	S.C.	Reference
					LD_{50} (mg/kg)	
				Route of administration		
Mouse	M	153	121	121	121	Woodard (65)
	F	178	121	131	154	Woodard (65)
	M	81	—	98	—	Lawrence (40)
Rat	M	60	112	61	66	Woodard (65)
	F	52	104	71	66	Woodard (65)
	M & F	72	—	56	—	Goldblatt[a]
	F	77	—	—	—	Johnson (32)
	M	71	—	64	—	Lawrence (40)
Rabbit	M	63	79	89	100	Woodard (65)
	F	63	79	89	100	Woodard (65)
	M & F	—	—	85	(Dermal) 68	Lawrence (40)
Dog	F	25	—	—	—	Taylor (57)

[a] Brit. J. Indust. Med. 1 : 213 (1944).

easily absorbed through the intact skin. The LD_{50} produced by topical administration was comparable to that from IP or oral administration (40). The "no effect" daily dose in the feeding studies conducted by Ambrose (3) was found to be about one-half the oral LD_{50} of ETCH as defined by later studies. Recently, Carson and Oser (14) reported that rats, dogs, and monkeys fed up to 45 mg/kg/day for 90 days exhibited no adverse signs. This dose level represented about 60% of the oral LD_{50}. Lawrence et al. (39) showed a "no adverse effect" in a group of rats who received 10% of the LD_{50} dose or 6.4 mg/kg IP daily for 30 days. This finding agrees with Johnson (32) who found that a lifelong intake of 12% of the acute oral LD_{50} or about 9 mg/kg/day produced no adverse effects. These latter studies, particularly those of Johnson (32), show that small doses of ETCH are detoxified rapidly in animals. However, if the amounts become too high and sufficient quantities reach intracellular sites, toxic manifestations will result.

A potential local or systemic toxic hazard might be present if sufficient ETCH or ETO is present in devices that have not been sufficiently degassed and such devices are used repeatedly over a period of time on a patient. The doses from such exposures represent a form of subacute toxicity which could involve dermal penetration with primary irritation, intradermal, intramuscular, and ophthalmic irritation, and potential tissue toxicity. These forms of subacute toxicity will be reviewed in a later section on residue limits.

DETECTION PROCEDURES FOR ETO, ETG, AND ETCH IN GASEOUSLY STERILIZED MATERIALS

After ETO was introduced in the late 1920s as a grain fumigant, wet chemical methods were employed for determinations of residual ETO as a gas or in aqueous solutions (41). Phillips and Kaye (47), in their classic series of papers in 1949 on the factors and kinetics of ETO sterilization, reviewed these chemical determinations which were slight modifications of one basic procedure. ETO was reacted in salt solutions containing standardized acid to form ETCH and metallic hydroxides. The amount of acid consumed as determined by titration with standard base is a measure of the initial ETO content. Later, Critchfield and Johnson (19) described a colorimetric assay of ETO (and ETG) following its conversion to formaldehyde.

The above chemical methods generally allow for elution of the absorbed epoxide by aeration and its entrapment in a reaction solution. These methods were found to be unsatisfactory for most medical products because a relatively small percentage of the ETO absorbed by the plastic was actually recovered. Even so, Royce and Moore (52) in 1955 and Perkins and Lloyd (46) in 1961 were able to confirm the absorption of 15,000 ppm of ETO into gum rubber while the latter group also showed the absorption and elution over time of 22,000 ppm of ETO from Tygon tubing (46). Later, Gunther (25) reported 94 % recovery of the 69,700 ppm of ETO solvated by a pure gum rubber sample. He eluted the ETO by distillation of the sample in monochlorobenzene which was collected in a receiving medium and titrated with a standard hydrogen bromide solution using crystal violet as an indicator. This method has been found tedious and somewhat low in recovery with various plastics, but Gunther's report definitely established the very high levels of ETO and propylene oxide which could be absorbed by rubber and plastics. Concurrently, Adler (1) demonstrated ETG residues in all samples (including steroids, antibiotics, and vitamins) of experimental batches sterilized by 10 % (by weight) ETO diluted with 90 % CO_2. He measured residual ETO by gas–liquid chromatography (GLC), while ETG and total glycol (i.e., ETG plus ETO as glycol) were measured by a modification of the chromotropic acid reaction after the removal of interfering substances by extraction or by ion exchange.

Up until 1965, only the glycols and residual ETO were reported as residues in materials treated with this epoxide. Then Wesley et al. (62) showed that fumigation of foods with ETO or propylene oxide can result in the formation of chlorohydrins. His group steam-distilled the food to remove the suspected chlorohydrins and then analyzed the distillate by chemical or gas chromatographic (GC) means. Ragelis et al. (48) sub-stantiated the formation of chlorohydrins in flour and pepper after fumi-gation with either ETO or propylene oxide. Gas chromatography of the ether extracts followed by infrared analysis and nuclear magnetic resonance were used to confirm the identity of the ethylene and propy-lene chlorohydrins (49). In 1968, Ben Yehoshua and Krinsky (6) found acetone to be a good solvent for extraction of ETO and its residues from dates prior to GC quantitation of the extracts. Thus, in the last 10 years there has been a shift away from wet chemical determinations to more sensitive and reproducible quantitative results with either GC or GLC.

The report by Cunliffe and Wesley (20) in 1967 on the formation of ETCH in polyvinyl plastics previously sterilized with ionizing radiation and subsequently resterilized by gaseous ETO escalated the need for rapid and accurate determinations of residues in plastic materials. The issue of toxicity from plastics used in medical devices resulted in the formation of a Z-79 Subcommittee on Medical Plastics of the American National Standards Institute (ANSI) in December, 1967, and the for-mation of a Z-79 Subcommittee on ETO Residues in April, 1968 (50). This latter group, which met quarterly for the next two years, and the Sterile Disposable Device Committee (SDDC) of the Health Industries Association concurrently started discussions as to the best procedures to detect and quantitate ETO, ETG, and ETCH from gaseously sterilized plastics. A subcommittee of the SDDC chaired by D. J. Cleary (17) initially recommended an acetone extraction procedure of 24 hr duration followed by GC analysis. Since that time, however, other members of this group have individually reported on the use of vacuum and/or aqueous extraction as useful techniques for certain types of materials.

When one looks at a list of medical items (Table 4) which are com-mercially treated with ETO, it is obvious that each product will have to be individually investigated to determine which extraction procedure is most efficient and reproducible. Thus, Matsumoto et al. (42) have deter-mined ambient aeration times for catheters through GC assays of residual ETO in water extracts from such products. Water extraction is slow and approximately 3 % of the ETO is converted to ETG during a 3 day extraction period (63). Recently, Spitz and Weinberger (55) have reported on a GC method for the analysis of ETO (acetone extract) and the simultaneous determination of ETG and ETCH in aqueous extracts from cellulosic materials. Later, Weinberger (61) described a co-sweep

Table 4 Examples of medical/surgical supplies known to be processed with ethylene oxide

Venoclysis (IV) sets	Eye droppers and cups
Procedure packs	Arterial shunts
Suture removal kits	Surgical gloves
Room air filters	Disposable diapers
Heart pacers and controls	Nonwoven fabrics (drapes)
Lymphography sets	Anaesthetic solutions
Plastic syringes, tubing and tubes	Urethral lubricant
Swabs and tongue blades	Otic drops and suspensions
Cotton and plastic bandages	Ophthalmic suspensions
Urinary drainage sets	Surgical jellies
Colostomy sets	Benzalkonium chloride
Dropper bottles and assemblies	solution and swabs
Vaginal irrigation sets	Sanitary napkins
Urinary catheterization trays	Baby supplies
Peritoneal dialysis trays	Plastic brushes
Heart catheters	Plastic sponges
Middle ear prosthesis	

extraction technique applied to aqueous extracts of these materials followed by GLC analysis. Whitbourne et al. (64) found increased recoveries of ETCH from polyvinyl chloride, synthetic rubber, and latex rubber when such ETO-sterilized materials were extracted under vacuum and the extracts condensed in a cold trap and then assayed by GLC as compared to water or acetone extracts so analyzed (Table 5). Brown (9) has reported on residue levels of ETO and ETCH in a variety of surgical materials (Table 6) extracted with p-xylene, the desired constituents isolated by column chromatography, the ETO converted to ETCH on a Celite column, and the eluates assayed by GLC. Mogenhan et al. (43) described an ETO residue determination which utilized vacuum extraction and condensation in a cold trap prior to GC assay of the revaporized ETO. A distinct advantage of the vacuum method is that very low levels of ETO can be detected since sample size can be increased without limit which is not the situation with liquid extraction methods, either water or acetone, which were also tested in their study.

Some investigators (4) have used the weighing method to study the toxicity of ETO residues in gas sterilized materials. Whitbourne (63) has found that this method gives erroneous values for specific residues, particularly when such residues are less than 200 ppm. The poor sensitivity for individual extractives in weight determinations can be attributed to the following factors: water absorption during sterilization; loss

Table 5 Effect of extraction procedure on recovery (in ppm) of ethylene chlorohydrin from sterilized materials[a]

Material	Water extraction	Acetone extraction	Vacuum extraction
P.V.C. (A)	207	188	323
P.V.C. (B)	112	48	142
Synthetic rubber	NR[b]	NR	0.59
Latex rubber	NR	NR	0.45

[a] From Whitbourne et al. (64).   [b] NR = no recovery.

Table 6 GLC detection of ethylene oxide or ethylene chlorohydrin in surgical materials from commercial or experimental sources[a]

Item	Material	Aeration status[b] (days)	Extraction time[c] (hr)	ETO (ppm)	ETCH (ppm)
Heart catheters	Dacron	C	72	NR[d]	2.0
		C	72	NR	3.0
		1	72	NR	27
Tubing	Polyethylene	C	48	NR	NR
Transfusion unit	P.V.C.	C	1	—	1.5
Penrose tubing	Rubber	1	24	NR	7.1
Surgeons' gloves	Rubber	1	72	2.4	1.9
		1	72	3.1	1.9
		2	1	—	13
		8	1	—	11

[a] From Brown (9).

[b] C means item was obtained from commercial sources or hospital central supply. Aeration status is unknown.

[c] Extraction solvent was p-xylene.   [d] NR = no recovery.

during aeration of absorbed gases used to dilute (decrease flammability) of sterilant; loss of volatile materials (plasticizers) from the plastic sample; and gain in weight from the formation of ETG and di-ethylene glycols. Because absorption of some gases could occur simultaneously with loss of other gaseous constituents, the results of weighing determinations can only be a rough guide as to what is happening to the residues.

FACTORS REGULATING THE ABSORPTION AND ELUTION (DEGASSING) OF ETO AND ITS REACTION PRODUCTS FROM PLASTIC MATERIALS

Rubber, plastics, and natural fabrics such as cotton are usually considered to be relatively inert to the presence of H_2O. However, this is not the situation when these materials, particularly rubber and some plastics such as polyvinyl chloride (P.V.C.) are exposed to organic solvents. Ethylene oxide is a cyclic ether and has most of the solvent properties associated with ether compounds. It is absorbed by all rubbers, most plastics, and many textile materials. The amount of ETO absorbed by rubber and plastics is regulated in part by the type of plastic and varies for modifications of the basic formula of that plastic. Table 7 lists some ranges of absorbed ETO for several types of rubbers and plastic following a standard ETO sterilization cycle at 130 F. The subsequent factors have been found by various investigators to influence the absorption and degassing of toxic residues, particularly ETO, from gaseously sterilized products: (*a*) type of material; (*b*) physical dimensions and exposed surface areas of materials; (*c*) packaging of the item; (*d*) sterilization variables to include time, temperature, gas concentration, type of gas diluents (CO_2 or fluorocarbons), and moisture; and (*e*) air movement (exchange) and temperature around the degassing item.

Table 7   Extent of ethylene oxide absorption by plastic and rubber materials during a standard gaseous sterilization cycle[a, b]

Material	Residue Level (*ppm*)
P.V.C.	10,000–30,000
Polystyrene	15,000–25,000
Polyethylene	5,000–10,000
Polypropylene	15,000
Natural rubber	20,000–35,000
Synthetic rubber	20,000
Silicone rubber	15,000–20,000

[a] From Ernst and Whitbourne (22).

[b] Cycle parameters are 650 mg/liter, 50% relative humidity, at 130 F for 4 hr.

PHYSICAL DIMENSIONS AND TYPE OF MATERIAL

The data in Table 7 point to P.V.C. and natural rubber as the materials with the greatest propensity to solvate ETO. The next important variables are the thickness and mass of the item and its surface area. Samples of the same mass of a given plastic will have different final absorption values and different gas elution curves depending on the

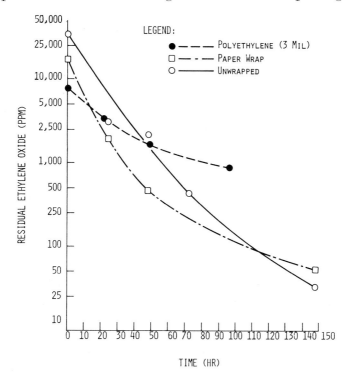

LEGEND:
● — — — POLYETHYLENE (3 MIL)
□ — · — PAPER WRAP
○ ——— UNWRAPPED

Figure 1 Effect of various packaging materials on ethylene oxide absorption and elution for P.V.C. endotracheal tubes sterilized with standard hospital cycle (650 mg/liter, 50% relative humidity, 130 F, for 4 hr).

degree of exposed surface area. If the surface area exposed is constant, then a thicker item will degas more slowly because the gas has penetrated to a greater depth and requires longer to migrate to the surface.

PACKAGING

The elution curves in Figure 1 depict the effect of the permeability of packaging on the total amount of ETO absorbed and its rate of degassing from P.V.C. endotracheal tubes. The more permeable wraps allow higher final absorption values but enable a faster rate of elution of the solvated ETO. Similar data were presented to the Z-79 Subcommittee on ETO Residues for comment. This group recommended that P.V.C. wrap should not be used since it delays elution of ETO. Nylon film is not very permeable to ETO, and its use as packaging for ETO-sterilized articles was also discouraged.

STERILIZATION FACTORS

At a fixed ETO concentration the longer a plastic item is exposed to the gaseous sterilant the greater the absorption. The total amount absorbed slopes off with a plateau being reached as the capacity of the plastic to solvate the gas is reached (22). According to Ernst and Whitbourne (22) absorption is inversely proportional to temperature, i.e., the absorption rate for the sterilant gas decreases as temperature increases. Their data show that the amount of ETO absorbed is in direct proportion to the concentration of the sterilizing gas. Both they and Kereluk and Lloyd (35) present evidence that pure ETO systems can result in higher levels of absorbed ETO than do ETO systems with diluent gases and that materials exposed to systems employing pure ETO can require longer aeration periods at ambient temperatures than do materials from other ETO systems. Mogenhan et al. (43) and Gunther (26) note that the diluent gases, either CO_2 or fluorocarbons, are absorbed by rubber and plastic materials. Fortunately, these gaseous diluents do not influence the absorption or desorption of ETO but may have an effect on the removal of other substances (plasticizers).

Humidity is a very important factor since it influences both the absorption and degassing of ETO from plastics. Ernst and Whitbourne (22) show that high moisture levels during ETO sterilization will cause greater absorption of ETO into P.V.C. Furthermore, high moisture levels will cause increased amounts of reaction products to form, i.e., more ETG and ETCH.

Some of the above factors have been utilized to derive a mathematical equation for the absorption of ETO by P.V.C. (22). The amount absorbed, A_c, is directly proportional to the concentration:

$$A_c = k(C - I)$$

where k is the absorption constant, C is the concentration, and I is a baseline intercept and thus also a constant. The absorption rate, A_t, decreases, but is proportional with time:

$$A_t = k \log_{10} t + C \text{ or } (C = A_t \text{ at } t = 1)$$

where k is the absorption rate constant for a specific concentration, t equals time, and C is a constant equal to A_t at $t = 1$. Figure 2 is a plot based on this equation where the ETO absorbed by P.V.C. is calculated against time for an exposure to a concentration of 1200 mg/liter, 50 % RH, and 130 F (54 C). The absorption exhibits first-order reaction kinetics with time.

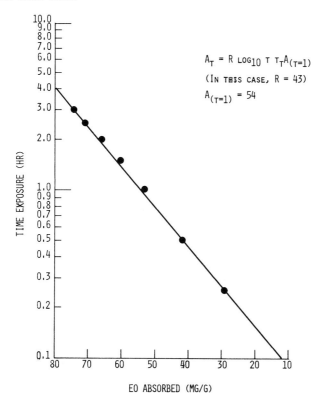

Figure 2   Ethylene oxide absorbed as a function of time.

DEGASSING TEMPERATURES AND AIR EXCHANGES

Unlike absorption, which is inversely proportional to temperature, the elution of ETO is directly proportional, i.e., elution rates increase with temperature and the amount of time required for aeration is decreased (22, 26). Kereluk and Lloyd (35) have presented an extensive series of charts on the dissipation of ETO and its diluent gases from rubber, vinyl plastic, and polyethylene at ambient temperatures and 50 C. Their data support the analysis of Ernst and Whitbourne (22) as shown in Figure 3 which depicts the linear release of residual ETO under forced aeration at 130 F (54 C) versus the rather exponential elution under ambient room conditions. In these experiments the P.V.C. endotracheal tubes were wrapped in 3 mil polyethylene. If the plastic item had been wrapped in a more porous type of package, aeration would have occurred at approximately 0.7 times the value found for polyethylene wrapping. It should also be noted that the aeration rate at 130F

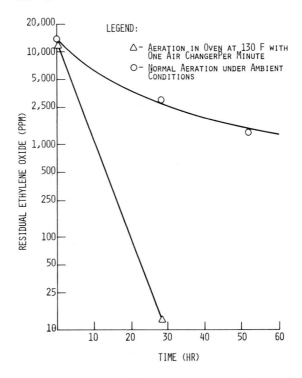

Figure 3 Effect of high temperature–high air flow aeration on ethylene oxide content of P.V.C. endotracheal tubes packaged in 3-mil polyethylene film.

was one air change per min in the degassing chamber. Such air exchanges should not be thought of as equivalent to the repeated vacuum cycles discussed by Thomas and Longmore (58), which are less efficient in the removal of ETO than are forced aeration cycles (51).

A mathematical analysis of the elution of absorbed ETO from P.V.C. has been presented by Ernst and Whitbourne (22). The elution rate, A_t, is exponential for a specific temperature and is given by the following equation:

$$A_t = A_0 e^{-kt} \text{ or } \log A_t = \log A_0 e^{-kt}$$

where A_0 is the starting absorption concentration, k is the elution rate constant, and t equals elution time. Although this latter plot will tend to tail near its terminal end, the curve for practical purposes is an exponential function.

It has been assumed by most practitioners of gaseous sterilization that the elution of ETO would allow for concomitant release of ETG and ETCH. Johnston (33), however, has presented data for nonwoven fabric samples and multicomponent devices which portray the elution of ETO over a 27 day period, but the ETG and ETCH levels either reached a plateau or even increased slightly by the end of 27 days. His results should be compared with those of Brown (9) presented in Table 6 which show the presence of ETCH in surgical materials picked up by the FDA from commercial channels.

AERATION PERIODS AND RESIDUE LIMITS FOR ETO-STERILIZED MEDICAL ARTICLES

In 1961, a review article by the author on gaseous sterilization (10) cited published reports of human injury from ETO residues and indicated the unpublished occurrence of other tissue reactions thought to be due to these residues. Further suspicion of the potential of ETO residues to cause human injury was given by Hirose et al. (28) who reported on the hemolysis of blood upon exposure to different types of plastic tubing which had been sterilized with ETO. The hemolytic effect from ETO-sterilized plastic tubing was transient in that it was maximal immediately after sterilization and not evident following 7 days of aeration of the tubing. Clarke et al. (16) confirmed these findings using plastics, gaseous sterilization equipment, and chemicals manufactured in Australia. The picture became further complicated when Cunliffe and Wesley (20) in 1967 detected ETCH in distilled water washings from radiation-sterilized P.V.C. tubing that had been resterilized with ETO. Shortly thereafter, O'Leary and Guess (45) demonstrated the toxicity of various ETO-sterilized plastics to tissue cultures and the hemolysis of human blood in ETO-sterilized disposable syringes.

During the past decade there were occasional reports of patient injury and recalls of drugs and devices by the FDA because of problems related to residual ETO or its reaction products (50, 5, 56, 27, 23). After the Z-79 Subcommittee on ETO Residues began its meetings in early 1968, other unpublished or suspected instances of patient reactions from ETO residues were indicated by several committee members. It became

personally obvious that some guidance on the time needed to aerate
ETO-treated supplies before use would have to be given to hospital
operators of gaseous sterilization equipment.

The following aeration times for ETO-sterilized rubber and plastic
items were offered (13, 11) for the guidance of hospital personnel:
(a) glass, paper, and thin rubber articles—hold 24 hr at room temperature; (b) gum rubber (thicker than $\frac{1}{4}$ inch) and polyethylene articles—
hold 48 hr at room temperature; (c) all other plastics except P.V.C.—
hold 96 hr at room temperature; (d) P.V.C. items—hold 7 days at room
temperature; and (e) aeration at 50–54 C in a properly designed aerator
—hold 12–16 hr or follow manufacturer's instructions. The discussions
of the Z-79 Subcommittee on ETO residues were a significant aid in
the formulation of these suggested aeration times since some of the
elution data discussed in the previous section were presented to this
group prior to formal publication.

Even though a few degassing curves have now been derived for the
elution of ETO from several plastic materials, the problem of determining a safe residue level for this substance as well as for ETG and
ETCH still remains. Subacute or chronic toxicity data are needed to
determine the doses of these compounds that man can tolerate and thus
allow a back calculation of safe residue levels in ETO-sterilized products.
Fortunately, the SDDC of the Health Industries Association contracted
with the Woodard Research Corp. for acute and limited chronic toxicity
studies of the three residues of concern (65). In addition, two other
groups, one under the leadership of Autian (21, 40, 39, 24) and the
other under Guess (24), have recently completed studies on the acute,
limited chronic, and tissue reactions to ETCH.

RESIDUE LIMITS FOR ETO

After data from the toxicity studies cited above became available, the
Z-79 Subcommittee on ETO Residues met in late 1971 for discussions
of a safe residue limit for ETO. A proposal was made to this subcommittee that an interim residue guideline of 25 ppm be established for
this substance in disposable plastic devices. This limit was derived
through the following assumptions and calculations:

1. The data in Table 8 from the limited chronic toxicity studies of the
   Woodard Research Corp. show an approximate "no effect" level
   of 6 mg/kg/day from 30 days of daily subcutaneous injections in dogs
   and rats. This was the lowest level of ETO assayed in the study.

2. However, some hematological changes were noted in both animal species and 2/4 dogs had ectopic hematopoiesis of the spleen at this dose level. Therefore, it was decided to take one-half of the above-cited dose as an assumed "no effect" dose level, i.e., 3 mg/kg/day.
3. A 10-fold safety factor (or 1/10 of the dose calculated in 2. above) was then applied to yield an assumed safe level of 0.3 mg/kg/day for man.
4. For a 70-kg man the safe daily dose was estimated to be 21 mg.
5. As a worst case situation it was postulated that the blood of a patient could be exposed to approximately one lb or 500 g of plastic film or tubing in an extracorporeal bypass operation or renal dialysis. If this amount of plastic film contained 25 ppm of ETO and all of this ETO were to be released into the patient's blood, the dose of ETO would be 12.5 mg or 60 % of the estimated safe dose (500 g times 0.025 mg/g yields 12.5 mg).
6. For a child weighing 30 kg, the estimated safe daily dose of ETO is 9 mg. A dose of 12.5 mg as calculated for the worst case situation in 5. above would exceed the estimated safe dose by 40 %.

However, it was the consensus of the Z-79 Subcommittee based on the data in Table 8 plus those of Andersen (4) that an interim residue guide-line of 250 ppm of ETO be established for plastic items.

RESIDUE LIMITS FOR ETG

Based on data presented in Table 9 and on the prior discussion of acute toxicity of ETG (Table 2), it appeared that 50 mg/kg/day was an approximate "no effect" level for dogs and rats. Since there were some slight hematological changes noted in the animals at this level, it would appear that one-half of this dose or 25 mg/kg/day is a more prudent "no effect" level. For a 70 kg man this yields an estimated daily safe dose of 175 mg (70 times 2.5 mg/kg) if a 10-fold safety factor is applied to this assumed "no effect" dose. If, as a worst case situation, the blood of a patient is exposed to 500 g of plastic film or tubing as described in the fifth item, above, containing 250 ppm of ETG and all of that ETG was released into the blood stream, a dose of 125 mg (500 times 0.25 mg/g) or 70 % of the estimated safe daily dose would occur.

While it is generally thought that plastic items containing less than 1000 ppm of ETG pose only a very remote chance of a patient response, this may not be the situation with an infant. For example, one of our FDA District Laboratories detected the presence of at least 1000 ppm

Table 8 Summary table on tissue irritation and subacute toxicity of ethylene oxide[a]

Animal	Test site[b]	Maximal concentration tested	Highest no-effect concentration	Total dose of ETO at no-effect level (mg)
		Tissue irritation study (one injection)		
Rabbit	IM	2%	2%	10
	ID	2%	0.2%	0.6
	Eye	10%	2.1%	2
	Dermal	5%	1%	5
Guinea pig	SC	1%	0.1%	0.05
		Subacute toxicity study (30 days with SC injection daily)		
Rats	Body wt	54 mg/kg	6 mg/kg	(lowest concentration tested)
Dogs	Body wt	54 mg/kg	6 mg/kg	
Rats	Hematology[c]	54 mg/kg	6 mg/kg	
Dogs	Hematology[c]	54 mg/kg	6 mg/kg	(some changes)
Dogs	Histopathology	54 mg/kg	6 mg/kg	(2/4 dogs—spleen: ectopic hematopoiesis)

[a] From Woodard and Woodard (65).
[b] IM = intramuscular; ID = intradermal; SC = subcutaneous.
[c] Hematology includes leucocyte counts and clinical chemistry of blood.

of ETG (1 mg/g) in an ETO-sterilized disposable diaper. If it is assumed that an infant would have six diaper changes per day and that each diaper weighs 80 g, then the total amount of ETG present during these six diaper changes is 480 mg. If 20 % of this amount would pass through the baby's skin, then there is a reasonable probability that over a period of time that toxic manifestations could be present. As yet, there exist no governmental or Z-79 Subcommittee guidelines for ETG residue levels in ETO-sterilized materials.

RESIDUE LIMITS FOR ETCH

At the time that the SDDC undertook its contract toxicity studies with the Woodard Research Corp., it was generally felt that ETCH was the potentially more toxic member of the three residues of concern. Indeed, the data in Table 3 on acute toxicity and in Tables 10 and 11 for limited chronic toxicity and tissue response tend to support this original supposition.

Table 9   Summary table on tissue irritation and subacute toxicity of ethylene glycol[a]

Animal	Test site[b]	Maximal concentration tested	Highest no-effect concentration	Total dose of ETG at no-effect level (mg)
		Tissue irritation study (one injection)		
Rabbit	IM	10%	10%	50
	ID	5%	5%	15
	Eye	100%	10%	10
	Dermal	5%	2%	10
Guinea pig	SC	1%	1%	0.5
		Subacute toxicity study (30 days with SC injection daily)		
Rats	Body wt	450 mg/kg	50 mg/kg	(lowest concentration tested)
Dogs	Body wt	450 mg/kg	50 mg/kg	
Rats	Hematology[c]	450 mg/kg	50 mg/kg	(elevated leucocytes)
Dogs	Hematology[c]	450 mg/kg	50 mg/kg	(increased neutrophils)
Dogs	Histopathology	450 mg/kg	50 mg/kg	(1/4 dogs—spleen: ectopic hematopoiesis)

[a] From Woodard and Woodard (65).

[b] IM = intramuscular; ID = intradermal; SC = subcutaneous.

[c] Hematology includes leucocyte counts and clinical chemistry of blood.

The results of Guess (24) show that ETCH is not a primary skin irritant and actually passes through the intact skin of rabbits without visible evidence of tissue toxicity. However, when the compound is injected under the skin or into muscle tissue, or comes into contact with mucosal membranes, it can be extremely damaging. Contrariwise, with dilution the toxicity to tissues declines rapidly so that a concentration of 1:50 (2%) usually shows no evidence of tissue injury. Carson and Oser (14) reported a "no effect" level of 45 mg/kg/day for rats, dogs, and monkeys fed ETCH for 90 days. Taylor et al. (57) in a chronic feeding study of 23 weeks' duration with rats reported a "no effect" level of 15 mg/kg/day for ETCH. In the subacute studies reported by Lawrence et al. (39) an IP dose of 6.4 mg/kg/day for 30 days was found to be the "no effect" level in rats. They calculated that on this basis no medical device should be capable of releasing to a 70 kg man an amount

Table 10 Summary table on tissue irritation[a] of ethylene chlorohydrin

Animal	Test site[b]	Maximal concentration tested (%)	Highest no-effect concentration (%)	Total dose of ETCH at no-effect level (mg)	Reference
Rabbit	IM	2	2	10	Woodard (65)
	IM	100	1	1	Guess (24)
Rabbit	ID	5	2	6	Woodard (65)
	ID	100	1	2	Guess (24)
	ID	100	1	2.4	Lawrence (40)
Rabbit	Eye	50	10	10	Woodard (65)
	Eye	100	10	10	Guess (24)
	Eye	100	1.25	1.5	Lawrence (40)
Rabbit	Dermal	5	1	5	Woodard (65)
	Dermal	100	20	40	Guess (24)
	Dermal	100	Absorbed too rapidly	—	Lawrence (40)
	Penile mucosa	100	1	2	Guess (24)
Guinea pig	SC	1	0.5	0.25	Woodard (65)

[a] Irritation from one injection.
[b] IM = intramuscular; ID = intradermal; SC = subcutaneous.

Table 11 Summary table on subacute toxicity of ethylene chlorohydrin

Animal	Test parameter	Maximal concentration tested (mg/kg)	Highest no-effect concentration (mg/kg)	Remarks	Reference
		Study of daily SC doses for 30 days			
Rats	Body wt	27	3	3 mg/kg was lowest level tested	Woodard (65)
Dogs	Body wt	27	3		
Rats	Hematology	27	3	High leucocyte counts	
Dogs	Hematology	27	3	1/4 dogs at 3 mg/kg level had ectopic hematopoiesis of spleen	
Dogs	Histopathology	27	3		
		Study of daily IP doses for 30 days			
Rats	Body wt	12.8	6.4	7/12 deaths at 12.8 mg/kg	Lawrence (39)
Rats	Gross pathology	12.8	12.8	Increased organ wt	
		Study of IP doses, 3 times per week, for 12 weeks			
Rats	Body wt	32	32		Lawrence (39)
Rats	Food consumption	32	32		
Rats	Hematology	32	32		
Rats	Histopathology	32	32		

equal to 448 mg per day. However, they further cautioned that it was dangerous to extrapolate rodent data to man and that every attempt should be made to reduce ETCH concentrations in plastic and rubber items to a minimum and, if possible, to a zero level.

In the chronic toxicity studies reported by the Woodard Research Corp. (Table 11) dogs and rats received subcutaneous injections for 30 days. At the lowest ETCH level tested (3 mg/kg/day) some of the animals showed slight hematological changes and 1/4 dogs had ectopic hemato-poiesis of the spleen. If one-half of this level or 1.5 mg/kg/day is taken as the "no effect" level and a 10-fold safety factor applied, then a 70 kg man should not be exposed to a daily dose (70 times 0.15 mg/kg) exceeding 10.5 mg of ETCH. If the blood of a patient is exposed to 500 g or plastic film or tubing containing 25 ppm or ETCH and all of the ETCH is eluted into the blood stream, then a dose of 12.5 mg (500 times 0.025 mg/g) would be received—approximately 20% greater than the estimated daily safe dose. Of course, this hypothetical "worst case" situation would not be expected to occur on a daily basis for any patient. In my opinion a properly ETO-sterilized and aerated plastic item should not contain more than 25 ppm of ETCH on the average when introduced into patient practice.

SUMMARY

In view of the data for ETO residues for commercially sterilized plastic items which was discussed but not published by the Z-79 Subcommittee on ETO Residues and which is also indicated by the data in Table 6, it is suggested that the main hazard from ETO residues is not in commercially sterilized items but primarily in hospital-treated materials. Since hospitals are active practitioners of gaseous sterilization but do not have the facilities to conduct residue determinations as does a commercial disposable device manufacturer, the problem is then posed to the fabricators of gaseous sterilizing equipment as to what aeration times they recommend or what aeration equipment they sell to enable hospitals to reach acceptable residue levels.

One U.S. manufacturer of ETO sterilizers has stated that the final judgment on safe aeration times is the responsibility of those concerned with the medical or surgical applications of these ETO-treated articles and materials and the circumstances under which these are to be employed. It is my contention that the manufacturers of ETO sterilizers had (and still have) the responsibility to inform their clients of the dangers to patients from ETO residues and not to wait for complaints of patient injury from the users of ETO sterilizers before admitting that ETO residues could be a problem. Another U.S. manufacturer of portable ETO sterilizers has recognized this responsibility and published tables of recommended ambient aeration times versus the aeration times needed in its aerator.

A third U.S. manufacturer has published ETO residue limits for three classes of medical items along with ambient aeration times versus the holding times for articles in its aerator to reach these residue limits (15). For class 1 items which have direct contact with sensitive body tissues and fluids such as implants and equipment used in extracorporeal bypass operations, the recommended limit for ETO as a residue is 25 ppm. For class 2 items which contact the patient's skin such as gloves and face masks, the residue level is suggested to be 250 ppm. For class 3 items through which gases are passed such as anesthesia units or respirators, the firm recommends aeration to a level of 1000 ppm or less of ETO. This company's approach is more realistic and will assure the continued use of gaseous sterilization for in-hospital processing of materials.

Gaseous sterilization processes have provided much health benefit due to a decrease incidence of bacterial infections through the availability and use of sterile disposable supplies. Since our standards of health have been raised by the introduction of this new sterilization technology into industry and hospitals, it behooves all of us associated with this sterilization process to minimize the risk of patient injury from any gaseous sterilization residues. There is a need for a continuing dialogue as to safe residue limits for all ETO-sterilized supplies.

References

1. Adler, N. 1965. Residual ethylene oxide and ethylene glycol in ethylene oxide sterilized pharmaceuticals. J. Pharm. Sci. **54**: 735–742.
2. Allen, R. C., H. Meier, and W. G. Hoag. 1962. Ethylene glycol produced by ethylene oxide sterilization and its effect on blood-clotting factors in an inbred strain of mice. Nature **193**: 387–388.
3. Ambrose, A. M. 1950. Toxicological studies on compounds investigated for use as inhibitors of biological processes. Archives Indust. Hyg. Occupat. Med. **2**: 591–597.
4. Andersen, S. 1971. Ethylene oxide toxicity. J. Lab. Clin. Med. **77**: 346–356.
5. Anesthesia Study Committee of the N.Y. State Society of Anesthesiologists. 1969. Hazards associated with ethylene oxide sterilization. New York State J. Med. **69**: 1319–1320.
6. Ben-Yehoshua, S., and P. Krinsky. 1968. Gas chromatography of ethylene oxide and its toxic residues. J. Gas Chromatog. **6**: 350–351.

7. Blood, F. R. 1965. Chronic toxicity of ethylene glycol in the rat. Food Cosmet. Toxicol. **3**: 229–234.

8. Blood, F. R., G. A. Elliott, and M. S. Wright. 1962. Chronic toxicity of ethylene glycol in the monkey. Toxicol. Appl. Pharmacol. **4**: 489–491.

9. Brown, D. J. 1970. Determination of ethylene oxide and ethylene chlorohydrin in plastic and rubber surgical equipment sterilized with ethylene oxide. J. Assoc. Off. Anal. Chem. **53**: 263–267.

10. Bruch, C. W. 1961. Gaseous sterilization. Annual Rev. Microbiol. **15**: 245–262.

11. Bruch, C. W. 1971. Are your disposables safe? Hospitals (J.A.H.A.) **45**: 138–146.

12. Bruch, C. W., and M. K. Bruch. 1970. Gaseous disinfection. pp. 149–206. In M. Benarde [Ed.], *Disinfection*. Marcel Dekker, Inc. New York.

13. Bruch, C. W., and M. K. Bruch. 1971. Sterilization. pp. 592–623. In E. W. Martin [Ed.], *Dispensing of medication*. Mack Publishing Co. Easton, Pa.

14. Carson, S., and B. L. Oser. 1969. Oral toxicity of ethylene chlorohydrin (Abstract). Toxicol. Appl. Pharmacol. **14**: 633.

15. Castle Co., Division of Sybron Corp., Rochester N.Y. 1971. Aeration chart No. 4041 (dated Dec. 1, 1971).

16. Clarke, C. P., W. L. Davidson, and J. B. Johnston. 1966. Hemolysis of blood following exposure to an Australian manufactured plastic tubing sterilized by means of ethylene oxide gas. Australian–New Zealand J. Surg. **36**: 53–56.

17. Cleary, D. J. 1969. Analysis of ethylene oxide sterilant residues. pp. 156–161. In the *Proceedings of the 1969 HIA Technical Symposium*. Health Industries Association. Washington, D.C.

18. Code of Federal Regulations. 1971. Sterilization of drugs by irradiation. Section 3.45 of Title 21, U.S. Govt. Printing Office. Washington, D.C.

19. Critchfield, F. E., and J. B. Johnson, 1957. Colorimetric determination of ethylene oxide by conversion to formaldehyde. Anal. Chem. **29**: 797–800.

20. Cunliffe, A. C., and F. Wesley. 1967. Hazards from plastics sterilized by ethylene oxide. Brit. Med. J. (2), 575–576.

21. Draize, J. H., G. Woodard, and H. O. Calvery. 1944. Methods for the study of irritation and toxicity of substances applied to skin and mucous membranes. J. Pharmacol. Exp. Therap. **82**: 377–390.

22. Ernst, R. R., and J. E. Whitbourne. 1971. Toxic residuals. In the *Study of the requirements, preliminary concepts, and feasibility of a new system to process medical/surgical supplies in the field*, pp. 46–57, Appendix pp. 1–2, Contract No. DADA17-70-C-0072. U.S. Army Medical R & D Command, Washington, D.C. (Defense Documentation Center Accession No. AD890320 and AD890321).

23. Food and Drug Administration, FDA Weekly Recall Reports, July 5–11, 1967, Item No. 5; Nov. 25–Dec. 1, 1969, Item No. 9.

24. Guess, W. L. 1970. Tissue reactions to 2-chloroethanol in rabbits. Toxicol. Appl. Pharmacol. **16**: 382–390.

25. Gunther, D. A. 1965. Determination of adsorbed ethylene and propylene oxides by distillation and titration. Anal. Chem. **37**: 1172–1173.

26. Gunther, D. A. 1969. Absorption and desorption of ethylene oxide. Amer. J. Hosp. Pharm. **26**: 45–49.

27. Hanifin, J. M. 1971. Ethylene oxide dermatitis. J. Amer. Med. Assoc. **217**: 213.
28. Hirose, T., R. Goldstein, and C. P. Bailey. 1963. Hemolysis of blood due to exposure to different types of plastic tubing and the influence of ethylene oxide sterilization. J. Thoracic Surg. **45**: 245–251.
29. Hollingsworth, R. L., V. K. Rowe, F. Oyen, D. D. McCollister, and H. C. Spencer. 1956. Archives Indust. Health **13**: 217–227.
30. Jacobson, K. H., E. B. Hackley, and L. Feinsilver. 1956. The toxicity of inhaled ethylene oxide and propylene oxide vapors. Archives Indust. Health **13**: 237–244.
31. Jamison, A. 1968. Irradiated food: FDA blocks AEC, Army requests for approval. Science **161**: 146–148.
32. Johnson, M. K. 1967. Detoxification of ethylene chlorohydrin. Food Cosmet. Toxicol. **5**: 449.
33. Johnston, D. 1971. Survey of ethylene oxide residue. pp. 185–202. In the *Proceedings of the 1971 HIA Technical Symposium*. Health Industries Association. Washington, D.C.
34. Joyner, R. E. 1964. Chronic toxicity of ethylene oxide: A study of human responses to long-term low-level exposures. Archives Environ. Health **8**: 700–710.
35. Kereluk, K., and R. S. Lloyd. 1969. Ethylene oxide sterilization. J. Hosp. Res. **7**: 7–75.
36. Kotin, P., and H. L. Falk. 1963. Organic peroxides, hydrogen peroxide, epoxides, and neoplasia. Radiat. Res., Suppl. **3**: 193–211.
37. Latven, A. R., and H. Molitor. 1939. Comparison of the toxic, hypnotic, and irritating properties of eight organic solvents. J. Pharmacol. Exp. Therap. **65**: 89–94.
38. Laug, E. P., H. O. Calvery, H. J. Morris, and G. Woodard. 1939. The toxicity of some glycols and derivatives. J. Indust. Hyg. Toxicol. **21**: 172–201.
39. Lawrence, W. H., K. Itoh, J. E. Turner, and J. Autian. 1971. Toxicity of ethylene chlorohydrin II. Subacute toxicity and special tests. J. Pharm. Sci. **60**: 1163–1168.
40. Lawrence, W. H., J. E. Turner, and J. Autian. 1971. Toxicity of ethylene chlorohydrin I. Acute toxicity studies. J. Pharm. Sci. **60**: 568–571.
41. Lubatti, O. F. 1932. Determinations of ethylene oxide. J. Soc. Chem. Indust. **51**: 361–367T.
42. Matsumoto, T., R. M. Hardaway, K. C. Pani, C. M. Sater, D. E. Bartak, and P. M. Margetis. 1968. Safe standard of aeration for ethylene oxide sterilized supplies. Arch. Surg. **96**: 464–470.
43. Mogenhan, J. A., J. E. Whitbourne, and R. R. Ernst. 1971. Determination of ethylene oxide in surgical materials by vacuum extraction and gas chromatography. J. Pharm. Sci. **60**: 222–224.
44. Morris, H. J., A. A. Nelson, and H. O. Calvery. 1942. Observations on the chronic toxicities of propylene glycol, ethylene glycol, diethylene glycol, ethylene glycol mono-ethyl-ether, and diethylene glycol mono-ethyl-ether. J. Pharmacol. **74**: 266–272.
45. O'Leary, R. K., and W. L. Guess. 1968. Toxicological studies on certain medical grade plastics sterilized by ethylene oxide. J. Pharm. Sci. **57**: 12–17.

46. Perkins, J. J., and R. S. Lloyd. 1961. Applications and equipment for ethylene oxide sterilization. pp. 78–92. In *Recent developments in the sterilization of surgical materials* (Pharmaceutical Society of Great Britain symposium). Pharmaceutical Press, London.

47. Phillips, C. R., and S. Kaye. 1949. The sterilizing action of gaseous ethylene oxide I. Review. Amer. J. Hyg. **50**: 270–279.

48. Ragelis, E. P., B. S. Fisher, and B. A. Klimeck. 1966. Note on determinations of chlorohydrins in foods fumigated with ethylene oxide and with propylene oxide. J. Assoc. Off. Anal. Chem. **49**: 963–965.

49. Ragelis, E. P., B. S. Fisher, and B. A. Klimeck. 1968. Isolation and determination of chlorohydrins in foods fumigated with ethylene oxide or propylene oxide. J. Assoc. Off. Anal. Chem. **51**: 709–715.

50. Rendell-Baker, L. 1969. Medical users' views of ethylene oxide sterilization problems. pp. 208–218. In the *Proceedings of the 1969 HIA Technical Symposium*. Health Industries Association, Washington, D.C.

51. Roberts, R. B., and L. Rendell-Baker. 1972. Ethylene oxide sterilization (letter to editor). Anaesthesia **27**: 237.

52. Royce, A., and W. K. S. Moore. 1955. Occupational dermatitis caused by ethylene oxide. Brit. J. Indust. Med. **12**: 169–170.

53. Sexton, R. J., and E. V. Henson. 1950. Experimental ethylene oxide human skin injuries. Archives Indust. Hyg. Occupational Med. **2**: 549–564.

54. Sollman, T. 1957. *A manual of pharmacology*, 8th ed. W. B. Saunders Co. Philadelphia, pp. 129–130.

55. Spitz, H. D., and J. Weinberger. 1971. Determination of ethylene oxide, ethylene chlorohydrin, and ethylene glycol by gas chromatography. J. Pharm. Sci. **60**: 271–274.

56. Superior Court, San Luis Obispo County, California. 1969. Rhodes vs. Paso Robles War Memorial Hospital (Ethylene oxide facial burns from anesthesia mask), Docket No. 33696.

57. Taylor, J. M. 1969. Unpublished FDA data to evaluate the safety of Food Additive Petition 9H-2398; Fed. Register **34**: 5857 (1969).

58. Thomas, L. C., and D. B. Longmore. 1971. Ethylene oxide sterilization of surgical stores. Anaesthesia **26**: 304–307.

59. Treon, J. F. 1967. Alcohols. pp. 1409–1496. In D. D. Irish and O. W. Fasset [Eds.], *Industrial hygiene and toxicology*. Interscience Publishers. New York.

60. Walpole, A. I. 1958. Carcinogenic action of alkylating agents. Annals N.Y. Acad. Sci. **68**: 750–761.

61. Weinberger, J. 1971. GLC determination of ethylene chlorohydrin following co-sweep extraction. J. Pharm. Sci. **60**: 545–547.

62. Wesley, F., B. Rourke, and O. Darbishire. 1965. The formation of persistent toxic chlorohydrins in foodstuffs by fumigation with ethylene oxide and propylene oxide. J. Food Sci. **30**: 1037–1042.

63. Whitbourne, J. E., C. Eastman, and R. R. Ernst. 1971. A study of the analytical determination of ethylene oxide. pp. 174–184. In the *Proceedings of the 1971 HIA Technical Symposium*. Health Industries Association. Washington, D.C.

64. Whitbourne, J. E., J. A. Mogenhan, and R. R. Ernst. 1969. Determination

of 2-chloroethanol in surgical materials by extraction and gas chromatography. J. Pharm. Sci. **58**: 1024–1025.

65. Woodard, G., and M. Woodard. 1971. Toxicity of residuals from ethylene oxide gas sterilization. pp. 140–161. In the *Proceedings of the 1971 HIA Technical Symposium*. Health Industries Association. Washington, D.C.; also complete *Study Report of Toxicity of Ethylene Oxide Glycol, and Ethylene Chlorohydrin*, Woodard Research Corporation, 1971, is available from HIA.

5

Packaging of Sterile Medical Products

DENNIS B. POWELL, PH.D.

RWP Flexible Packaging Limited
Bristol, United Kingdom

THE PRIME FUNCTION of a package containing a presterilized medical item is to ensure that the sterility of the contents is maintained up to the time the package is intentionally opened and that provision is made for the contents to be removed without contamination. Failure to achieve this aim negates the efforts of bacteriologists to control sterilization methods and the standards of sterility that have been set. A recent recommendation, previously mentioned in this volume, that any sterilization procedure should achieve a statistical probability of not more than one nonsterile article occurring in one million articles processed, loses its practical significance if the package fails to achieve a similar standard. In order to achieve such standards, many factors involved in the design and manufacture of a package must be carefully considered and the major ones are listed as follows:

1. Suitability of packaging material for the sterilization method.
2. Resistance of the material to bacteria.
3. Strength of package.
4. Type of package.
5. Testing of the package.
6. Type of opening.

Although this list of the factors involved, is not complete, it probably includes the major ones encountered. These factors have not been listed in any order of importance as this would be extremely difficult. Many of these items are interdependent and, in many instances, failure to overcome one problem will negate the whole package function.

SUITABILITY OF PACKAGING MATERIAL
FOR THE STERILIZATION METHOD

Although materials suitable for all methods of sterilization are available, care must be taken in selecting the correct material for the sterilization method to be used since each process imposes certain limitations.

The steam process demands adequate air and moisture permeability of material and, because of the high temperatures involved, many thermoplastic materials cannot be used. Nevertheless, certain thermoplastics such as high-density polyethylene, polypropylene, and nylon are suitable. Medical grade paper is the most widely used material for steam sterilization and is often used in conjunction with heat-resistant plastic materials.

The gas process does not restrict the use of thermoplastic materials because it is carried out at low temperatures, but the permeability of the packaging material is a very important factor. This limitation is often not due to gas penetration but rather air permeability; most gas processes involve vacuum cycles which can impart considerable physical stresses on the package if entrapped air in the package is not easily removed. Because there is no standard gas process in use, it is essential that the packaging material be selected and tested in the cycle for which it is intended.

Radiation sterilization offers the widest choice of packaging materials; high temperatures are not involved so that many thermoplastic materials can be used and, since radiation penetrates all common packaging materials, the permeability factors associated with the steam and gas processes are not relevant. Some materials can be affected, however, such as polypropylene, which can lose strength and discolor, and polyvinylchloride which tends to discolor and yield free hydrochloric acid. Nevertheless, radiation-resistant grades of these polymers are available.

Since no packaging material is a single chemical entity, many materials are available commercially in different chemical forms, although they may be classified as a single product. For example, a common thermoplastic material can contain different plasticizers, stabilizers, and slip additives in various proportions. These small variations may result in different end results when the materials are sterilized. This is further complicated when packaging converters combine basic raw materials in different ways using various adhesives, etc. It is most important, therefore, that guidance be obtained from the packaging manufacturer; preferably the packaging material should be subjected to the sterilization process and thoroughly tested before it is regularly used.

RESISTANCE OF THE MATERIAL TO BACTERIA

A detailed examination of the bacterial permeabilities of packaging materials has not been carried out, probably because of the difficulties of measuring this property under practical conditions. The most important factor affecting bacterial permeability is the frequency and size of pinholes in the packaging material. Ideally the package material chosen for an application should be completely free of pinholes. Pinholes are frequently found in single-ply materials which should be employed only in thicknesses where the occurrence of pinholes is very remote. Coatings will often effectively fill in pinholes that occur in a base material, and when two plies of material are laminated together not only will the laminant tend to fill in pinholes but it is also unlikely that pinholes in one ply will occur directly opposite those in another ply to produce a continuous hole.

In theory, only pinholes that are smaller than the smallest known bacterial cell can be tolerated, but in practice this standard may be unnecessary. An investigation (18) using a sizegrading, split-sampler technique of the size distribution of airborne particles carrying various species of bacteria and fungi found in hospital and office premises has shown that most organisms associated with human disease were usually found on particles in the range 4–20 μ equivalent diameter. Many fungi, however, appeared to be present in the air as single spores. There must also be a force to drive organisms through pinholes in a package to render the contents nonsterile. It is well known that paper packages held in humid storage conditions or in direct contact with water stand considerable risk of contamination by bacteria growing through the paper. The use of waterproof packaging materials is, therefore, always to be preferred, and sterile packages should, wherever possible, be stored in dry and good storage conditions, particularly if they are made in any part from uncoated paper. Water is not, however, the only driving force that can promote the passage of bacteria through pinholes in a package. Pressure differences between the inside and outside of a package can cause ingress of airborne bacteria. These pressure differences can be caused by temperature changes, the opening of cupboards and drawers, impact during transport, or simply by handling so that a "bellows effect" is produced.

Therefore, although no standards exist which control the frequency or size of pinholes that can be tolerated in packaging materials, it is important to develop and use techniques for determining pinholes. Also it is necessary to measure pinholes in packaging materials that have been flexed, abraded, and creased, since these actions can cause pinholes in materials which are pinhole-free when examined in sheet form.

Paper is probably the most frequently used packaging material that is susceptible to pinholes. It is essential, therefore, that only high quality papers specially developed for the medical market should be used for packaging sterile products, and regular control measurement of pinhole size should be carried out. Paper is a very good filter medium because of its fibrous structure in which the cellulose fibres mesh into an irregular network. Actual holes should not occur in good quality papers, but irregular-shaped passages through the fibres do exist and paper technologists call these pores, rather than pinholes. Measurements of maximum pore size give a good indication of the bacterial filtration properties of paper. A simple and rapid method of measuring the maximum pore diameter of a sheet of paper is based on the dioxane method described by Corte (4). The method as described can be used as a convenient control technique, but it must not be assumed that the actual pore size as measured will have a direct relationship to the passage of bacterial cells. For example, papers with a pore size distribution of 10–14 μ have been tested as filters to carbon particles measuring 0.5 μ and have been found to prevent the passage of these particles.

In the United Kingdom, the Department of Health and Social Security has produced specifications for paper used in various hospital applications. These papers must pass a test procedure specified in British Standard B.S.2577:1955, which measures the filtration properties of papers to a continuous flow of methylene blue particles. The apparatus is complicated and the standard is not expressed in terms of pore size. Nevertheless, paper mills can produce papers to a specification which is acceptable for hospital application.

The most objective test is to measure the bacterial resistance of papers. This can be done by drawing a bacterial aerosol through a paper sample subjected to a pressure differential. The disadvantage of this technique is that the air porosity of the paper sample dictates the volume of air passing through the sample. The porosity of a paper can vary significantly during manufacture, but this characteristic may have little effect on actual bacterial resistance. This porosity variable can, however, be overcome by introducing a flowmeter into the apparatus used.

A method for testing papers when wet for bacterial penetration has been described by Harbord (13). Test samples of paper are subjected to direct contact with a bacterial suspension for 2 hr, and any bacteria that have penetrated the samples are counted after incubation. It is considered that only papers with a NIL penetration rate are satisfactory since the test procedure simulates conditions that can be found in practice. This method is used as a quality control technique, but suffers from the usual problems associated with bacterial testing, those of time and cost.

Materials containing films, coatings, and laminations are commonly used for packaging disposable products because they are conveniently used on automatic packaging machines and they give good physical protection to a product as well as moisture resistance. There are several techniques available for detecting pinholes in these materials, and a useful review of the methods used has been given by Becker (2). The methods involve the penetration through the pinholes and the subsequent detection of liquids, light, electrical or corona discharges, and gases. Liquids provide an efficient and rapid method for detecting pinholes. The liquids are generally colored with a suitable dye and must have good wetting properties; benzene and ethyl alcohol have been found to be suitable and a small amount of detergent solution is often added when water is used. Becker quotes that pinholes with diameter $10\ \mu$ can be detected when ethyl alcohol is used at a test pressure of 2 mm Hg. The method can be used with plastic-coated papers, where a liquid that wets well will penetrate the plastic coating by capillary pressure and come into contact with the capillary system of the paper so that capillary force alone causes penetration of the liquid and no external pressure is required.

The most common gas method used is based on the diffusion of ammonia through pinholes in the test material and subsequent detection on a paper impregnated with an ammonia-sensitive reagent placed the other side of the test piece. Pinholes with a diameter of down to $5\ \mu$ can be detected by this method. Davis (9) has described this method fully and has used paper coated with ferrous ferrycyanide (Turnbull's blue) as the ammonia-sensitive reagent which changes to a white color on contact with ammonia gas. The same principle can be used for detecting and measuring pinholes in plastic films by subjecting the film to ammonia on one side and hydrochloric acid on the other. Small white spots of ammonium chloride form where pinholes occur and these can be marked, the ammonium chloride washed away, and the pinholes measured under a microscope.

Light can be used only for testing fully opaque materials. Large pinholes can be detected by observation against a bright light source or the material can be covered by a photosensitive paper on one side and exposed to bright light on the other side. Pinholes as small as $5\,\mu$ can be easily detected with this technique.

Electrical methods of detecting pinholes are based on a spontaneous electrical discharge in air, and there are two variations of the technique. The first method utilizes a sparkover between a brush electrode and a plate or roller electrode, and is particularly useful to packaging manufacturers since the pinholes can be detected in a continuously moving web of material. The material runs over a metal roller and a metal wire brush is positioned directly above the roller. A potential provided from a high voltage supply is passed across the electrodes. Pinholes are immediately detected by small sparks, and instruments can be incorporated in the circuit to give visual or acoustic signals of occurrence of pinholes. It is thought that this technique detects pinholes with a diameter of less than $5\,\mu$. An essential feature of the method is that the test material must have an adequate resistance; all plastic films have this property except films such as regenerated cellulose and cellulose acetate which contain high proportions of water. The second electrical method operates at a lower voltage so that sparkover does not occur but a corona discharge takes place through any pinholes. The pinholes are observed where a luminous discharge occurs, and measurement of the corona discharge is approximately proportional to the number of pinholes.

A new technique has recently been described (15) which relies on the electrolytic oxidation of a colorless redox indicator, benzidine, so that the black oxidation product formed gives a precise picture of pinholes occurring in a test film on a white millipore filter. Large pinholes can be seen with the naked eye, but small pinholes down to a diameter of $1\,\mu$ are observed with a microscope. The method is described as a rapid technique for the detection and size determination of pinholes and could be a very useful additional technique to those already mentioned for determining pinholes in plastic films and coatings.

Although there are several methods for determining pinholes in packaging materials, it must be realized that only small samples are tested by these techniques. The statistical significance of results obtained by these methods compared with the amount of packaging materials in use is very limited but, nevertheless, they serve to eliminate certain materials which could otherwise have been considered for packaging sterile products and they also enable spot checks to be made on materials in current use as to the frequency of pinhole occurrence.

STRENGTH OF PACKAGE

It is very difficult to define the physical strength characteristics required for a sterile package, but the ultimate aim is to ensure that the sterility and function of the contents are not impaired by damage to the package. There is no doubt that many sterile items are insufficiently protected against physical damage. A visual examination of packaged sterile items distributed to a group of hospitals has shown that of 2546 packages inspected from various manufacturers 6.4 % were found to be defective; and of 2400 syringe packages examined, 1.2 % were similarly imperfect (8). It was found that approximately half of these defects were due to bad seals and it is not known if these faults were due to non-sealing at the time of manufacture or to seals that had opened during subsequent transit. Christensen (3) has also stated that it is not uncommon to find approximately 10 % of packaged sterile items with holes in the packages caused by various means.

There are many factors which have to be taken into consideration when determining the physical strength characteristics required by a package. The size, weight, and shape of the product are extremely important considerations. For example, Crawford (5) has described an experiment in which a hundred 20-ml syringes, each weighing approximately 20 g, were packaged in thick polyethylene bags and then packed in a strong transport carton. The carton was dropped on the floor from a height of a meter, and almost all the polyethylene bags were found to have been punctured by the syringe. This type of problem can largely be overcome by restricting movement which may be accomplished by using smaller bags to limit the movement of the product in the primary pack and also containing the packages in a smaller outer container or placing more packages in the containers. The product can also be designed so that sharp edges which could damage the package are eliminated. The movement of packages within a container is extremely important since the packages move against one another and can cause abrasive perforation. Because of this, the ancillary packaging such as dispenser cartons and transport containers must be carefully considered, bearing in mind the product, its primary package, the method of transport, and the storage conditions that are likely to be encountered. All these factors must be computed before the primary and ancillary packaging can be selected and a final decision can be made only after thorough distribution and market tests.

Probably the most frequent weakness found in package construction

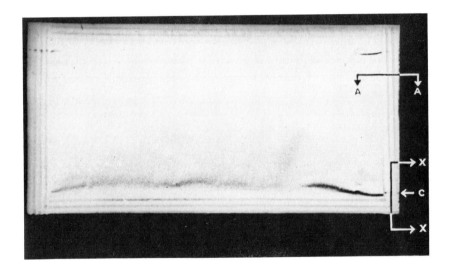

Figure 1

occurs in the package seals. These weaknesses are often seen to occur at the same location of a seal area and they may be caused by a fault in the sealing mechanism. It is useful in these instances to make thin sections of the faulty area of the seal and examine them under a microscope; the sections may be stained to aid examination. For example, a thin section of a package made from paper/foil/polyethylene has been taken at right angles to the direction of the seal (A–A, Figure 1). In this instance the

seal has been well made so that the interface of the polyethylene surfaces
are completely fused (Figure 2). To produce a seal of this type the materials must be brought together in the heat sealing plates under the correct
conditions of temperature, pressure, and dwell; if the plates are of the
crimping type as in Figure 1, then the crimping jaws must be perfectly
aligned. This is one of the most important factors to examine when a

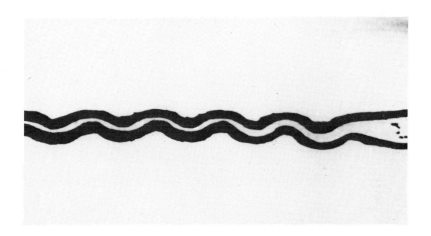

Figure 2

packaging machine is set up to ensure good heat seals; if the jaws are
out of line, then no adjustment of temperature, pressure, or dwell will
produce efficient seals. Figure 3 shows a section through a seal made with
jaws that are not aligned. It will be seen that the material has been so
badly sheared that it is almost fractured and holes have been produced
between the polyethylene interfaces. Although penetration of bacteria
is not possible through these holes because of the direction in which

the crimp seal has been made (see Figure 1), some seals are made with the crimp seals at right angles to the package, and in this case great care must be taken with jaw alignment to prevent holes.

It is desirable that the two faces of materials to be sealed should be presented completely flat to the heat sealing plates. If this is not done,

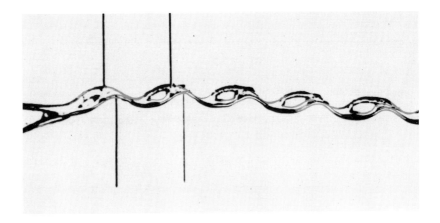

Figure 3

creases may be produced. Figure 4 shows a section taken in the direction X–X through the crease which is seen at point C in Figure 1. A large hole is visible through the heat seal and it may be possible for bacteria to enter the package by this means. It may not always be possible to avoid creases completely; it is then desirable to use a heat sealing medium which will flow out and fill in minor irregularities (e.g., polythene and ionomers). If preforming is not used, it is an advantage to use material with good flexibility for packaging bulk items, since, to avoid an excessively large package, sufficient material must be available to stretch over the product to allow seals to be made without too much creasing.

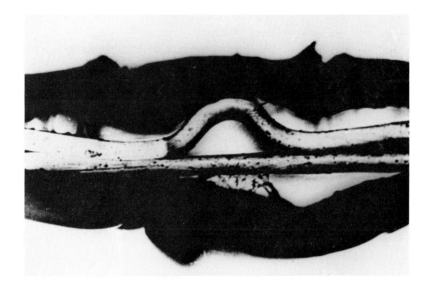

Figure 4

TYPE OF PACKAGE

Rigid containers made from fibreboard, plastics, metals, and glass are all suitable if the correct sterilization technique is used. Very few commercial applications, however, utilize rigid containers because of the relatively high unit cost and the difficulty of automatically filling. Rigid containers, nevertheless, have two useful characteristics: physical protection to the contents, and methods of opening which enable the contents to be removed without contamination. Rigid containers are used on a commercial scale for packaging hypodermic syringes and needles and, to a more limited extent, for catheters. The pharmaceutical industry also uses rigid containers extensively for packaging sterile products, particularly liquids.

Flexible package techniques are, however, most commonly used for the commercial packaging of medical items. The main reasons for this are availability of automatic packaging machinery, wide choice of materials, ease of pack identification, and low unit cost. The basic disadvantages are the amount of material required to pack a three-dimensionally shaped product, consistency of making seals, provision of methods to open the package, and the physical protection of the primary pack is not generally as strong as provided by rigid containers.

The main methods of packing medical items using flexible materials can be well illustrated by taking as an example the packaging of a disposable hypodermic syringe:

(1) One type of package is sealed on four sides (Figure 5). This package style is suited for automatic packaging, and a wide range of materials are available, both in single ply and combinations. The pack is made from two webs of material which can be the same or dissimilar, which allows various types of "peel-open" packages to be produced. A disadvantage of this package for bulky products, such as a syringe, is that a large area of material must be used and, since four seals are made, this increases the care that must be taken to ensure integrity of the seals. A variation on this method is to use a single-folded web of material which is wrapped around the product and then sealed on the remaining three sides (one long seal and two cross seals). This variation does reduce the area of material used, but limits the types of peel-open devices that can be used.

(2) The simplest method is to package the syringe in a preformed tube of flexible material such as polyethylene lay-flat tubing (Figure 6). This type of package has the advantages of using a small area of material and only two seals have to be made. A disadvantage of the method is the limited number of materials available in this form; they are used generally in single-ply form and, therefore, have the inherent weaknesses associated with single-thickness materials. An additional disadvantage is that the method does not lend itself to automatic packaging.

(3) An alternative method is to use one web of material which is formed into a tube by producing a long seal in the direction of the material (Figure 7). This can be done by wrapping the material around a metal tube on a vertical filling machine; a seal is then made across the material, a syringe dropped into the tube formed, and a further cross seal made at the top to complete the package. This type of package is

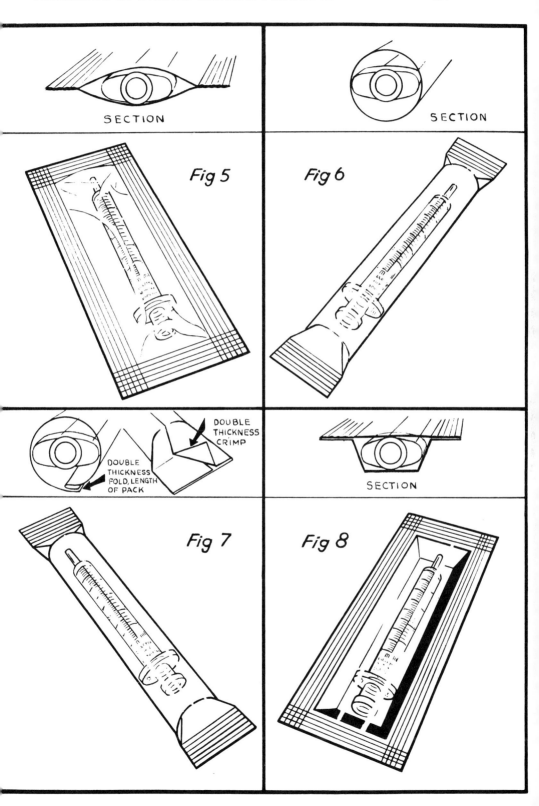

SECTION

SECTION

Fig 5

Fig 6

DOUBLE
THICKNESS
CRIMP

DOUBLE
THICKNESS
FOLD, LENGTH
OF PACK

SECTION

Fig 7

Fig 8

more commonly made by wrapping the material around the syringe in the horizontal plane while the long seal is made and the two cross seals are subsequently produced. The latter method is normally carried out on a continuous flow system and lends itself to high packing speeds. This system utilizes less material than in method (1) and only three seals have to be made. Nevertheless, great care must be taken in making the cross seals where the long seal and cross seals meet, because four thicknesses of material have to be welded together (see Figure 7). Since there is a change of material thickness across the sealing face, there is a danger of leaving a small channel at the point of changeover from two to four plies of material.

(4) A further method is to preform one web of material to form a dish into which the syringe is placed, then a further web of material is fed over the top of the dish and heat-sealed on all sides (Figure 8). The advantages of this method are the economy in use of material and that perfectly flat faces are presented for heat sealing. This type of packaging has always been attractive for packaging three-dimensional products, but its general usage has been limited by the materials that could be easily thermoformed (these also were normally only available in single-ply form) and there were few automatic machines available to produce such a package. This situation has changed radically in the last few years so that the method is becoming very popular. Several types of machines are now available, laminated webs have been developed that can be thermoformed, and materials are now produced which can be used as a peelable lid. The base tray can be rigid, semi-rigid, or flexible and the top web is easily printed for carrying information. The forming tools for the base web can be changed very quickly on some machines so that a rapid change from packing one product to another can be achieved. Stresses on the heat seals are limited by this technique because the package is formed around the product and, although Figure 8 shows a rectangular tray, this can be designed so that the dish conforms to the shape of the product.

As already stated, there is a wide range of flexible packaging materials available for use in the methods described, and combinations producing opaque, transparent, or window packs can be used. The window pack, i.e., one side opaque and one side transparent, is very popular since the opaque surface can be used to print brand names and information for the user in a distinct form, whereas the transparent window enables the contents to be seen as an important check on the information printed on the other side. The size of the package is always an important consideration since sterilization cost depends a great deal on the space taken up by the product. It is sensible to do away with unnecessary material, but sufficient material must be used to prevent heat seals having to stand excess strain. Also, if a peelable type of opening is required, then some form of tab must be provided. Fortunately, the problem of package size is usually self-solving, since as more automatic packaging machines are used it is impossible for the machine to make an acceptable package with insufficient material.

The final type of package chosen for a product is dictated by many factors, such as materials, method of opening, etc., and before a product is offered commercially on a large scale many of these factors can be investigated by a limited market test utilizing preformed packages and manually packing the product. Premade bags, pouches, and trays are available for such tests.

It is very important in selecting the type of package to remember that sufficient area be provided to enable product identification and instruction details to be clearly printed. It is a common complaint of hospital staff that insufficient attention is taken of these factors.

TESTING OF THE PACKAGE

There are several methods of testing the integrity of a package and, since there are no officially recognized methods of determining this, manufacturers tend to use methods which they consider best suited for testing their own products. There are few nondestructive test methods so that most tests are carried out on a selected number of packages which have statistical significance.

A simple method for detecting faults in packages made of water-resistant materials is to immerse the pack under water and slowly squeeze the package by hand. Air bubbles will appear if a leak is present. A variation on this test is to immerse the package in water, which preferably contains a wetting agent, contained in a desiccator and a vacuum then drawn on the dessicator; again air bubbles appear from the package if there is a hole.

A common gas technique for detecting holes in packages utilizes ammonia as a test medium. A piece of cotton wool or tissue impregnated with ammonia is inserted into a package which is premade and finally sealed or as it is being made on a packaging machine; care must be taken to ensure that the ammonia-impregnated tissue does not contaminate the seals when they are formed. The package is then placed in a desiccator containing hydrochloric acid and a vacuum drawn; the formation of ammonium chloride fumes indicate faults in the package.

A very common test method used is to subject a package to a vacuum of 20 in. Hg in a desiccator. The vacuum is held for a set time, usually a minute, and the behavior of the package is observed. A perfect package inflates, remains turgid as long as the vacuum is held, and returns to a normal appearance when the vacuum is released. Packages with gross faults will not inflate, and those with minor leaks will possibly inflate but will appear shrunken when the packages are returned to atmospheric pressure. Only packages made of air-impermeable materials can be satisfactorily tested by this technique. The volume of air in the package, the rate at which the vacuum is drawn, and the time that it is held are variables which can affect the result of the test, but these can be controlled and the technique can be used as a regular test method for the production of a standard product.

Colored liquids are also used. One technique is to inject the liquid into the package, tape over the injection hole, and then shake the liquid, which normally has good wetting properties, around the package; faults are detected visually where the liquid has "searched out" holes. A slight variation on this technique is to cut the package in half and then partially fill both halves of the package with the test liquid which again indicates faults. Frohnsdorff (12) has described a nondestructive test using a dilute fluoresceine solution for examining rigid needle containers. The plastic needle cases are immersed in the fluoresceine solution in a vacuum chamber and a vacuum of 10 in. Hg drawn and held for 5 min. The vacuum is released and the containers are held for a further 5 min before they are washed and lightly centrifuged. The containers are placed on a conveyor, passed through a darkened chamber illuminated with ultraviolet light, and faulty units are detected by bright fluorescence and rejected. Solid particles, such as carbon black and anthracene, have also been used as a test media. The method normally used is to place a package in a desiccator containing a layer of the test media; a vacuum is drawn and then suddenly released. The package is removed from the desiccator, the outer surface of the package is carefully cleaned, and then is opened for examination. Any carbon black particles that have entered the package can be seen visually; anthracene particles are observed under ultraviolet light.

The ultimate test of a sterile package is to subject it intentionally to bacteriological contamination under stress and determine if the contents have been contaminated. Two methods that have been used to carry out such a test have been described (8). The first method involves subjecting a test package contained in a respirator to alternating positive and negative pressures to simulate the changes in temperature and atmospheric pressure that a package might experience during storage. A pump, connected to the respirator, produces an alternating pressure at a rate of 20 cycles/min and the test package is subject to this procedure for 2 hr in a suspension of an organism, *Serratia marcescens*, that has been injected into the respirator. After this cycle, the contents are tested for the ingress of the organism. The second method simulates rough handling that packages might experience during transport by subjecting packages in rotating drums which contain the same microorganism (this organism is used because it is easily recognized). The drums, constructed with three right-angled plates inside, are rotated at 2 cycles/min for 2 hr. After this process, the packages are carefully removed from the drum and the outside surfaces of the packages are swabbed with a solution of 0.5 % chlorhexidine in 70 % alcohol and left for 30 min. The contents of the packages are then removed aseptically and incubated in a suitable culture media.

It is essential that packages should be withdrawn from the market at regular intervals for sterility testing. Great care may have been taken at the time of manufacture to produce a sterile product, but factors of transport and storage, not discovered in initial market tests, can nullify all the control efforts that have been made during manufacture of the product. Such examinations can often reveal weaknesses in the integrity of the package and these can then be rectified.

TYPE OF OPENING

The weakest link in the sterility chain—from manufacturer to patient —is almost certainly the opening of the package and removal of the contents. It is difficult to assess the degree of contamination that occurs when this exercise is carried out, but reference to some published work can indicate the minimum level that can be expected.

During a series of bacteriological experiments designed to evaluate various wrapping materials and containers for packaging surgical dressings (1), the bacteriological efficiency of the packaging materials was measured by the degree to which its contamination rate exceeded a "blank" or "zero" figure. The "zero" figure was measured by using test swabs contained in tins that had been sterilized in hot air; 518 control swabs were tested and 20 gave positive cultures so that a "zero" contamination rate of 3.8 % was obtained for these experiments. A further series of experiments, carried out by three industrial laboratories on the radiation sterilization of disposable syringes (16), utilized syringes treated at 10 Mrad for determining the "zero" contamination levels of the laboratories. These "zero" levels were found to be < 0.1 % in two laboratories and < 0.6 % in the third, but the authors pointed out that these low figures were achieved by the aid of laminar airflow cabinets and using double packaging of the syringes.

These experiments, since they were carried out by trained bacteriologists, would indicate that in practice it is reasonable to expect that contamination levels in the order of 1–5 % can be expected when a singly wrapped product is removed from its package. If this order of contamination is experienced, then the sterilization standard of one in a million, previously mentioned, is largely negated; it is essential then that packages be designed with opening devices that enable the product to be removed with the least possible chance of contamination.

For many years it was considered essential by several bacteriologists (14, 6) that a sterile article should not be drawn over a nonsterile edge so that cutting or tearing were not methods of opening a flexible package that should be encouraged. Nevertheless, recent comments (8, 3) indicate that cutting open a package, even with unsterile scissors, offers slight risk in contaminating the sterile products when it is withdrawn. Unfortunately, statistical data to show if the unsterile edge of a cut package is of practical significance are not available. However if a package is to be cut open, then either sterile or nonsterile scissors must be provided. The provision of sterile scissors for opening every package does not appear to be practical considering the very large number of prepackaged sterile items that are in current use, and it is inconceivable to suggest to a nurse that she may use nonsterile scissors to start a sterile procedure.

Probably the easiest way of opening a flexible package is to provide a method of tearing and this technique has been widely used, particularly for packaged syringes. This method may require the introduction of starting aids such as a notch, but an essential feature for this type of opening to be successful is that the material should have a low degree of stretch on tearing. A tear tape or string incorporated into a package might be considered as a further tearing aid, but such a method inevitably increases the risk of imperfect sealing. An alternative approach is to break the package open by pressing the object through the wall of the package. This method cannot be universally employed, but has been used successfully for needle packages where the hard hub of the needle facilitates the breaking of the material. A bacteriological assessment of this type of package has been carried out and it has been found that out of two series of needles with 400 in each series from two different manufacturers, 7 % and 1.5 % needles were contaminated when the hub of the needle was pressed through the package (7).

It has been suggested (8, 3) that the most important factor in opening a sterile package is the bacteriological aerosol that is created when a package is torn or pulled apart and this may contaminate the contents. The aerosol is particularly important when the outer surface of the package is covered with dust particles. The practical significance of the aerosol effect has not been determined since there are no published bacteriological experimental data to enable this factor to be assessed. The effect, however, has been illustrated by dusting the outer surface of packages with a fluorescent powder, opening the package, and then observing under ultraviolet light how the particles settle on the contents (11).

It is very difficult to envisage any method of opening a package which does not cause an aerosol effect since the movement of hands and the "bellows" effect that is produced when a package is held in the hand and opened will certainly produce an aerosol of some degree. Nevertheless, since the aerosol effect almost certainly exists, a sterile package and the method of opening should be designed in such a way that the dangers of an aerosol should be limited.

One of the most popular ways of avoiding this and also limiting the possibility of contaminating the sterile item by handling, is to employ a double package. It is preferable that the inner wrap should not only protect the contents during the opening of the outer wrapper, but it should be easily opened without tearing or cutting before the contents are withdrawn. In many instances the inner wrap need only be folded over like an envelope. An outer wrap where the packaging material can be peeled away from the article so that at no time does the contents touch the outer surfaces of the package has a distinct advantage. Nevertheless, peelable packages must be provided with tabs which can be held to facilitate the peeling action of the package. There is a distinct danger that dust can collect in the tab opening and come into contact with the contents when the package is peeled apart. This danger can be largely overcome by folding over both edges of the tabs so that dust cannot collect in between the tabs; this may not be necessary if other ancillary packaging is used which limits dust contamination.

In principle, therefore, it would appear that an initial target for presterilized items should be a package designed with a folded inner wrap and securely sealed peelable outer wrap with the opening tabs folded over.

Several methods of producing a peelable package have been employed. The most common method is the controlled rupturing of paper fibre. A heat seal is produced between a paper surface and another web of material which is coated with a thermoplastic heat sealing medium. The two webs of material are peeled apart, and paper fibres in the area of the heat seal are broken so that the package is opened. It is very essential with this method that the paper surface be carefully selected so that limited fibre rupture occurs and not paper tearing. Also rigid control of the heat sealing medium and the sealing conditions must be maintained. This method of opening has been criticized because a cloud of paper fibres might be created which, although sterile, should not be allowed to contaminate the contents. The importance of this factor has not been determined, but its significance should be limited if suitable papers and double packaging are utilized.

Several fully peelable systems which do not involve fibre tearing have been developed. One system (10) utilizes heat-sealable lacquer coatings which can impart peeling qualities to polyethylene-to-polyethylene heat seals. The lacquer coatings split when the package plies are peeled apart and this system is used extensively for radiation sterilized packages. Another system (19) suitable for radiation sterilization actually relies on radiation degradation of polypropylene-to-polypropylene heat seals.

Peelable seals have been produced by heat-sealing two different polymer systems together, but this technique generally involves very stringent heat control and makes this system unreliable for automatic packaging. Peelable packages have also been made by combining two plies of paper with a cohesive latex system so that, when the package is peeled open, all the sealant is transferred from the surface of one ply to the other so that reclosure cannot be made; this package construction can be steam-sterilized. Many other peelable systems have been developed and a recent article (17) indicates the considerable amount of development work being carried out by packaging manufacturers to produce a large range of peelable packages suitable for the medical market. Peelable seals can be made in various ways, but it is often forgotten that such seals are a compromise between a complete weld and no seal at all, and in an effort to produce good peelable seals the strength and integrity of the seals are sometimes ignored. A well-sealed package is the first essential and peelable seals are a secondary requisite.

It can be said that the sterility of a packaged product is dependent on the integrity of the package in which the sterilized item is contained. Packaging is, therefore, of the same order of importance as the method that is used to sterilize the product. Unfortunately, there is no such thing as a perfect package into which a range of products can be contained. The package requirements for each item must be independently assessed. Many of the problems that are encountered in selecting and testing a sterile package have been considered in this paper, but it must be recognized that even a perfect package will probably not satisfy the standards that bacteriologists would like to achieve.

Packaging manufacturers can provide a very wide range of materials and package designs suitable for presterilized disposable products. However, the greater assistance of bacteriologists, particularly in the area of opening the package, would help packaging manufacturers ensure that they fully contribute to the main objective of the hospital services and the manufacturers of presterilized medical products—to provide acceptable products which can be used with the highest degree of confidence to the benefit of the patient.*

References

1. Alder, V. G., and F. I. Alder. 1961. J. Clin. Path. **14**: 76–79.
2. Becker, K. 1963. Proc. Patra Packaging Conf. Oxford. 226–235.
3. Christensen, E. A. 1970. J. Danish Hospitals. **10**: 107–109.
4. Corte, H. 1965. Das Papier. **19** (7): 346–351.
5. Crawford, C. G. 1970. Nord-Emballage. **3**: 32–36.
6. Cunliffe, A. C. et al. 1963. Lancet. **ii**: 582–583.
7. Darmady, E. M. et al. 1961. J. Clin. Path. **14**: 55–58.
8. Darmady, E. M. et al. 1968. Packaging for Radiosterilization (Proc. Symp. U.K. Panel for Gamma and Electron Irradiation, London). pp. 16–21.
9. Davis, E. G. 1969. CSIRO Fd Preserv. Q. **29** (2): 35–39.
10. Douglas, E. A., and J. W. Scarrott. U.K. Patent No. 1,093,671.
11. Fallon, R. J. 1963. Lancet. **ii**: 785.
12. Frohnsdorff, R. S. M. 1968. Packaging for Radiosterilization 79. (Proc. Symp. U.K. Panel for Gamma and Electron Irradiation, London). pp. 39–52.
13. Harbord, P. E. 1968. Packaging for Radiosterilization (Proc. Symp. U.K. Panel Gamma and Electron Irradiation, London). pp. 60–61.
14. Hare, R., P. J. Helliwell, and R. A. Shooter. 1961. Lancet **i**: 774.
15. Huldy, H. J. 1970. Verpakking. **22** (5): 278–284.
16. Ley, F. J. et al. 1972. J. Appl. Bact. **35** (1): 53–61.
17. Modern Packaging 1972. **45** (4): 24–27.
18. Noble, W. C., O. M. Lidwell, and D. Kingston. 1963. J. Hygiene Camb., **61**: 385–391.
19. Powell, D. B. U.K. Patent No. 1,123,072.

* I would like to thank the International Atomic Energy Agency for permission to use in this paper abstracts from an article I have written in greater detail for the Radiation Manual that the I.A.E.A. expect to publish later this year.

6

Biological Control of Industrial Gamma Radiation Sterilization

J. D. M. WHITE

Group Development Manager
Johnson & Johnson Ltd., England

THE BIOLOGICAL control of sterilization cannot be discussed without first defining sterilization or sterility. The theoretical definition is of no help as an absolute negative cannot. be proved. Sterility in practice is therefore a matter of informed judgment and cannot be a mathematical fact. This situation is recognized in the definition of sterility generally held today in the United Kingdom, a sterile item being defined as one that has been manufactured under suitable microbiologically controlled conditions and has been subjected to an approved method of sterilization.

On first sight this definition may sound vague, but when considered in depth it is a realistic statement of the three essential elements involved. These are approval in the judgment of expert and authoritative opinion of (1) the sterilizing process; (2) the methods used to control it; and (3) the microbiological control of the manufacturing process prior to sterilization.

The Scandinavians prefer what is apparently a rather different definition of practical sterility which has been expressed as follows (4): "After complete sterilization there should, at the most, be only a risk of specified magnitude that viable microorganisms might still remain on the treated material." The Danes have particularized this definition to "a very low probability that the articles in question have more than one viable microorganism per 10^6 units." This type of definition on the surface appears to be more precise than that used in the U.K., but in fact on detailed analysis it is again based on expert judgment of efficacy and not pure mathematical fact. However, the concept is valuable to use as an image of the desired safety margin to be achieved in sterilization.

The third type of practical definition of sterility in use today is that in which a sterile item is considered to be one which, having been sterilized by an acceptable method, meets the criteria for sterility stipulated in an official standard or pharmacopoeia. This definition requires no comment.

In the definition of practical sterility no particular method of sterilization has been considered, since any concept of sterility must be universally applicable to all methods of sterilization if it is to be logically coherent. In considering the control of a sterilization process, this situation is no longer true as the particular features and facets of each process have to be considered separately. The following discussion on biological control therefore relates only to gamma irradiation. In particular, it relates to gamma irradiation of products which present a generally biostatic environment to their microbial flora. This discussion will be applicable to most medical devices, surgical dressings, and dry pharmaceuticals. Many of the points in this discussion will be pertinent to sterilization by accelerated electrons and to products which allow active growth of their flora, but this will not be universally true and it should be borne in mind.

METHODS

Microbiological control can be exercised at three stages in the manufacture of a sterile item: (a) presterilization; (b) sterilization; and (c) post sterilization. This again is true of all methods of sterilization. The differences in approach to the control of the various methods of sterilization lie in the distribution of effort between three stages to obtain maximum control over the final sterile item.

PRESTERILIZATION CONTROL

Presterilization is the most recent stage to receive close attention, but many would agree it is one of the most important. The significance of initial contamination level on sterilization has been recognized for a considerable time (8).

Christensen et al. (3) in 1966 put forward a method of using initial contamination counts in irradiation sterilization and this was embodied in the Danish Health Authorities' recommendations for radiosterilized products in 1968. In essence, this method takes a specific inactivation factor for the process at a standard sterilization dose and then limits the average initial contamination count to a fixed figure to give a 1 in 10^6 safety margin on the final sterile item. Allowance is made to increase the sterilization dose within limits if the initial count is above the desired maximum level.

The use of initial contamination counts as a presterilization control looks very attractive, as it appears to put irradiation sterilization on a mathematical basis. However, this is not really true as the final mathematics are based on judgment decisions involved at a deeper level in the logic of the concept. For instance, a judgment is involved in the use of mean initial contamination count as the basis of control rather than the median, three standard deviation upper limit or some other statistical parameter, of the original population. Table 1 which represents a hypothetical situation, demonstrates how samples can be different and still possess the same mean.

Table 1 Samples with different contamination counts and the same means

	Initial contamination count										Mean	Median	3× S.D.
Sample A	25	30	70	10	75	90	85	15	5	95	50	50	108
Sample B	10	1	0	0	3	2	478	0	1	5	50	1.5	451
Sample C	10	29	150	0	3	2	250	50	1	5	50	7.5	252

Judgment must also be exercised in selecting the microbiological reference preparation from which the inactivation factor for the sterilizing process is to be computed. It is considered by Christensen et al. (4) and others that the resistance of microorganisms in such a standard preparation should be greater than the resistance of all pathogenic organisms and at least as great as the resistance of all generally occurring microorganisms in the relevant environment. The relevant environment must be a matter of judgment and yet can have a dramatic effect on the resistance of the organism in question. The point that must be borne in mind with this method is that the final mathematics are only as accurate and valid as the assumptions and results on which they are based.

It is unfortunate that the Danish technique embodies the idea of higher doses for higher initial contamination levels, as this might give the impression of running counter to current thinking with regard to good manufacturing practice. If there is one thing of which we can be sure, it is that all involved in the manufacture of sterile products must strive to produce items with the minimum initial contamination level that contemporary technology will allow.

It is this thought that dominates our attitude to presterilization control. Initial contamination counts are extremely valuable in monitoring the manufacturing process prior to sterilization. The technique can be applied to materials, component parts and the packaging that go to make the final product as well as the final product itself. In this way, potential problem areas can be highlighted and appropriate action taken. The mean and variance of the initial contamination level should be taken into account when considering the significance of the values obtained.

Counts should be carried out on a routine basis but it is impossible to recommend a frequency as this will be governed by the nature of the product, the manufacturing process, the raw materials and past experience. Skill must be exercised to direct the microbiological control effort where it can do most good. This approach cannot be stressed too strongly as it is a waste of time to blindly follow a set plan. A product that has been produced by a well designed process for a number of years will require only a modest level of initial contamination testing, whereas during the initial period of production of a new product, frequent testing is desirable.

Mean initial contamination counts should not be treated as precise facts; they are merely indications of the likely average level of microbial contamination. Even with frequent testing, the sample sizes that can be employed are small relative to the numbers involved with mass produced items, such as plastic disposable syringes, and hence we have an inadequate knowledge of the initial contamination level of the whole population. This situation is not assisted by the apparent number of changes in initial contamination level where (a) short (individual fliers); (b) medium (daily trends); and (c) long term (seasonal) variations can be identified.

Ironically, the situation is equally difficult for special medical devices made in small numbers, where to obtain an accurate knowledge of the initial contamination level, an unacceptably high proportion of the total output would have to be tested. These remarks are not intended to undermine the value of initial contamination counts. They are merely to indicate the restraints that must be imposed on how actual figures are used. Initial contamination counts in the hands of a competent and enquiring control microbiologist are one of the most powerful tools at his disposal in controlling plant hygiene at the presterilization stage, and hence confidence in the final sterile item. They should be used together with aerial counts and personnel checks to control overall plant hygiene.

This comment can be considered to be equally true of all the methods of sterilization, although in our opinion, irradiation sterilization, because of one of its inherent advantages, lends itself to a recently proposed method that offers an even more powerful tool to the control microbiologist. This method is the substerilizing dose technique proposed by Tallentire et al. (9).

Tallentire et al. appreciated that the information obtained from sterility testing could be enormously increased if the technique was applied to items that had received known fractions of the total sterilizing process. They also realized that gamma irradiation sterilization was particularly well suited to this approach as substerilizing doses can be conveniently and accurately given to test items. They examined model systems of contaminated items and the effect on their microbial populations of increasing irradiation dose. They suggest that this approach may form the basis of a microbiological quality control system. Samples of the items in question would be subjected to substerilizing doses, and hence the sterility safety margin predicted for the bulk population, after sterilization at the standard dose.

If Tallentire et al. can successfully develop their technique to practical realization, then my contention that sterility cannot be mathematically based will be proved wrong. I sincerely hope that this will be the case, but past experience indicates that even with this new attack on the problem we will have to make some assumptions for lack of full information regarding the system with which we are dealing, and hence judgment will once more have to be applied.

Ley et al. (6) have reported their findings on the use of substerilizing doses to examine plastics disposable syringes. These findings demonstrated some of the value of the substerilizing dose approach to presterilization control, although the results they obtained were insufficient to enable predictions to be made regarding the safety margin at the standard sterilizing dose.

Recently we have had the opportunity to examine contaminated cotton rolls by the substerilizing dose technique (Harboard et al.). A batch of small cotton rolls was received from a supplier with a high initial contamination count. These rolls were rejected by Microbiological

Control but it was appreciated that other than in number, the contaminating flora on the cotton rolls was typical of bleached cotton products, and hence these items represented a good opportunity to examine the irradiation of this flora by substerilizing doses.

The cotton rolls in question weigh approximately 0.25 g, and a random sample of 40 indicated an average contamination level of 1884 organisms per roll. Results ranged from 500 to 7500 organisms per roll. Samples were irradiated by A.E.R.E., Harwell with gamma rays from a Cobalt 60 source, at a number of substerilizing doses. In addition, samples were also irradiated at 10 Mrad to act as controls during laboratory testing. All samples were subjected to a seven day sterility test. The results obtained in this study are shown in Table 2.

Table 2   Irradiation of contaminating flora on cotton rolls by substerilizing doses

Dose (Mrad)	Number of sample groups irradiated	Number of cotton rolls per sample	Number of sample groups contaminated	Percentage of sample groups contaminated
0.1	100	1	100	100
0.25	400	1	176	44
0.35	300	5	60	20
0.4	100	5	11	11
0.5	300	5	20	6.66
0.55	100	5	1	1
0.6	300	5	0	0
10.0	200	1	0	0

At several substerilizing doses, grouped samples were used to increase the sample size without adding to the volume of testing. The number of individual rolls likely to have been contaminated in these groups was calculated by probability theory. The 95 % confidence limits for the results were derived by the method of Clopper & Pearson (5). Table 3 shows the final calculated results, both in terms of numbers of rolls contaminated and as percentages, at each dose. It is obvious that despite the high level of initial contamination, gamma irradiation deals effectively with the microbial flora present. It is interesting that these findings approximate those predicted by Tallentire et al. (9).

The above examples demonstrate how substerilizing doses can be used to investigate particular aspects of the microbiology of an item to be sterilized. For normal microbiological control we are currently evaluat-

Table 3 Probability of contamination of cotton rolls

Dose (Mrad)	No. of cotton rolls tested	Probable no. of cotton rolls contaminated			Probable % of cotton rolls contaminated		
		Found	Upper 95% limit	Lower 95% limit	Found	Upper 95% limit	Lower 95% limit
0.1	100	100	100	96	100	100	96
0.25	400	176	192	156	44	48	39
0.35	1500	66.12	84.15	51.66	4.41	5.61	3.44
0.4	500	11.45	19.45	5.2	2.29	3.89	1.04
0.5	1500	20.88	34.59	12.3	1.39	2.31	0.82
0.55	500	1	5.2	0	0.20	1.04	0
0.6	1500	0	9.06	0	0	0.60	0

ing a more pragmatic approach to the use of substerilizing doses which recognizes that judgment has still to be exercised in assessing the significance of the findings but attempts to maximize the amount of information available on which to base such a judgment.

In our technique, no attempt is made to derive an inactivation curve for the product's flora. Only two substerilizing doses are used; these we call the *challenge* and *pathfinder* doses. The actual doses are not fixed, but can be altered to take account of the varying circumstances surrounding each product. Typically, the doses are 1.25 and 0.25 Mrad, respectively.

The challenge dose samples are intended to provide the major proportion of the information necessary to make the judgment that an acceptable safety margin should be achieved by sterilizing the product with the standard sterilizing dose, i.e. the process is in control. The pathfinder samples are used to pinpoint the area on which to concentrate microbiological control resources if a potential problem is indicated.

The basic method is to take three equal groups of randomly selected samples of actual product, in their package. The package may be overwrapped to facilitate aseptic handling in the laboratory but this in no way invalidates the standard nature of the item and the inside of its package. Two of the groups of samples are gamma irradiated at the challenge and pathfinder doses whilst the third is irradiated at 10 Mrad to act as a known sterile control. All three sample groups are then sterility tested. The 10 Mrad samples are used to monitor accidental laboratory contamination during sterility testing.

First-class sterility testing technique is most important as an accidental contamination rate of 1 in 10^3 is necessary to obtain real benefit from this method of control. To achieve accidental contamination rates during sterility testing of this order requires great attention to detail and imagination in the design of the technique used to present the packaged product for sterility testing. This is particularly so when the product has a complex physical form.

As in conventional sterility testing, the desired result with the challenge samples is no growth at the end of the sterility test, or rather not a statistically significant number of samples showing growth as compared to the 10 Mrad controls. Naturally, as good microbiological practice, all positive results in both the challenge and control samples should be investigated to indicate the nature of the organism and whether it is likely to have been an accidental laboratory contaminant.

If no positive results are obtained with the challenge samples, then the significance of this finding can be judged in the light of the known inactivation curves available for specific organisms, particularly the *resistant organisms*. The term *resistant organism* is used here to cover inherently radioresistant organisms and organisms which have had resistance conferred upon them from the environment in which they have been placed. Before any realistic judgment can be made, the challenge samples size should be greater than 10^2, and 10^3 should be the minimum objective. This sample size means that except in specific circumstances, such as the initiation of a new production process, this method of presterilization control cannot be applied on a batch basis, but rather it is a continuous, sequential technique of control covering a reasonable period of production.

An example will demonstrate how challenge sample results can provide a basis for judging the acceptability of the safety margin of a sterile item. Assume that 10^3 challenge samples are taken from a production line which has a mean initial contamination level of 50 organisms per item and no positive results are found on testing. Now the hypothesis can be made that the initial microbial flora is composed of a particular resistant organism and the validity of this hypothesis examined in the light of the actual sterility test findings. This hypothesis can be repeated to cover any relevant resistant organism and so build a picture of how well the sterilizing process deals with the microbial flora of the item in question.

For the example, the hypothesis can be made that only 1 % of the initial flora has equivalent resistance to *Streptococcus faecium* A_2l as studied by Christensen (2). At 1.25 Mrad this organism, under the particular conditions of test, had an inactivation factor of 10^1. In these circumstances if the hypothesis had been correct, on average, 50 positive results should have been found in the 10^3 challenge samples. However, no positives were found. Indeed, at the most we should find two or three false positives. Therefore, it can be concluded that the original hypothesis is incorrect and that if organisms are present of equivalent resistance to *Strep. faecium* A_2l, then their numbers must have been lower than assumed.

In a semiquantitative way it is possible to go further and estimate the probable maximum concentration, in the initial flora, of any resistant organism for which an inactivation curve is known, and hence estimate the likely order of the safety margin for the item after sterilization at the standard sterilizing dose. The probability (q) of any specific resistant organism (i) being in the initial flora can be taken to be:

$$q_i < \frac{Ic_i \times 10^{-3}}{\bar{x}}$$

where Ic_i is the inactivation factor, at the challenge dose, for organism (i) and $\bar{x}$ is the mean initial contamination count. The overall safety margin (P) at the standard sterilizing dose can similarly be taken to be:

$$P_i > \frac{Ic_i \times 10^{-3}}{Is_i}$$

where Is_i is the inactivation factor at the standard sterilizing dose of the organism. A uniform distribution of the flora has to be assumed and 10^{-3} is taken as the limiting discrimination of the sterility test.

However, it should be stressed that the challenge dose method of presterilization control is not strictly mathematically based, and at best it is a semiquantitative way of judging the relevance of published inactivation curves of resistant organisms to a particular production process.

One advantage of the challenge dose method is that the test tends to become increasingly discriminating the more resistant the organism. This is due to the fact that inactivation curves for resistant organisms are generally characterized by an initial shoulder (A) or a gentle slope (B) (Figure 1).

If a resistant organism were found whose inactivation curve (C) had a steep initial slope and a pronounced tail, this would be difficult to control by the challenge sample method. However, experience to date suggests that this form of inactivation curve must be uncommon. In addition, the presence of this type of organism should be indicated by the pathfinder samples.

A second possible weakness with the method is the perennial problem of how representative the samples of the total population are. This is covered to a reasonable degree by the sequential nature of the method. Challenge samples tested over a period of several months must represent most of the variations that occur under normal manufacturing conditions. However, this type of sample will not necessarily detect unusual

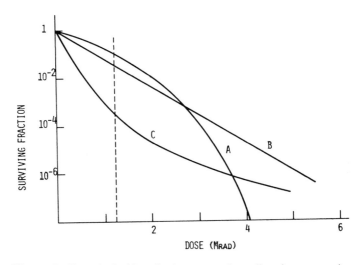

Figure 1   Hypothetical inactivation curves for radioresistant organisms.

circumstances that last for a brief period of time but whose occurrence by definition must be rare. The method has the advantage that, as it uses the relatively simple sterility test technique, sample size can be larger than with counting techniques.

The results obtained by Ley et al. (6) on disposable plastic syringes can be appraised by the challenge dose method. Table 4 is an abstract from their paper. The very low number of positive results obtained at 1.25 Mrad clearly indicates that the occurrence of highly resistant organisms must be rare for each of the three manufacturers. It therefore can be concluded that the production processes are in control.

Similarly, the results we obtain with our contaminated cotton rolls can be considered by the challenge dose method. In this case the challenge dose can be taken as 0.6 Mrad, and as we have 1500 sterility test

Table 4   Results of challenge dose method test on disposable plastic syringes

Manufacturers	Dose (Mrad)	No. of syringes positive	No. of syringes tested
A	1.25	3	1050
	10.00	3	1200
B	1.25	1	2400
	10.00	0	4400
C	1.25	0	540
	10.00	0	1020

results without a positive, clearly the number of resistant organisms present must at the most be minimal. The situation is therefore indicated as being in control and an adequate safety margin should be obtained at the standard sterilizing dose.

However, the cotton rolls were rejected as the initial contamination level was higher than that obtainable by current good manufacturing practice. I think this demonstrates our philosophy to presterilization control. No one piece of information should be allowed to dominate but an overall judgment made on all the information available. As with all rigorous methods of microbiological control, the challenge dose method is demanding on resources. Use and time will demonstrate how valuable an aid it is to making a judgment on the acceptability of a sterile item.

In addition to the results previously reported, we have used the method in a pilot study to examine a range of gamma radiation sterilized Ward Procedure Packs. These packs contain a variety of items, including surgical dressings. So far 1291 challenge samples have been examined and no positive results found. We are encouraged by our work to date with the challenge dose method, and consider the concept deserves further in-use evaluation.

The pathfinder samples are given their minimal dose to inactivate organisms of low resistance, as these are of no consequence as far as the sterility of the final product is concerned. Each of the positive pathfinder samples is examined to type the organism present and so determine whether there are any known potentially resistant organisms on the product. If necessary, specific organisms can be investigated for their inherent resistance by the well established techniques.

If a pathogenic organism is found of possible high resistance, further investigation is necessary. It is not possible to be dogmatic about the form of this investigation as it would depend on the previous microbiological history of the product and the overall circumstances of the situation together with the frequency with which the organism is found, the status of its pathogenicity, etc. It should be borne in mind that the finding of a pathogen of possible resistance in a pathfinder sample does not constitute a failure, assuming that the challenge sample results were negative, as the latter are the basic control. Pathfinder sample results should be used as a means of concentrating microbiological investigational efforts at the point at which they can be of greatest value.

If a resistant pathogen is found in the pathfinder samples and the same organism occurs on a challenge sample, this would require immediate and intensive investigation and corrective action taken before sterile product could continue to be released from production. The accumulative results over a period of time of the organisms found in pathfinder samples can be used to review the practical significance of any newly discovered resistant pathogenic organisms. Pathfinder sample results, in conjunction with initial contamination counts, aerial counts and personnel hygiene checks, should be used to monitor overall plant hygiene.

Finally, the determination of the relative biological efficiency of the radiosterilization plant can be considered a part of presterilization control. The evidence available to date suggests that there may be differences in microbiological efficiency between different radiosterilization units. However, if differences exist between different gamma radiation units using cobalt 60 sources, these are likely to be exceedingly small and consequently of no significance. Differences between accelerated electron and gamma radiation plants do appear to be significant, especially with the higher energy accelerated electron units; but even so, such differences are likely to be small in terms of the sterilizing dose.

The determination of the relative biological efficiency of a plant is desirable, but this can be carried out only by using microbiological reference standards that have been fully developed and approved by national health authorities. As is the case with any reference standard, microbiological reference standards and the techniques for using them must be beyond reproach if they are to be of any value. A strain of *Streptococcus faecium* $A_2 1$ (ATTC. 19581), spores of a strain classified as *Bacillus sphaericus* $C_1 A$ and a *Coli bacteriophage* $T1$ have been proposed as reference standards (4).

STERILIZATION CONTROL

Gamma radiation sterilization in a well designed and well operated plant is intrinsically a highly reproducible process. It also has the unique advantage over other methods of sterilization that basically only one parameter has to be controlled to ensure reproducibility of the process. This is the absorbed dose.

Physical/chemical methods are readily available that can accurately measure absorbed dose, and correct plant operation is also easy to monitor. Under these circumstances biological control of the actual sterilization process becomes unnecessary. This fact received early recognition by the Ministry of Health in the United Kingdom (7) and biological control of irradiation sterilization is not required in the U.K. This view is held in a number of other countries but biological control is still required by some.

Biological control takes the form of biological indicators or monitors. These are standardized test pieces incorporating a high population of a single species of organism, of a resistant type. There are two basic types of biological indicators: inoculated carriers, and inoculated products and simulated products. Both types of indicator have one function in common, that is to measure that the desired dose of radiation has been absorbed during sterilization. However, initially the inactivation of any biological indicator has to be calibrated against absorbed dose measured by chemical or physical means. Hence the biological indicator in this case is a secondary standard. As biological techniques, in any case, are less precise than physical/chemical dosimetry, the use of the latter form of control over the absorbed dose is much to be preferred.

Inoculated product indicators have a second function, and that is to validate the biological efficacy of each and every sterilization cycle with reference to the product being sterilized. The concept is good but, unfortunately, the creation of the indicator introduces a number of unknown factors, and so the results obtained cannot be directly related to the standard product without making the assumption that these factors are insignificant. For instance, the very act of introducing the test organism to the product distorts the microenvironmental history of the product, as compared with the standard production item. If product indicators are used, this distortion must be assumed to be of no consequence.

The use of inoculated product indicators is of value with some methods of sterilization, but their use to control gamma radiation sterilization, with its high degree of reproducibility, is superfluous. It is

far better to devote microbiological control resources to the initial vali-
dation of the sterilizing process for the product and subsequently to
presterilization control, leaving control over the reproducibility of the
sterilization process to physical/chemical dosimetry.

POSTSTERILIZATION CONTROL

Poststerilization control, in which the actual product is sterility tested
after sterilization, is one of the earliest forms of biological control exercised over a sterile product. Many authors have pointed out the severe
limitations on the information obtained from sterility testing (10).

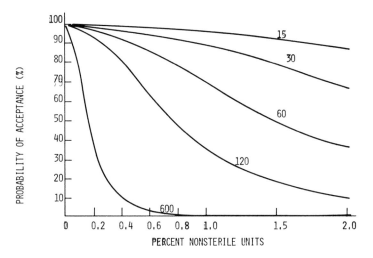

Figure 2 Probability of acceptance of lots having stated percent of nonsterile units
with different sample sizes. (C. Artandi)

These limitations arise for two reasons. First, the laws governing
statistical sampling demand enormous sample sizes if confidence limits
of the magnitude of 1 in 10^6 are to be realized, and in practical terms
these would be impossible to achieve on a batch basis. The problem has
been illustrated in many different ways. In Figure 2 Artandi (1) represents it graphically for a model system with uniform contamination.
Even with a sample size of 600, it would be seen that a lot will be accepted
10 % of the time with a contamination rate of 1 in 2.5×10^2.

Second, current laboratory techniques do not enable sterility testing
to be carried out with a significantly better rate of accidental laboratory
contamination than 1 in 10^3. Hence the confidence obtained from
sterility testing must be orders of magnitude short of that desired.

One argument in favor of sterility testing in the past (11) has been that although the method cannot demonstrate a high sterility safety margin, at least it indicates that the product has been through a biocidal process. Today a number of products manufactured with the best techniques of modern technology would pass a conventional sterility test before being sterilized, and hence this argument must now carry little weight.

In a well-designed gamma irradiation plant, it is easy to ensure that all products to be sterilized passes in the correct manner through the plant which, coupled with good sterile label control, can obviate any possibility of confusion occurring between sterile and nonsterile product. In these circumstances, there can be no reason for carrying out sterility testing on gamma radiation sterilized products, and to do so is to waste microbiological control resources which, as has already been stressed, should be concentrated on presterilization control.

SUMMARY

In summary, two points should be stressed. First, judgment in the light of expert opinion has to be exercised in accepting a sterilizing process for a product. Indeed, judgment has also to be used in a wider field than just microbiology, covering material science, toxicology and clinical need, to assess the best approach to sterilizing a particular product. Second, there can be no substitute for a well informed, intelligent, enquiring control microbiologist, fully conversant with the manufacturing process to be controlled, to ensure that adequate safety margins are maintained for a sterile item. Such microbiological control efforts should be concentrated on the presterilization stage of manufacture, and this is especially true in the case of gamma radiation sterilization.

References

1. Artandi, C. 1972. Microbiological control before and after sterilisation: Its effect on sterility assurance. Presented at the I.A.E.A. Working Group Meeting on Recommended I.A.E.A. Code of Practice, Risö, Denmark.
2. Christensen, E. A. 1970. Radiation resistance of bacteria and the microbiological control of irradiated medical products. pp. 1–13. In *Sterilisation and preservation of biological tissues by ionising radiation.* STI/PUB/247, I.A.E.A. Vienna.
3. Christensen, E. A., N. W. Holm, and F. Jaul. 1966. *The basis of the Danish*

choice of dose for radiation sterilisation of disposable equipment. Risö Report No. 140. Danish Atomic Energy Commission Research Establishment. Risö, Denmark.

4. Christensen, E. A., L. O. Kallings, and D. Fystro. 1969. Microbiological control of sterilisation procedures and standards for the sterilisation of medical equipment. Ugeskr. Laeg. **131**: 2123–2128.

5. Clopper, C. J., and E. S. Pearson. 1934. The use of confidence or fiducial limits illustrated in the case of the binomial. Biometrika **26**: 404–413.

6. Ley, F. J., B. Winsley, P. Harbord, A. Keall, and T. Summers. 1972. Radiation sterilisation: Microbiological findings from subprocess dose treatment of disposable plastic syringes. J. appl. Bact. **35**: 53–61.

7. Ministry of Health, London. 1963. Methods of controlling the operation of cobalt 60 radiation plant used for sterilising process.

8. Rubbo, S. D., and J. F. Gardner. 1965. *A review of sterilisation and disinfection.* Lloyd-Luke. London. pp. 10–12.

9. Tallentire, A., J. Dwyer, and F. J. Ley. 1971. Microbiological quality control of sterilised products: Evaluation of a model relating frequency of contaminated items with increasing radiation treatment. J. appl. Bact. **34**: 521–534.

10. Sampling procedures and statistical aspects. 1963. pp. B1–B32. In *Council of the Pharmaceutical Society of Great Britain*, Round Table Conference on Sterility Testing. London.

11. Savage, R. H. M. 1961. Interpreting the results of sterility tests. pp. 190–198. In *Sterilisation of Surgical Materials*. The Pharmaceutical Press. London.

PART TWO

Regulatory Review

7

Factors Determining Choice of Sterilizing Procedure

CARL W. BRUCH, PH.D.

Chief, Drug-Device Microbiology Branch
Food and Drug Administration
Washington, D.C.

F OR A LL sterilizing processes (except sterile filtration-aseptic fill procedures), microorganisms die at a rate which is approximately logarithmic, i.e., in physical chemical terms, a first-order chemical reaction. A plot of such inactivation kinetics down to microbial survivor levels expressed as negative logarithms reveals that sterilization is a probability function (5). Logarithmic death rates and associated probabilities of survivors have been an integral part of food canning processes in the U.S. since the early 1920s (1). However, for the past half century the drug and medical device industry as well as hospitals have relied on the assay of a small sample of sterilized product as the way to insure process effectiveness. To interrelate the degree of sterility assurance obtained by these two differing approaches will not be attempted in this brief paper. Suffice it to say, the *U.S. Pharmacopeia* (*USP*) XVIII finished product sterility tests, which usually utilize a sample size of 20 items, can only detect a contamination level of 15% with a 95% confidence rate. This corresponds to an approximate probability of survivors of 10^{-1}. Contrariwise, the use of biological indicators (BI) allows the estimation of survival levels of 10^{-6} or less.

DEFINITIONS OF STERILIZATION

If one relies on finished product sterility tests as the means to assure sterility of lots of processed materials, then sterilization can be defined as the process by which living organisms are removed or killed to the extent that they are no longer detectable in standard culture media in which they have previously been found to proliferate. This concept conveys the idea that the biological procedures used to assay sterility can be as important as the process used to achieve this condition.

If sterilization (except for sterile filtration-aseptic fill procedures) is approached as a probability function, then sterilization is the process by which anticipated levels of microbial contaminants in a load of materials are exposed to that number of D values (time for 90 % kill) for the sterilant being utilized so that the probability of a survivor is $< 10^{-6}$. Such calculations can be made when the levels and resistance (expressed as D values) are known for the natural contaminants carried in a load of materials to be processed (5) or can be derived from the use of product-carried BI (2).

A BI is defined as a preparation of microorganisms, usually bacterial spores, which is carried either directly by some of the items to be sterilized (product-carried) or by adventitious carriers such as filter paper, threads, or porcelain cylinders, and which serves as a challenge to the efficiency of a given sterilization cycle.

SPECIFIC FACTORS REGULATING CHOICE OF STERILANT

The above discussion and definitions implicitly state the objective of any sterilizing process (destruction or removal of microorganisms), the mathematical relationships defining that process, and the certainty with which that objective can be measured. With such a brief overview, the specific factors regulating the selection of a sterilizing agent for a given product can now be examined in the order of their importance: nature of product and effects of sterilant thereupon; legal acceptability or requirements for a product treated by a particular process; economics of the sterilizing process; and parameters of sterility assurance tests for each sterilizing procedure.

NATURE OF PRODUCT AND EFFECTS OF STERILANT

Except for incineration, steam sterilization under pressure (110–130 C) is the most efficient sterilant (2). However, many heat-labile biochemical substances (vitamins, amino acids, antibiotics, etc.) as well as many plastics cannot tolerate moist or dry heat. Thus, low temperature sterilization methods that operate at temperatures of less than 60 C, such as ionizing radiation and gaseous ethylene oxide (ETO), are needed to process many disposable devices, while sterile filtration is required for heat-sensitive pharmaceuticals. Furthermore, any residues generated by a sterilant must be held to such levels that pose no hazard to the patient using that product.

LEGAL ACCEPTABILITY AND REQUIREMENTS AFFECTING PRODUCT WHEN TREATED BY A PARTICULAR PROCESS

All new drugs in the U.S. (unless "grandfathered") require pre-clearance for safety and efficacy before marketing. Since the method of sterilization can affect the safety and potency of any drug required to be sterile (all parenteral and ophthalmic products), the sterilization process, including sterility assurance procedures, must be acceptable to the Food and Drug Administration (FDA). For sterile drugs other than certifiable antibiotics, the sterility tests listed in the drug compendia (*USP* and *National Formulary*) are considered as minimal acceptable requirements. Separate sterility test procedures for certifiable antibiotics are published by the FDA (6).

Because the use of ionizing radiation on organic materials in solution can generate changes in the treated molecules with new potential for toxicity, the FDA requires an approved new drug application (NDA) for all drugs, including injectables, ophthalmic products, surgical sutures, and surgical dressings, sterilized by this procedure (7). In view of the high cost of the necessary animal toxicity test data to be supplied in such a NDA, ionizing radiation has found little utility for the sterilization of drugs in the U.S., except for surgical sutures and dressings, which are medical devices traditionally accepted as drugs.

The use of ionizing radiation on cosmetics or medical devices does not require such preclearance for safety and efficacy since these products are regulated by different sections of the Food, Drug and Cosmetic Act. This situation means that "after the fact" control is used to regulate the safety and efficacy of these products. The FDA assumes the burden of proof in a court of law to provide evidence of actual or potential harm to consumers before such products can be removed from the marketplace. Fortunately, a sizeable bank of knowledge and data have been built up over the past two decades on the use of ionizing radiation on plastics and medical devices. No evidence of human (or animal) injury has been attributable to the use of ionizing radiation with sterile-disposable devices.

The situation regarding the use of ETO as a sterilant poses several issues. Manufacturers of some over-the-counter (OTC) drugs and many disposable devices have utilized this sterilant and marketed their products without preclearance for safety and efficacy. It is known that sizeable amounts of ETO can be absorbed by plastics and then released following sterilization. Various forms of dermal injury from bandages, shoes, anesthesia masks, and rubber gloves as well as blood hemolysis have resulted from desorbed ETO (4). A limited review of the extent of use of this sterilant with OTC drugs is foreseen.

Over the past four years the Z-79 Subcommittee for Ethylene Oxide Residues of the American National Standards Institute (ANSI) has reviewed the hazard from the use of this sterilant on plastics and has published interim residue limits for ETO per se in plastics and disposable devices. This subcommittee will also publish tentative guidelines for residue limits for ethylene chlorohydrin and ethylene glycol in disposable plastic products. The greatest hazard from such residues occurs in materials sterilized by hospitals and not properly degassed. At the present there exist no governmentally established standards for ETO residues in drugs or devices.

ECONOMICS OF THE STERILIZING PROCESS

Sterilization with steam under pressure is usually considered the most economical (and most efficient) sterilant. While dry heat is cheap, its effects on product and packaging are too severe for general industrial use. When a given sterilization process and associated equipment are expected to be used for many years, it is generally accepted that a radiation sterilization process is cheaper than sterilization with gaseous ETO. However, size of initial investment is much reduced with an ETO process as contrasted with the equipment and facilities required for an ionizing radiation process. A process employing sterile filtration with aseptic filling is usually considered the most expensive process because of high personnel, maintenance, and sterility control regimens.

PARAMETERS OF STERILITY ASSURANCE TESTS

In view of the high sterilizing efficiency associated with steam under pressure, the USP requires only a sample size of 10 finished product items from each lot for sterility testing. These are incubated for 10 days if the item is a solid and 7 days if a liquid. No advantage accrues from the use of BI with this sterilant.

With sterilizing agents other than steam under pressure and aseptic fill procedures, the USP requires that there be 40 finished product tests (actually 20 items with liquids) which are incubated for 14 days. With the use of 10 adventitious BI per sterilization lot (load), the number of product sterility tests is reduced to 20, and the incubation time is lowered to 10 days. With product-carried BI only 10 such inoculated product items need be tested, and the incubation time is 7 days. Since product-carried BI can be used with ETO and ionizing radiation processes, these latter procedures can now compete on a favorable basis with the sterility assurance parameters, i.e., number of product sterility tests and incubation times, associated with steam sterilization under pressure.

SUMMARY

The safety and efficacy of a medical item are affected by the choice of sterilizing agent. The basic issue with efficacy is that the product meet certain performance standards (potency and stability with pharmaceuticals) following sterilization. Drugs which require a NDA before marketing are reviewed for the possibility of an effect of the sterilizing process on drug potency and quality. With medical devices the burden of proof for efficacy before marketing rests with the manufacturer since preclearance is not required.

The basic safety issue is that the product be sterile and nontoxic following sterilization. The sterility tests described in the drug compendia (*USP* and *National Formulary*) are considered to be minimal requirements to be met before an item is marketed. The only sterilant for which a legal mandate exists to prove nontoxicity is ionizing radiation applied to drugs. No governmental standards exists for the presence of ETO residues in medical products, but the Z-79 Subcommittee of ANSI is in the process of publishing interim guidelines for such residues in plastic materials and devices.

References

1. Bigelow, W. D. 1921. The logarithmic nature of thermal death time curves. J. Infectious Dis. **29**: 528–536.
2. Bruch, C. W. 1971. Are your disposables safe? Hospitals J.A.H.A. **45**: 138–146.
3. Bruch, C. W. 1972. Sterility assurance: Finished product tests vs. biological indicators. Australian J. Pharm. Sci.
4. Bruch, C. W. 1973. Sterilization of plastics: toxicity of ethylene oxide residues. In this volume. Ch. 4.
5. Bruch, C. W., and M. K. Bruch. 1971. Sterilization. pp. 592–623. In E. W. Martin [Ed.], *Dispensing of medication*. Mack Publishing Co. Easton, Pa.
6. Code of Federal Regulations. 1971. Sterility test methods and procedures. Sec. 141.2 of Title 21. U.S. Government Printing Office. Washington, D.C.
7. Ibid. Sterilization of drugs by irradiation. Sec. 3.45 of Title 21.

8

Control of the Manufacture and Sale of Disposable Plastics in the United Kingdom

ALEXANDER BISHOP

Scientific and Technical Branch
Ministry of Health and Social Security
London, England

INTRODUCTION

THERE ARE, at the present time, no direct statutory requirements in the United Kingdom for the manufacture or sale of sterile medical devices. The Medicines Act, 1968, provides for the control of medicinal products and certain other substances and articles through a system of product licenses and certificates and the licensing of firms and persons engaged in the manufacture or assembly of such products or in wholesale dealing in them. The products subject to the act are those that fall within the definition of a medicinal product, and those brought within the licensing provision by statutory orders under the act. A product license is needed for relevant dealings in any products to which the act applies. In addition, anyone manufacturing or assembling relevant products has to hold a manufacturer's license which covers the activity in question. Anyone dealing with such products, other than as a manufacturer or retailer, must hold a wholesale dealer's license. Licenses are issued by the licensing authority which consists of the Health and Agriculture Ministers of the United Kingdom. Licensing of human medicines is handled in the Department of Health and Social Security.

Medical devices are not at present included in these arrangements, but

Section 104 of the act gives ministers powers to specify any class of articles which are not medicinal products (as defined in the act) but are manufactured, sold, supplied, imported or exported for use wholly or partly for a medicinal purpose—a fairly comprehensive description of the plastics disposables—and may direct that specified provisions of the act shall relate to them.

It would clearly be quite improper to hazard a guess as to whether this power will be invoked to embrace sterile medical devices. Nevertheless the Department of Health and Social Security has, for many years, exercised a considerable measure of control over the manufacture and importation of some plastics single-use products and a general supervision over many more. Some blood transfusion equipment and surgeons' gloves, for example, are purchased by central contract for the whole hospital service whereas others are subjected to a system of approval. Many, it may be suspected, escape control altogether usually because they are produced by firms not manufacturing products already subject to approval. Approved firms are well aware of department requirements and apply them to all their sterile products.

The vast majority of plastics products for single use supplied individually wrapped in a sterile condition are subjected to cold methods of sterilization, usually exposure to ethylene oxide or irradiation. Both methods, at least when practicable processes are considered, are dependant for their efficiency on a low initial bacterial contamination on the article to be sterilized. Control of the conditions of manufacture thus becomes an important part of the control of the sterilizing process, and surveillance of these conditions forms an important part of any attempt to assess the probability of the process finally yielding a sterile product. It is extremely difficult for individual hospitals to make meaningful assessments of the sterility of these products from their own resources. No reliance can be placed on "sterility tests" performed on a small number of randomly obtained samples by personnel not routinely engaged in this form of testing. The errors of the test will greatly outweigh the probability of detecting an unsterile article.

The introduction of a wide range of plastics materials for the manufacture of these single-use articles requires assessment of the suitability of the material for its purpose, the investigations including such sources of misunderstanding and contention as testing for toxicity and pyrogenicity. In these matters also the hospital is entirely in the hands of the manufacturer who may be a very small firm without facilities for this kind of testing or even without knowledge of the necessity for it.

LISTS OF APPROVED MANUFACTURERS

It is for these reasons—and also in order to be reasonably certain that the articles are manufactured to acceptable standards, that they are suitable for their intended use and that their quality is properly controlled—that the Department of Health and Social Security has instituted the "approval" scheme mentioned earlier. An Approved List of manufacturers of sterile single-use hypodermic syringes and needles has been in operation for some time, with both British and foreign manufacturers being considered for inclusion in it. Similar lists of approved manufacturers of sterile catheters are being drawn up and it is intended to extend the scheme to other sterile plastics articles.

Two factors particularly assist us in maintaining this surveillance without the sanction of legislative authority. In the first place the major use of the great majority of these products is in hospitals and, second, the Hospital Service in the United Kingdom is centrally financed, thus providing considerable scope for central contracting and approval of products.

The basis of the approval is an inspection of the manufacturer's premises and methods to assess his ability to supply reliably and consistently a satisfactory article in a sterile condition. The prerequisites for approval are:

1. Suitable premises, a well conducted sterilising process and adequately supervised personnel;
2. Satisfactory quality control exercised over the product at all stages of manufacture.

It cannot be emphasised too strongly that the existence of agreed standards and specifications are essential in any control system. There is little point in providing a biologically safe syringe—sterile and non-toxic—if it leaks. When we first interested ourselves in the manufacture of intravenous catheters we found it more difficult to ensure that they would not break off in use than to satisfy ourselves of their sterility.

ENVIRONMENTAL CONTROL IN MANUFACTURING

The facilities used for the complete process of manufacture, assembly, packaging, and sterilization must be designed to ensure the minimum bacterial contamination of the product. This means that the premises must be supplied with adequately filtered air, and positive air pressure should be provided in clean areas. Apparatus and fittings must be designed to allow easy cleaning and the avoidance of accumulation of dust. Regular microbiological checks are made on the bacterial contamination of all working surfaces, the atmosphere and the product at different stages of assembly. Staff engaged in all stages of the manufacturing process are supervised with respect to their personal hygiene and systematic or local disease. It is most important that a competent microbiologist having adequate laboratory facilities accept responsibility for the bacteriological aspects of the manufacturing process. The microbiologist must be answerable directly to the Board.

CONTROL REQUIREMENTS FOR RADIATION STERILIZATION

The sterilizing process control will differ with the method. In the case of irradiation, physical evidence that the approved radiation dose has been received by each article is sufficient. We approve the irradiation plant on the basis of requirements for dosimetry and the keeping of records which were drawn up in consultation with the United Kingdom Atomic Energy Authority (UKAEA). When the plant is commissioned the dosimetry is performed under the supervision of experts provided by UKAEA. In general this involves checking the distribution of dose throughout each package, in particular the regions of minimum dose; the relationship between package density and speed of conveyor for the given minimum dose; and the functioning of the process time-recording devices on the conveyor system. Dosimetry studies are carried out after changes in the source and, of course, routine checks are required during normal operation of the plant. A device must be fitted to the plant to record the number of packages treated (and their rate of treatment) while the source is exposed and the total number of packages passing through the plant whether the source is exposed or not. A log is kept of the density or weight of all packages treated in the plant and changes in the conveyor speed. A logbook recording change of source strength is also required to be kept. With electron accelerators the relevant machine parameters must be continuously and automatically monitored and recorded. Alarm systems must give warning of variations exceeding agreed limits and shall prevent the inadvertent passage through the plant of doubtfully sterile material.

CONTROL REQUIREMENTS FOR ETHYLENE OXIDE STERILIZATION

Unfortunately physical control of an ethylene oxide sterilizing process is not practicable; many factors, such as gas concentration and humidity, are very difficult to measure and even more difficult to specify with any certainty. Such a process must be monitored by means of contaminated control preparations containing known numbers of organisms in a form known to be resistant to the process. Their number must be related to the probable number of organisms in the load to be sterilized and to the size of the chamber. They should be inserted in those parts of the load that experiment has shown to be most difficult of access to the gas. Great care has to be exercised in the choice of bacteriological medium used to culture them after processing as it is only too easy to observe apparently sterile cultures when absence of growth is due to unsuitable medium rather than nonviable organisms.

Although we see little point in them when applied to products sterilized by methods amenable to physical control, sterility tests are carried out on batches of articles sterilized by ethylene oxide as an additional check and in order to detect the adventitious occurrence on the articles to be sterilized of organisms in large numbers or, perhaps, in a very dry or resistant form. The sterilizing process must be under the control of the same microbiologist who is responsible for the environmental conditions in the manufacturing plant. Full records of all sterilized batches are required and a quarantine system must be maintained for those awaiting bacteriological clearance. Evidence is required of the reduction of levels of residual gas.

TOXICITY CONTROL

Whatever method of sterilization is used the manufacturer is required to provide full details of the formulation of the materials from which the product is made, their source and any test procedures which demonstrate that they are nontoxic. There are, as yet, no officially recognized methods for testing for toxicity applied to all these products. A committee of the British Standards Institution is currently working on this problem. Information is requested about the packaging materials, the method of sealing and the tests that have been applied to them. The firm must inform the department's inspectorate of any significant change in materials or methods of manufacture and of changes in responsible staff.

SUMMARY

To be effective such an approval scheme involves constant vigilance and continuing surveillance of manufacturers. Fortunately, however, it is in the interest of industry to encourage it. There are few more discouraging experiences for a competent and responsible manufacturer than to be defeated in a competitive bid in favor of a product which may be not only inferior to his own but may be cheaper simply because the firm manufacturing it economized on essential environmental conditions during its manufacture and on the quality control exercised over it.

It is fair to add that the fact that most sterile single-use articles currently purchased by British hospitals are now of an acceptable standard is due in no small measure to the cooperation that we have received from manufacturers and their willingness to meet our requirements even when these have been, perhaps, rather more rigorous than those to which they were accustomed and where often the only compulsion to meet them was their own desire to do the job properly.

9

Ten Years of Sterile Products Control in Belgium

B. J. A. HUYGHE

Inspector General
Ministry of Health
Brussels, Belgium

THE BELGIAN medical law of March 25, 1964, regulates the manufacture, importation, wholesale distribution, and dispensing of sterile medical products. Paragraph two of the first article of this law specifies that:

The King can render applicable all or part of the provisions of the present law to articles and materials which are claimed to possess curative or preventative properties or which fulfill curative or preventative functions in the art of healing.

The Royal Decree of June 6, 1960, relative to manufacture, preparation, and wholesale distribution and dispensing of medicines, specifies the nature of the articles and instruments that are subject to pharmaceutical control. This regulation has been modified a number of times in order to add sterile injection, perfusion, transfusion or drainage devices, as well as probes, catheters, other containers, tubings, needles, and droppers. In effect it now covers all articles that are claimed to be sterile and are intended to be used for injection, perfusion, transfusion or drainage, as well as all sterile materials intended for medical and obstetrical intervention.

At the time of its publication, the Royal Decree was aimed only at sterile materials for perfusion, transfusion or drainage. In 1962, when sterile disposable injection materials began to appear on the Belgian market, the field of application of the Royal Decree of June 6, 1960, was extended to include sterile injection materials as well. Since that time, the use of disposable sterile materials has broadened considerably, and the users of medical and pharmaceutical materials have seen many new sterilized products come on the market. Consequently, in 1969 a new revision of the decree was necessary in order to include "all sterile materials for injection, perfusion, transfusion or drainage, as well as probes, catheters, i.e., all containers, tubing, needles, droppers, and all articles labeled as sterile and intended for use in injection, perfusion, transfusion or drainage, as well as any materials marked sterile intended for use in medical or obstetrical intervention."

It should be made clear that the provisions of the Royal Decree of June 6, 1960, are equally applicable to:

1. Surgical ligatures, i.e., all sterile threads, of any nature whatsoever, utilized in surgery.

2. Sterile bandages, i.e., all absorbent or carded material of any nature which is labeled as sterile.

By virtue of this ruling, those concerned with the preparation, trade, and wholesale distribution of these articles, as well as importation, whether with a view toward fabrication or preparation in Belgium, or whether with a view toward distribution or wholesale marketing in Belgium, are required to obtain an authorization issued by the Minister of Public and Family Health. This authorization lists the articles for which the authorization is valid as well as the places where operations are performed.

The holder of an authorization for manufacture, preparation, or import of regulated material is required:

1. To communicate to the Minister of Public and Family Health with the help of formularies set up by the Inspection of Pharmacy: (a) the common name of the product, (b) the composition, and (c) the analytical methods.

2. To ensure that the fabrication, industrial preparation, and distribution of sterile materials is handled by persons who are free of contagious disease and in locations reserved exclusively for these operations.

3. To ensure that the places of fabrication and preparation and the warehouses for finished products are isolated from premises where chemical products or substances other than those covered by the Royal Decree might be handled or stored.

4. To ensure that the materials, apparatus, and containers intended for use in the fabrication, preparation, transporting, and preserving of sterile articles, as well as premises and warehouses, are maintained in such a manner that the nature of the sterile articles is not altered.

5. To prevent delivery of these products to market before their conformity (sterility) to the laws and regulations has been attested to through analysis by the industrial pharmacist attached to the establishment or by a laboratory which is recognized by the Minister of Public and Family Health.

6. To state on the outside of the package and on other boxes or containers holding the products the authorization number assigned by the Minister of Public and Family Heath as well as the manufacturers lot number. This number, set up according to a code fixed by the Minister of Public and Family Health, is common to all articles originating from the same fabrication process and subjected to a common process of sterilization. Consequently, the lot number for sterile materials is limited by the capacity of the sterilizer. The lot number is made up of five figures representing the date of manufacture or sterilization of the lot of medical materials. The first two figures are the last two digits of the date of year of manufacture. The third figure, consisting of one of the letters from A to L, indicates the month of manufacture with A indicating January and L indicating December. The fourth and fifth figures, consisting of two digits from 01 to 31, indicate the day; for example, a lot sterilized on the 27th of May, 1972, would bear the number 72 E 27. A problem has existed in establishing the lot number with products exposed to continuous sterilization processes, e.g. gamma rays. Belgian officials have ruled that all the products sterilized during a one-week period may bear the same lot number. Nevertheless, control of sterility must be effected on one sampling taken on *each day* of sterilization. In addition, any changes in the source of irradiation must be brought to the attention of the Belgian courts.

7. To guarantee, when the shelf life is not stated, that the stability of the product is within limits mentioned on the label. It is essential to note that throughout the duration of validity of a product (a maximum of five years) the industrial pharmacist must keep available for Pharmaceutical Inspection a sample of the products the conformity of which he has certified. This sample must be sufficiently large to allow for any confirmatory examinations that may be necessary. Moreover, the samples must be sealed by the industrial pharmacist and authenticated by his signature.

8. Not to sell, offer for sale, or distribute "medicines" except to other holders of authorization and to dispensary pharmacists. This regulation, however, does not apply to products that, by reason of their nature or characteristics, do not lend themselves to the possibilities of normal

pharmaceutical distribution; the list and the method of distribution of these are fixed by the Minister of Public and Family Health.

Moreover, the flasks, tubes, and other containers holding such materials must bear the following label information in at least one of the national languages:

(a) full reference about the nature of the product and any information that the Minister of Public and Family Health specifies;
(b) on the exterior packaging, complete information relative to modes of use and preservation.

As stated above, the holder of an authorization is obliged to withhold market delivery of sterile products until after their sterility has been certified through analysis, either by the industrial pharmacist attached to the firm or by a laboratory recognized by the Minister of Public and Family Health.

The following are the sterilization methods recognized by the Belgian Pharmacopoeia. The mode of sterilization in all cases must be compatible with the nature and use of the product.

Sterilization may be accomplished by:

(a) exposure to flame;
(b) dry heat for at least 1 hr at temperatures between 160 C and 180 C;
   (b1) dry heat for $1\frac{1}{2}$ hr at a temperature of 150 C;
(c) dry heat for 2 hr at a temperature of 120 C;
(d) exposure for 1 hr to a flowing steam;
(e) saturated steam for 30 min in an autoclave at a temperature of 120 C taking care that all air is expelled and that an excess of water is avoided during the operation;
(f) immersion in a boiling water bath for 1 hr;
(g) boiling for $\frac{1}{2}$ hr utilizing a container equipped with a reflux condenser, both having been previously sterilized;
(h) heating for 1 hr at a temperature of 80 C on each of three successive days; or at a temperature of 60 C for 1 hr on each of five successive days;
(i) for thermolabile substances the aseptic assembly process may be utilized (for this, the material and necessary containers as well as the products are separately sterilized by suitable methods, and the assembly or filling is carried out by aseptic means);
(j) filtration through a bacteriological filter;

(*k*) contact with gases under controlled conditions of exposure time, temperature, humidity and gas concentration (this method is particularly applicable to certain antibiotics and to plastic items used for transfusion and perfusion);

(*l*) ionizing radiation (the materials to be sterilized are exposed to X-rays, gamma rays, or cathode rays so that each item is exposed to a radiation dose not less than 2.5 megarads [Mrads]).

It is significant to point out that the Belgian Pharmacopoeia also specifies that all articles for sterilization be cleaned carefully beforehand and that all handling be done with the maximum of cleanliness to avoid as much as possible the introduction of contaminating agents.

Articles made of rubber must be sterilized according to *d, e, f, k,* or *l;* glass or porcelain objects, according to *a, b, c, d, e,* or *f.*

Metal articles must be treated according to *a, b, c,* or *f.* In the *f* case, however, it is advisable to add one or two standard-sized jars of sodium carbonate or borax and then wash in sterile water.

Bandaging materials must be sterilized according to *e.* Before sterilization they must be packaged in special metallic containers having holes which can be closed off immediately after sterilization. Alternatively, the bandage materials must be packaged in a material which will allow the passage of steam, while effectively protecting the articles against subsequent contamination. The sterilization must be conducted in such a manner that the required temperature during the time prescribed is obtained throughout the mass. During sterilization of bandages it is necessary to ensure the complete penetration of steam at 120 C. Controls must be either with thermocouple temperature readings or by sterility tests. The latter must indicate that the desired temperature was attained and maintained for the minimal period of time.

The Belgian Pharmacopoeia stipulates requirements for sampling for sterility testing.

A lot of materials is defined as being made up of the total number of containers holding a given substance that has been submitted to the same process of sterilization in the same apparatus. Regardless of the number of units that make up the lot, one takes at random at least ten samples for products sterilized by wet heat under pressure, and at least twenty for products sterilized by any other method.

Sterility tests must be done with all necessary aseptic precautions. In no instance, however, may the operations be performed directly under ultraviolet light or in an area treated with aerosol disinfectants.

Adequate controls for working conditions, for the sterility of the materials, for the culture media, and for the materials utilized for the test must be established for each series of experiments. The Pharmacopoeia also describes the media to be utilized as well as the duration and the conditions of the test.

The above constitutes a brief sketch of the legal requirements relating to sterile articles marketed in Belgium.

One might question if such regulations are necessary. The answer is positive, as the following will demonstrate. The aim of the legislation is to guarantee to the physician, or to those who use the product, that articles labeled as sterile are indeed sterile.

An investigation conducted in the laboratories recognized by the Minister of Public and Family Health has proved the need for verifying the sterility of articles labeled as "sterile." Since the enforcement of the Royal Decree in 1960, more than 7000 lots of sterile items have been sterility-tested by these laboratories. More than 90 of these lots were found not to be sterile. Among the products found to be contaminated were: tubing, duodenal probes, pediatric probes, urinary bags, cups, surgical gloves, syringes (with or without needles), bandages, kits for perfusion or transfusion, valves, and catheters. The means used to treat these materials were by ethylene oxide, accelerated electrons, gamma rays, and steam.

Special note should be made of the quality of packaging used for these materials. On numerous occasions inspection revealed the packaging to be of marginal quality. In several instances, the contamination found was due to slight defects in the seams, to seals with openings allowing bacteria to enter, or to plastic packaging material that was too light and showed tears or openings.

It is appropriate, finally, to point out to the manufacturers of disposable sterile products that the packages and the materials they contain should satisfy the following criteria:

1. Plastic packaging material should allow for effective sterilization of the equipment without being altered.

2. Packages, under normal conditions of use, should be impervious to moisture, air, chemicals, and microorganisms.

3. Packaging materials should be sufficiently transparent for visual verification of the contents.

4. All materials and surfaces in contact with biological liquids, tissues, etc., should be chemically and physically inert and incapable of causing any alteration whatsoever.

5. Plastic materials should contain no heavy metals or metal compounds.

6. Disposable sterile products should be sterile, nontoxic, and nonpyrogenic.

It is my recommendation that each country organize a similar control program with the aim of safeguarding the health of its population. I call on all countries manufacturing or sterilizing similar articles offered as sterile to set up effective control systems.

PART THREE

Sterilization Technology

10

The Effects of Radiation Sterilization on Plastics

DAVID W. PLESTER, B.SC., PH.D., A.R.I.C.

Plastics Division
Imperial Chemical Industries
London, England

INTRODUCTION

THERE ARE many different kinds of atomic radiations, but they may be classified into two basic groups: neutral particle radiation and charged particle radiation. The interaction of neutral particles with matter generally yields energetic charged particles, so the observed radiation effects of both types of particle are similar even though the original radiation may have been neutral. For sterilization purposes the radiations of practical importance are high-energy electrons, which are negatively charged, and gamma rays which can be regarded as electromagnetic radiation and neutral. Although both radiations give rise to essentially similar effects, there are important differences in their behavior. The distance to which particles penetrate matter depends largely on their type and whether they are charged or not and only slightly on their energy. Gamma rays possess a much greater penetration ability than do high-energy electrons. As considerably greater dose rates can be achieved from electron sources than with gamma rays from ^{60}Co decay, however, the sterilizing time is correspondingly shortened. In the remainder of this discussion the term *radiation* will be used to mean both high-energy electrons and gamma rays except where an explicit distinction is made.

No induced radioactivity arises in materials irradiated with ^{60}Co gamma radiation or with electrons of energies up to 5 Mev.

141

Radiation with energies below 5 Mev affects primarily the electrons of matter on which it impinges. Collisions with nuclei can be ignored. The charged particle gradually loses energy passing through the absorbing material, the energy being dissipated by excitation or ionization of the atoms or molecules concerned. The subsequent alterations in molecular structure govern the changes in physical and chemical properties of the material. As they are not necessarily deleterious these changes are referred to as radiation effects rather than radiation damage.

The processes of excitation and ionization of an organic molecule leads to one or more of a number of effects. Gas evolution, polymerization, crosslinking, degradation and double-bond formation have all been observed, and all lead directly to changes in physical properties. These effects are relevant too to the results of irradiating polymers. A polymer may undergo chain scission, the molecules being broken into smaller fragments, or crosslinking may take place with the formation of larger molecules. Very low molecular weight fragments, i.e., gases, and unsaturation are important side results of these reactions.

Polymers preferentially crosslink or degrade depending on their chemical structures. Conflicting results have been found with a few materials, but a general empirical conclusion for polymers with carbon chains is that crosslinking occurs if each carbon carries at least one hydrogen atom, whereas if a tetra substituted carbon is present scission takes place. Both crosslinking and degradation may occur in the same polymer simultaneously, although usually one process predominates. This explains why, for example, both gas evolution and increases of molecular weight may be observed together.

STERILIZATION DOSE

For the purposes of this assessment it is assumed that the dose required for radiation sterilization is 5 Mrad. This adequately covers the range of doses that are used or proposed and allows some latitude for inexactness in application. The effects of higher doses are included as well because of possible repeated sterilization. For practical purposes it can be assumed that effects of resterilization are cumulative and additive.

EFFECTS ON PLASTIC PROPERTIES

GENERAL

Plastics are synthetic organic materials of high molecular weight which at some stage in their production are capable of being shaped and subsequently capable of retaining that shape. The polymer molecules are made up of a large variable number of repeating monomer units and may be straight or branched, either randomly or regularly. The arrangement of molecules may also be random or regular, giving zones of low or high crystallinity. Virtually all plastics contain small amounts of other ingredients to confer to each particular technical properties, and in a few cases these amounts approach 30 % by weight. These ingredients are normally simple chemicals of low molecular weight.

All plastics are affected by ionizing radiation; the only variables are the type of effect and the size of dose necessary to produce it. Not only do they behave as other organic substances but, owing to their high molecular weight, drastic changes in the physical properties of plastics may be exhibited as a result of only minor chemical modifications. As the chemical reactions are taking place in a solid medium, and an ill-defined one too, it is difficult to predict behavior on a theoretical basis. Certain additives have a protective action and can reduce the effect of radiation on plastics. These may either be energy absorbers or chemical reactants which combine with radiation-produced free radicals. The atmosphere in which irradiation takes place often modifies the effects. In particular, differences are usually observed between the behavior in the presence or absence of oxygen. Findings, however, are not consistent; with some plastics degradation is enhanced in the presence of air, whereas for others it is reduced. Thin specimens are likely to be more affected because oxygen is freely available; with bulky items the oxidation process, except at very low dose rates, will be diffusion-controlled. Post-irradiation effects have been also noted, presumably because of the persistence of free radicals in the material following exposure to radiation.

The observed effects on plastics properties are varied but, most importantly, involve mechanical characteristics. Polymerization and crosslinking increase the molecular weight and therefore lower the mobility of molecules and reduce creep. This may raise the tensile strength, depending on the normal mechanism of tensile breaking, and does increase the hardness and brittleness. Impact strength usually decreases or remains relatively unchanged. Radiation-induced degradation, on the other hand, by lowering the molecular weight, detracts from most of the valuable properties associated with plastics. Tensile, impact, and shear strengths all are reduced and so is the elongation at break. Often embrittlement occurs even though the material may have become somewhat softer. Crystallinity can increase in polymers that undergo scission, there being less restraint on the shortened molecules, causing a rise in density.

An obvious effect of radiation on many plastics is the development of color; in some cases the material will become opaque after prolonged exposure. Most materials turn yellow or brown, but the dose at which discoloration becomes noticeable varies widely. The extent and amount of color development may vary on storage after irradiation, either increasing or diminishing with time, and are usually affected by the presence of oxygen.

Much of the literature dealing with the effects of radiation on plastics is concerned with mechanisms especially under extreme exposures. The behavior at sterilizing doses has in many cases to be determined by interpolation. Information presented here has been gathered from a number of general sources (7, 12, 13, 23), but specific further references are quoted where appropriate.

OLEFINE POLYMERS

Polyethylene Both low- and high-density forms of polyethylene are resistant to single-dose radiation sterilization and can withstand, without substantial change in mechanical properties, doses up to at least 100 Mrad (23).

Polyethylene in general crosslinks on irradiation, although there is a chain scission mechanism as well (5). The average molecular weight increases and the crystallinity decreases. The effect on mechanical properties is complex; e.g., the tensile strength first increases with dose up to about 10 Mrad, then decreases slowly, returning to its original value at 100–150 Mrad. The elastic modulus behaves in an opposite manner, first falling then rising again. Impact strength begins to fall at 70 Mrad, reaching zero at 500 Mrad (9). Gas permeability changes are small (17), there being no alteration at 10 Mrad and about 50 % reduction after 100 Mrad (16).

As would be expected radiation brings about a reduction in solubility. Even after only a 5 Mrad dose the solubility in xylene at 25 C is reduced to half that of unirradiated material.

Polypropylene Polypropylene is readily affected by radiation and is borderline in stability to single-dose sterilization. Thus it is one of the more interesting materials for consideration especially as its combination of mechanical properties make polypropylene useful for many biomedical applications (20).

Both chain scission and crosslinking result from irradiating polypropylene although, in the presence of air, oxidative degradation is an important effect as well. The rate of diffusion of oxygen into the material may be rate controlling. Items irradiated at high dose rates, such as can be achieved by electron beams, may therefore show much less damage than those treated at low dose rates. Crosslinking is evidently the major factor at low doses because the impact strength suffers an immediate fall followed by a slow decay over a period of months. Even after 2.5 Mrad the impact strength can decrease eventually by more than 50%. Discoloration also occurs in polypropylene, often a noticeable yellow after single-dose sterilization, which although aesthetically objectionable may be masked by the incorporation of a trace of blue pigment.

Because of the radiation sensitivity of polypropylene the small differences between the products of different manufacturers and indeed the various formulations on each manufacturer's range can be important. The changes referred to do not necessarily go together; thus a grade which discolors severely does not always embrittle nearly so much in comparison. The purity of the polymer, the stabilizers used (19), the fabrication process, and the shape of the final article all are relevant to suitability for radiation sterilization. The onset of brittleness, e.g., is much less severe with simple moulded shapes than for the more complex ones such as hypodermic syringe barrels where there is some locked-in strain.

Currently, therefore, some polypropylene items can satisfactorily withstand a radiation sterilization dose; others are not yet good enough. It is essential to evaluate performance after storage and not merely immediately following exposure.

Poly(4-methyl pentene) Little information is available, although radiation effects could be predicted as similar to those in polypropylene. In fact poly(4-methyl pentene) seems to be rather more resistant and can be regarded as unaffected by a single sterilization dose although unsuitable for repeated exposure.

Copolymers Both ethylene-vinyl acetate copolymer and ethylene ethyl acrylate copolymer are satisfactory for radiation sterilization.

Indeed, the latter has been found more resistant than polyethylene itself (21).

Polystyrene   This is the most radiation-stable of the common moulding plastics, and large doses are required to bring about significant effects. The aromatic rings in the structure appear to provide a protective action towards radiation effects, and the plastic is largely unaffected up to doses of 500 Mrad. The so-called high-impact polystyrene is somewhat less stable towards radiation, but nevertheless is still among the more resistant of plastics.

Styrene-acrylonitrile   Styrene-acrylonitrile copolymers (SAN) are not as resistant to radiation as polystyrene itself, but are still fairly stable (21) and well able to resist a number of sterilization doses.

ACRYLIC POLYMERS

Poly(methylmethacrylate)   Poly(methylmethacrylate) can satisfactorily withstand a single radiation sterilization dose both in the high molecular weight cast sheet form and as a moulded item. It is not, however, suitable for repeated doses. The effect of radiation is degradation both in the ester side chains and in the main chain of the molecule. Hence mechanical strength is affected, the tensile strength, e.g., being lowered by 50 % at about 20 Mrad and thereafter decreasing rapidly. The material eventually becomes brittle and cracks may appear.

A yellow discoloration develops in poly(methylmethacrylate) during radiation doses as low as 0.5 Mrad and the optical transmittance falls by one-third at 5 Mrad (24). This coloring tends to fade following subsequent storage in air although no postirradiation recovery seems to occur in mechanical properties. Certain additives can give a degree of protection against the degradation of poly(methylmethacrylate) (3).

VINYL POLYMERS

Poly(vinyl chloride)   Poly(vinyl chloride) is suitable for single-dose radiation sterilization both in its unplasticized and plasticized forms. The mechanical properties begin to show some change above 15 Mrad so that repeated dosing is not advisable.

In general the polymer crosslinks in the absence of air and degrades if oxygen is available. Thus degradation may be observed upon irradiation of thin films but is confined to the surface of thicker articles. Poly(vinyl chloride) discolors at quite low doses, 2 to 3 Mrad, the shade and intensity of color varying with the presence of different plasticizers and stabilizers. It is interesting that, in contrast to the behavior of poly(methylmethacrylate), the discoloration of poly(vinyl chloride) intensifies upon subsequent storage. The inclusion of sodium stearate is reported to be effective in reducing discoloration, whereas the use of organotin stabilizers promotes color development (26). These tin stabilizers also seem to inhibit crosslinking.

Differences have been noted between the effects of radiation on unplasticized and plasticized poly(vinyl chloride) and also between compositions containing different plasticizers. However, the differences are slight and probably not significant in a consideration of sterilization although one study (11) has shown a relatively good resistance to radiation in material plasticized with DOP, presumably dioctyl phthalate.

A more important effect is the liberation of hydrochloric acid with the corresponding production of unsaturation. The effect is reduced by the stabilizers always present in commercial compositions but some hydrochloric acid is available for further reaction. The subsequent sterilization by ethylene oxide of poly(vinyl chloride) previously treated by radiation has been reported to cause formation of the toxic agent ethylene chlorhydrin (14). Such resterilization should therefore be avoided (4).

Vinyl chloride copolymers   Copolymers appear to be less resistant to radiation than poly(vinyl chloride) itself and to undergo degradation rather than crosslinking. Vinyl chloride/vinyl acetate copolymer, for example, shows a threshold effect at 1.4 Mrad (10) and could not be regarded as suitable for radiation sterilization.

Poly(vinylidene chloride)   This too is less stable than the vinyl chloride polymer. The mechanical properties start to be affected at 4 Mrad (10), hence, although it may just withstand radiation sterilization, this procedure is not recommended.

FLUORINATED POLYMERS

Poly(tetrafluoroethylene)   In contrast to its resistance to heat and to chemical attack poly(tetrafluoroethylene) is extremely sensitive to radiation. Effects on tensile strength have been observed at doses as low as 0.1 Mrad although there is much less damage in the complete absence of oxygen (25). This plastic is therefore quite unsuited to radiation sterilization.

Others   Poly(chlorotrifluoroethylene) and fluorinated ethylene/propylene copolymer are both more resistant to radiation effects than poly(tetrafluoroethylene). Only limited data are available on these products, by they can probably withstand one-dose sterilization without undue change.

POLYAMIDES

No great difference has been noted in the effect of radiation on various types of polyamide: nylon 66 and nylon 6. All are suitable for sterilization although not for many repeat doses. Polyamides crosslink and lose crystallinity upon irradiation causing a slow increase in tensile strength but a much more rapid drop in impact strength. The latter characteristic falls to half its initial value after a dose of about 20 Mrad. Films and fibers are more affected mechanically than thick mouldings possibly because the loss of strength arising from the reduction in crystallinity is more important for thin section material than the accompanying increase in strength caused by crosslinking. Also the presence of oxygen substantially increases the effects of radiation, and such changes will in practice be more important for thin section material.

POLY(ETHYLENE TEREPHTHALATE)

Poly(ethylene terephthalate) is suitable for radiation sterilization whether in film or fiber form. Mechanically it can withstand at least 100 Mrad although discoloration occurs at lower doses. Crosslinking is the major effect of radiation but radiation-induced oxidation can be important too in the presence of air.

CELLULOSE ESTERS

Cellulose acetate is relatively unaffected by radiation doses up to 10 Mrad and may therefore be sterilized by this means. The tensile strength is reduced by 50 % at about 40 Mrad (10). Other esters such as the propionate, the acetate-butyrate, and the nitrate behave similarly. Cellulose itself undergoes scission under the influence of radiation more rapidly than its esters and ethers.

THERMOSETS

Phenol formaldehyde and urea formaldehyde are both reasonably stable towards radiation and suitable for irradiation sterilization. PF is the more resistant of the two resins being largely unaffected at 100 Mrad, but color changes may occur below this. Cellulose fillers such as wood flour and paper are relatively more affected by radiation and generally lower the resistance of the resins containing them.

Epoxy resins are very stable and usually satisfactory up to 500 Mrad. In the form of thin films or coatings they are, however, more susceptible to radiation degradation in air. Comparisons of epoxy resins cured with different reagents show that aromatic amines give products that are much more resistant to radiation than those prepared with aliphatic curing agents (2).

Polyester resins have good stability too, being resistant up to around 100 Mrad, and may indeed be cured using radiation (23).

MISCELLANEOUS PLASTICS

Acetals   Polyformaldehyde and acetal copolymers are sensitive to radiation and cannot be recommended as suitable for sterilization. Of the two the copolymer has somewhat better resistance (18) but radiation above about 1 Mrad brings about unacceptable changes.

Polycarbonate   Polycarbonate can satisfactorily be given a single-dose sterilization exposure (22) but tends to become brittle much above 2.5 Mrad.

Acrylonitrile-Butadiene-Styrene   ABS is much less resistant than the styrene-acrylonitrile (SAN) materials (21) but nevertheless is sufficiently stable to be suitable for a single sterilization dose.

Poly(phenylene oxide)   Modified PPO is reported to exhibit good radiation resistance (21).

Some important properties are summarized in Table 1.

EFFECTS ON OTHER MATERIALS

To complete this survey some very brief information is included to indicate the radiation stability of selected other materials for quick reference and also to put the behavior of plastics into context.

RUBBERS

Conventional rubber compounds exhibit about a 50-fold variation in their resistance to deterioration in tensile strength and ultimate elongation brought about by radiation. Damage is reduced in the absence of oxygen, but is greatly accelerated if irradiation takes place under conditions of stress. Table 2 shows the general effect of radiation on

Table 1   Summary of relative resistance of plastics to radiation

Plastic	Resistance to radiation	Suitability for sterilization	
		One dose	Several doses
Polyethylene (HD and LD)	Good	Yes	Yes
Polypropylene	Fair	Borderline	No
Poly(4-methylpentene)	Fair	Yes	No
Ethylene/vinyl acetate	Good	Yes	Yes
Polystyrene	Excellent	Yes	Yes
SAN	Good	Yes	Yes
Poly(methylmethacrylate)	Fair	Yes	No
Poly(vinyl chloride)	Fair	Yes	No
Poly(vinylidene chloride)	Poor	No	No
Poly(tetrafluoroethylene)	Very Poor	No	No
Polyamides	Fair	Yes	No
Poly(ethylene terephthalate)	Good	Yes	Yes
Cellulose acetate	Fair	Yes	No
Phenol formaldehyde	Good	Yes	Yes
Urea formaldehyde	Good	Yes	Yes
Epoxy resins	Excellent	Yes	Yes
Acetal copolymers	Poor	No	No
Polycarbonate	Fair	Yes	No
ABS	Fair	Yes	No
Poly(phenylene oxide)	Good	Yes	Yes

Table 2   General effect of radiation on types of rubber in unstressed state

Material	Comments
Polyurethane rubber	Excellent stability up to 500 Mrad
Natural rubber	Good stability up to 100 Mrad
Butadiene styrene rubber (SBR)	Good stability up to 100 Mrad
Nitrile rubber	Good stability up to 100 Mrad
Silicone rubber	Poly(dimethylsiloxanes) stable up to 10 Mrad and methylphenyl silicones rather more stable
Neoprene rubber	Stable up to 10 Mrad
Butyl rubber	Unstable above 1 Mrad

various types of rubber (23) in an unstressed state, although stability can be influenced by the nature of antioxidants and fillers present.

TEXTILES AND FIBERS

Owing to differences in assessing radiation effects and relating changes in fiber characteristics to those of the resultant textiles there is some conflict in the literature about radiation tolerance. A suggested maximum exposure level for common fibers (8) is:

$$
\left.\begin{array}{l}
\text{Polyester fibers} \\
\text{Acrylic fibers}
\end{array}\right\} \text{50 Mrad}
$$

$$
\left.\begin{array}{l}
\text{Wool} \\
\text{Viscose Rayon} \\
\text{Silk} \\
\text{Cellulose acetate}
\end{array}\right\} \text{20 Mrad}
$$

$$
\left.\begin{array}{l}
\text{Nylon} \\
\text{Cotton}
\end{array}\right\} \text{1 Mrad}
$$

Work on the sterilization of sutures (6), however, showed a reduction in breaking strength of cotton surgical sutures of only 15–20 % because of radiation and demonstrated that radiosterilization was an acceptable procedure. Absorbable gut sutures and nonabsorbable sutures of silk, polyester and nylon are not affected in tensile strength by 2.5 Mrad (15).

ADHESIVES AND CEMENTS

Adhesives and cements behave upon irradiation in a manner generally similar to the plastics or reinforced plastics on which they are based. Structural adhesives such as the epoxy and phenolic resins and polystyrene systems (1) have excellent radiation resistance which is further improved when inorganic fillers are present. The glass fiber in reinforced resins, e.g., provides substantial further protection. Vinyl type adhesives —a common one is polyvinyl acetate—have moderate radiation resistance which is adequate for single-dose sterilization. Pressure-sensitive adhesives undergo oxidative breakdown readily and are not recommended for sterilization by radiation (23).

References

1. Aitken, A. D. 1965. Application of adhesives in nuclear technology. Sheet Metal Ind. **42**: 736.
2. Aitken, I. D., and K. Ralph. Feb:, 1960. Some effects of radiation on cast epoxy resin systems. Report AERE–R–3085. Atomic Energy Research Establishment.
3. Alexander, P., and D. J. Thoms. Nov., 1958. Protection provided by added substances against the direct action of ionising radiation. Radiation Research, **9**: 509.
4. The Anaesthesia Study Committee of the New York State Society of Anaesthesiologists. 1969. Hazards associated with ethylene oxide sterilisation. N.Y. State Journal of Med. **69**: 1319.

5. Baskett, A. C., and C. W. Miller. 1954. Nature Lond. **174**: 364.

6. Blouine, F. A., and J. C. Arthur. 1964. Radiation sterilised cotton surgical sutures. Am. Dyestuffs Reptr. **53**: (23) 33.

7. Bolt, R. O., and J. G. Carrol. 1963. *Radiation effects on organic materials.* Academic Press. New York.

8. Ibid., p. 444.

9. Bopp, C. D., and O. Sisman. June, 1951. Physical Properties of Irradiated Plastics. USEAC Report ORNL–928, Oak Ridge National Laboratory.

10. Bopp, C. D., and O. Sisman. 1955. Nucleonics, **13**: 28.

11. Chapiro, A. 1956. J. Chim. Phys. **53**: 895.

12. Chapiro, A. 1962. *Radiation chemistry of polymeric systems.* Interscience. London.

13. Charlesby, A. 1960. *Atomic radiation and polymers.* Pergamon. London.

14. Cunliffe, A. C., and F. Wesley. May, 1967. Hazards from plastics sterilized by ethylene oxide. Brit. M. J. **2**: 575.

15. Horibe, Takashi, Kibuchi, Hiroshi, Fujii, and Masamuchi. 1968. Sterilisation of surgical sutures by gamma rays. Eisei Shikanjo Hokutu, **86**: 41. Chem. Abs. 1969: 125037k.

16. Mayers, A. W., C. E. Rogers, V. Stammett, and M. Szwarc. May, 1957. Permeability of polyethylene to gases and vapours. Mod. Plast. **157**: 34 (9).

17. Moore, P. W. 1968. Evaluation of polyethylene ampules as containers for radiation sterilised solutions. Aust. At. Energy Comm. Report AAEC/TM–444.

18. Mozisek, M. Mar., 1970. Effects of ionising radiation on the properties of acetal resins. Plaste u Kaut. **17**: 177.

19. Nechitailo, N. A., P. I. Sanin, L. S. Polak, and J. Pospisil. 1968. Alkyl derivatives of pyrocatechol as stabilisers in gamma-irradiated polypropylene. J. Polym. Sci. *C*, No. 16, Pt. 6, **3433**.

20. Plester, D. W. 1970. The effects of sterilising processes on plastics. Biomed. Eng. **5**: 443.

21. Popovick, B. Oct., 1970. Effects of gamma radiation on polymers. SPE Journal. **26**: 54.

22. Radiation and plastics in medical use. Mar., 1968. Mod. Plast. **45**: 48.

23. Radiation stability of materials. Mar., 1965. Radiosotopes Review Sheet G1. Wantage Research Laboratory, UKAEA.

24. Schmidt, D. L. Mar., 1958. Effects of gamma radiation on aircraft transparent materials. Wright Air Development Center, Report WADC–TR–56–557, Pt. II.

25. Wall, L. A., and R. E. Florin. 1959. J. app. Polymer Sci. **2**: 251.

26. Wippler, C. 1959. Rev. gen. Caoutchouc. **36**: 369.

11

Design of Radiation Sterilization Facilities

R. EYMERY

Commissariat à l'Energie Atomique
France

FROM THE BEGINNING of this century, the efficiency of X-rays in the destruction of microorganisms was recognized (10). Fifty years later the development of the nuclear industry made possible the production of sources of radiation powerful and inexpensive enough to make this method attractive. Their technology is now well established, their working safety is good, and their use offers extremely interesting guarantees.

IONIZING RADIATIONS AND THEIR INTERACTIONS WITH MATTER

The use of ultraviolet radiation for surface sterilization is well known. The radiations we are concerned with here are much higher in energy. Whereas ultraviolet rays do not exceed a few tens of electron volts, gamma rays or accelerated electrons have energies in the region of one million electron volts. At such energy levels, and for organic materials or those which have a low atomic number, the interaction of these radiations with matter is essentially marked by ionization phenomena, i.e., the breaking off of an electron from the electronic cloud of an atom. The energy necessary to break this link is about a few tens of electron volts. When accelerated electrons are concerned, the ionization is direct. The incident particle, negatively charged, transmits its energy to the electrons of the medium in the course of successive shocks; a few tens of thousands of atoms will be ionized the full length of the particle's path, which, in water, for example, can be a few centimeters.

153

The conditions of the interaction of the electrons with the substance make it possible to define a depth of maximum penetration. The energy transferred to the medium by a beam of parallel electrons varies with the depth, reaching the maximum when the depth is half the maximum penetration depth (Figure 1). Since the loss of energy of the incident particles is essentially due to the shocks with the electrons of the medium, it will be proportional to the number of electrons present per volume unit, or approximately proportional to the density of the irradiated material. That is why, in Figure 1, the transferred energy is given in

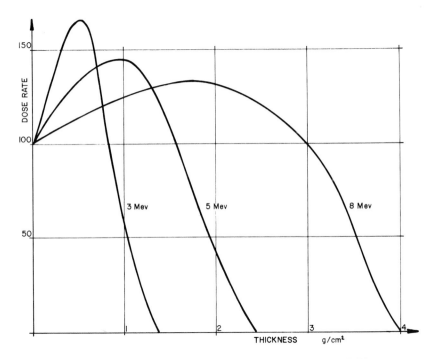

Figure 1   Penetration of an electron beam. (*Source*: Ref. 8.)

function of a thickness which is expressed in grams per square centimeter. These curves are nearly valid for all substances which do not contain any elements with a very high atomic number.

Even though gamma rays are one of the products of a nuclear transmutation, whereas X-rays result from the interaction of accelerated electrons with substances having a high atomic number, no difference in nature exists between them, and the conditions of absorption by the matter are exactly the same. The probability of interaction of these

particles not electrically charged, called *photons*, with the atomic nucleus
or with the electrons is very small. On the other hand, the energy transferred in the course of a shock is generally a large portion of the initial
energy and the electron "broken off" in this way is capable itself of
causing secondary ionizations. Moreover, most often the photon will be
found to deviate significantly from its initial trajectory. Therefore the

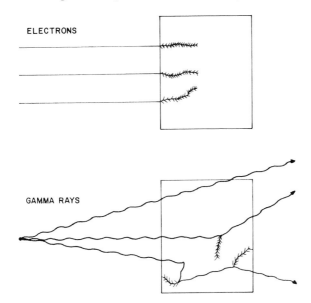

Figure 2 Interaction of electrons and gamma rays with matter.

photons have a relatively large, angular path, in the region of a few
tens of centimeters in water. At each change of direction this path is
marked by small zones of ionization due to the secondary electrons. The
random nature of the trajectory of the particles is much more apparent
for the photons than for the electrons because the number of shocks is
relatively small: about ten, for example (Figure 2). It is not possible to
define a maximum path for photons.

The attenuation of a beam of photons is exponential and a good idea
of its penetration is given by the numerical values of the thickness of
the substance which reduces a particle flux to $\frac{1}{10}$ of its initial value
(see Table 1). When its organic substances are concerned, the attenuation is nearly proportional to the density.

There is one point which deserves special attention among the problems involved with the use of these radiations for radiosterilization: Is

Table 1	Ten value thickness for various materials (in centimeters) (*Source* **Ref. 11**)			
Source	*Water*	*Concrete*	*Iron*	*Lead*
Cobalt 60	35.5	17.3	5.6	3.4
Caesium 137	27.4	12.7	4.1	1.8

there a risk that this radiation might induce a certain radioactivity into the treated substances? It is true that particles of very high energy can produce an activation of certain elements, but it has been clearly shown (12) and verified experimentally that the activation due to the photons and electrons below 5 Mev is insignificant, on the one hand because its probability is very small, and on the other hand, because the nuclides formed, when there are some, decay rapidly, thus quickly bringing the induced radioactivity to a level lower than the natural radioactivity.

It is perhaps useful here to recall the definitions of the units relative to ionizing radiation:

1. The electron volt, ev, and its multiples, the kiloelectron volt, kev, and the mega electron volt, Mev, are used to measure the energy of a particle.
$$1 \text{ ev} = 1602 \times 10^{-12} \text{ ergs.}$$

2. The rad and its multiples krad and Mrad are units of measurement of the energy transferred by a beam of particles to the substance.
$$1 \text{ rad} = 100 \text{ erg/g.}$$

3. The curie is the quantity of radioelement in which the number of disintegrations per second is 3.7×10^{10}.

4. The power of the sources of radiation can also be given in kilowatts.
$$1 \text{ kw} = 6.24 \times 10^{15} \text{ Mev/sec.}$$

DOSIMETRY FOR INDUSTRIAL RADIOSTERILIZATION

The purpose of dosimetry is to measure the energy transferred by radiations to treated material. What is important in radiosterilization is not so much the dose received but rather the destruction of the micro-organisms induced. Consequently, to ensure good functioning of the process, bacteriological controls are instituted. These controls were the subject of a recommendation of the International Atomic Energy

Agency (7) which emphasized that, to a certain extent, the resistance of microorganisms to radiation depends on their environment. Unfortunately, this method involves a rather impressive task for each measurement, and automation does not seem very likely (3).

Dosimetry by physical or chemical means is usually easy to use, relatively precise, and reliable. Therefore it is employed systematically for routine controls and to complement bacteriological controls. The comparison between the dose measured by these means and the effect on the microorganisms can be interesting. The qualities that a good dosimetric system must have are:

1. It must be independent of the dose rate and only record the total dose received.
2. It must be small in size and independent of the radiation energy, at least in the considered energy range.
3. Like all other means of measurement, it must be precise, reliable, and reproducible.

The irradiation industry had to choose from numerous systems available. Calorimetric methods are to be considered first, since our concern is to measure the absorbed energy. They have proven to be inadequate for gamma irradiation because the energy flow is too small. On the other hand, they give good measurement of the energy transferred by a beam of electrons. The calorimeters are, however, too large to insert in the packages to be irradiated so as to measure the local variations in dose.

The oxidation of iron sulfate in solution by irradiation is a phenomenon which is easily reproducible, precise, and not sensitive to the energy of the particles and the moderate dose rates encountered in the gamma installations. The use of iron sulfate enables measurement of integrated doses much lower than those necessary in radiosterilization, but in a gamma installation the dose received is inversely proportional to the speed of the conveyor. Dosimetric measurements can therefore be made at high speed with a sensitive dosimeter as well as at low speed with a less sensitive dosimeter. In practice dosimetry with iron sulfate is relatively complex and is more of a reference dosimeter than a systematic one.

Numerous dosimeters are available for systematic measurements. Their accuracy is around $\pm 5\%$, their volume is small, and the measurement is most often done by an optical transmission reading at a determined wave length. Finally, their cost is low. The most well known are:

1. The transparent polymethylmetacrylate, with a reproducibility reaching 2 %. It is in the form of small plaquettes 1 mm thick.
2. The colored polymethylmetacrylate, the reading of which can be done with simple means.
3. The polyvinyl chloride in film 0.2 mm thick.

Normal precautions can be taken to ensure that the irradiation installation functions correctly; there is, however, always risk of an incident against which extraordinary precautions must be taken. For example, the possibility exists that a nontreated package can be accidentally set among those which have been treated. To avoid this, it is useful to put a colored sticker on each package. The color of this sticker should change distinctly at the moment of irradiation.

BIOLOGICAL EFFECT OF THE IONIZING RADIATION

The biological effect of ionizing radiation involves special characteristics which need to be known before the optimum conditions of sterilization of a product can be defined. When a microbial culture is submitted to the effect of a radiation, one notices an exponential reduction in the number of germs which survive with respect to the dose received (Figure 3). If we designate by D_{10} the dose which causes the reduction of the microbial population to $\frac{1}{10}$ of its initial value, this dose does not generally depend on the initial contamination.

The mechanism of radiation effect is still subject to discussion. There are two theories: (1) that of the direct effect which supposes that the death of a microorganism is due to the destruction of a vital molecule; and (2) that of the indirect effect which supposes that death is due to the chemical action of compounds formed by the radiation.

The exponential reduction of the number of germs makes it impossible to define a dose for absolute sterilization. It is only possible to say that a determined dose brings about a determined reduction for a certain microorganism. Moreover, it is impossible to state that no germ has survived the treatment; it can be said only that the probability of finding a surviving germ, under controlled conditions, is, for example: 10^{-3} or 10^{-6}. Therefore we are led to the notion of the probability of sterility which can sometimes appear surprising. We must remember, however, that it is not possible to be sure of sterility. When sterility tests are made on samples, one does not determine whether the batch is sterile or not, but rather a certain probability of sterility for this batch.

If radiosterilization offers only a certain probability of sterility, it is essential to know if this probability is sufficient, taking into account the intended use of the product, especially if it is comparable with the guarantees offered by other methods. Therefore, it is conceivable that the dose necessary to ensure a satisfactory sterility varies, on the one hand, with the initial contamination and, on the other, with the final

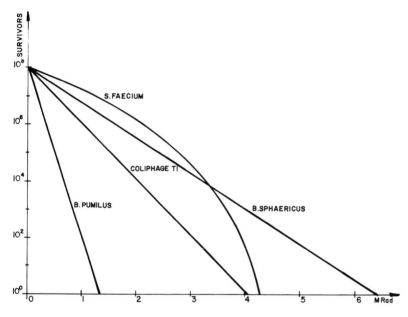

Figure 3   Inactivation curves for various microorganisms. (*Source*: Ref. 3.)

use of the product. This is of special interest for the radiosterilization of pharmaceutical products which, at the beginning, are almost germless and to which it is often impossible to give large doses.

As for disposable articles, systematic tests for contamination before sterilization have been carried out in different countries (5). Satisfactory doses of sterilization determined by bacteriologists vary from 2.5 to 4.0 Mrad. It seems difficult to make an industrial installation of gamma irradiation operate so that the dose distributed varies with the products treated. Most installations in service in the world have been set up so that the minimum dose received by the product is 2.5 Mrad.

IRRADIATION FACILITIES USING GAMMA RADIATIONS

THE SOURCE OF RADIATION

Radioisotopes for industrial irradiation   Radioisotopes offer very interesting nuclear features: cobalt 60 and caesium 137 have the decay diagram as shown in Figure 4. Compared with other radiation sources, these radioisotopes offer the following characteristics:

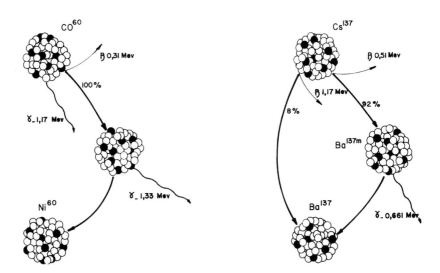

Figure 4   Decay scheme of cobalt 60 and caesium 137.

1. The release of radiation is continual and cannot be hindered by any known means.
2. The flux of photons released by a source decreases, with respect to the time, in a perfectly regular and exponential way.
3. The energy of the particles released is well defined and cannot be modified by the user.

Since the gamma radiation is extremely penetrating as well, the essential interest of gamma radiosterilization lies in the possibility of reproducing, in an almost certain way, the state of treatment practically without concern that any incident, either mechanical or human, can disturb it.

Elementary sources Cobalt 60 is obtained by neutronic irradiation in a nuclear reactor from natural cobalt or cobalt 59. The irradiation can be done in a research reactor, a specialized reactor, or in a power reactor. Cobalt in the form of metal is fitted with an aluminum or stainless steel sheath before being put into the reactor so as to avoid all excessive contamination when it is removed. After their activation in the reactor, the cobalt elements are regrouped in order to build up the form of

Figure 5 Industrial sources made of small cobalt elements (Commissariat à l'Energie Atomique, France).

source desired (Figure 5). They are then set in a second sheath which is perfectly airtight and inactive. Weldings of these sheaths are done automatically in an argon atmosphere and are carefully tested. Then the sources are measured by means of ionization chambers or calorimeters. All the operations are done remotely through walls more than 1 m thick. Some manufacturers guarantee their sources for ten years against all corrosion risk.

The specific activity of these sources, i.e., the power emitted by each

gram of cobalt, depends on the conditions of irradiation. It is generally
between 15 and 80 curies/g. It begins to decay from the moment it comes
out of the reactor. After a certain time, called the "half life," the specific
activity is only half of the original value. In other words, in order to
maintain the gamma power released in an irradiation facility at an
almost constant level, it is necessary to put in new elementary sources
from time to time to compensate for the decay. Economic considerations
determine the frequency of source replenishment.

Caesium 137 is not a product voluntarily obtained by neutronic
irradiation. It is an obligatory by-product of the fission of uranium 235.
An atom of caesium 137 is produced in the proportion of 6 % from the
fission of a nucleus. Therefore it is a free radioisotope from the start. It
is all the more interesting to use since, among the nuclear energy residues, it is a rather cumbersome element because of its long period and
the penetration of its radiation. Unfortunately, separation of caesium
137 from the other fission products, its purification, and its conditioning
(in the form of chloride), are expensive operations. At the present, the
cost of the energy released by caesium 137 is slightly greater than that
of the energy released by cobalt 60 in spite of the advantage of its long
period. For several years to come, the use of caesium 137 will be limited
to laboratory or mobile irradiators.

Source-holder set   The most widely used arrangement for radiosterilization of medical material is that of making the products to be irradiated
pass on both sides of a flat source (Figure 6), which is made up of a
stainless steel support on which the elementary or elementary group
sources are set. Most frequently the source-holder is vertical to minimize
the risk of incident if an object falls on the source-holder. A certain
number of free spaces are provided on the source-holder to permit
ulterior loading without removing the old sources for at least a few
years. In fact, during the study of the installation, the complete program should be planned for future recharges because after a few years
the activity of the different elements constituting the source panel will
not be uniform. Their arrangement plays an important role in ensuring
a good dose uniformity in the products to be irradiated and the highest
output from the installation. How the sources are set on the source-
holder depends on the means of stocking adopted for the source. For a
large facility the source activity may reach two millions curies.

Self-absorption   Whatever the arrangement adopted, a fraction of
the radiation is absorbed by the source itself and by its covering. It is

desirable to have the smallest fraction possible. In a flat source panel, only the radiation released laterally is used for sterilization. The remainder, released in other directions near the source plane, is unused radiation. Therefore it is important to minimize the fraction of useful radiation which will be absorbed. From this point of view, the thin flat sources have a certain interest. With a thin source which is 3 mm thick

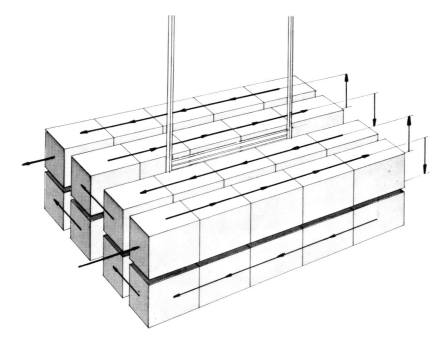

Figure 6 General disposition of packages around a source.

(1 mm of cobalt 60 and 1 mm of stainless steel on both sides) the difference between the energy released perpendicular to the biggest side of the real source and the energy which would be released by a theoretical source without self-absorption is insignificant.

With a cylindrical source having a diameter of 6.35 mm covered with a steel sheath 1 mm thick, the irradiation released laterally is reduced by 7 %.

ARRANGEMENT OF PACKAGES TO BE IRRADIATED

For the best absorption of the radiations released by the source, the radiation source must be surrounded as completely as possible by the products to be irradiated. Moreover, the wider the material, the greater will be the fraction of radiation absorbed. But this energy must be absorbed usefully. Irradiation at a dose greater than that needed is a waste of energy and can sometimes be harmful to the products being treated. Therefore the package size must be limited, and the packages must be arranged on several levels on both sides of the source. Each package will successively pass on each of the lines of irradiation (Figure 6). A similar arrangement is adopted in height.

Figure 7a Irradiation facility using a horizontal conveyor (built by H. S. Marsh Ltd., U.K.).

Irradiation conveyor Depending on the type of factory production, the products to be sterilized may be irradiated in their normal dispatch cartons or, alternatively, placed in special containers used only for irradiation. One of two arrangements is generally used:

1. *Horizontal displacement conveyor with vertical permutation of the packages* (Figures 7a and 7b). The packages occupy successively all possible positions on the same horizontal plane; they are then transferred to another level where they also occupy successively all possible positions. For horizontal movement, either a system of rollers or slides on which the packages are moved by pushing or a

165

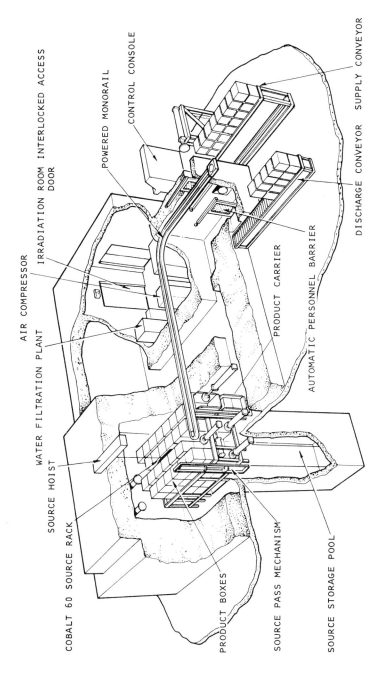

COBALT 60 SOURCE RACK

SOURCE HOIST

WATER FILTRATION PLANT

AIR COMPRESSOR

IRRADIATION ROOM INTERLOCKED ACCESS DOOR

POWERED MONORAIL

CONTROL CONSOLE

SUPPLY CONVEYOR

DISCHARGE CONVEYOR

AUTOMATIC PERSONNEL BARRIER

PRODUCT CARRIER

SOURCE STORAGE POOL

SOURCE PASS MECHANISM

PRODUCT BOXES

Figure 7b Irradiation facility using a horizontal conveyor (built by Atomic Energy of Canada, Ltd.).

set of aerial rails on which suspensions are hung can be used. The vertical transfer of the packages is quite complicated.

2. *Vertical displacement conveyor with lateral permutation of the packages* (Figure 8). The packages are suspended by two chains which make them pass several times in front of the source. After a complete

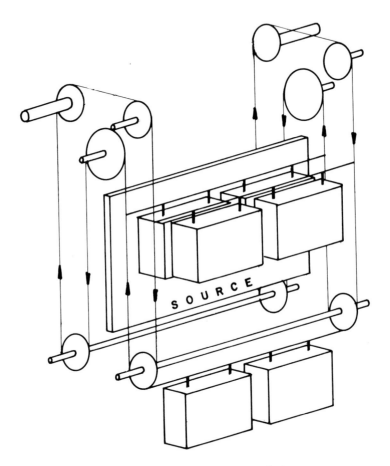

Figure 8 Sketch of a facility with a vertical conveyor.

circuit, the packages are laterally pushed to occupy a second position on the conveyor which ensures a uniform dose. In any event, both sides of the packages successively face the source.

The choice of conveyor is dictated by the desirability of maximum product output and the need to minimize mechanical complications.

Whatever the chosen principle is, there must be a satisfactory mechanical hold, the structure of which should shield minimally the packages being irradiated.

The dose received by the packages will be inversely proportional to the speed of the conveyor. The speed must be regulated with precision. It must be decreased periodically to allow for the source decay.

Material and equipment The structural materials must be capable of resisting corrosion, especially near the source. It is almost impossible efficiently to grease the mechanical parts. The equipment must be made of materials not liable to deterioration. Most plastics are quickly destroyed by radiation. Only polystyrene and polyethylene can withstand high doses.

The package or carrier displacements are made by pneumatic jacks which can be placed in the cell, hydraulic jacks, or electric motors which should be sheltered from the radiation. Various arrangements can be used to ensure that the operations are correctly performed. The control of the time spent for the execution of certain transfer operations which are especially critical enables functioning abnormalities to be revealed before they have serious consequences.

Feeding conveyor The conveyor which completes the transfer of the packages into the cell and out of it after irradiation must pass through a biological protection. The feeding conveyor can function independently of the irradiation conveyor or both may be more or less closely connected. Most often the feeding conveyor is an overhead conveyor. One carrier is sufficient for the entry and exit. The carrier transports a package to be irradiated to the cell interior and then returns a package which has received the treatment. Finally, at the exterior of the installation, different conveyors ensure the connection with other points of the factory as well as a stocking device which enables an automatic functioning of the installation during the night or even over the weekend.

BIOLOGICAL PROTECTION

During storage The intensity of radiation near the source is so great that the lethal dose for man would be reached within a few seconds. Therefore, it is necessary to provide a shield that must always be situated between the source and the personnel. The suitable thickness is about 30 cm of lead, or 150 cm of concrete, or 5 m of water. Even though it is possible to irradiate products at the bottom of a pool, this method is not applicable for industrial installations because the efficiency is low. Irradiation is accomplished in air; therefore, in normal functioning, the irradiation chamber is separated from the exterior by a thick concrete wall, and the access to the chamber is prohibited to personnel.

The transfer of products to be irradiated can, however, be done continuously by passage through a maze having a certain number of angles so as to reduce not only the direct radiation from the source but also radiation scattered by the wall, which is often significant. Passage in this labyrinth is prohibited to personnel and is protected by various safety devices, e.g., a pit filled with water over which the carriers pass. Less cumbersome but also more complex solutions with mobile protection parts have sometimes been used, e.g., revolving doors.

Source storage   When it is necessary to go inside the cell for maintenance or after incidents, the source should be placed in a position called "storage." The source will be separated from the irradiation chamber by an absorbing shield. The storage can be either in a pool dug in the irradiation chamber floor or in a slot surrounded by concrete and supplied with a removable plug. Often the plug is connected to the source-holder and it places itself in position at the moment the source enters into the storage shaft (Figure 9).

Generally the "pool" solution is used for large installations. This set-up enables an easier recharge of the sources and ensures their cooling. The recharge is done by sinking an ordinary transport container to the bottom of the pool and manipulating the sources under water by means of special, long tongs. Since the pools must be capable of resisting earthquakes, they are not joined to the block of concrete which constitutes the main shielding. The pool water is checked and eventually treated so as to eliminate corrosion of the sources.

For average-sized installations, dry storage is normally used because it is more economical than the pool. In this instance, the source-holder is supplied with horizontal slides onto which the sources can be pushed passing through the protection concrete in a special shaft. It is necessary to have an adapted transport container provided with a barrel placed in front of the shaft passing through the protective wall (Figure 10). All the source housing holes will then be brought successively in front of this shaft, and the elementary sources can be pushed from the container onto the source-holder. Old sources can be evacuated in the same way.

SAFETY SYSTEM

A safety system is based on the following principles:

1. Access of the cell is prohibited when the source is in irradiation position.
2. The source cannot be put in irradiation when access to the cell is permitted.
3. The operator is obliged to make sure that no one is inside the irradiation chamber before closing the door.

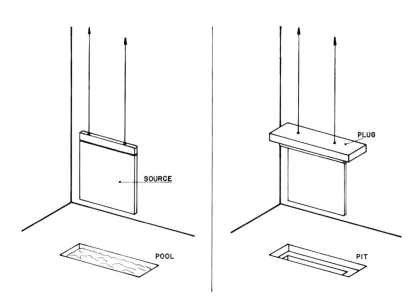

Figure 9 Source storage.

The first two principles are ensured by a mechanical safety system that is usually made up of unremovable key locks. For exceptional maneuvers this device can be bypassed by using a special key. Then the security relies on a sound alarm which goes off automatically if the door is open when the level of radiation reaches a certain threshold.

The third principle implies that the operator must enter the cell. He can close the door only after pushing a button inside the cell. He has only a few minutes to do so, after which he can no longer close it unless he reenters the cell and repeats the procedure.

These main devices for protection against personnel irradiation are complemented by other devices designed to eliminate other risks:

1. Control of contamination of the atmosphere and the pool water.
2. Fire detectors.
3. Dropping of the source in the event of a conveyor malfunction.
4. Ban to enter the cell if the ozone level is too high.

Figure 10   Container for loading a dry storage source (The Radiochemical Center, H. S. Marsh, Ltd., U.K.).

TECHNICAL-ECONOMIC STUDY OF A
GAMMA IRRADIATOR

Precise definition of the user's needs is the starting point in the study of an irradiation facility. The treatment capacity required serves as a basis for the definition of the source, making a reasonable hypothesis for efficiency. But also necessary at the beginning is to foresee, as much as possible, future developments; short-term growth of the initial capacity can strongly encourage the choice of one solution rather than another.

The size and density of the packages, if fixed, are essential elements of the study; secondary factors can also be important, as, for example, the value of the products. In fact, the material treated is expensive since the quantity in irradiation is several cubic meters. Its value must be taken into account as an initial investment.

If all the parameters are not fixed, various solutions should be examined and, for each one, the output should be determined by a geometrical study.

Geometrical study   Radiation is absorbed better by any substance as its density becomes higher. As a result, for the same geometrical arrangement of the products to be irradiated, the output is even higher as the density becomes greater. Therefore, the possibility occurs that changing the packaging can increase the output.

For a given substance, the maximum acceptable dose (overdosing) can be fixed first in relation to the eventual deterioration of the substance. When the density is fixed, it is possible to determine the optimum package thickness that permits maximum efficiency while respecting the limit imposed by the overdosing. (For the numeric values obtained see Ref. 4.) For packages 46 cm thick, irradiated on both sides, the efficiency varies from 18 % for a density of 0.1 to 36 % for a density of 0.25, whereas under the same conditions the rate of maximum dose/minimum dose goes from 1.30 to 1.35. It is impossible to calculate in an accurate and fast manner the dose in a gamma irradiator. In fact, the phenomena of radiation interaction with matter are too complex to enable the formulation of a convenient equation. Exact calculations have been made for simple cases, for example, for a point source in an infinitely homogeneous medium. In an irradiator the sources are not point in nature, and the irradiated medium is finite and heterogeneous. Calculation methods do, however, give an approximate determination of sufficient doses so as to allow us to choose the best solutions.

Economic study   The investments to be considered are, first, those associated with civil engineering. Generally their amount is not influenced by the choice of irradiation conveyor. On the other hand, how the source is stored can be important. The second element of the initial investment concerns the mechanical parts, the conveyors, the safety system and the equipment. The third element is the cost of the initial source which is considered as an investment. Since the source is recharged periodically, its use does not decrease its value; it would be desirable that the producing organizations of the sources envisage the possibility of either taking back the used sources or renting them.

The operating expenses include, other than the return on the investments, the recharge of the source which, for cobalt 60, is annually about 14 % of the cost of the source at its nominal activity. In fact, as a natural consequence of the decay, the actual power of the source is always greater than its nominal power which is reached only the day before a new replenishment. Finally, the price of labor can vary by important proportions according to the degree of automation of the installation. With completely automated systems, the labor measurements can be reduced to a few relatively untrained people.

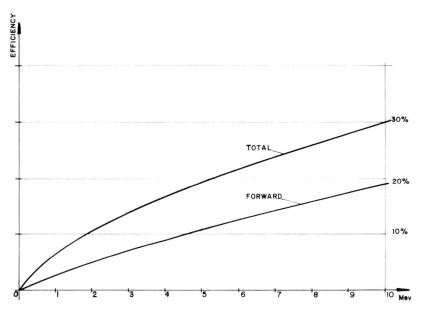

Figure 11   Electron X-ray conversion efficiency. (*Source*: Ref. 9.)

RADIOSTERILIZATION BY ELECTRON ACCELERATORS

DESCRIPTION AND FUNCTIONING

Even though accelerated electrons can produce high-energy X-rays when they are stopped in a dense target, the efficiency of this energy conversion is too small to envisage its use in industrial radiosterilization (Figure 11). Direct use of accelerated electrons, even though their use has some inconveniences in comparison to gamma rays, can also have an economic advantage in the high power range. These installations are much less numerous than those using radioisotopes. Generally they have a higher power. The different parts which make up an electron accelerator are:

1. The low-energy electrons source.
2. The zone of acceleration in which there is a static or high-frequency electric field.
3. The zone for shaping the beam.

The set is in an enclosed space which is kept under a constant vacuum. The electron beam is formed into a screen by alternating lateral deviation. This beam passes through the wall of the enclosed space through a very thin sheet of metal called a *window*. Under this window, the beam may be used for the treatment.

Figure 12   Electron accelerator for radiosterilization (C.A.R.I.C., France).

Two types of machines can be used in radiosterilization. One is the electrostatic machine—the most well-known type is the Van de Graaf. The high-voltage source ensures acceleration of the electrons. High voltage is provided by a mechanical device, a charge carrier which can be a belt or a revolving cylinder. It can also consist of a set of transformers and rectifiers. The high voltage is either continuous or alternating at a low frequency (Figure 13).

The other is the linear accelerator. Linear accelerators have a cylindrical acceleration space in which circular electrodes are submitted to a voltage of very high frequency. The power oscillator is synchronized with the command impulse of the electron gun. Puffs of electrons follow each other in the acceleration axis. The beam is scanned with a relatively low frequency compared with that of electronic impulses so that the zones irradiated at each impulse will overlap.

Features of the irradiation   The electronic beam of the machine scans a certain width, for example, about 60 cm. The beam thickness is however very small, about a centimeter. The packages to be irradiated move perpendicularly on the plane of the beam. All the width cannot be used; it must be limited to the zone where the irradiation is uniform (Figure 14). Therefore the power of the beam is extremely concentrated and the dose rate is several thousand times greater than that encountered in a gamma irradiator.

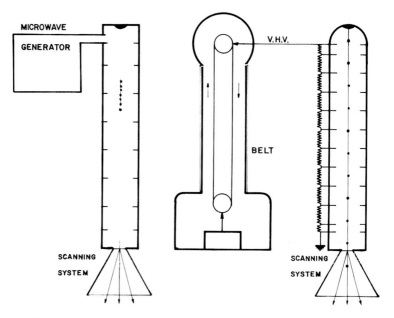

Figure 13   Schematic diagrams of electron accelerator. Left: linear accelerator, right: Van de Graaf accelerator.

We have seen (Figure 1) that the curves of the electron penetration are very much a function of their energy. For a package, it is therefore possible to determine the energy sufficient to attain a satisfactory irradiation, i.e., when the dose received under the package is identical to that received on the surface. In view of the shape of the penetration curves, this condition implies that all the interior of the package will have received a greater dose. This determination is done experimentally. This is possible only if the package thickness, or rather its equivalent thickness in a substance of density 1, does not exceed a certain limit which corresponds to the maximum energy available. Over this limit, it is possible to think of a double irradiation by turning the package over, but in this case, there is no means of directly controlling the dose reaching the center of the package.

The beam power is established at the maximum level possible taking into account the desired energy. The dose rate on the package is then determined and the package speed is immediately deduced from this. The practical efficiency is in the region of 30 to 40 %.

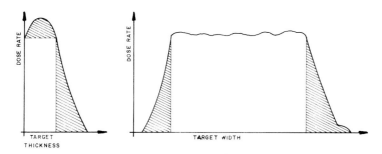

Figure 14 Energy loss in accelerated electron processing.

Loss of energy (Figure 14) is due to:

1. The electrons which pass through the package without yielding all their energy;
2. the use of only the central part of the beam;
3. the overdosing of one part of the package; and
4. the irregularities of package loading.

Regulating the apparatus   The values of the main parameters must be permanently verified. The measurement of the electron current can be made by devices which do not intercept the beam; for example, plates placed on both sides of the beam collect electrons backscattered by the window, their number being proportional to tne intensity of the incident beam. Different methods also enable continuous measurement of the electron energy, in particular to verify that the desired deviation is actually obtained.

Protection, safety system   For an accelerator, the irradiation chamber should be in size and in thickness of concrete about the same as for a gamma irradiator. There is no need of source storage, since the machine can be stopped. The principles and setup of the safety system are the same as those for gamma radiation.

COMPARISON TO THE GAMMA SOURCES

Available power   The power of a gamma source can be adjusted rather well to the needs of the user. Moreover, it is desirable to do so, since the cost of the source and its periodic recharge is exactly proportional to the power. Remember that the power radiated by 100,000 curies of cobalt 60 is 1.5 kw. The maximum power of an accelerator, on the other hand, is fixed at the time of the purchase. An eventual increase of the capacity is impossible. Therefore for a company which is beginning to use radiosterilization, it is advisable to be equipped with an apparatus, the capacity of which goes well beyond the initial needs. Moreover the purchase price is not at all proportional to its power. The power of machines used in radiosterilization is generally from 3 to 10 kw.

Utilization efficiency   The efficiency of the facilities varies with the irradiated product and its packaging. Without being able to give numeric values, it can be considered that electron accelerators generally have an efficiency slightly higher than that which can be expected from a gamma source.

Maintenance factor   Most users acknowledge that installations using gamma sources are so mechanically simple that the maintenance is reduced to a minimum. It can be considered that they are available 95 % of the time. Real utilization time for an accelerator is more debatable, because even with methodic maintenance the risks of breakdown are not to be overlooked.

Conditions of irradiation   The size of certain medical accessories— disposable hemodialysers, for example—is such that irradiation by accelerated electrons is eliminated from the beginning. In most cases, one or the other of these processes can be used. However, the penetration of gamma radiation and the regularity of the flow of the source are such that it is not necessary to systematically check each package to be sure that it has been suitably irradiated. It is advisable to do this if an accelerator is used because the least variation of the machine or the least variation in density or loading of packages could lead to an underdosing.

Labor cost   Very little labor is needed to ensure the functioning of a gamma irradiator which can be entirely automated. The functioning of an accelerator, the dosimetry of the packages, the maintenance of the machine require not only more personnel but also more qualified personnel. It would be pretentious to want to draw up general conclusions from these few remarks. It seems, on the contrary, that the interest of one or the other of these processes strictly depends on the specific conditions of the company: more or less volume treated, foresight of production development, more or less variety of products, regularity of manufacture, presence of qualified personnel in the company.

DESIGN OF THE PRODUCTS
AND PACKAGING

When a producer of medical material thinks about adopting radiosterilization, he must make a comprehensive examination of the process and the modifications that this method will bring to his manufacture.

The need for reducing initial contamination to a minimum is important. No sterilization process can be considered to produce sterile items unless strict hygienic conditions are observed.

The question arises as to the resistance of the component materials to radiation. Some substances are not noticeably modified by radiation; others are, either in an apparent way or not visibly at first investigation.

Packaging is an important factor (13). Though one of the recognized advantages of radiosterilization is that packages can be treated through the wrapping, this wrapping must be strong enough to stay airtight until it reaches the hands of the final user. Though the generally used sheets make efficient barriers when they are new, it is not always the same for the closings. Even though it is difficult to foresee a wrapping which can withstand all mechanical attacks coming from the exterior, it ought to be required that at least it will withstand rather well the action of its contents.

Packaging in dispatch boxes also ought to be studied carefully, especially in the case of gamma irradiation. Recall that for a given density and a maximum relation of heterogeneity of the imposed dose, there is a package thickness which ensures the maximum output. The radiosterilization installation is not only made up of elements of a set. It must be integrated into a production line all stages of which will have been reexamined so as to obtain from this method all of the guarantees it can give.

SUMMARY

To set up an irradiation installation which functions in good technical and economical condition, a careful examination of numerous factors is necessary. The determination of the minimal dose for sterilization of medical items involves a good knowledge of the bacterial contamination before treatment. The choice of the maximal dose should be made in relation to the function of the resistance to the radiation of the substance to be treated. The arrangement of irradiation depends strictly on the packaging of the products and in particular their apparent density.

After a brief review of the general characteristics of radiation, the installations and its method of working were described.

The gamma irradiation installation includes a certain number of lines on both sides of a flat source. Various solutions are usually possible; the choice depends on technical and economical factors. Different types of conveyors as well as methods for the protection of personnel have been described. The electron accelerators present special problems. Here some elements were given for the comparison of the two types of sources. Finally, it was emphasized that the acceptance of radiosterilization involves modifications of the other stages of production.

References

1. Artandi, C., and W. Van Winkle. 1965. Comparison of electron beam and gamma irradiation plants. Isotopes and Radiation Technology. **2** No. 4.
2. Attix, F. H., and E. Tochilin. 1969. *Radiation dosimetry.* Academic Press. New York.
3. Benazet, F., and C. Godard. Problemes bacteriologiques poses par la radio-sterilisation des appareils medico-chirurgicaux en matiere plastique et par son controle. Bulletin d'Information A.T.E.N. No. 93, p. 19.
4. Brown, M. G. 1967. *Radiosterilization of medical products.* IAEA. Vienna, p. 381.
5. Cook, A. M., and R. J. Berry. 1967. *Radiosterilization of medical products.* IAEA. Vienna, p. 295.
6. Goldblith, S. A. 1967. *Radiosterilization of medical products.* IAEA. Vienna, p. 3.
7. IAEA. 1967. *Recommended code of practice for radiosterilization of medical products.* Vienna.
8. Icre, P., and F. Petit. 1967. *Radiosterilization of medical products.* IAEA. Vienna, p. 367.
9. Koch, H. W., and E. H. Eisenhower. 1965. *Radiation preservation of foods.* Publication 1273. National Academy of Sciences–National Research Council. Washington, D.C., p. 172.

10. Minck, F. 1896. Munchener Medizin Wochensch. **5**: 101.
11. Price, B. T. et al. 1957. *Radiation shielding*. Pergamon. New York, p. 37.
12. Rogers, F. 1964. *Activity induced in food by electron, X-rays and gamma irradiation*. AERE R 4601. London.
13. U.K. Panel on Gamma and Electron Irradiation. Packaging for Radiosterilization. Symposium 1968. London.
14. Van Winkle, W., et al. 1967. *Radiosterilization of medical products*. IAEA. Vienna, p. 169.

12

Ethylene Oxide Gaseous Sterilization for Industrial Applications

ROBERT R. ERNST

Senior Staff Scientist
The Castle Company
a Division of the Sybron Corporation
Rochester, New York

INTRODUCTION

THE EFFICACY of ethylene oxide (EO) as a sterilant has been confirmed by many investigators subsequent to the basic evaluations by Phillips (1949) and Kaye and Phillips (1949). The use of EO has since become universal in hospitals and industry to sterilize heat or moisture-sensitive materials. Because its highly diffusive nature and its permeability make it possible to sterilize through sealed plastic wrapping films, shipping cartons, and containers, it became a highly desirable process for the sterile-disposable (single-use) medical devices industry.

As a result, growth of the industry and of the demand for EO processing had a parallel increase. The sheer volume of materials sterilized by EO far exceeds any other sterilizing process for medical products.

Ethylene oxide is the simplest epoxy compound having the formula: $\underset{\diagdown O \diagup}{CH_2 \text{----} CH_2}$. It is an extremely reactive, colorless gas with a boiling point of 10.8 C at atmospheric pressure. Manufactured in the U.S.A. on a large scale, it is primarily used in the synthesis of organic polymers. It is available in an undiluted form as a liquid under mild pressure or diluted with either carbon dioxide or chlorofluorohydrocarbons. The diluent gases are inert biologically, and are added to make a nonflam-

181

mable mixture. Ethylene oxide is flammable and can be highly explosive in the pure form. Its range of flammability as a mixture in air extends from 3.6 % to 100 % by gaseous volume. The gas is also mildly toxic. Its inhalation toxicity is similar to that of household ammonia. However, its presence is more tolerable than ammonia, which is a severe lacrimator. Therefore, the danger exists that toxic levels may not be as readily noticed in the environment. On the other hand, it is highly unlikely that toxic levels would persist in any environment. Its presence is hardly detectable since its greater density generally confines it to floor level, and its high diffusivity allows it to leak out rapidly through the minutest floor-level openings. The gas should not, however, be vented from a sterilizer into a confined space.

Ethylene oxide has been designated the most ideal gaseous sterilizing agent. The distinct advantages are listed as follows:

1. Materials sterilized with EO are not generally exposed to damage, especially from heat and moisture. Thus, a great variation of materials are sterilizable by this means.
2. Products may be sterilized already packaged for shipment, since EO will permeate sealed films and sealed cartons.
3. Although the agent is mildly toxic, it has the ability to vaporize from materials very rapidly, leaving no residue in most cases.
4. It is highly diffusive and will penetrate areas not reached by liquids or steam.
5. Although it is highly reactive, its degree of reactivity is low enough to provide sterilization in the presence of high levels of organic matter.
6. Although the process is complex, requiring knowledge and good equipment for greatest efficiency, sterilization can be achieved by astute knowledgeable users in such simple equipment as plastic or rubber bags, metal drums, or jars.

The following are disadvantages, which in most cases are not seriously limiting:

1. Ethylene oxide is more expensive to use than heat.
2. It requires more attention than heat or radiation processing.
3. Monitoring is necessary for each cycle because of its complexity.
4. It is sometimes necessary to determine whether or not residues of sterilant or reaction products persist in treated materials.

It has been mentioned many times (Ernst and Doyle, 1968) that sterilization by gaseous EO is substantially more complex than steam processes, although all sterilization processes are complex and possess definable limitations. However, because of its complexity many mysteries and misconceptions (Ernst, 1971) have resulted leading many to discontent, discouragement, and unjust denunciation of the EO process.

The following factors represent the interrelated parameters for which consideration must be given, since they are directly or indirectly related to sterilization efficacy and efficiency:

1. Temperature of sterilization
   a. Permeation and distribution of heat
2. Humidity
   a. Environmental dryness and storage conditions of product and packaging
   b. Humidifying method which will enhance or inhibit permeation and diffusion of moisture
   c. Distribution of moisture relative to air and sterilant gases, and stratification
   d. Maintenance of moisture levels
3. Gas concentration
   a. Gaseous mixture used
   b. Means of providing concentration
   c. Distribution of EO, inert gases, air, and moisture
      (1) Stratification of gases
      (2) Diffusion and permeation barriers
4. Product and packaging
   a. Cleanliness
   b. Storage conditions relative to dryness and contamination
   c. Special treatments which would afford protection for contaminating organisms
   d. Density of packaging
   e. Permeability of
      (1) Moisture
      (2) EO
      (3) Heat
   f. Damage
      (1) Vacuum-pressure changes
         (a) Bursting
         (b) Implosion or crushing
      (2) EO residuals, polymers, and reaction products
   g. Protective effects; laminates, antistatic agents, crystal formation

5. Sterilizer loading
   a. Density
   b. Positioning

Additionally, the listed interrelationships are affected by operational sequence, degree, and limits.

INACTIVATION KINETICS

As in most other sterilizing processes, the order of death by EO is exponential. Figure 1 shows the inactivation curves for various exposure temperatures for paper strips containing 1 million spores per strip at

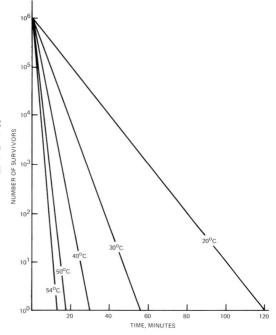

Figure 1 Inactivation rates at various temperatures for *Bacillus subtilis* var. *niger* spores on paper strips in gaseous ethylene oxide at 1200 mg/liter and 40% relative humidity.

40% relative humidity and 1200 mg/liter ethylene oxide. Many have shown the exponential nature of spore inactivation by EO (Kereluk and Lloyd, 1969; Kereluk et al., 1970).

An Arrhenius plot of rate constant for inactivation of *Bacillus subtilis* var. *niger* spores are shown in Figure 2. The calculated activation energy for the system, $E_0 = 26,000$ cal/mole which is within the range of intermediate bond strengths for organic molecules. Amaha and Sakaguchi

(1957) determined the thermodynamic relationships and the activation energies by heat for the inactivation of spores of *Bacillus natto*, *Bacillus megatherium*, and *Bacillus mycoides*, comparing these with similar data for protein denaturation of hemoglobin, trypsin, and pancreatic lipase. The range of values of E_0 of 40,800 to 77,300 cal/mole was favorably comparable to values from Wang, Shearer, and Humphrey (1964) who determined the Arrhenius activation energy for the inactivation of *Bacillus stearothermophilus* spores: $E_0 = 83,600$ cal/mole. Urbakh (1961)

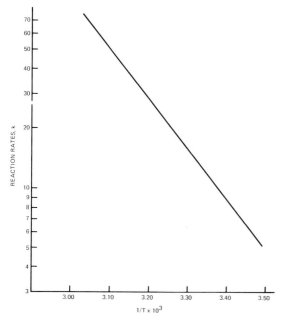

Figure 2 An Arrhenius plot of inactivation rate constants for *Bacillus subtilis* var. *niger* spores determined from the curves of Figure 1.

determined that the number of broken chemical bonds from the kinetics of protein denaturation is related to at least one labile site. The activation energy for the EO system is considerably less, and could reasonably reflect the activation energy for an alkylation reaction as it relates to DNA or RNA inactivation.

CONCENTRATION AND TEMPERATURE EFFECTS

Ernst and Shull (1962) first discovered that death became zero order at high levels of concentration. Thermochemical death time curves are shown in Figure 3 for 440, 880, and 1580 mg/liter in the temperature range of 18–57 C.

The results demonstrate a diminishing concentration dependence with increase in temperature (37–57 C) and confirm the low temperature (20–37 C) characteristics previously reported. Time-temperature relationships were determined for the sporicidal activity of various concentrations of vapor phase ethylene oxide admitted to a humidified, evacuated chamber (50 mm Hg abs, 30–50 % relative humidity). Spores of *Bacillus subtilis* var. *niger*, air dried on glass beads, were used as the

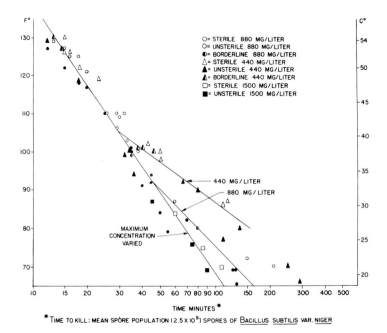

Figure 3   Thermochemical death time curves for spores of *Bacillus subtilis* var. *niger*. (From Ernst and Doyle, 1968. Biotech. and Bioeng. **10**: 1–31. By permission, Interscience Publishers, John Wiley & Sons, Inc., New York.)

test organism. The data reveal a logarithmic time-temperature curve of maximum slope exhibiting the characteristics of a zero order reaction above minimum concentrations. As the concentrations of ethylene oxide gas is reduced below these minima, the reaction becomes first order and individual nonparallel logarithmic time-temperature curves result which diverge from the curve of maximum slope at a specific temperature for each concentration. The temperature coefficients for the sterilizing action of ethylene oxide, calculated from the divergent logarithmic time-temperature killing curves, are 3.2 for 440 mg/liter, 2.3 for 880 mg/liter, approaching a Q_{10} of 1.8 as a limit.

Within the range of limiting concentrations, the reaction rate change for each 10 C rise in temperature, Q_{10}, was in exact agreement to Phillips's (1949) Q_{10} of 2.74, which was determined from Ct 90 values (molar concentration of gas multiplied by the time for 90 % inactivation). El Bisi et al. (1963) determined a Q_{10} of 1.5 nearly equivalent to our limiting Q_{10} of 1.8. Opfell et al. (1959) also found that doubling the concentration had a negligible effect on the rate of inactivation.

Values of Q_{10} decrease with increasing temperature in normal chemical reactions. Rahn (1945) indicated Q_{10} values of 2, 3, and 4 at 20–30 C for normal chemical reactions and 1.36, 1.62, and 18.4 at 170–180 C. For dry heat sterilization a Q_{10} of 1.6 could be expected for the range of 170–180 C. For steam denaturation of proteins, however, Q_{10} values go from 10, 20, and 100 at 50–60 C to 4.8, 7.7, and 23.0 at 120–130 C. Thus, the Q_{10} range for the EO reactions are within the values one would expect for normal chemical reactions.

THE EFFECT OF RELATIVE HUMIDITY

Although the basic parameters for ethylene oxide sterilization are established they are sometimes difficult to attain in practice where the principle limiting factor is moisture availability. Bruch and Bruch (1970) make the following statement concerning the importance of moisture: "A theme that runs through most of these kinetic investigations on EO inactivation is that moisture appears to be the most critical variable for this process after a minimal EO concentration and temperature are established."

The role of moisture in gaseous sterilization with EO was established by Kaye and Phillips (1949). Paradoxically there are conflicting opinions as to actual optimum relative humidity requirements in the ethylene oxide sterilization process. The Kaye and Phillips (1949) data show an optimal relative humidity in the vicinity of 33 %; whereas Ernst and Shull (1962), Perkins and Lloyd (1961), Mayr (1961), and Kereluk et al. (1970) presented data to show that sterilizing efficiency increased with increased relative humidity. A conflict does not actually exist. The methods or test procedures were entirely different and represented diverse conditions. Phillips' optimal low-level relative humidity requirement was based on work where microorganisms and their carrier materials were allowed to equilibrate with respect to their relative humidity environment. In this case the optimal was determined at 33 % relative humidity at 25 C.

A model system was proposed by Ernst and Doyle (1968) which

would logically explain why an optimal relative humidity is indicated under experimental conditions, whereas a high relative humidity is generally required in practice. It is hypothesized that water molecules carry ethylene oxide to reactive sites. In practice either water or EO increases the permeation of the other through plastic films depending upon their polar or nonpolar character.

The fact that ethylene oxide acts as a "carrier" for moisture through nonpolar and normally hydrophobic films having low moisture permeations was frequently observed in the Castle Process Laboratory. When a sealed polyethylene bag was placed into a sterilizer conditioned

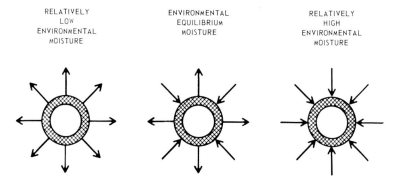

RELATIVELY   ENVIRONMENTAL   RELATIVELY
LOW   EQUILIBRIUM   HIGH
ENVIRONMENTAL   MOISTURE   ENVIRONMENTAL
MOISTURE   MOISTURE

Figure 4 Model representing the dynamic exchange of water by bacterial spores unequilibrated with their environmental moisture. (From Ernst and Doyle, 1968. Biotech. and Bioeng. **10**: 1–31. By permission, Interscience Publishers, John Wiley & Sons, Inc., New York.)

at 54 C in a high relative humidity, little if any moisture diffused through the polyethylene film. However, on addition of EO to this system, globules of water were found on the inside of the polyethylene bag indicating that EO acted as the carrier for the diffusion of moisture through the polyethylene film. Conversely, water aids the permeation of ethylene oxide through polar type films (e.g., nylon and cellophane) which normally allow water to readily permeate but are slow to diffuse EO.

The model system is portrayed in Figures 4 and 5. Spores are characterized with respect to their immediate environment and relative moisture content as compared with the gross environment surrounding them with respect to available moisture. The arrows represent the dynamic exchange of moisture. In Figure 4 the "contaminated sites" are represented as having equal amounts of moisture, but are not in equilibrium with their gross environment. On the left is represented a relatively low environmental moisture with respect to the site. The exchange of moisture is outward, away from the spore. In practice this condition is very limiting to the sterilization process. On the right is shown the opposite effect of a high environmental moisture. The dynamic exchange of water is primarily toward the site. This represents the most ideal situation in practice. In the center is represented the equilibrium (steady-state) condition which is intermediate in effectiveness. Figure 5 is the second part of the model showing in all three cases situations where the spore and its immediate environment (the site) is in equilibration with

RELATIVELY
DRY SPORE
LOW RH

INTERMEDIATE
"OPTIMAL" RH

RELATIVELY
WET SPORE
HIGH RH

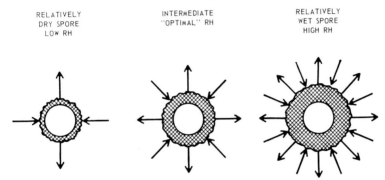

Figure 5   Model representing the dynamic exchange of water by bacterial spores equilibrated to different levels of environmental moisture. (From Ernst and Doyle, 1968. Biotech. and Bioeng. **10**: 1–31. By permission, Interscience Publishers, John Wiley & Sons, Inc., New York.)

its surroundings with regard to moisture exchange. Represented on the left is a relatively dry site in low environmental moisture under steady-state conditions. There is little exchange of moisture in and out of the spore. In practice we know this situation is very limiting for sterilization. On the right, the opposite situation shows a relatively wet site in an environment of high available moisture and equilibrated therewith, representing a high rate of interchange of moisture between the site and its surroundings. It was suggested by Phillips (1961) that a zone of high moisture would have a diluting effect on EO reducing its availability to the cell, especially when the EO environment is minimal. The model represented by the central figure would agree with the optimal relative humidity designated by Phillips.

Experience has shown that, although Phillips's basic parameter is correct, for all practical purposes it is more realistic to base sterilization processes on the first consideration for two primary reasons: (1) Usually sterilization processes are carried out at higher than ordinary room temperatures, producing a condition which, as described above, presents materials to be sterilized which are moisture deficient with respect to an established relative humidity environment; (2) usually materials to be sterilized, except for exposed surfaces, have wrapping, matrices, and the like which present diffusion barriers. And although the optimal 33 % relative humidity is desirable at the site of bacterial surfaces, a much higher than optimal level must exist as a driving force to achieve this goal. Fick's diffusion law applies where, all other factors being constant, the rate of diffusion across a barrier is directly proportional to the

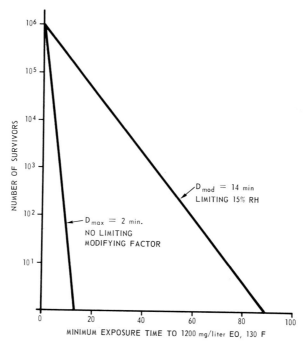

Figure 6 Survivor curves of *Bacillus subtilis* var. *niger* spores on paper strips under optimal (D_{max}) conditions vs. limiting 15% relative humidity (D_{mod}).

concentration gradient across the barrier (the gradient in this case being moisture in the sterilizer versus moisture at the bacterial site).

$$m = \Delta A(C_2 - C_1)\, t/h$$

where m = mass of substance diffused; Δ = coefficient of diffusion; A = cross-sectional area; $(C_2 - C_1)$ = concentration gradient across a thickness, h; t = time, an important and necessary factor.

Figure 6 portrays the rate-limiting effect of low moisture levels in the sterilizer (in this case under conditions of below optimal equilibrium) of 15 % relative humidity. D_{max} represents a rate curve determined from end-point determinations. A D value represents the time necessary to inactivate 90 % or one log of a population, based on the exponential rate curve. D_{max} determined from end-point data represents the safest rate value for calculating sterilization times. D_{mod} represents the modified rate from end-point determinations under the condition of limiting relative humidity. Parametric studies, where rate curves were determined by classical means for various concentrations, relative humidities and temperatures, have shown that at higher-than-ambient temperatures, the relative humidity is the most critical variable (Ernst and Doyle, unpublished data).

DESICCANT DRYING OR IN-CRYSTAL OCCLUSION

Gilbert et al. (1964), extending the work of Phillips (1961), found that severely desiccated bacterial spores, vegetative cells, and T-1 bacteriophage could not be sterilized in EO, even when exposed at 33 % relative humidity. The resistant microorganisms reacted normally and were easily sterilizable when rehydrated. However, the desiccated state could not be readily overcome by high relative humidity levels unless exposed to 100 % relative humidity or intentionally wetted.

Doyle and Ernst (1968) found a significant decrease in resistance with subsequent washings of spore suspensions of *B. subtilis* var. *niger* as seen in Figure 7. Conversely, the degree of cleanliness of the spore suspension was more significant than the relative dryness in EO resistance, and that "dirty" spore suspensions dried on a solid surface (aluminum foil) indeed showed a much higher order of resistance than the same suspension on porous paper. The aluminum carriers containing unwashed spores were unsterile even after a 48-hr exposure to optimal conditions at 1200 mg/liter at 40 % relative humidity and 130 F.

Figure 7 shows that desiccant drying does not effectually increase resistance of the spores whether adequately cleaned or not, but rather, in the case of insufficiently cleaned spores, desiccant drying slightly decreases resistance. The author presumes that organisms may have been occluded in crystals which produced the unsterilizable desiccation effect reported by others. We have discovered in our laboratory that with asbestos (some papers are presumed to include asbestos) a dissolvable recrystallizable substance occludes spores within the reforming crystals on subsequent drying.

Cleanliness of materials to be sterilized is an extremely important consideration. The presence of organic matter itself will not ordinarily defeat but will reduce sterilizing efficiency, unless in-solid or in-crystal occlusion is severe enough to stop diffusion of moisture (Royce and Bowler, 1961). Figure 8 shows crystals of calcium carbonate having spores in high numbers occluded within them. The release of the spores from the dissolving crystals are shown in Figure 9. Since these crystals are only very slightly dissolvable in ordinary water, this condition, which would be prevalent in soil, goes generally undetected by standard

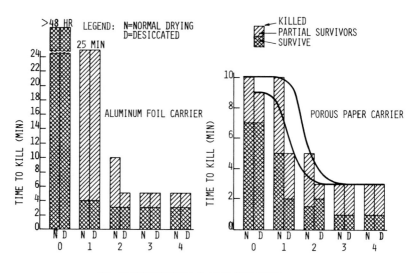

NO. OF RESUSPENSIONS IN DISTILLED WATER

Figure 7 Effects of relative cleanliness and degree of dryness on the resistance of *Bacillus subtilis* var. *niger* spores to gaseous ethylene oxide. (From Ernst and Doyle, 1968. Biotech. and Bioeng. **10**:1–31. By permission, Interscience Publishers, John Wiley & Sons, Inc., New York.)

culturing techniques. Ernst and Doyle (1968) found that spores protected in this way could not be sterilized by ordinary exposures to either steam, EO, or dry heat. Dry heat required an increased exposure time of about 9 times, and steam 900 times to sterilize effectively an equivalent number of spores. Of recent concern has been the potential of having materials contaminated with bacteria occluded in NaCl crystals and its effect of defeating sterilization by ethylene oxide. Indeed, it is the author's firm conviction that the so-called effect of desiccant drying defeating sterilization by EO, was an artifact consisting of the formation of NaCl or other crystals around bacteria. This artifact required dissolution of the crystal structure by wetting to affect sterilization. In

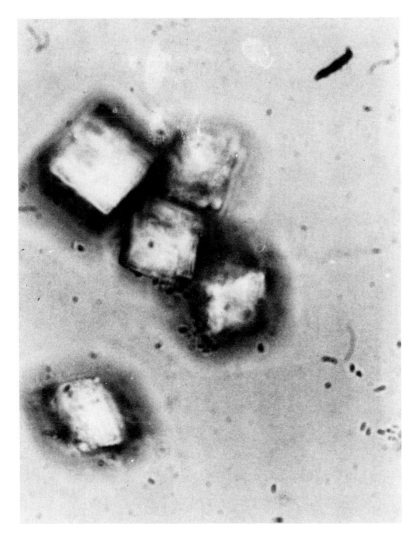

Figure 8 Crystals of calcium carbonate, 100 microns per side, containing an average of 100 spores each.

the case of the possible existence on a product of a few salt crystals which, by slim chance, contained microbial contamination, the crystals would, even then, conceivably dissolve and reform in a dynamic fashion, releasing the contamination in the relatively high moisture of the EO sterilizer. Never in *ordinary* sterilizing practice would one expect to find the state and degree of contamination as indicated by some misleading experiments.

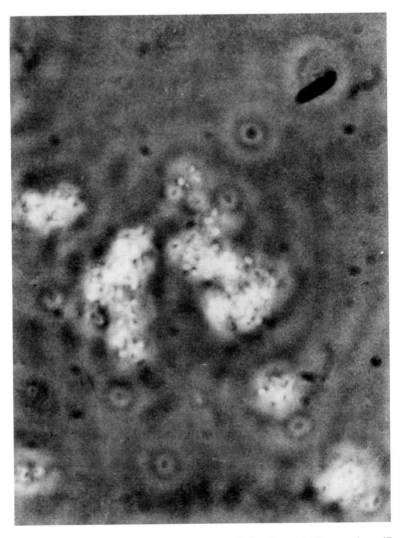

Figure 9 Dissoluting crystals releasing spores of *Bacillus subtilis* var. *niger*. (From Ernst and Doyle, 1968. Biotech. and Bioeng. **10**: 1–31. By permission Interscience Publishers, John Wiley & Sons, Inc., New York.)

ENVIRONMENTAL DRYNESS

Desiccant drying, which we feel is primarily artifactual, is therefore of little concern in practice. However, environmental dryness may severely affect EO sterilization for other reasons. Moisture absorbable materials such as paperboard boxes, paper and cloth wrappings, and certain plastic films (nylon and cellophane) to a lesser extent, but still of concern, polyethylene and other plastic surfaces such as coiled tubing, tend to compete for moisture with the contaminating microbial population we seek to destroy. The outer layers or wrappers soak up moisture so rapidly and preferentially as not to allow any residual to effectively sterilize the product, especially if these materials are stored in dry environments. Our modern heating and air conditioning are the principal factors in producing the effect of severely drying out the materials stored in such environments. It is the dryness associated with the mass of material and its overwhelming demand for moisture in a *competitive* sense that is the crux of the moisturizing problem.

From our experimentation and experience as discussed above, we can summarize with the following statements:

1. That the relative dirtiness is a considerable factor in decreasing sterilizing efficiency.
2. That desiccated spores of those we tested are somewhat easier to kill than nondesiccated, excluding the spores occluded in crystals or a hard organic crust.
3. Spores occluded in crystals cannot be killed by EO unless the crystal dissolves. This effect has never been observed by the author *in practice*. Adequate provision for humidification, according to the McDonald principle (1962), would dissolve any chance crystals which may contaminate a product. However, crystalline materials and certain powders which contain occluded bacteria would not be sterilizable in a gaseous EO process.
4. Air pockets or strata will tend to delay but not defeat sterilization by EO.
5. Environmental dryness may be severe enough to defeat sterilization by EO because dried out wrappings, boxes, etc., compete for moisture in the sterilizer.

Ernst et al. (1969) also noted the presence of chemically reactive barriers. Cyclohexylamine, a corrosion inhibitor, and Orvus-K (Proctor and Gamble), a neutral anionic synthetic detergent used on plastic as an antistatic agent, greatly extend the time required to EO sterilize a surface treated with such compounds.

In concluding this discussion on the sterilization parameters and limiting factors in EO gaseous sterilization, it is worthy to note that a significant delineation is often necessary between theory and practice, as we pointed out. A notable example is that, although by experiment it is definitely easier to kill spores on porous surfaces than hard surfaces

(Ernst and Doyle, 1968; Kereluk et al., 1970), in practice in industry, large massive loads of cotton, cloth, or paper products are much more difficult to sterilize than a large load of nonporous materials, principally for the moisture competition effect.

Points to be considered to avoid problems:

1. Materials to be sterilized should be clean and free of organic debris.
2. The storage and manufacture of materials to be gas sterilized should be in an environment maintained in excess of 40 % relative humidity, especially during excessively hot and cold periods.
3. Humidity must be properly controlled in the sterilizer to assure a relative humidity as high as possible short of wetting materials. There should be a sufficient soaking or "dwell" period of at least 30 min, depending on the nature of the load. The McDonald (1962) process, or a modification thereof, utilizing prehumidification should always be used. Anything short of it is an invitation to trouble. Environmental conditions prior to gas exposure are inadequate to replace the prehumidifying stage in the sterilizer. This is the *most important* step in the sterilization process.
4. The admission of the sterilant gases to the sterilizing chamber should be via a heat-exchanger to assure proper vaporization and heating of the gas. For a 130 F operation, the incoming EO temperature should be 150 F in the gaseous phase.

   The inflowing liquid sterilant would vaporize slowly in the chamber space causing freezing conditions within that portion of the chamber. The cold inflowing and vaporizing sterilant would therefore collapse and even freeze out the prehumidifying moisture leaving a residual desert environment which could result in sterilization failure. Adding the unvaporized sterilant for the same reason produces temperature gradients and gaseous stratification (Ernst and Doyle, 1968).
5. Use only wrapping materials which provide good and rapid permeation to moisture, air and gas (paper, polyethylene, Tyvek[R] are good candidates). Nylon and cellophane are poor, and should be avoided.
6. Avoid the severe conditions which will tend to facilitate the formation of toxic residues and damaging polymers. This subject is discussed elsewhere in this volume by Dr. Carl Bruch.

INDUSTRIAL STERILIZATION PROCESSES

The most efficient sterilizing process, based on the considerations listed above, is that of McDonald (1962) and is shown on a pressure-time graph of Figure 10. The sequential stages are listed. Of minor importance is the operating pressure which determines the EO gaseous concentration. What is most important is the strategic placement of moisture under vacuum to provide the best dynamics for heat and moisture permeation. This can best be accomplished under vacuum. Where the operating temperature is 54 C or higher, the degree of vacuum is critical for highest efficiency. This would be 26 inches Hg vacuum or higher based on the thermodynamic relationship of saturated moisture.

Why is it so important to strategically place moisture, that is to concentrate it near to but not directly on the sterilizing site? Ernst et al. (1970) presented four reasons why it is important to prehumidify under vacuum to strategically place moisture prior to adding the sterilant gas:

Figure 10   Pressure changes in various stages in ethylene oxide sterilization, the McDonald (1962) process. The dashed line represents the Air Displacement process, a modification of McDonald to preserve packaging integrity. By permission, Parenteral Drug Association, Inc., Philadelphia.

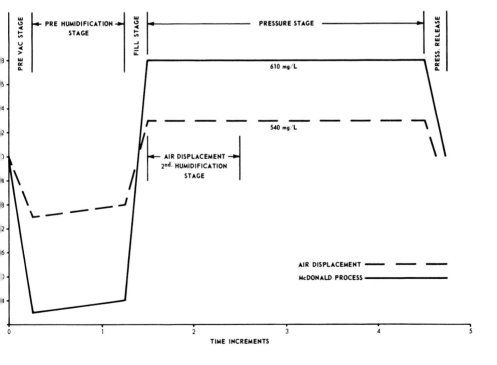

1. The number of water molecules in even a highly humidified environment is overwhelmed by the greater number of EO molecules.
2. The diffusivity of EO far surpasses that of water vapor. If EO and water were equally dispersed, the EO would permeate into and through materials preferentially, leaving moisture behind.
3. Water readily reacts with both EO and the diluents CO_2 and Freon 12, the latter presumably by hydrogen bonding in the gaseous state, rendering the moisture ineffective as well as reducing the efficiency of EO itself. Large molecular aggregates are formed by H-bonding which can sometimes be seen as a vapor cloud which is heavier than air. This state also is conducive to the formation of toxic residues and damaging polymers.
4. Molecular interference such as air pockets and expanded heat-sealed plastic bags prevents the effective permeation of water vapor.

Molecular interactions can seriously interfere with diffusion of moisture and EO, as occurs by attempting to sterilize such with pure EO under vacuum. Air in the lumen of coiled tubing is also a limiting condition, not so much for EO, but for the permeation of heat and moisture. Air is a great barrier for diffusion of heat and moisture in EO, but not as severe as in steam sterilizers. Air stratification can severely delay EO sterilization if the air strata is great enough in depth, such as might occur in industrial sterilizers where no attempt is made to remove air. The delaying effect is directly related to diffusion path length vertically. Thus, it would be most severe in industrial sterilizers having a large vertical dimension (Ernst et al., 1970).

The relative ease by which products sealed in various packaging films are sterilizable has been determined by Doyle et al. (1970) to be in the following increasing order of resistance: polyethylene and polyvinyl chloride (the least resistant to achieve sterilization), nylon, cellophane/polyethylene laminate, phenoxy, mylar/polyethylene laminate (the most difficult to permeate). Although increasing the thickness of the film is also a limiting factor, for polyethylene film, increasing thickness from 1 to 4 mils (Kereluk et al., 1970) does not appreciably change the barrier effect as much as the theoretical consideration may imply. However, increasing the thickness of nylon and some other difficult-to-permeate films does limit the permeation rate of the sterilizing gaseous components and therefore affect the concomitant ease of sterilization.

THE MCDONALD (1962) PROCESS AND AIR DISPLACEMENT

It remained for an engineer of the Castle Company, Robert McDonald, extrapolating Kaye and Phillips's (1949) data and by astute experimentation, to develop a basic process, now referred to as the McDonald process. It has been improved upon, but not basically changed. It has been compromised, but for reasons of preserving packaging integrity rather than for preserving efficiency.

Figure 10 graphically presents the pressure-vacuum changes that occur in the various steps of the McDonald process. A modification of the McDonald process, the Air Displacement process, is also shown. The sequential steps of the McDonald process are as follows:

1. *Temperature setting.* This is usually around 130 F (54 C). From Ernst and Shull (1962a), sterilizing efficiency can be increased and exposure time reduced by increasing the temperature. Roughly, sterilizing time may be reduced by one-half for every 30 C rise in temperature. However, the problem of moisturizing makes it necessary to compromise the temperature to prevent excessive wetting of materials which would result at higher temperatures because of the necessity to maintain a temperature-dependent relative humidity level of at least 35%. To increase temperature above 130 F would require decreasing relative humidity to prevent wetting. The overall effect of decreasing relative humidity is greater in reducing sterilizing efficiency than the opposing effect of temperature.

2. *Evacuation.* The sterilizer is evacuated to about 27 inches Hg. This provides optimal conditions for moisturizing and heating.

3. *Humidifying.* Generally steam is introduced to the evacuated chamber and controlled by some means to provide a high level of relative humidity in the chamber (usually 45–85%). These conditions are maintained for a period of time depending on size and density of load and other factors. This is called the "dwell" (it is a soak period). Time is required for moisture to permeate depending on the "driving force" also (20 min–2 hr). The rule is to provide moisture much in excess of the minimal 35% relative humidity, but short of wetting materials. The higher relative humidity levels provide a driving force for diffusion and also contain valuable elements of heat. The advantages of this strategic placement of moisture, referred to as *pre-humidification,* have been discussed. It cannot be overemphasized, however, that prehumidification in the sterilizer chamber has such distinct value and importance that it cannot be replaced by pre-

humidification outside of the chamber. Sometimes it is important to precondition goods under moisture and heat in the external environment. However, the prehumidification-under-vacuum step of the process is not to be avoided. It is indeed *the most important step* of the entire sterilization sequence.

4. *Introduce sterilant gases to a predetermined pressure or concentration.* There are several gaseous mixtures used. The most prominent at present is the "12-88" mixture (12 % EO by weight or 27.3 % by volume in fluorocarbon-12). In some cases, 10 % EO in carbon dioxide is used. The pressure for operating with fluorocarbon mixtures is usually 8 psig (630 mg/liter concentration) and for carbon dioxide, 25 psig (450 mg/liter). The pressures may vary depending on the EO concentrations desired. The various EO sterilant mixtures will be compared on practical grounds in a following section.

5. *Timing at operating pressure.* This will vary considerably depending on type of packaging, on density of load and total load volume, and whether a sterilizer has some means of circulating gas. For large industrial sterilizers the time is usually between 3 and 16 hr.

6. *Reducing pressure, exhausting sterilant gases.* At this point, sterilization has been accomplished. However, to protect personnel in confined spaces the sterilant gases should be pumped or vented out of the working area. As an additional precaution flushing is desirable to reduce the EO concentration to the environment. The danger to personnel is minimal even if vented into the working space, since EO dissipates so rapidly. Thus, extreme measures are not warranted.

Most damage to packaging results in this stage due to the reduced pressure. For example, a heat-sealed polyethylene bag will absorb moisture and EO sterilant gases which add their partial pressures to the interior of the bag already containing air expanded by heat. This added pressure will often cause the bags to burst and lose their integrity during the pressure reduction stage.

Sometimes packaging places severe constraints upon the sterilization process which may not be avoidable. To preserve packaging integrity, a modification of the McDonald sterilizing cycle was designed, since most distortion and damage to packaging occurs during vacuum-pressure changes.

The Air Displacement process is a best compromise of the most efficient McDonald process which is designed to work within the limits of the constraints of the packaging, whereby distortion, bursting or implosion effects are entirely obviated. This is, however, at the expense or loss of some efficiency of the McDonald process.

The Air Displacement process is a modification of the McDonald process. Similar sequential steps are shown in Figure 10, and are described as follows:

1. *Temperature setting.* As described for McDonald, 130 F.
2. *Evacuation.* The sterilizer is evacuated to the limit short of producing packaging damage. The package must be tested to determine its vacuum limit. For example, let us assume that a vacuum in excess of 10 inches Hg will produce package bursting. Therefore, the pre-evacuation setting will be 10 inches Hg. The rule of thumb is to go as high in vacuum as the packaging will allow for good strategic placement of moisture.
3. *Humidifying.* As described for the McDonald process.
4. *Introduce the sterilant gases to slight positive pressure.*
5. *Air venting.* This begins as the sterilant gases continue to fill the chamber. The relative density of the sterilant 12-88 mixture is about 4 times that of air. Thus, the air can be effectively squeezed out vertically upward.
6. *Pressurize chamber to operating pressure.* The air venting has ceased and gas continues to fill chamber to operating pressure. The selected pressure is variable and is dependent upon the packaging limitations. Implosion of packages can be prevented by controlling the input rate. Sometimes it is necessary to operate at low pressures to prevent crushing of certain types of materials. However, the most critical factor is usually package bursting due to reducing pressure when the pressure differential is excessive. Generally, if care is exercised to work within the vacuum limits of packages, bursting will most often occur at the end of the cycle during the pressure-reducing or post-vacuum stages. The reasons why package bursting is more severe when pressure is reduced at the end of the cycle are as follows:
   a. Usually the resident air in a hermetically sealed package will not escape. This resident air will acquire heat and will expand.
   b. Humidification will add moisture to the system.
   c. The permeating sterilant gases will add significantly to increase internal pressures. If we subjected the package to a post vacuum of 10 inches Hg we would add an additional $\frac{1}{3}$ atmosphere, and most assuredly burst the package. The rule of thumb to keep

the final pressure within bounds, which generally works, is to divide the vacuum by three as follows:

$$\text{Operating pressure} = \frac{\text{inches of vacuum}}{3}$$

in psig as the lowest whole number. For our example:

$$P = \tfrac{10}{3} = 3 \text{ psig.}$$

As indicated by Ernst and Shull (1962 a) where other conditions are optimal, especially relative humidity and temperature, the concentration (which is pressure dependent) is of relatively minor importance. One would observe that sterilization at 2 psig (480 mg/liter) is just as effective and rapid as at 8 psig (660 mg/liter).

7. *Timing at selected pressure.* Pressure (3 psig in our example) is variable depending on loading volume and density, and whether or not there is a means of circulating gas. Gaseous circulation aids considerably in efficiency of moisturizing and heating, as well as for avoiding air stratification.

8. *Reduce to atmospheric pressure.*

9. *Flushing.* We recommend flushing with filtered air as in the McDonald process.

The Air Displacement process utilizes the best distinctive features of the McDonald process within the constraining limits packaging places upon it. Placement of moisture is most effective at 26 inches of Hg vacuum (negative pressure) or less for sound physical reasons. Compromising the vacuum as we do in air displacement reduces the moisturizing and heating effectiveness, depending upon the degree. Although 26 inches or greater is optimal, 20 inches is better in effectiveness than 10 inches, and 10 is better than zero, etc. Thus, although the Air Displacement is less efficient than the McDonald process, it is greatly more efficient than another recently devised commercial process. This process, the Pressure Balance process (PB) (Gunther, 1971), was also designed to reduce package bursting, and is shown as a pressure-time curve in Figure 11. Figure 12 compares the heating effectiveness of the three processes mentioned. Heating is almost directly related to humidification. Ernst et al. (1970) (Figure 12), show the comparative heating effectiveness of the various industrial processes, demonstrating the McDonald cycle to be by far the most effective and Air Displacement (in one modification) to be of intermediary effectiveness with PB process relatively less effective than both.

An industrial EO gaseous sterilization process (compared in Table 1) uses pure or nearly 100 % EO, which is flammable and may be explosive. This principal disadvantage is one of grave concern. The explosive force of the undiluted EO is presumed to be 50 times greater than a purely oxidation reaction would indicate. Thus, the use of undiluted EO requires the use of highly explosion-proof equipment. Generally, underwriters or government agencies require a remote location and special buildings for the operation of this equipment. Insurance costs tend to be high, and skilled knowledgeable personnel are required for the operation of such equipment.

The principal advantage for the use of undiluted EO is its relatively low cost. Another advantage is the fact that a pressure vessel is not required beyond the capability of high-vacuum containment. The use of the undiluted sterilant additionally provides very high concentration at less than atmospheric pressure.

Because of the necessity to achieve and maintain relatively high-

Figure 11   Pressure changes in various stages of EO sterilization representing the Pressure Balance (or Gunther (1971)) Process. From Ernst et al. (1970). By permission, Parenteral Drug Association, Inc., Philadelphia.

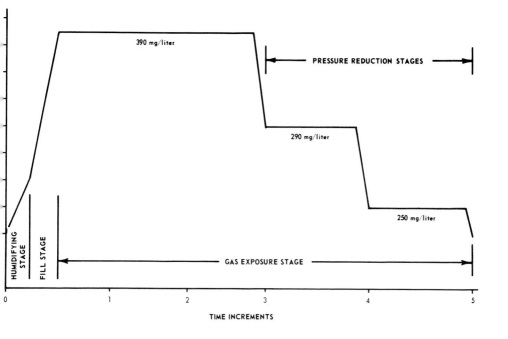

Table 1 Relative positive and negative features by comparison of four industrial sterilization processes

Characteristic	Process designation[d]			
	McDonald	Air displacement	Pressure balance	Pure EO
A. Overall sterilizing efficiency[a]	+++	++	+	+++
B. Factors affecting efficiency				
1. Humidifying potential	++++	++		++
2. Heating potential	++++	++	+	+
3. Air removal potential (prevent stratification)	+++	++++		++++
4. Permeation into sealed-in air pockets	++++	++	+	++++
5. Possible high gas concentration	+++	+++	+	++++
C. Negative and deleterious factors[b]				
1. Requirement for gas circulation	H.B.[c]	H.B.	A.R. ----	N.R.
2. Package bursting potential	----	-		--
3. Package compression potential	-		----	---

[a]
+ + + + (or nearest optimal) Highest order for efficiency
+ + + High order for efficiency
+ + Intermediate order for efficiency
+ Poor order for efficiency
Blank space (or least optimal) Very poor order for efficiency

[b]
- - - - Greatest deleterious effect
- - - High order of deleterious effect
- - Intermediate deleterious effect
- Low order of deleterious effect
Blank space No deleterious effect

[c] H.B., Highly beneficial
A.R., Absolute requirement
N.R., Not recommended; however, it would be highly desirable for better heat and moisture distribution

[d] McDonald and Pure EO are traditional processes
Air displacement is a compromise of McDonald to preserve packaging integrity
Pressure balance is a compromise process to preserve packaging integrity

vacuum levels, package bursting and distortion is prevalent. Sometimes to reduce this potential, special venting arrangements must be made in packaging, or, frequently, sealing is effected after sterilization, allowing for possible poststerilization recontamination. Its inflexibility in this regard is a distinct disadvantage. Another disadvantage is the molecular interference associated with distended packaging, limiting the moisturizing and heating so important to an efficient sterilization. Thus, for many applications, despite the higher gaseous concentration (Ernst and

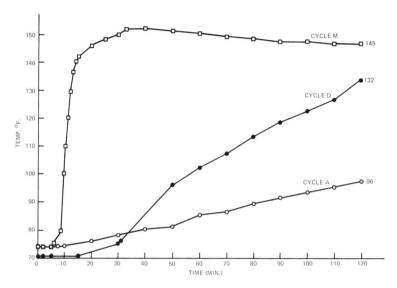

Figure 12 Comparison of heating characteristics of three sterilization processes. From Ernst et al. (1970). By permission, Parenteral Drug Association, Inc., Philadelphia.

> *Note.*—Cycle M = McDonald Process
> Cycle D = Air Displacement
> Cycle A = Pressure Balance

Shull, 1962a), the diluted fluorocarbon mixture and some CO_2 mixtures tend to provide higher sterilizing efficiencies.

When one considers the higher cost for equipment and insurance plus the extreme danger, the lower gas cost seems to shrink to relative insignificance. Generally the use of undiluted or flammable mixtures are restricted to traditional installations. There seems to be an accelerating trend to use the much safer, and hardly less efficient, and questionably more costly 12-88 mixture.

Since it was stated that humidification under vacuum is the most important step in EO sterilization, a word is in order here respecting the four systems compared in Table 1. Strategic placement of moisture and moisturizing effectiveness have been discussed. But it is repeated here that its greatest potential is at or above 26 inches of Hg vacuum, at 130 F, and is less effective proportionately with lesser vacuums, and least effective at atmospheric pressure or under positive pressures. A driving force is necessary which attains best at the optimal vacuum level. Also a soak period or dwell, which is the characteristic of the McDonald principle, is of great importance. The PB process is notably deficient in both areas.

The most effective heating and humidifying is being done in inter-mediate size sterilizers being used mainly in hospitals or small volume process applications. Henfrey (1961; reaffirmed by Henry, 1963) de-veloped a steam-bleed principle which introduced steam in a steady flow as a chamber was being evacuated. This provided optimal heating and moisturizing in concert with effective air removal as applied to high vacuum steam sterilization. At some point a steady-state equilibrium attains at which the exhausting rate exactly matches the inflowing rate of steam. This point has a temperature-pressure relationship that matches the steam tables. Sterilizer manufacturers astutely use this principle for rapid heating and humidifying in the prevacuum, prehumidifi-cation sequence of the McDonald EO process. Sometimes it tends to overmoisturize but heating and moisturizing are rapid and optimal for sterilization. Keep in mind the fact that a driving force is necessary. This is provided by the nearly saturated level produced by the rate-controlled steam input. The wetting potential is reduced by providing a slight superheat, by maintaining a jacket temperature somewhat above the steam temperature at the vacuum level. Thus, one can control the relative humidity at less than 100 % levels. The indicated relative humidity might be in the range of 75 to 90 % levels, although the sterilizer is actually filled with superheated steam. The steam of course is the best heat-transfer medium. Nonetheless, a heating and moisturiz-ing lag occurs depending again on size and/or density of loading which requires a dwell or soak period to be effective. The dwell in this case is dynamic, as flow *in* matches flow *out* at a specific vacuum.

Under the conditions described above, EO sterilization, which is mainly limited because of moisturizing effects as compared to steam sterilization, has the potential of being as effective, and in many cases even more effective, than steam sterilization. EO sterilization has at-tained a stage of effectiveness and efficiency second to none, especially when one considers that more materials and greater quantities are sterilized in the medical and related industries by EO than by any other process.

References

1. Amaha, M., and K. Sakaguchi. 1957. The mode and kinetics of death of the bacterial spores by moist heat. J. Gen. Appl. Microbiol. **3**: 163–192.
2. Bruch, C. W., and M. K. Bruch. 1970. Gaseous disinfection. pp. 149–206. In M. A. Benarde [Ed.], *Disinfection*. Marcel Dekker, Inc. New York.
3. Doyle, J. E., and R. R. Ernst. 1968. Influence of various pretreatments (carriers, desiccation and relative cleanliness) on the destruction of *Bacillus subtilis* var. *niger* spores with gaseous ethylene oxide. J. Pharm. Sci. **57**: 433.
4. El Bisi, H. M., R. M. Vondell, and W. B. Esselen. 1963. Kinetics of bacterial activity of ethylene oxide in the vapor phase. III. Effect of sterilant temperature and pressure. p. 13. *Bacteriological Proceedings 1963*. Abstracts. The 67th Annual Meeting of the American Society for Microbiology.
5. Ernst, R. R. 1971. Mysteries and misconceptions related to sterile processing in hospital and industry. A consultant's viewpoint. pp. 44–58. *Proceedings of the HIA Technical Symposium "Sterile Disposable Devices: Present and Future."* Sponsored by the Sterile Disposable Device Committee of Health Industries Association, Washington. Available from the Health Industries Association, 1225 Connecticut Ave., N.W., Washington 20036.
6. Ernst, R. R., and J. E. Doyle. 1968. Limiting factors in ethylene oxide gaseous sterilization. Dev. Ind. Microbiol. **9**: 293–296.
7. Ernst, R. R., and J. E. Doyle. 1968. Sterilization with gaseous ethylene oxide: A review of chemical and physical factors. Biotech. and Bioeng. **10**: 1–31.
8. Ernst, R. R., J. Mogenhan, J. Whitbourne, and K. West. 1970. The air displacement process in industrial ethylene oxide sterilization. Bulletin of the Parenteral Drug Association. **24**: 119–133.
9. Ernst, R. R., and J. J. Shull. 1962a. Ethylene oxide gaseous sterilization. I. Concentration and temperature effects. Appl. Microbiol. **10**: 337–341.
10. Ernst, R. R., and J. J. Shull. 1962b. Ethylene oxide gaseous sterilization. II. Influence of method of humidification. Appl. Microbiol. **10**: 342–344.
11. Ernst, R. R., K. L. West, and J. E. Doyle. 1969. Problem areas in sterility testing. Bulletin of the Parenteral Drug Association. **23**: 29–39.
12. Gilbert, G. L., V. M. Gambill, D. R. Spiner, R. K. Hoffman, and C. R. Phillips. 1964. Effect of moisture on ethylene oxide sterilization. Appl. Microbiol. **12**: 496–503.
13. Gunther, D. A. 1971. Balanced pressure process of sterilization. U.S. Patent 3,589,861.
14. Henfrey, K. M. 1961. Drayton Castle Technical Bulletin No. 1. Drayton Castle Ltd. West Drayton, Middlesex, England.
15. Henry, P. S. H. 1963. Residual air in the steam sterilization of textiles with pre-vacuum. J. Appl. Bacteriol. **26**: 234–245.
16. Kaye, S., and C. R. Phillips. 1949. The sterilizing action of ethylene oxide. IV. The effect of moisture. Am. J. Hyg. **50**: 296–306.

17. Kereluk, K., R. A. Gammon, and R. S. Lloyd. 1970. Microbiological aspects of ethylene oxide sterilization. I. Experimental apparatus and methods. Appl. Microbiol. **19**: 146–151.
18. Kereluk, K., R. A. Gammon, and R. S. Lloyd. 1970. Microbiological aspects of ethylene oxide sterilization. II. Microbial resistance to ethylene oxide. Appl. Microbiol. **19**: 152–156.
19. Kereluk, K., R. A. Gammon, and R. S. Lloyd. 1970. Microbiological aspects of ethylene oxide sterilization. III. Effects of humidity and water activity on the sporicidal activity of ethylene oxide. Appl. Microbiol. **19**: 157–162.
20. Kereluk, K., R. A. Gammon, and R. S. Lloyd. 1970. Microbiological aspects of ethylene oxide sterilization. IV. Influence of thickness of polyethylene film on the sporicidal activity of ethylene oxide. Appl. Microbiol. **19**: 163–165.
21. Kereluk, K., and R. S. Lloyd. 1969. Ethylene oxide sterilization. A current review of principles and practices. J. Hosp. Res. **7**: 7–75.
22. Mayr, G. 1961. Equipment for ethylene oxide sterilization. pp. 90–97. In *Recent Developments in the Sterilization of Surgical Materials. Symposium.* Pharmaceutical Press. London.
23. McDonald, R. L. 1962. Method of sterilizing. U.S. Patent 3,068,064.
24. Opfell, J. B., J. P. Hohmann, and A. B. Latham. 1959. Ethylene oxide sterilization of spores in hydroscopic environments. J. Am. Pharm. Assoc. **48**: 617–619.
25. Perkins, J. J., and R. S. Lloyd. 1961. Applications and equipment for ethylene oxide sterilization. pp. 76–90. In *Recent Developments in the Sterilization of Surgical Materials. Symposium.* Pharmaceutical Press. London.
26. Phillips, C. R. 1949. The sterilizing action of gaseous ethylene oxide. II. Sterilization of contaminated objects with ethylene oxide and related compounds: Time, concentration and temperature relationships. Am. J. Hyg. **50**: 280–289.
27. Phillips, C. R. 1961. The sterilizing properties of ethylene oxide. pp. 59–75. In *Recent Developments in the Sterilization of Surgical Materials. Symposium.* Pharmaceutical Press. London.
28. Phillips, C. R., and Kaye, S. 1949. The sterilizing action of ethylene oxide. I. Review. Am. J. Hyg. **50**: 270–279.
29. Rahn, O. 1945. Physical methods of sterilization of microorganisms. Bacteriol. Revs. **9**: 1–47.
30. Royce, A., and C. Bowler. 1961. Ethylene oxide sterilization—some experiences and some practical limitations. J. Pharm. Pharmacol. **13**: 87T–94T.
31. Urbakh, V. Y. 1961. Thermodynamics of protein denaturation. Biofizika. **6**: 748–750.
32. Wang, D. I. C., J. Scharer, and A. E. Humphrey. 1964. Kinetics of death of bacterial spores at elevated temperatures. Appl. Microbiol. **12**: 451–454.

13

Formaldehyde Gas
as a Sterilant*

J. J. TULIS, PH.D.

Director
Microbiological Sciences Department
Becton, Dickinson Research Center
North Carolina

INTRODUCTION AND BACKGROUND

THE APPLICATION of formaldehyde gas for inactivation of microorganisms was practiced before the turn of the century. One of the first uses of formaldehyde as a wet vapor was to fumigate sick rooms (19). Pernot (17) in 1909 successfully sterilized surfaces of eggs in incubators by adding potassium permanganate to formalin. In 1939, Nordgren (16) summarized much of the early work concerning the efficacy of formaldehyde gas; later Walker (29) published an excellent book entitled, *Formaldehyde* which has served as a reference for many investigators. As the need for area sterilization and decontamination increased, vaporized formaldehyde was used more extensively as a space and surface sterilant. Effectiveness was demonstrated against bacteria, fungi, viruses, and rickettsia, as well as insects and other animal life (6). Three important factors associated with the efficacy of formaldehyde as a vaporized fumigant during this early period were elevated temperature, high relative humidity, and questionable penetrability (18). These factors were determined from the application of liquid formalin, whereby a wet vapor containing formaldehyde gas was generally produced.

In 1956, Kaitz (12) introduced a new application of formaldehyde gas

* The studies reported herein were conducted by the research staff of the Microbiological Sciences Department, Becton, Dickinson Research Center. Participating in the laboratory studies were the following personnel: D. J. Daley, Ph.D., K. W. Draper, D. C. Garnett, H. S. Lilja, R. N. Plaugher, J. L. Sliger, and L. A. Taylor. Their participation in these studies is gratefully acknowledged.

with a process that involved the depolymerization of the formaldehyde polymer, paraformaldehyde, to yield dry formaldehyde gas for use in area and surface sterilization. In 1961, Harry (7) confirmed the work of Kaitz by effectively ridding surfaces of poultry houses of bacterial life. Later Vineland Poultry Laboratories (28) reported many applications for surface sterilization using paraformaldehyde. In 1969, Taylor et al. (23) presented a broad spectrum of paraformaldehyde applications for surface sterilization and detoxification using dry formaldehyde gas. Studies at the Becton, Dickinson Research Center have demonstrated that by using paraformaldehyde, sterilization can be achieved at ambient relative humidity and temperature with no significant build-up of residuals or obvious damage to materials (26, 27). Aeration of an area can be achieved in a relatively short time period. In addition, it has been determined that the dry formaldehyde gas can penetrate closed areas and packaged material. The gas concentration can be controlled to any desired concentration by weighing exact amounts of the paraformaldehyde chemical. This new concept of gaseous formaldehyde sterilization is quite different from the early use of vaporized formaldehyde and has opened new vistas for polymer-resin research in the field of sterilization.

As the National Aeronautics and Space Administration (NASA) extends its exploration into space with an aim of landing spacecraft on the surface of planets such as Mars, sterilization becomes of utmost importance. With the imposed international constraints of spacecraft sterility prior to impact or landing on planetary bodies, NASA must have at its disposal dependable sterilization technology. Thus, a requirement was recognized for the development of methodology for the sterilization of electronic potting compounds and mated surfaces, which was later extended to spacecraft surfaces and the Technology Feasibility Spacecraft, an instrumented mock-up. Studies conducted at Becton, Dickinson and Company laboratories demonstrated the potential usefulness of organic chemicals containing a volatile chemical germicide for sterilization of medical–surgical devices and spacecraft materials. Specifically, it appeared feasible and practical that sterilant mixtures could be developed that would be relatively inactive at ambient conditions, but when placed at moderately elevated temperatures, would evolve sufficient amounts of sterilant to inactive large numbers of bacterial spores.

The rationale for our studies was based on the knowledge that various organic resins and polymers, when exposed to elevated temperature, will release potentially sterilizing quantities of gaseous formaldehyde.

The active formaldehyde evolves from the organic resin or polymer in such a manner that the rate of release, and therefore the sterilization process, is a function of time and temperature. The amount of sterilant gas and moisture released is extremely small, and contaminating micro-organisms are theoretically subjected to *in situ* sterilization without untoward effects on materials or surrounding areas.

In recent years there have been a number of attempts to produce coatings or product additives that will result in materials with "self-sterilizing" properties (9, 14). Generally, little or no success in achieving sterility has resulted from the use of nonvolatile or low-vapor-pressure chemicals (9). This is primarily because such chemicals usually require high moisture environments for maximum bactericidal activity (4, 8, 11), and even in this instance show only limited sporicidal activity. Conversely, some success has been experienced in the development of self-sterilizing materials that incorporate volatile-type disinfectants (9). Nevertheless, the usefulness of a volatile germicide is maximized if volatility is very low at ambient temperatures yet significant at elevated temperatures below 100 C.

Melamine (2,4,6 triamine—1,3,5 triazine) reacts under alkaline con-ditions with formaldehyde to give various methylol derivatives (21). Because six reactive sites are available, the hexamethylol melamine compound can be prepared. However, the most commonly used product is the methylated trimethylol melamine (21), the structure of which is below:

MELAMINE FORMALDEHYDE

Cationic resins can be formed with melamine formaldehyde under acidic conditions (20), which are used to impart wet strength properties to paper and shrink resistance properties to textiles.

The reaction products of urea and formaldehyde are a mixture of mono-methylol urea and di-methylol urea (20). The mono-methylol urea compound, with only one formaldehyde reactive group, is not as effective in imparting stability to cellulosic fabrics as is the di-methylol urea (21), the structure of which is shown below:

$$
\begin{array}{ccccccccc}
 & H & & H & & O & & H & & H \\
 & | & & | & & \| & & | & & | \\
HO - & C & - & N & - & C & - & N & - & C & - OH \\
 & | & & & & & & & & | \\
 & H & & & & & & & & H \\
\end{array}
$$

DIMETHYLOL UREA

Urea formaldehyde is used in the paper and textile industry to provide desired properties to these materials, either as a precondensate (i.e., mixture of mono- and di-methylol urea) which penetrates the cellulose fibers to form the three-dimensional resin *in situ* or as a partial condensate which does not penetrate the cellulose fibers but instead forms the three-dimensional resin on the fiber surface (20).

Aqueous urea formaldehyde solutions differ from formalin solutions by containing methylol ureas of low molecular weight and water-soluble urea formaldehyde condensates; some free and loosely bound hydrated formaldehyde (methylene glycol) is present (29). Aqueous formaldehyde (formalin) is composed mainly of methylene glycol and various polymeric hydrates (polyoxymethylenes); very little unhydrated monomeric formaldehyde is found (28).

Paraformaldehyde is defined as "a mixture of polyoxymethylene glycols containing from about 90 to 99 percent formaldehyde and a balance consisting primarily of free and combined water" (29). It is not a new compound, having been first prepared in 1859 (3) and named "paraformaldehyde" in 1888 (24). The chemical composition of paraformaldehyde is $HO-(CH_2O)-H$ where n may represent from 8 to 100 formaldehyde units. The major chemical properties of paraformaldehyde are listed in Table 1, Appendix. Because of the relative insolubility of paraformaldehyde in acetone, a property not exhibited by low molecular weight polyoxymethylene glycols, the majority of the polymeric forms of paraformaldehyde contain more than 12 formaldehyde units (29). In appearance, paraformaldehyde is a colorless solid, which may be flaky, granular, or a fine powder. At ambient temperatures, paraformaldehyde slowly vaporizes releasing monomeric formaldehyde gas probably accompanied by water vapor (16). The rate of depolymeriza-

Table 1 Biocidal properties of melamine formaldehyde

Melamine formaldehyde[a] (mg)	Microbial growth[b] after exposure at				
	22 C	35 C	45 C	60 C	125 C
2	+	+	+	+	−
4	+	+	+	+	−
6	+	+	±	±	−

[a] Per 100 cc air; 24 hr exposure.

[b] Biologic indicators with 1×10^5 *B. stearothermophilus* spores/strip suspended in sealed glass vessels.

tion is a function of heat and availability of polymeric end groups (29), since depolymerization occurs at the hydroxyl end groups as an "unzipping" reaction. Thus, paraformaldehyde composed of high molecular weight polymers will evolve gas more slowly than that composed of low molecular weight polymers, although the depolymerization rate is the same for both. The end result of polymer breakdown is the formation of water from the terminal methylene glycol residue. With improvements in processing, the paraformaldehyde manufactured today has a relatively narrow molecular weight range. This material is an excellent source of monomeric formaldehyde gas which can be produced in a temperature-controlled reaction. Because paraformaldehyde depolymerizes completely to yield pure monomeric formaldehyde there are no contaminating residues as found with formalin solutions (methanol and formic acid residues) or the various synthetic resins (complex resin residues).

We are convinced, as other investigators are, that numerous advantages accrue with the use of the dry gas as compared to the vaporized formalin. Among these are ease of handling, need for less material, no residues, insignificant adsorption and repolymerization, much better penetration, accurate quantitation, incorporation into carrier materials, and others. Formaldehyde gas will penetrate and adsorb onto various surfaces as a function of temperature, relative humidity, gas, concentration, and exposure time (2, 29). When proper exposure conditions are employed, a sterilized enclosure may be entered within 12 to 24 hours if sufficient ventilation is available (2). When formaldehyde gas is neutralized with ammonia gas to form hexamethylenetetramine, an enclosure may be entered within minutes or hours (23, 27). According to safety standards, 5 ppm of HCHO is allowable for personnel during a normal

8 hr workday (13). To efficiently accomplish this level following the use of formaldehyde for sterilization, a neutralization or rapid air-exchange system, probably coupled with a depolymerization process to eliminate adsorbed formaldehyde polymers, may be required.

EXPERIMENTAL PROCEDURES AND RESULTS

The laboratory test procedure used for evaluation of the biocidal properties of the various formaldehyde-liberating organic chemicals involved the placement of milligram amounts of sterilant additive into

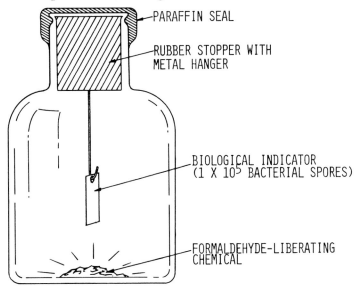

Figure 1 Test procedure for evaluation of formaldehyde-liberating chemicals.

100 cc glass vessels, the stoppers of which were affixed with metal hooks onto which the filter paper spore strips were attached (Figure 1). Stoppered vessels were sealed with paraffin prior to placement in incubators or ovens at temperatures ranging from ambient to 125 C for evaluation of the sterilizing efficiency of the various additives as a function of time and additive concentration. Trials were conducted in triplicate and each parametric point was repeated a minimum of two times; the majority were repeated more often. Spore strips were assayed for viability by inoculation into Trypticase Soy Broth (TSB) with appropriate incubation temperature (60 C for the thermophilic sporeformer *Bacillus stearothermophilus* and 37 C for the mesophilic sporeformer

Bacillus globigii) for periods of at least four days with daily observation for presence of growth. Positive cultures were examined for possible contaminating microorganisms in order to eliminate false positives.

Empirical evidence was obtained which indicated that the polymeric form of formaldehyde, paraformaldehyde, was considerably more effective as a sterilizing agent than were the formaldehyde-resins. As indicated in Table 1, although 1×10^5 bacterial spores could be killed by exposure to melamine formaldehyde (at 6 mg/100 cc air) for 24 hr at 45 or 60 C, it was not effective at lesser concentrations. Inactivation was not achieved at any of the concentrations used at 22 or 35 C within 24 hr and inconsistencies in killing were observed in replicate tests. By comparison, when using paraformaldehyde under similar test conditions but at much lower concentrations (1 mg/100 cc air), routine sporicidal activity was achieved within 72 hr at 22 C, 14 hr at 35 C, 5 hr at 60 C, and 1 hr at 125 C (Table 2).

Table 2   Biocidal properties of paraformaldehyde[a]

Time (hr)	Microbial growth[b] after exposure at			
	22 C	35 C	60 C	125 C
0.5	+	+	+	+
1	+	+	+	−
3	+	+	+	−
5	+	+	−	−
7	+	+	−	−
14	+	−	−	−
72	−	−	−	−

[a] 1 mg/100 cc air.
[b] Biologic indicators with 1×10^5 *B. stearothermophilus* spores/strip suspended in sealed glass vessels.

Due to the viscous nature of urea formaldehyde and general insolubility in organic solvents, aqueous solutions of this resin were prepared for evaluation of sporicidal activity. Preliminary studies showed that 1–3 ml of a 50 % urea formaldehyde solution were sporicidal within 24 hr at 22, 35 or 60 C. The feasibility of using aqueous urea formaldehyde, which is a mixture of low molecular weight methylol ureas and urea formaldehyde condensates, as a sterilizing spray was demonstrated by the inactivation of 1×10^5 bacterial spores on aluminum strips following the spray application of a 1 % urea formaldehyde solution. Sprayed strips were air dried and then placed at 45 or 60 C for 1, 2, or 3 hr;

complete kill of bacterial spores was achieved in 1 hr at both 45 and 60 C.

The comparative inactivation of two sporeforming bacteria, *B. stearo-thermophilus* and *B. globigii*, by formaldehyde gas from melamine formaldehyde or paraformaldehyde (2 mg/100 cc air) at 125 C is shown in Table 3. The spores of both *Bacillus* species were inactivated within about 1 hr by paraformaldehyde, whereas at least 3 hr were required for comparable inactivation by melamine formaldehyde. No significant differences in spore resistivity to formaldehyde were indicated by these studies.

Table 3 Inactivation of *Bacillus stearothermophilus* and *Bacillus globigii* by melamine formaldehyde or paraformaldehyde at 125 C

| | Microbial growth after indicated exposure | | | |
| | Melamine formaldehyde[b] | | Paraformaldehyde[b] | |
Time[a] (hr)	*B. stearothermo-philus*[c]	*B. globigii*[c]	*B. stearothermo-philus*[c]	*B. globigii*[c]
0.5	+	+	+	+
1.0	+	+	−	±
1.5	+	+	−	−
2.0	+	±	−	−
2.5	+	±	−	−
3.0	−	±	−	−

[a] Exposure time in sealed glass vessels.
[b] 2 mg/100 cc air.
[c] 1×10^5 spores/strip.

The methodology employed in the determination of formaldehyde gas loss from melamine formaldehyde or paraformaldehyde as a function of time and temperature included series of accurate weight assays using an analytical digital Mettler balance. Appropriate control samples were routinely included in all trials. Individual experimental points were assayed in triplicate and repeated at least twice; 100 mg samples of resin or polymer were used in aluminum weighing pans. The studies on loss of formaldehyde gas from various carrier-sterilant mixtures were conducted in a similar manner. Results were corrected for any weight loss recorded for control discs.

A summary presentation of data on the loss of formaldehyde from paraformaldehyde and melamine formaldehyde at temperatures from 45 to 125 C and exposure periods of 1 hr through 7 days is shown in

Table 4   Loss of formaldehyde from paraformaldehyde and melamine formaldehyde at elevated temperatures

Exposure time (hr)	Percent loss at indicated exposure temperature							
	45 C		60 C		90 C		125 C	
	PF	MF	PF	MF	PF	MF	PF	MF
1	—	—	1.0	2.0	19.5	4.0	95.1	5.8
2	—	—	1.7	2.4	36.0	5.6	98.1	9.0
3	—	—	4.3	2.6	41.3	5.4	98.6	9.2
4	—	—	5.4	3.0	45.6	5.6	98.8	10.0
5	—	—	7.5	2.6	47.3	8.4	99.0	9.8
6	—	—	11.3	2.8	52.3	9.0	99.5	10.6
12	—	—	12.7	3.6	56.3	7.2	100.0	19.2
24	5.7	—	24.0	3.0	82.0	9.8	—	19.8
48	14.1	4.4	38.9	3.4	95.5	9.6	—	20.8
72	23.5	4.4	49.5	10.0	98.1	11.0	—	21.2
168	54.2	6.8	73.4	10.8	99.8	14.4	—	24.2

Table 4. Significant differences in gaseous evolution from the two formaldehyde-liberating chemicals as a function of temperature were
observed. At 60 C approximately 10 % loss of formaldehyde occurred
within 6 hr from the pure chemical paraformaldehyde with a 73 % loss
observed after 168 hr. In comparison, the loss of gaseous formaldehyde
from melamine formaldehyde at 60 C after 6 hr was approximately 3 %.
Formaldehyde release continued until 72 hr, when a 10 % loss was
recorded and did not increase significantly throughout the 168 hr exposure period. At 90 C exposure approximately 52 % loss of formaldehyde took place within 6 hr from paraformaldehyde as compared to 9 %
from melamine formaldehyde. At 168 hr, when all available formaldehyde had evolved from paraformaldehyde, only 14 % loss was observed
for melamine formaldehyde. At 125 C exposure, the comparative losses
of formaldehyde as a gas from paraformaldehyde and melamine
formaldehyde were respectively 95 % and 6 % after 1 hr, 98 % and 9 %
after 2 hr, 98 % and 10.5 % after 6 hr, and 100 % and 24 % after 7
days. The findings indicated that paraformaldehyde completely de-
polymerized and vaporized at 125 C within several hours, whereas
after 7 days exposure, melamine formaldehyde had lost approximately
one-fourth of available formaldehyde residue.

Studies on the addition of various chemical sterilants to potting
compounds and other carrier substances were conducted with the use of
specific amounts of resin or polymer and sterilant carrier. The sterilant-
carrier combinations were mixed thoroughly and then allowed to cure

as required. In each case, a negligible weight loss occurred during the curing period. The concentrations of the polymer, paraformaldehyde and the synthetic resins, melamine formaldehyde and urea formaldehyde, were calculated on a weight/volume basis to insure the availability of equal numbers of formaldehyde molecules in corresponding samples of sterilant-carrier systems.

For verification of internal sterility of potting compounds, biologic indicators were placed within 0.5 mil plastic (Teflon) pouches, sealed, and then embedded in potting compound or carrier material, with or without additive, prior to the curing process (Figure 2). RTV-3140, a

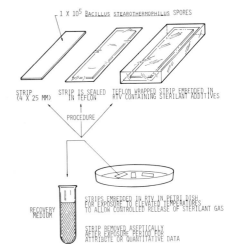

Figure 2 Embedding procedure for verification of internal sterility of potting compound.

Dow-Corning flight-approved potting compound, was used extensively as a candidate electronic material during these studies. The actual method of embedding involved the use of 25 ml uncured carrier-sterilant mixtures, one-half of which was placed into petri plates. From three to nine sealed biologic indicators were then placed onto the surface of the uncured carrier-sterilant mixture and the remainder of the 25 ml volume poured over the plastic pouches containing the bacterial spores. The plates were allowed to cure at ambient temperature for 72 hr prior to further evaluation at elevated temperatures. Control studies indicated that sufficient formaldehyde gas was not generated during the curing process to inactivate the biologic indicators. During subsequent internal sterilization trials, the embedded spores were subjected to various time-temperature exposure periods, after which the strips were removed aseptically and assayed by qualitative or quantiative procedures. Qualitative assays were made by inoculation of spore strips into TSB.

Quantitative assays were made by introducing spore strips into 18×150 mm screw cap test tubes containing glass beads in 10 ml distilled water. The strips were agitated for at least 15 sec on a Vortex mixer which resulted in complete disintegration of the strips. After a series of tenfold dilutions, aliquots of each dilution were plated in triplicate in Trypticase Soy Agar (TSA). Colony counts were recorded after incubation at 60 C for 48 hr.

Table 5 Microbial inhibition by potting compound-sterilant mixtures

| | *Inhibition zones*[a] *(mm) with indicated additive* | | | | | |
| | *Paraformaldehyde* | | *Melamine formaldehyde* | | *Urea formaldehyde* | |
Organism	1%	5%	1.9%	9.5%	2.1%	10.6%
B. globigii	25	34	10	16	10	16
S. marcescens	15	26	10	12	10	10
K. pneumoniae	21	29	10	10	10	15
S. aureus	32	44	16	20	15	20
E. coli	17	26	10	17	10	10

[a] Modification of classical antibiotic sensitivity procedure; discs 10 mm in diameter.

For zone inhibition tests, using a modification of the antibiotic disc sensitivity procedure, sterilant-carrier discs were placed on TSA plates previously inoculated with 24 hr cultures of microorganisms. Included in these studies were *B. globigii, Serratia marcescens, Klebsiella pneumoniae, Staphylococcus aureus,* and *Escherichia coli.* Zone inhibition readings were made at 24, 48, and 72 hr after inoculation; zone diameters were measured in millimeters. Results from these studies are presented in Table 5. Discs containing 1% paraformaldehyde displayed good inhibition against all test microorganisms with zones of 15 to 32 mm diameter. At 5% paraformaldehyde, inhibition zones of 26 to 44 mm diameter were observed. Similarly prepared discs containing melamine formaldehyde or urea formaldehyde showed inhibition only against *S. aureus* at 1% available formaldehyde with 16 mm and 15 mm diameter zones, respectively. At 5% available formaldehyde, the melamine formaldehyde discs were somewhat more inhibitory than the urea formaldehyde discs, displaying inhibitory properties against all test organisms except *K. pneumoniae.* Urea formaldehyde discs showed no inhibition against *S. marcescens* and *E. coli.*

Shown in Figure 3 are the comparative losses of gaseous formaldehyde from paraformaldehyde-RTV and melamine formaldehyde-RTV discs at 90 C and the resultant progressive decrease in biocidal activity which transpired. The average inhibition zones after 1, 2, 4, and 6 hr prior exposure of paraformaldehyde-RTV to 90 C were 23, 22, 16 and 12 mm in diameter; no biocidal activity was evident after 24 hr. The zones of inhibition produced by melamine formaldehyde-RTV discs, although not as large initially as those produced by the paraformaldehyde-RTV

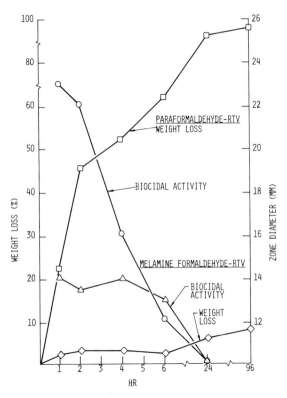

Figure 3   Loss of formaldehyde and biocidal activity from paraformaldehyde-RTV and melamine formaldehyde-RTV at 90 C.

discs, were indicative of a slower rate of loss of biocidal activity throughout the 24 hr exposure period.

Quantitative studies were conducted at ambient temperatures using 1×10^5 *B. stearothermophilus* spores embedded in RTV-3140 containing 1 % paraformaldehyde. Without exception, the data obtained revealed an initial plateau period of four to six days during which no loss of viability occurred. Subsequently, exponential inactivation took place with a *D* value of approximately 60 hr (Figure 4). In comparison, no reduction in spore population was observed in RTV-3140 containing 1.9% melamine formaldehyde or 2.1% urea formaldehyde during the same curing period. Moreover, no significant reduction in spore population was observed upon exposure of the latter two compounds to 60 C for time periods up to 6 hr. Studies conducted with 0.1% paraformaldehyde

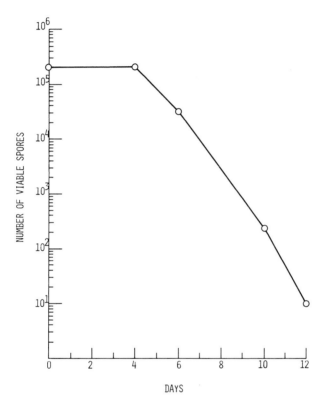

Figure 4   Inactivation of *Bacillus stearothermophilus* spores on strips embedded in RTV-3140 containing paraformaldehyde (1%) during curing at 25 (± 2) C.

in RTV-3140 at 60 C revealed complete inactivation of 1×10^5 *B. stearothermophilus* spores within 24 hr exposure (Figure 5). These results indicated significant differences in the rate of release of formaldehyde from the three compounds despite the fact that all contained equivalent amounts of available formaldehyde residue. No loss of viability was observed in control samples during the same time-temperature exposure. Additional studies conducted at 60 C on the inactivation of 1×10^5

spores of *B. stearothermophilus* embedded in compound 3547 (Chem Seal Corp.) containing various sterilant additives (Figure 6) revealed complete inactivation of spores in mixtures containing 1 % paraformaldehyde after 24 hr exposure. In comparison, samples containing 2.1 % urea formaldehyde were inactivated after 48 hr and insignificant inactivation was observed in samples containing 1.9 % melamine formaldehyde after the same time period.

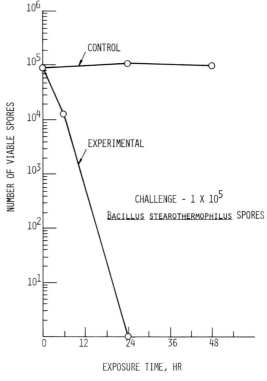

Figure 5 Internal sterilization of RTV-3140 containing 0.1% paraformaldehyde at 60 C.

Summary data on the inactivation of RTV-embedded bacterial spores as a function of additive, additive concentration, time, and temperature are shown in Table 6. Appreciable differences between the time required for apparent sterilization of RTV potting compound were observed when comparing additive and temperature, whereas, the fivefold difference in additive concentration did not affect the kill rate significantly.

Studies on the addition of formaldehyde-liberating chemicals to paper as a carrier revealed that sterilizing activity was a function of time and temperature. Representative data using melamine formaldehyde at temperatures from 60 to 125 C and exposure periods of 1 to 6 hr are

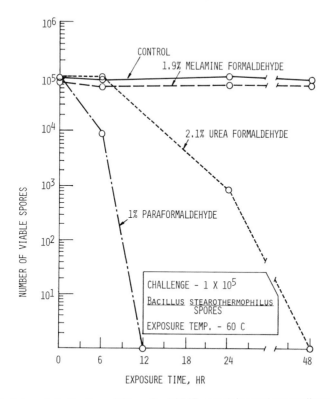

Figure 6 Internal sterilization of Chem Seal 3547 containing various sterilant additives.

Table 6 Summary on inactivation of embedded bacterial spores by formalde-hyde-liberating additives

Exposure temperature	Time required to achieve internal sterility (hr)[a]			
	Melamine formaldehyde		Paraformaldehyde	
	9.5%	1.9%	5%	1%
45 C	~96	>96	24	24
60 C	36	~72	2	6
90 C	1	2	$\frac{1}{4}$	$\frac{1}{2}$

[a] 1×10^5 *Bacillus stearothermophilus* spores used as challenge.

presented in Table 7. The majority of screening and evaluative studies on the sterilizing efficacy of various sterilants were conducted with the use of surgical blade foil packets as the test system. As indicated, complete inactivation of 1×10^6 *B. globigii* spores could be achieved at 110–125 C within 1 hr whereas 6 hr were required when the exposure temperature was reduced to 70–80 C.

Table 7   Sterilizing activity[a] of melamine formaldehyde sized paper[b] at various temperature-time relationships

Tempera-ture (°C)	Spore survival after indicated exposure					
	1 hr	2 hr	3 hr	4 hr	5 hr	6 hr
125	−	−	−	−	−	−
120	−	−	−	−	−	−
110	−	−	−	−	−	−
100	±	−	−	−	−	−
90	±	±	−	−	−	−
80	±	+	±	+	±	−
70	+	+	±	±	±	±
60	+	+	+	+	+	+

  [a] Evaluated by use of foil blade packets containing test paper inserts and spore strips (1×10^6 *Bacillus·globigii* spores/strip).
  [b] 0.64% formaldehyde.

Table 8 shows the effectiveness of five different additives against test spores of high and low ethylene oxide resistivity when exposed at 37 C for 8 hr. Data indicated that insufficient formaldehyde gas was liberated at 37 C to effect sterility of the more resistive *B. globigii* spores.

Table 8   Sterilization activity of selected formaldehyde additive papers against bacterial spores of different ethylene oxide resistivity

Test paper[a]	% CH_2O	Percent survival of Bacillus globigii spores of indicated resistivity	
		Low[b]	High[c]
Cymel 301	0.787	0	0
C-Tron 300	2.64	17	50
UF-Concentrate 85	1.90	17	83
Methyl carbamate	1.88	17	83
Paraformaldehyde	0.125	17	100
Controls	0.000	100	100

  [a] Exposure—37 C, 8 hr.
  [b] ETO LD_{50}—8 min.
  [c] ETO LD_{50}—15 min.

Information presented in Table 9 shows the sterilization cycles that could be used with either Cymel 301 or paraformaldehyde to sterilize surgical blades. The minimum time required to kill 1×10^6 bacterial spores was 1 min at 125 C, 5 min at 90 C, $1\frac{1}{2}$ hr at 60 C, and 11 hr at

Table 9 Sterilization cycles using paraformaldehyde or Cymel 301 prepared in paper rolls[a]

Exposure cycle time		Spore survival after indicated cycle temperature				
(min)	(hr)	125 C	90 C	60 C	45 C	37 C
1		−				
2		−				
3		−				
4		−				
5		−	−			
10			−			
15			−			
30			−			
	1			∓		
	1.5			−		
	2			−		
	3			−		
	10				∓	+
	11				−	−
	12				−	−

[a] Paraformaldehyde (1.03 % CH_2O). Cymel 301 (1.42 % CH_2O).

45 and 37 C. An obvious increase in time with decrease in temperature exposure was observed.

Data shown in Table 10 reveal the extreme rapidity with which sufficient formaldehyde gas can be generated to affect *in situ* sterilization

Table 10 In-line sterilization employing formaldehyde-liberating paper inserts

Exposure time (sec)	Temperature (°F)		Distance of infrared lamps from package (in.)	Percent spore survival with indicated additive	
	Inside package	Outside package		Paraformaldehyde	Cymel
5	113	106	1	40	
10	135	122	1	20	
15	182	135	1	0	
30	210	184	1	0	100
45	242	226	1		0
60	280	280	1		0
5	100	97	2	40	
10	122	116	2	20	
15	131	136	2	0	100
30	186	188	2	0	80
45	236	239	2		20
60	256	268	2		20

of surgical blades. Infrared lamps were used as the source of thermal energy. Time periods as short as 15 sec were found sufficient to liberate the sterilizing gas inside the package where the temperature reached 130–180 F. Paraformaldehyde-treated inserts were more effective than those treated with Cymel, although the time differential, when using a distance of 1 in. from lamp to package, was only 30 sec to obtain sterility.

Table 11 Formaldehyde gas inactivation of *Bacillus subtilis* var. *niger* spores on filter paper

Time of exposure[a] (min)	Survival of indicated challenge		
	1×10^5	1×10^6	1×10^7
5	Tntc[b]	Tntc[b]	Tntc[b]
10	250	Tntc[b]	Tntc[b]
15	70	Tntc[b]	Tntc[b]
20	36	528	Tntc[b]
25	6	394	Tntc[b]
30	30	338	Tntc[b]
35	16	323	Tntc[b]
40	0	269	271
45	0	54	68
50	0	6	58
55	0	0	6
60	0	0	0

[a] *Test conditions.* Formaldehyde: 3.5 mg/liter.
Temperature: 28 C.
Relative humidity: 84%.
[b] Too numerous to count.

Quantitative data presented in Tables 11 and 12 show the inactivation of bacterial spores inoculated onto filter paper or stainless steel surfaces and subjected to formaldehyde gas as evolved from paraformaldehyde. Although the relative humidity was elevated to 84%, the conditions of exposure were essentially ambient. Large populations of spores were destroyed in less than 1 hr by exposure to 3.5 mg/liter of dry formaldehyde gas. The specific role (and requirement) for moisture in the inactivation of microorganisms by formaldehyde has been the subject of research by Becton, Dickinson and others (10, 22, 26, 27). We find that high relative humidity is not a prerequisite for good microbial inactivation and can be a deterrent due to the increased repolymerization of

Table 12   Formaldehyde gas inactivation of *Bacillus subtilis* var. *niger* spores on stainless steel surfaces

Time of exposure[a] (*min*)	Survival of indicated challenge				
	1×10^5	1×10^6	1×10^7	1×10^8	1×10^9
5	10	15	26	Tntc[b]	Tntc[b]
10	0	0	2	1	1
15	0	0	8	1	1
20	0	0	0	2	3
25	0	0	0	0	3
30	0	0	0	0	3
35	0	0	0	0	155
40	0	0	0	11	0
45	0	0	0	0	0
50	0	0	0	2	0
55	0	0	0	0	0
60	0	0	0	0	0

[a] *Test conditions.*   Formaldehyde: 3.5 mg/liter.
Temperature: 28 C.
Relative humidity: 84%.
[b] Too numerous to count.

monomeric formaldehyde at high relative humidity levels. The adsorption or repolymerized formaldehyde on materials is a direct function of increased relative humidity.

Findings presented in Table 13 are the condensed data from 20 separate trials structured for establishment of optimal chamber cycle parameters using formaldehyde gas as the sterilizing vehicle. Four different surfaces (stainless steel, rubber, glass, and plastic) were inoculated with approximately 1×10^6 bacterial spores, packaged within cloth or paper, and exposed to formaldehyde gas at the indicated concentrations. Relative humidity and temperature were ambient and exposure time was 1 or 2 hr. Although complete sterilization of all test pieces was not achieved in any of these experimental trials, good microbial inactivation was observed in most. It must be acknowledged that these were marginal cycle parameters and that the microbial challenge used in these studies was rather formidable. Thus, a longer exposure period or increased gas concentration would be expected to result in reproducible and reliable sterilization of packaged materials. The concentration of formaldehyde gas used in these trials (1 to 3.5 mg/liter) was considerably less than when employing ethylene oxide, where concentrations of 500 to 1000 mg/liter are routinely used.

Table 13 Formaldehyde gas sterilizer data

Formaldehyde gas concentration (mg/liter)	Time (min)	Temp (°C)	RH (%)	Percent survival using indicated wrapped surfaces[a]							
				Stainless steel		Rubber		Glass		Plastic	
				Cloth	Paper	Cloth	Paper	Cloth	Paper	Cloth	Paper
1.06	120	34–41	35	100[b]	100[b]	40	30	20	30	20	40
1.75	120	35–41	20	100[b]	100[b]	80	100	60	40	20	40
2.8	120	34–40	50	100[b]	0[b]	0	20	0	0	0	0
2.8	120	36–52	50	20	20	0	0	0	20	0	0
3.5	60	35–36	50	20	40	0	20	20	40	0	0
3.5	120	37–55	45	100[b]	90[b]	10	0	10	0	10	0
3.5	120	31–64	50	7	0	0	0	0	0	0	0

[a] Surfaces inoculated with 1×10^6 *Bacillus subtilis* var. *niger* spores and packaged with standard hospital wrap.

[b] Stainless steel samples in these trials inoculated with 1×10^7 spores onto surfaces containing oily residue.

Data presented in Table 14 are indicative of the penetrability of dry formaldehyde gas through various thicknesses of polyethylene film. Thus, low molecular weight monomeric formaldehyde could penetrate plastic barriers in sufficient quantities to inactivate contained microorganisms. Although complete kill of spores was not obtained when the barrier was increased (greater mil thickness polyethylene) or when microbial challenge was increased, chemical indicator studies conducted in conjunction with microbial inactivation revealed that good penetration of formaldehyde gas occurred.

Table 14 Sterilizing activity of formaldehyde gas as determined by penetration of polyethylene film

Barrier (mil thickness)	Inactivation of indicated spore population[a]				
	10^2	10^3	10^4	10^5	10^6
1	+	+	+	±	−
2	+	±	−	−	−
4	+	−	−	−	−
6	±	−	−	−	−
8	−	−	−	−	−

[a] +, complete inactivation of all samples; ±, complete inactivation of some samples; −, incomplete inactivation of all samples.

Exposure conditions. Formaldehyde: 3.5 mg/liter.
Temperature: 34–54 C.
Relative humidity: 50 %.
Contact time: 2 hr.

Additional representative studies on the penetrability of formaldehyde gas are presented in Table 15. These studies were conducted in conjunction with the sterilization of a spacecraft mock-up for NASA and are indicative of the variable penetrability of formaldehyde gas through various barrier materials. Conditions of temperature and relative humidity were essentially ambient; the gas concentration ranged from 1.47 to 1.62 mg/liter and the exposure time was 6 hr.

Shown in Figure 7 are the results of quantitative studies on inactivation of bacterial spores by formaldehyde gas as a function of barrier material and thickness. Exponential inactivation of barrier enclosed spores occurred with D values of 90, 105, and 135 min for 3 and 6 mil polyethylene or cellophane, respectively. Ambient conditions of relative

Table 15 Penetrability of formaldehyde gas through various barrier materials

| Type of barrier material | Percent sterility of indicated spore populations[a] | | | |
	10^4	10^5	10^6	10^7
Polyethylene film, 2 mil	100	100	62.5	75
Polyethylene film, 4 mil	100	100	62.5	75
Polyethylene film, 5 mil	50	75	50	50
Polyethylene film, 6 mil	37.5	50	37.5	50
Cellophane, double thickness	0	0	0	12.5
Latex rubber	—	—	75	—
Glassine paper	87.5	75	87.5	62.5
Cotton plug	100	75	87.5	62.5
Polystyrene flask, screw capped	87.5	100	75	75

Test conditions. Gas concentration, 1.60–2.08 mg/liter; temperature 86–90 F; % relative humidity, 47–48; exposure time, 12 hr.

[a] *Bacillus subtilis* var. *niger.*

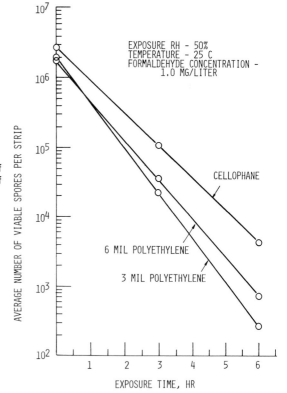

Figure 7 Inactivation of barrier-enclosed spores of *Bacillus subtilis* var. *niger.*

humidity and temperature were maintained and the formaldehyde gas concentration was 1 mg/liter. D values for naked spores exposed to 1 mg/liter formaldehyde at ambient conditions have ranged from 90 to 120 min, indicating that the polyethylene film did not inhibit the ingress of sterilizing gas.

Several formaldehyde gas exposure trials wherein ammonia gas was used for neutralization of the formaldehyde are depicted in Figure 8.

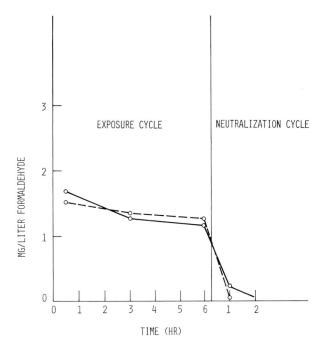

Figure 8 Formaldehyde concentrations during exposure and ammonia neutralization cycles.

Levels of formaldehyde gas through the 6 hr cycle after thermal depolymerization of paraformaldehyde were approximately 1.5 mg/liter. One to 2 hr after neutralization the levels of formaldehyde were reduced sufficiently to allow entry of personnel into the chamber. The reaction product of formaldehyde and ammonia was the harmless compound, hexamethylenetetramine.

Summary data in Table 16 presents findings on the formation and retention of formaldehyde residuals on various materials. Assays for the detection of residual formaldehyde on test pieces were conducted immediately after exposure and after holding 7 days under ambient condi-

Table 16   Summary of data obtained from assays of formaldehyde residuals on various test pieces

% RH	Cycle parameters Temp. (°C)	Cycle parameters Exposure time (hr)	Gas conc. (mg/l)	Materials tested	Amount of residual immediately after exposure (μg/gram)[a]	Amount of residual after 1 week holding
70	25	18	1.1	Cotton swab	338	0
				Glass strip	0	–
				Steel strip	0	–
				Plastic strip	0	–
70	25	3	1.1	Cotton swab	1960	0
				Glass strip	0	–
				Steel strip	0	–
				Plastic strip	0	–
70	40	3	1.1	Cotton swab	1040	0
				Glass strip	0	–
				Steel strip	0	–
				Plastic strip	0	–
70	40	1.5	1.1	Cotton swab	1140	0
				Glass strip	0	–
				Steel strip	0	–
				Plastic strip	0	–
50	40	1.5	1.1	Cotton swab	1136	0
				Glass strip	0	–
				Steel strip	0	–
				Plastic strip	0	–
50	25	3.0	1.1	Cotton swab	840	0
				Glass strip	0	–
				Steel strip	0	–
				Plastic strip	0	–
50	47	18	10.0	Latex rubber	55	0
				Silicone rubber	0	–
50	25	18	1.0	Filter paper	8000	0
70	25	6	1.0	Filter paper	4900	0
30	25	3	1.0	Filter paper	570	0
50	43	18	8.4	Polystyrene[b]	24	<1
50	50	18	6.4	Polystyrene[b]	30	<1
50	50	18	18.0	Polystyrene[b]	29	5
50	50	18	18.0	Polystyrene[b]	55	<1

[a] Measurements of materials tested
  Stainless steel: 15× 50 mm, 3.96 g   Filter paper: 0.3 g
  Glass: 15× 50 mm, 2.75 g   Latex rubber: 1.0 g
  Polypropylene: 15× 50 mm, 1.21 g   Silicone rubber: 1.0 g
  Cotton swabs: 0.3 g   Polystyrene: 1.0 g
[b] Enclosed in paper barrier.

tions using a modification of the chromotropic acid technique (30). Immediately after exposure to 1.0 mg/liter of gas, hard surface items such as stainless steel, glass, and polypropylene plastic showed no trace of formaldehyde. In comparison, porous materials such as filter paper and cotton contained relatively high concentrations of formaldehyde. However, no residue was detected after holding these samples under ambient conditions for 7 days. When polystyrene or rubber materials were exposed to increased concentrations of 6–18 mg/liter of gas, very little or no residue was detectable after 7 days. These results indicated that residual formaldehyde should not be a significant factor with respect to hard surfaces. The varying residual levels that may occur in or on porous materials such as cloth, paper, and soft rubber should dissipate readily with aeration at ambient or elevated temperatures.

A listing of materials, items, and areas found to be compatible with formaldehyde gas is presented in Table 17. It is important to recognize

Table 17 Compatibility of materials, items, and areas with formaldehyde gas[a]

Materials	Items	Areas
Stainless steel	Furniture	Research laboratories
Carbon steel	Laboratory equipment	Mobile laboratory trailers
Aluminum	Animal cages	Truck trailers
Galvanized metal	Laminar flow equipment	Aircraft
Other metallic surfaces	Biological cabinets	Ships
Glass	Biodetection devices	Apollo modules
Rubber	Air sampling devices	Spacecraft mock-up
(natural and synthetic)		
Formica	Medical devices	Test chambers
Polyethylene	Medical kits	Animal facilities
Polypropylene	Balances	Aseptic assembly areas
Polystyrene	Microscopes	
Cellophane	Cameras	
Mylar	Optical equipment	
Lucite	Clothing	
Cloth	Bedding	
Paper	Toilet articles	
Potting compounds	Surgical drapings and packs	
Paint	Disposable dinnerware	
Synthetic fabrics	Diving equipment	
Wood	Athletic equipment	
	Electrical equipment	

[a] Formaldehyde gas concentrations maintained at minimum effective sterilization or decontamination levels.

that compatibility of the indicated listing was determined by unimpaired operation or no obvious corrosive or degradative effects. The levels of formaldehyde used ranged from 1 to 10 mg/liter with exposure periods of 1 to 24 hr. This highly diversified listing is indicative of the potential applicability of dry formaldehyde gas as evolved from paraformaldehyde or synthetic resins for the sterilization or decontamination of materials, items, and areas without untoward effects.

DISCUSSION

Studies conducted at Becton, Dickinson and Company on the potential application of formaldehyde-liberating compounds in the successful sterilization of diversified materials have indicated that the overall concept is entirely feasible. Research was conducted on the inactivation of bacterial spores by the synthetic resins, melamine formaldehyde and urea formaldehyde, and the organic polymer, paraformaldehyde, both as pure chemicals and as additives to potting compounds and paper.

Without exception, the use of paraformaldehyde as a potential sterilant, in comparison with the synthetic resins, proved to be significantly more effective. These results were not unexpected since paraformaldehyde is a better source of monomeric formaldehyde than are the synthetic resins. It was apparent from the studies, also, that the inactivation process per se was strictly a function of available formaldehyde gas. Analysis of data on the biocidal activity of controlled quantities of paraformaldehyde at ambient and elevated temperatures in conjunction with data on the evolution of formaldehyde gas from paraformaldehyde as a function of time and temperature provided information on the maximal molecular amounts of formaldehyde gas required to inactivate microbial spores. Empirical evidence indicated that 1×10^5 bacterial spores suspended in a 100 cc sealed vial and exposed to 1 mg paraformaldehyde would be inactivated within 5 hr. During this time approximately 7.5 % of the available paraformaldehyde vaporized, i.e., about 75 μg. The number of formaldehyde molecules dispersed in the 100 cc volume were 1.5×10^{18} or $1.5 \times 10^4/\mu^3$. Assuming that the spores were evenly distributed within the spore strip volume and the individual bacterial spore occupied 6 μ^3, 9×10^4 molecules of formaldehyde (4.5×10^{-12} μg) were required to inactivate the spore.

The important aspect of these analytical calculations, which are based on experimental data, is that the findings from studies on spore inactivation by paraformaldehyde at ambient temperature, where the time required for inactivation was considerably prolonged and rate of gaseous evolution considerably different, resulted in comparable findings; i.e., approximately 6×10^4 molecules of monomeric formaldehyde (3×10^{-12} μg) were required to inactivate the individual bacterial spore. In addition, studies wherein paraformaldehyde-RTV discs were subjected to elevated temperature prior to biologic evaluation of residual sporicidal activity supported observations on the molecular relationship of formaldehyde gas to spore inactivation. In these studies, discs containing 3.1 mg paraformaldehyde were exposed to 125 C for 1 hr during which time approximately 95 % (2.95 mg) of added paraformaldehyde had vaporized leaving a residue of approximately 150 μg. These discs were then used for evaluation of sporicidal activity by placement into 100 cc sealed vessels containing biologic indicators and subjected to 125 C for specified time periods. Results showed that a 1 hr exposure period at 125 C was sufficient to effect sterility. During this time period approximately 60 % or 90 μg of the residual paraformaldehyde had vaporized. Thus, approximately 1×10^5 molecules of monomeric formaldehyde (5×10^{-12} μg) were required to inactivate each bacterial spore.

Additional supportive evidence was provided upon analysis of inactivation data when using melamine formaldehyde at 125 C. With the use of 2 mg melamine formaldehyde in a 100 cc volume, 1×10^5 bacterial spores were inactivated in 3 hours. Based on studies of gaseous evolution at 125 C, 9.5 % of the available formaldehyde had been released during this time period. Because only 53 % of the melamine formaldehyde molecule is comprised of formaldehyde residues, calculations showed that approximately 100 μg were released into the 100 cc volume. Therefore, the number of formaldehyde molecules dispersed per cc of volume was 2×10^{16}. Using this information and the previous calculations on spore volume, the number of monomeric formaldehyde molecules required to inactivate an individual bacterial spore was 1.2×10^5 (6×10^{-12} μg formaldehyde). Thus, the maximal number of monomeric formaldehyde molecules required to inactivate the bacterial spore when using paraformaldehyde at ambient temperature or 60 C, when using residual paraformaldehyde from heat-treated RTV-sterilant discs by exposure to 125 C, or when using melamine formaldehyde at 125 C were similar; i.e., 6×10^4, 9×10^4, 1×10^5, and 1.2×10^5, respectively. Comparative weight relationships were 3×10^{-12}, 4.5×10^{-12}, 5×10^{-12}, and 6×10^{-12} μg formaldehyde per bacterial spore, respectively. These are conservative values and it is fully recognized that the minimum molecular quantities of monomeric formaldehyde gas required to inactivate a bacterial spore may be lower since certain assumptions were made regarding spore distribution and size in the calculations. Since the mechanism of spore inactivation by gaseous formaldehyde is unknown, a priori this information appeared extremely significant. Because 6×10^4 to 1×10^5 molecules of formaldehyde gas were required to inactivate a bacterial spore, it could be hypothesized that for inactivation to occur a large number of intracellular sites would have to be attacked by formaldehyde. The obvious intracellular target molecules appear to be the enzymes, of which there are numerous specific copies found intracellularly.

Formaldehyde reacts, in general, with proteins by hardening them and decreasing their water-sensitivity (29). Specifically, these tanning effects are due mainly to the crosslinkage of protein chains by methylene bonds containing reactive groups (1). The various protein residues involved in reactions with formaldehyde include primary amino and amido, guanidyl, secondary amide, indole and imidazole groups, mercaptan radicals, and phenolic nuclei (29). Formaldehyde also reacts with nucleic acids and the contribution of these reactions to spore inactivation cannot be discounted. It has been demonstrated that the inactivation of viruses by formaldehyde can result from an aldehyde–nucleic acid reaction (5). Neely (15), in studies on the action of formaldehyde on microorganisms, stated that inactivation may be due to unbalanced growth with the subsequent formation of 1,3-thiazine-4-carboxylic acid. Thus, both nuclear and cytoplasmic elements may be impaired by the action of formaldehyde.

Data from studies on the loss of monomeric formaldehyde from synthetic resins, paraformaldehyde, and potting compound-sterilant mixtures suggested that internal sublimation of sterilants with outward diffusion of vaporized formaldehyde transpired. During this process of evolution of sterilizing gas, embedded bacterial spores were subjected to *in situ* inactivation with the resultant sterilization of the entire component. Experimental verification for internal sterilization of potting compound was subsequently obtained by employing the spore-embedding technique described. Inactivation of 1×10^5 embedded bacterial spores was achieved at temperatures ranging from 45 to 90 C within relatively short time periods with the use of melamine formaldehyde or paraformaldehyde as the sterilant additive.

The concept of a "self-sterilizing" potting compound has been demonstrated. Procedures were developed that should ensure the internal sterility of electronic components. The applicability of this development to the NASA spacecraft sterilization program could result in a reduction of the total encapsulated microbial burden on spacecraft, thereby allowing a shorter and less thermally destructive therminal heat sterilization cycle. Also this technique might be applicable to the preparation of sterile science instruments being designed for use in other planetary explorations.

Research on the application of the unique sterilizing process (25) employing paper packaging materials as carriers for volatile sterilant has been underway at Becton, Dickinson for more than 4 years. The patented process, trademarked as "Aldesteri" has been used successfully to sterilize diverse medical, surgical, and laboratory devices and instruments and home consumer items. It is a self-sterilization process where the active sterilant is the molecular amount of monomeric formaldehyde gas liberated by thermal exposure of packaged materials. The Aldesteri process is simple, reliable, safe, economical, and highly efficient. We believe it to be the most noteworthy contribution to the sterilization field in recent years.

References

1. Anson, M. L., and J. T. Edsall. 1945. *Advances in protein chemistry*. Vol. II. Academic Press. New York, pp. 278–336.
2. Braswell, J. R., D. R. Spiner, R. K. Hoffman. 1970. Appl. Microbiol. **20**: 765–769.
3. Butlerov, A. 1859. Ann. **111**: 245, 247–248.
4. Dunklin, E. W., and W. T. Lester. 1961. Soap, N.Y., **27**: 127.
5. Fraenkel-Conrat, H. 1954. Biochem. Biophys. Acta. **15**: 307–309.
6. Glick, C. A., G. G. Gremillion, and G. A. Bodmer. Oct., 1959. Proc. 10th Animal Care Panel. Washington, D.C., pp. 29–31.
7. Harry, E. G. May, 1961. The Vet. Record, **73**: 522, 526.
8. Hoffman, R. K. 1951. Proc. Chem. Spec. Manuf. Assoc. New York.
9. Hoffman, R. K., S. Kaye, and C. E. Feazel. 1959. Official Digest, Fed. of Paint and Varnish Prod.
10. Hoffman, R. K., and D. R. Spiner. 1970. Appl. Microbiol. **20**: 616–619.
11. Hoffman, R. K., S. B. Yeager, and S. Kaye. 1955. Soap and Chem. Spec. **31**: 135.
12. Kaitz, C. July 25, 1961. U.S. Patent 2,993,832. Poultry and egg fumigation process.
13. Manufacturing Chemists Assoc. Apr., 1960. Chem. Safety Data Sheet, SD–1.
14. Morris, E. J., and H. M. Darlow. 1959. J. Appl. Bacteriol. **1**: 64–72.
15. Neely, W. B. 1963. J. Bacteriol. **86**: 445–448.
16. Nordgren, G. 1939. Acta Path. Microbiol. Scand. (suppl.), **40**: 21–34.
17. Pernot, E. F. 1909. Oreg. Agr. Expt. Sta. Bul. 103.
18. Phillips, C. R. 1961. pp. 746–765. In C. F. Reddish [Ed.], *Antiseptics, disinfectants, fungicides and sterilization*. Lea and Febiger. Philadelphia.

19. Schmidt, A. Aug. 8, 1899. U.S. Patent 630,782. Disinfecting by means of formaldehyde.
20. Skelly, J. K. Jan., 1965. Chem and Ind. pp. 50–56.
21. Solomon, G. L. Dec., 1968. Proc. Amer. Assoc. Textile Chemists and Colorists, Amer. Dyestuff Reporter. pp. 29–34.
22. Songer, J. R., D. T. Braymen, R. G. Mathis, and J. W. Monroe. 1972. H.L.S. 9: 46–55.
23. Taylor, L. A., M. S. Barbeito, and G. G. Gremillion. 1969. Appl. Microbiol. 17: 614–618.
24. Tollen, S. B., and F. Mayer. 1888. Ber. 21: 1566, 2026, 3503.
25. Tulis, J. J., L. A. Taylor, and G. B. Phillips. 1971. Bact. Proc. p. 11.
26. Tulis, J. J., D. J. Daley, H. S. Lilja, and K. W. Draper. 1971. Bact. Proc. p. 15.
27. Tulis, J. J., L. A. Taylor, and D. J. Daley. 1971. Bact. Proc. p. 15.
28. Vineland Poultry Laboratories. Fumigation with Formaldegen. Bulletin R5–767030, Vineland, N.J.
29. Walker, J. F. 1964. *Formaldehyde*, Vol. III. Van Nostrand Reinhold. New York.
30. West, P. W., and B. Z. Sen. 1956. Anal. Chem. 153: 177–83.

Table 1, Appendix   Properties and characteristics of paraformaldehyde

Appearance	White solid (fine powder, coarse granules and flakes)
Explosive limits	For dust, the minimum explosive concentrations are 32 mg of paraformaldehyde per liter of atmosphere containing over 8.6% by volume of oxygen
Flash point	Tag. closed cup 71 C (160 F) approximately; Tag. open cup 93 C (199 F) approximately
Autoignition temperature	300 C (572 F) approximately
Density	1.46 gm/ml approximately
Density, bulk	About 0.8 to 1.0 gms/ml
Heat of combustion	120.5 Kcal per mol. equivalent of formaldehyde
Melting point range (sealed tube)	120–170 C (248–338 F) depending upon the degree of polymerization
Odor	Pungent
Ash %	0.01 maximum
Formaldehyde	95
Solubility	Very slowly soluble in cold water; soluble in hot water; soluble in aqua ammonia or water containing alkalies or mineral acids. Very slowly soluble in methanol; soluble in hot methanol. Insoluble in hydrocarbons or carbon tetrachloride
Threshold limit	5 ppm or 6 mg/m^3.

14

Heat Sterilization

I. J. PFLUG, PH.D.

School of Public Health
University of Minnesota

INTRODUCTION

HEAT STERILIZATION is an old and proven art which during the last half century has become more sophisticated with the incorporation of analytical and statistical procedures into its design and evaluation. The development of techniques for measurement of the resistance of microorganisms to heat destruction processes, new knowledge regarding the behavior of microorganisms when subjected to different types of heat stress, and the general maturing of the biologic sciences all have contributed to a better understanding of heat sterilization processes. Although analytical tools have been available to the microbiologist for use in the evaluation and design of sterilization processes, there has been a tendency to continue to make final decisions on the basis of biologic tests or previous experience. The trends of this era with higher production-line speeds, more automation of production equipment, and a desire on the part of the consumer and government for a more reliable final product are now causing changes in old ways and attitudes. In the future, more of the available scientific and engineering knowledge will be used in the evaluation, design, and control of sterilization processes.

The material is presented with the hope that it will encourage a more analytical treatment of sterilization processes. This paper will deal with heat sterilization in four sections: (1) statistics and sterilization processes; (2) heat destruction of bacterial spores; (3) determining the lethality of sterilization processes; and (4) commercial sterilization cycles.

HEAT DESTRUCTION OF BACTERIAL SPORES

INTRODUCTION

In the heat destruction of bacterial spores, we are dealing with destruction of life at the single-cell level. Today we are relating heat stress and the death of the entire microorganism. In the future we expect to be able to relate the quantity of heat energy to changes in vital cell molecules that lead to the ultimate cessation of organized cell metabolism or death of the cell.

Schmidt (1954) states, "The only single practical criteria of the death of microorganisms is the failure to reproduce when, as far as is known, suitable conditions for reproduction are provided. This means that any organism which fails to show evidence of growth when placed under what are considered, in the light of our present knowledge of bacterial nutrition and growth requirements, adequate growth conditions, is considered dead." As is pointed out so well by Schmidt, death is defined as the loss of the cell's ability to reproduce. In the destruction of cells and spores of microorganisms by heat, the end objective is to destroy the life processes. We are not satisfied, however, to simply discuss rates of death or factors that influence conditions for death. We feel that it is important to try to understand more about the basic mechanism that causes death so that we are better able to predict destruction rates for conditions that we have not been able to duplicate in the laboratory.

In this discussion of the death of microorganisms, the lethal agent is heat, or more precisely, a molecular energy state that is capable of producing changes in the cell that prevent the cell from reproducing either by direct effects on the reproductive mechanism or by disrupting cellular metabolic systems that provide energy and chemical inter-mediates for reproduction. In discussing the death of microorganisms brought about by high temperatures, our discussion will center on the bacterial spores which are the biological units that are most able to tolerate high temperatures for comparatively long periods of time.

MATHEMATICAL MODELING

Simple logarithmic model (constant temperature)   Thermal resistance of microorganisms is important in all sterilization processes. For thermal resistance data to be amenable to analytical treatment there must be accepted theories of the death of microorganisms. The logarithmic order of death of microorganisms fills such a need. In the logarithmic order of death, cells die in a geometric progression where in each equal successive time interval the same fraction of remaining viable cells die. The logarithmic model for microbial destruction is described by the expression

$$\log N_U = \frac{-U}{D} + \log N_0$$

where N_0 is the initial microbial population; D is the microbial destruction rate, the time to reduce the population by 90 % at temperature T; N_U is the population after U minutes of heating. If the logarithm of the number of survivors is plotted versus time, the resulting curve (commonly referred to as a survivor curve) is a straight line.

The simple logarithmic model requires that the survivor curve be a straight line where $y_0 = N_0$. Failure of an experimentally determined survivor curve to meet these criteria indicates that the data does not completely fit the model. However, the model itself imposes several restrictions on the experimental program:

1. The spores of the suspension being evaluated must be genetically, chemically, and physically uniform.
2. The conditions of the heat destruction test must be constant and identical on a test-to-test basis.
3. The overall handling procedures including the media, incubation temperature, and recovery method must be identical and constant.

It is very difficult to control all of these variables to a degree where the variation will not affect the shape of the survivor curve. When a non-linear survivor curve is obtained the question must be raised whether variations in the experimental protocol are responsible for the unique shape of the survivor curve.

In many instances, bacterial spores are more sensitive to physical and chemical conditions than our measuring and controlling instrumentation. A deviation from a straight line does not mean that the model has failed; it may indicate that we are unable to control the physical system closely enough to test the model.

If the experimentally determined survivor curve is not a straight line passing through N_0 it usually has a straight line portion and an initial phase showing either a higher or a lower death rate than the subsequent steady-state portion of the curve. A typical straight line semilogarithmic survivor curve is shown in Figure 1. A survivor curve characterized as being concave downward is shown in Figure 2; a concave upward curve is shown in Figure 3.

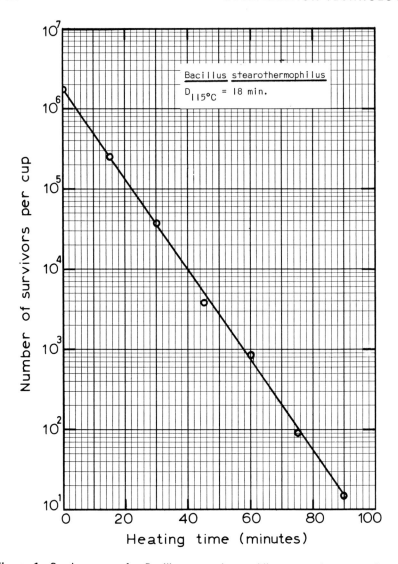

Figure 1 Survivor curve for *Bacillus stearothermophilus* spores in saturated steam at 115 C.

In our laboratory we recently introduced the term *intercept ratio* (IR) which is expressed as

$$IR = \frac{\log y_0}{\log N_0}$$

where y_0 is the y-intercept of the straight line model and N_0 is the initial number of spores per test unit of the experiment. Hopefully, the IR

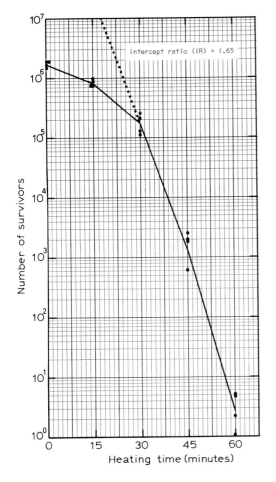

Figure 2 Survivor curve at 90 C for *Bacillus subtilis* var. *niger* spores in water.

value will make possible the organized characterization of survivor curves where y_0 of the survivor curve is larger or smaller than N_0. In Figure 2 the y-intercept value is larger than N_0, therefore IR > 1, whereas in Figure 3, the intercept value is smaller than N_0 and IR < 1.

The simple logarithmic model does not fit all experimental data; however, no model has been developed to date that will fit all data. A number of models have been developed that are supposed to be superior, but we still recommend the use of the simple logarithmic model because of its simplicity and utility.

Temperature coefficient model   In some heat sterilization processes the lethal effect must be integrated over a range of temperatures; in other sterilization applications it must be possible to determine an equivalent

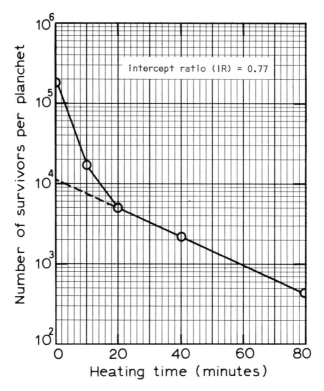

Figure 3 Dry heat survivor curve for *Bacillus subtilis* var. *niger* spores on stainless
steel strips. Ethanol spore suspension. Strips equilibrated for 24 hr at 40%
relative humidity at 23 C; sealed in thermal death time cans and heated in
an oil bath at 115 C.

process at another temperature. Both of these situations require the
use of a temperature coefficient model.

The temperature coefficient of a process is the change in the rate of
the process with a change in temperature. The Q_{10} value is widely used
by the scientific community as a measure of the temperature coefficient
of chemical and biological reactions. Q_{10} is defined as the change in the
reaction rate constant, k, for a change in temperature of 10C. In equation
form

$$Q_{10} = \frac{k_{(T+10\ \text{C})}}{k_T}.$$

The Q_{10} value of many chemical and biological reactions is two;
however, Q_{10} values for the heat destruction of bacteria are larger,
ranging from 2.2 to 4.6 for dry heat and 10.0 to 18.0 for wet heat.

(a) *Bigelow*. Bigelow (1921) observed that if the logarithm of the destruction time was plotted versus temperature on an arithmetic scale,

the result over the range of temperatures studied was a straight line. This method of plotting thermal resistance and thermal death time data must be judged as empirical. The simplicity of this type of analysis and the ready adaptation of the analysis to analytical manipulation has encouraged its use.

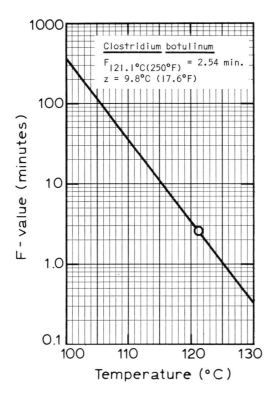

Figure 4 Thermal death time curve for *Clostridium botulinum* spores (data from Townsend et al., 1938, who applied correction to the data of Esty and Meyer).

The temperature coefficient model of Bigelow (1921) is shown graphically in Figure 4. The equation of this model is

$$\log F_T^z = \frac{1}{z}(T_B - T) + \log F_{T_B}^z$$

where T_B is the base temperature, $F_{T_B}^z$ is specified and T is the new temperature corresponding to F_T^z. The z value is a measure of the slope of the curve. It is also the number of degrees of temperature change necessary to change the D value by a factor of 10. The z value is related to $Q_{10\,C}$ by the equation

$$z\,C = \frac{\log Q_{10\,C}}{10}$$

The Bigelow temperature coefficient model is commonly called a thermal resistance curve if the logarithms of the D values are plotted versus the temperature. It is referred to as a thermal death time curve if the logarithms of the F values are plotted versus temperature.

The Bigelow model is empirical. The lack of a theory as to why thermal destruction data should respond and form straight lines when plotted in this manner caused researchers to look for a theory that could be used to reinforce this method of analysis or to develop another method of analysis that had a sound theoretical basis.

(b) *Arrhenius.* The Arrhenius analysis is a method for handling established kinetic data of either zero, first, or second order. In making an Arrhenius analysis the logarithm of k is plotted versus the reciprocal of the absolute temperature. The Arrhenius equation

$$k = A \exp\left(-\frac{E^*}{RT}\right)$$

where k = the specific reaction rate constant (time^{-1})

       A = a constant, the frequency factor (time^{-1})

    exp = exponential function of the Naperian base e

      E^* = activation energy

       R = gas constant

       T = absolute temperature

can be used to find activation energy since the slope of the curve resulting when k is plotted versus $1/T$ is the constant E^*/R. Integration between the limits $k = k_1$, at $T = T_1$ and $k = k_2$ at $T = T_2$ using base 10 logarithms and constant E^* will give:

$$\log \frac{k_2}{k_1} = \frac{E^*}{2.303R}\left[\frac{T_2 - T_1}{T_1 T_2}\right]$$

which can be used to determine the activation energy of the reaction from two values of D or k. The z value can be related to the energy of activation using the equation:

$$E^* = 2.303\ RT^2 z^{-1}$$

where E^* is the activation energy, R is the gas constant, and T is the absolute temperature.

(c) *Eyring.* In present-day chemical kinetics the fundamental equation of Eyring (1935) and Glasstone, Laidler, and Eyring (1941) is used instead of the generally empirical Arrhenius relationship. This relationship

$$k = \frac{RT}{Nh} \exp\left[\frac{\Delta S_a}{R}\right] \exp\left[\frac{-\Delta H_a}{RT}\right]$$

where N is Avogadro's number, h is Planck's constant, and ΔS_a is the entropy of activation change, is quite sophisticated and requires a large quantity of reaction rate data before meaningful results are obtained. The ΔH_a, the enthalpy of activation, of the Eyring equation is essentially equal to the experimental energy of activation of the Arrhenius equation. In general the same type of graph, $\log k$ versus $1/T$ is used in the Eyring analysis as is used in the Arrhenius analysis.

Summary of model considerations The straight line relationships of both the simple logarithmic thermal destruction model and the Bigelow temperature coefficient model hold only for a homogeneous culture of any single species of microorganism. The experimental semilogarithmic survivor curve of a mixed microbial population with several levels of heat-resistance will not be a straight line; it will be a curve determined by the relative D and N_0 values of the several microbial populations. In each population,

$$\log N_U = \log N_0 - \frac{U}{D_T^z}$$

Therefore, for populations 1, 2, 3, ...

$$(\log N_U)_1 = \left(\log N_0 - \frac{U}{D_T^z}\right)_1$$

$$(\log N_U)_2 = \left(\log N_0 - \frac{U}{D_T^z}\right)_2$$

$$(\log N_U)_3 = \left(\log N_0 - \frac{U}{D_T^z}\right)_3$$

The number of survivors after a heating time U, will be the sum of N_{U_1}, N_{U_2}, and N_{U_3}, when

$$(\log N_U)_1 + (\log N_U)_2 + (\log N_U)_3$$

$$= \left(\log N - \frac{U}{D_T^z}\right)_1 + \left(\log N_0 - \frac{U}{D_T^z}\right)_2$$

$$+ \left(\log N_0 - \frac{U}{D_T^z}\right)_3$$

It is believed that in a sterilization process dealing with natural contamination there will be one subpopulation that will exhibit relatively
large D values and, at the same time, have sufficient initial numbers
(N_0) to be the controlling population as far as achieving a final sterility
level. This subpopulation will fit the mathematical model, will have a
straight line survivor curve, and can be used as the basis for the sterilization process design.

MECHANISM OF SPORE DEATH*

It is generally believed today that the interruption of cellular function
by heat is due to denaturation of critical protein in the cell, although as
stated by Oginsky and Umbreit (1959), "We do not know, however,
whether the logarithmic order of death is an expression of the mono-
molecular reaction or protein denaturation or of a subsequent phenomenon." It is generally concluded that the denaturation of proteins
and nucleic acids is a function of the intramolecular hydrogen bonds
which are partly responsible for the spatial structure. A critical number
of these bonds must be broken before nonreversible denaturation occurs.
Cox and Peacocke (1957) assumed DNA (deoxyribonucleic acid) denaturation was a first-order reaction and calculated an activation energy
of 50 kcal in the temperature range 75 to 100 C; they observed that this
compared favorably with the 60 kcal value from earlier ultraviolet and
viscosity studies and the range 36 to 93 kcal reported by Doty and Rice
(1955). Cox and Peacocke (1957) also pointed out the need for successive
rupture of many hydrogen bonds; to denature the DNA of herring
sperm they estimated the number to be 5 to 8 if the activation energy
for rupture of the two hydrogen bonds linking a pair of bases is taken
as 6 to 10 kcal.

According to Cavalieri and Rosenberg (1957) who studied the role of
heat and acid in DNA denaturation: "Hydrogen bonds in DNA can be
cleaved reversibly, either thermally or by titration or by a combination
of both, until a certain minimum number of intact H-bonds remains.
Thereafter, the remaining bonds cleave spontaneously and irrever-
sibly.... This latter process has been called denaturation." They also
note that "the effect of heat and acid when present simultaneously, are
additive, and denaturation is apparently the same regardless of the
means by which the H-bonds have been broken." These observations
appear to parallel the effects of heat and acid on the thermal destruction

* This section has relied heavily on Pflug and Schmidt (1968).

of microorganisms. Cavalieri and Rosenberg (1957) observed that salt in low concentrations (they used 0.017 to 0.20 м NaCl) exerted a protective effect against hydrogen bond breakage; they also note that "chelating agents, such as glycine, exert a protective influence beyond that attributable to their contribution to ionic strength."

Denaturation and degradation are two different phenomena and while both may be produced by the same agent, in general, denaturation is a change in the spatial configuration, whereas degradation is a change in molecular weight. Historically, denaturation referred to solubility but in the words of Johnson et al. (1954): "denaturation has descended into the limbo of a popular rather than a scientific term; like the word life, it is convenient, useful, and full of meaning, but not susceptible of rigid definition." It is appropriate therefore to raise the question regarding the meaning of the general statement that microbial death is probably the result of a nonreversible heat-induced denaturation of critical genetic material in view of our meaning of denaturation which is: any change in the native structure resulting in loss of the ability to reproduce. Structurally, proteins and enzymes are specific, orderly polycondensations of amino acids through peptide linkages, whereas nucleic acids are polycondensations of ribose sugars through phosphate linkages. The resulting long chains assume a three-dimensional helical configuration which, according to Mirsky and Pauling (1936), are maintained through hydrogen bonding. The catalytic activity of enzymes and the ability of nucleic acids to reproduce themselves require critical spatial relationships.

Many chemical factors undoubtedly influence the thermal stability of the critical macromolecules of bacterial spores. Alderton et al. (1963 and 1964) have been able to reduce the heat resistance of *Bacillus megaterium* by pretreating the spores with acid, pH 1.1, stripping the cells to the hydrogen form. The reaction is reversible; heat resistance is increased by loading with metal cations. The rates of cation uptake suggest two binding sites: the initial rapid uptake rate exerts only a small effect on heat resistance with the later slow uptake producing a large increase in heat resistance. They observed that when unequalized spores with low initial heat resistance were heated in calcium buffers, concave upward survivor curves were obtained compared to straight line survivor curves for the fully equalized cells and concave downward curves when equalized spores were placed in a low pH buffer. These results indicate that the heat resistance of spores can change during the heating period if there are chemical changes in the spores. It is apparent from the literature that denaturation can be reversible or nonreversible. Reversible denaturation implies that under certain conditions the structure that has undergone change can be brought back to its native active state. Johnson et al. (1954), Hermans (1966), and others describe a large number of conditions where denaturation takes place but under certain post-stress conditions the protein can return to its native condition. The repair of ultraviolet-light-damaged DNA using certain cell extracts as reported by Elder and Beers (1965) is convincing evidence that genetic material can be damaged and still carry on functions provided correct chemical material is present in the media. We know that the transition from a helix to a random coil takes place in degrees, as pointed out by Hermans (1966); it is not necessarily an all or nothing transformation. We do not know how much change is required for cellular metabolic or reproductive processes to be blocked conditionally on one hand and totally on the other.

There appears to be an increasing amount of research data which supports the position that the death of microbial cells may not be a phenomenon that takes place instantly and is nonreversible but in the words of Amaha and Sakuguchi (1957), "that the death of bacterial spores by heat is a gradual chemical process which proceeds step-by-step with the time of heating and can be reversed at least in the first stage, under the proper conditions of subculture." Tischer and Hurwicz (1954) used the term *partially inactivated* to describe a condition that they believe may exist in the thermal destruction of microorganisms. These observations go hand-in-hand with the theory that death is due to denaturation of a critical molecule brought about by the disruption of hydrogen bonds and there is a level where denaturation is reversible. Rahn (1945) emphasizes that the chemical reaction of spores causing death must be basically a single molecule reaction; therefore, we must be dealing with the denaturation of a critical molecule that can be denatured in degrees, with degree of denaturation being a function of the heat treatment.

FACTORS AFFECTING THE HEAT RESISTANCE OF BACTERIAL SPORES

There are four general factors which affect the heat resistance of bacterial spores:

1. Inherent resistance due to the genetic makeup of the spore.
2. Environmental influences active during the growth and formation of the spores.

3. Environmental influences active during the time of heating of the spores.
4. Environmental influences which have certain affects subsequent to heating.

Inherent resistance manifests itself when different strains of the same species or general type of organism have widely different degrees of heat resistance even though they have been grown in the same medium and subjected to the same growth conditions. The biological indicator organism, *Bacillus stearothermophilus*, exhibits a D value of several min at 120 C whereas even the resistant strains of *Bacillus subtilus* exhibit a D value of only about 0.5 min at 120 C.

The environmental influences which are effective during the formation of spores are the growth temperature, the composition of the nutrient medium in relation to any one particular organism, and the age of the spores at the time of evaluation.

Environmental influences which are active during the heating of the spore suspension include variables such as pH, carbohydrate, protein and fat contents of the substrate, the nature of colloidal systems such as starch or soil, salt, and many other soluble organic or inorganic compounds which may be present, and the ionic strength of the solution.

The environmental influences that affect the outgrowth of spores subjected to a heat treatment include the nature of the recovery method, the chemical composition of the recovery medium, and the incubation temperature. For many species, heated spores are more selective in their nutrient requirements for outgrowth than are nonheated spores. This is usually attributed to heat damage to their metabolic and reproductive systems. The incubation temperature also becomes more critical with certain species following a heat treatment.

The dry heat resistance of bacterial spores is greatly influenced by the history of the spore in regard to water as well as the water content of the spores during the heat treatment. For example, if wet spores are dried to a water content of 2 % and then tested they will have a different death rate than very dry spores (i.e., < 0.5 % water content) which have been humidified to 2 % and then subjected to a heat treatment.

Specific details of the response of spores to these specific environmental influences are discussed in detail in the paper entitled "The Destruction of Microorganisms Using Dry Heat" by I. J. Pflug. The effects of all of these different factors are discussed in detail by Pflug and Schmidt (1968), Hersom and Hulland (1964) and other authors, so they will not be discussed here.

DETERMINING THE LETHALITY OF HEAT
STERILIZATION PROCESSES

INTRODUCTION

It is an axiom in the control sciences area that it must be possible to successfully measure the variable before it can be controlled. The control of a sterilization cycle requires that we are able to analytically evaluate the cycle. In this discussion the practical determination of the lethality of a sterilization cycle will be described in detail and illustrated using a typical example. The analysis will utilize the logarithmic model and the Bigelow (1921) temperature coefficient model that were described in the previous section of this report.

TERMINOLOGY AND SYMBOLISM

Temperature   Heat sterilization deals with temperature effects, consequently temperature is important; the symbol T will be used throughout this paper to indicate temperature. Subscripts applied to the T are used to denote specific temperature conditions such as:

T is temperature that is changing with time (degrees F or C)

T_0 is the initial temperature (degrees F or C)

T_1 is the heating medium temperature (degrees F or C)

T_2 is the cooling medium temperature (degrees F or C)

T_a is the intercept value of the heating curve straight-line asymptote (degrees F or C).

Time   Time is the second important element in heat sterilization. Time will conventionally be measured in minutes; however, we shall be dealing with time both on a practical or clock basis and on a theoretical basis. The symbol t will be used to indicate time that can be measured with a clock. Appropriate subscripts will be used with the symbol t to indicate particular time measurements. The symbol t_B will be used to denote the sterilization time of a heat sterilization process; the process time is measured starting from the time the autoclave reaches the sterilizing temperature and ending at the end of the heating period—when the steam is turned off and cooling media is added. The symbol t_h will be used to indicate heating times other than the sterilization times.

Equivalent time   Throughout our discussion of heat sterilization we will be dealing with a theoretical time variable that will be generally described as the equivalent time at a particular temperature. In dealing with the practical sterilization processes there will always be some heating lag and some cooling lag. It is not possible to instantly raise the temperature of an autoclave filled with product from 70 F to 250 F. The theoretical or equivalent times at a temperature are determined experimentally or mathematically to yield the time period, as far as heat effect is concerned, that the particular item under test was at the specified temperature. The following symbols are all units of theoretical time: D, D_T, F, F_0, F_T^z and U. They will be defined in the following discussion.

The survivor curve   In this analysis we will assume that spores subjected to a heat sterilization process will die according to the simple logarithmic model.

The symbol N is used to indicate microbial population in numbers of organisms. Specific terms used are:

N_0: the initial population in number of organisms per object, container or tube

N_U: the population in number of organisms per object, container or tube after heating time U.

The heating time U that is used with the number of organisms to locate a point on the survivor curve is the equivalent time that the organism was subjected to the heating medium temperature.

U: the equivalent time in minutes at heating medium temperature; $U = F_{T_1}$.

The slope of the survivor curve is an important unit; the D value is a measure of the slope and is defined as:

D, D_T the thermal resistance value in minutes at temperature T, the time to reduce a microbial population by 90 % at T.

The number of organisms per object, container or tube after heating time U can be calculated using the equation:

$$U = D(\log N_0 - \log N_U)$$

When the number of organisms in a test is too low to assay via a plate count, the most probable number technique of Halvorson and Ziegler (1933) is used. The number of replicate objects, containers, or tubes is indicated by n, the number showing growth by p and the number sterile by q. The most probable number of organisms N_U surviving after U min is found by the expression

$$N_U = \ln n/q$$
$$N_U = 2.303 \log n/q$$

When half of the replicate samples are positive and half negative $n/p = n/q = 2$, $N_U = 0.69$ and $\log N_U = -0.16$. In Table 1 are shown the relative survivors, N_U, as a function of the number of positive replicate units.

Table 1 Most probable number of survivors calculated using the equation
$$N = \ln \frac{r}{q} = 2.3029 \times \log_{10}(r/q)*$$

$r = 5$	$r = 10$	$r = 20$	$\dfrac{r}{q}$	$\log_{10}\dfrac{r}{g}$	N	$\log_{10}N$
		11	20.000	1.30103	2.9961	0.4766
	1	2	10.000	1.00000	2.3029	0.3623
		3	6.667	0.82391	1.8974	0.2782
1	2	4	5.000	0.69897	1.6097	0.2068
		5	4.000	0.60206	1.3865	0.1419
	3	6	3.333	0.52288	1.2041	0.0807
		7	2.857	0.45593	1.0500	0.0212
2	4	8	2.500	0.39794	0.9164	−0.0379
		9	2.222	0.34678	0.7986	−0.0977
	5	10	2.000	0.30103	0.6932	−0.1591
		11	1.818	0.25963	0.5957	−0.2250
3	6	12	1.667	0.22185	0.5109	−0.2918
		13	1.538	0.18709	0.4308	−0.3657
	7	14	1.429	0.15491	0.3567	−0.4477
		15	1.333	0.12494	0.2877	−0.5411
4	8	16	1.250	0.09691	0.2232	−0.6513
		17	1.176	0.07058	0.1625	−0.7892
	9	18	1.111	0.04575	0.1054	−0.9772
		19	1.053	0.02228	0.0513	−1.2900
5	10	20	1.000	0.00000	—	—

* Where r is the number of units per replicate treatment; q is the number of units negative. (Equation taken from Halvorson and Ziegler, 1933.)

The thermal resistance curve   The thermal resistance curve (Bigelow, 1921) for a microorganism is the curve that relates the D value at several temperatures. The basis of the thermal resistance and thermal death curves is discussed in the section on the temperature coefficient of spore destruction where a general equation for the Bigelow model was given. A more useful form of resistance curve equation is presented below:

$$\frac{D_T^z}{D_{250}^z} = 10^{\frac{250-T}{z}}$$

where $z =$ the change in temperature necessary for D_T^z of F_T^z to change by a factor of 10.

The thermal death time curve   The thermal death time curve differs from the thermal resistance curve in that a thermal resistance curve is by definition the time at different temperatures to destroy 90 % of the organisms, whereas the thermal death time curve is the time at several temperatures to produce some given level of sterilization effect. The terms D_T^z and F_T^z are related in that $F_T^z = kD_T^z$ in which k is selected to provide a given degree of preservation. The selection of k is somewhat academic since the value of F_T^z is usually based on prior sterilization experience. The equation of the thermal death time curve is:

$$\frac{F_T^z}{F_{250}^z} = 10^{\frac{250-T}{z}}$$

F = equivalent time in minutes to produce a given sterilization effect at 250 F

F_0 = equivalent time in minutes to produce a given sterilization effect at 250 F, $z = 18$ F

F_T^z = equivalent time in minutes to produce a given sterilization effect at T F for a given z

$F_{T_1}^z = U$ = equivalent time in minutes at heating medium temperature (T_1).

Characteristics of both the thermal resistance and thermal death time curves   The thermal resistance and thermal death time curves for a given organism evaluated under identical conditions are parallel. The Fahrenheit temperature difference required for the z value of the curve to change by a factor of 10 is used as the measure of the slope of the thermal resistance and thermal death time curves. (This is also the degrees F required for the curve to traverse one log cycle.) The symbol z is used to describe the direction of thermal resistance and thermal death time curves. A value of $z = 10$ C $= 18$ F is used extensively for the wet heat destruction of bacterial spores.

Examination of the thermal resistance or the thermal death time curve shows that the relative lethality at temperature T compared to a base temperature, for example, 250 F, is a function only of z. The lethal rate (L) in minutes at 250 per min at T is given by the relationship:

$$L = 10^{\frac{T-250}{z}}$$

Tables of lethal rates for a wide range of z values for base temperatures of 250 and 212 F and 120 and 100 C are given in Tables 2, 3, 4, and 5.

Table 2 Lethal rates, min at the 212 F reference temperature/min at *T* F

$$F^z_{212}/F^z_T = 10^{\frac{T-212}{z\,\mathrm{F}}}$$

Temp. F	Z Value 6 F	8 F	10 F	12 F	14 F	16 F	18 F	20 F	22 F	24 F
150,0	4,642E-11	1,778E-08	6,310E-07	6,813E-06	3,728E-05	1,334E-04	3,594E-04	7,943E-04	1,520E-03	2,610E-03
151,0	6,813E-11	2,371E-08	7,943E-07	8,254E-06	4,394E-05	1,540E-04	4,084E-04	8,913E-04	1,688E-03	2,873E-03
152,0	1,000E-10	3,162E-08	1,000E-06	1,000E-05	5,179E-05	1,778E-04	4,642E-04	1,000E-03	1,874E-03	3,162E-03
153,0	1,468E-10	4,217E-08	1,259E-06	1,212E-05	6,105E-05	2,054E-04	5,275E-04	1,122E-03	2,081E-03	3,481E-03
154,0	2,154E-10	5,623E-08	1,585E-06	1,468E-05	7,197E-05	2,371E-04	5,995E-04	1,259E-03	2,310E-03	3,831E-03
155,0	3,162E-10	7,499E-08	1,995E-06	1,778E-05	8,483E-05	2,738E-04	6,813E-04	1,413E-03	2,565E-03	4,217E-03
156,0	4,642E-10	1,000E-07	2,512E-06	2,154E-05	1,000E-04	3,162E-04	7,743E-04	1,585E-03	2,848E-03	4,642E-03
157,0	6,813E-10	1,334E-07	3,162E-06	2,610E-05	1,179E-04	3,652E-04	8,799E-04	1,778E-03	3,162E-03	5,109E-03
158,0	1,000E-09	1,778E-07	3,981E-06	3,162E-05	1,389E-04	4,217E-04	1,000E-03	1,995E-03	3,511E-03	5,623E-03
159,0	1,468E-09	2,371E-07	5,012E-06	3,831E-05	1,638E-04	4,870E-04	1,136E-03	2,239E-03	3,899E-03	6,190E-03
160,0	2,154E-09	3,162E-07	6,310E-06	4,642E-05	1,931E-04	5,623E-04	1,292E-03	2,512E-03	4,329E-03	6,813E-03
161,0	3,162E-09	4,217E-07	7,943E-06	5,623E-05	2,276E-04	6,494E-04	1,468E-03	2,818E-03	4,806E-03	7,499E-03
162,0	4,642E-09	5,623E-07	1,000E-05	6,813E-05	2,683E-04	7,499E-04	1,668E-03	3,162E-03	5,337E-03	8,254E-03
163,0	6,813E-09	7,499E-07	1,259E-05	8,254E-05	3,162E-04	8,660E-04	1,896E-03	3,548E-03	5,926E-03	9,085E-03
164,0	1,000E-08	1,000E-06	1,585E-05	1,000E-04	3,728E-04	1,000E-03	2,154E-03	3,981E-03	6,579E-03	1,000E-02
165,0	1,468E-08	1,334E-06	1,995E-05	1,212E-04	4,394E-04	1,155E-03	2,448E-03	4,467E-03	7,305E-03	1,101E-02
166,0	2,154E-08	1,778E-06	2,512E-05	1,468E-04	5,179E-04	1,334E-03	2,783E-03	5,012E-03	8,111E-03	1,212E-02
167,0	3,162E-08	2,371E-06	3,162E-05	1,778E-04	6,105E-04	1,540E-03	3,162E-03	5,623E-03	9,006E-03	1,334E-02
168,0	4,642E-08	3,162E-06	3,981E-05	2,154E-04	7,197E-04	1,778E-03	3,594E-03	6,310E-03	1,000E-02	1,468E-02
169,0	6,813E-08	4,217E-06	5,012E-05	2,610E-04	8,483E-04	2,054E-03	4,084E-03	7,079E-03	1,110E-02	1,616E-02
170,0	1,000E-07	5,623E-06	6,310E-05	3,162E-04	1,000E-03	2,371E-03	4,642E-03	7,943E-03	1,233E-02	1,778E-02
171,0	1,468E-07	7,499E-06	7,943E-05	3,831E-04	1,179E-03	2,738E-03	5,275E-03	8,913E-03	1,369E-02	1,957E-02
172,0	2,154E-07	1,000E-05	1,000E-04	4,642E-04	1,389E-03	3,162E-03	5,995E-03	1,000E-02	1,520E-02	2,154E-02
173,0	3,162E-07	1,334E-05	1,259E-04	5,623E-04	1,638E-03	3,652E-03	6,813E-03	1,122E-02	1,688E-02	2,371E-02
174,0	4,642E-07	1,778E-05	1,585E-04	6,813E-04	1,931E-03	4,217E-03	7,743E-03	1,259E-02	1,874E-02	2,610E-02
175,0	6,813E-07	2,371E-05	1,995E-04	8,254E-04	2,276E-03	4,870E-03	8,799E-03	1,413E-02	2,081E-02	2,873E-02
176,0	1,000E-06	3,162E-05	2,512E-04	1,000E-03	2,683E-03	5,623E-03	1,000E-02	1,585E-02	2,310E-02	3,162E-02
177,0	1,468E-06	4,217E-05	3,162E-04	1,212E-03	3,162E-03	6,494E-03	1,136E-02	1,778E-02	2,565E-02	3,481E-02
178,0	2,154E-06	5,623E-05	3,981E-04	1,468E-03	3,728E-03	7,499E-03	1,292E-02	1,995E-02	2,848E-02	3,831E-02
179,0	3,162E-06	7,499E-05	5,012E-04	1,778E-03	4,394E-03	8,660E-03	1,468E-02	2,239E-02	3,162E-02	4,217E-02
180,0	4,642E-06	1,000E-04	6,310E-04	2,154E-03	5,179E-03	1,000E-02	1,668E-02	2,512E-02	3,511E-02	4,642E-02
181,0	6,813E-06	1,334E-04	7,943E-04	2,610E-03	6,105E-03	1,155E-02	1,896E-02	2,818E-02	3,899E-02	5,109E-02
182,0	1,000E-05	1,778E-04	1,000E-03	3,162E-03	7,197E-03	1,334E-02	2,154E-02	3,162E-02	4,329E-02	5,623E-02
183,0	1,468E-05	2,371E-04	1,259E-03	3,831E-03	8,483E-03	1,540E-02	2,448E-02	3,548E-02	4,806E-02	6,190E-02
184,0	2,154E-05	3,162E-04	1,585E-03	4,642E-03	1,000E-02	1,778E-02	2,783E-02	3,981E-02	5,337E-02	6,813E-02
185,0	3,162E-05	4,217E-04	1,995E-03	5,623E-03	1,179E-02	2,054E-02	3,162E-02	4,467E-02	5,926E-02	7,499E-02
186,0	4,642E-05	5,623E-04	2,512E-03	6,813E-03	1,389E-02	2,371E-02	3,594E-02	5,012E-02	6,579E-02	8,254E-02
187,0	6,813E-05	7,499E-04	3,162E-03	8,254E-03	1,638E-02	2,738E-02	4,084E-02	5,623E-02	7,305E-02	9,085E-02
188,0	1,000E-04	1,000E-03	3,981E-03	1,000E-02	1,931E-02	3,162E-02	4,642E-02	6,310E-02	8,111E-02	1,000E-01
189,0	1,468E-04	1,334E-03	5,012E-03	1,212E-02	2,276E-02	3,652E-02	5,275E-02	7,079E-02	9,006E-02	1,101E-01
190,0	2,154E-04	1,778E-03	6,310E-03	1,468E-02	2,683E-02	4,217E-02	5,995E-02	7,943E-02	1,000E-01	1,212E-01
190,5	2,610E-04	2,054E-03	7,079E-03	1,616E-02	2,913E-02	4,532E-02	6,391E-02	8,414E-02	1,054E-01	1,271E-01
191,0	3,162E-04	2,371E-03	7,943E-03	1,778E-02	3,162E-02	4,870E-02	6,813E-02	8,913E-02	1,110E-01	1,334E-01
191,5	3,831E-04	2,738E-03	8,913E-03	1,957E-02	3,433E-02	5,233E-02	7,263E-02	9,441E-02	1,170E-01	1,399E-01
192,0	4,642E-04	3,162E-03	1,000E-02	2,154E-02	3,728E-02	5,623E-02	7,743E-02	1,000E-01	1,233E-01	1,468E-01
192,5	5,623E-04	3,652E-03	1,122E-02	2,371E-02	4,047E-02	6,043E-02	8,254E-02	1,059E-01	1,299E-01	1,540E-01
193,0	6,813E-04	4,217E-03	1,259E-02	2,610E-02	4,394E-02	6,494E-02	8,799E-02	1,122E-01	1,369E-01	1,616E-01
193,5	8,254E-04	4,870E-03	1,413E-02	2,873E-02	4,771E-02	6,978E-02	9,380E-02	1,189E-01	1,442E-01	1,695E-01
194,0	1,000E-03	5,623E-03	1,585E-02	3,162E-02	5,179E-02	7,499E-02	1,000E-01	1,259E-01	1,520E-01	1,778E-01
194,5	1,212E-03	6,494E-03	1,778E-02	3,481E-02	5,623E-02	8,058E-02	1,066E-01	1,334E-01	1,602E-01	1,866E-01
195,0	1,468E-03	7,499E-03	1,995E-02	3,831E-02	6,105E-02	8,660E-02	1,136E-01	1,413E-01	1,688E-01	1,957E-01
195,5	1,778E-03	8,660E-03	2,239E-02	4,217E-02	6,629E-02	9,306E-02	1,212E-01	1,496E-01	1,778E-01	2,054E-01
196,0	2,154E-03	1,000E-02	2,512E-02	4,642E-02	7,197E-02	1,000E-01	1,292E-01	1,585E-01	1,874E-01	2,154E-01
196,5	2,610E-03	1,155E-02	2,818E-02	5,109E-02	7,814E-02	1,075E-01	1,377E-01	1,679E-01	1,974E-01	2,260E-01
197,0	3,162E-03	1,334E-02	3,162E-02	5,623E-02	8,483E-02	1,155E-01	1,468E-01	1,778E-01	2,081E-01	2,371E-01
197,5	3,831E-03	1,540E-02	3,548E-02	6,190E-02	9,211E-02	1,241E-01	1,565E-01	1,884E-01	2,192E-01	2,488E-01
198,0	4,642E-03	1,778E-02	3,981E-02	6,813E-02	1,000E-01	1,334E-01	1,668E-01	1,995E-01	2,310E-01	2,610E-01
198,5	5,623E-03	2,054E-02	4,467E-02	7,499E-02	1,086E-01	1,433E-01	1,778E-01	2,113E-01	2,434E-01	2,738E-01
199,0	6,813E-03	2,371E-02	5,012E-02	8,254E-02	1,179E-01	1,540E-01	1,896E-01	2,239E-01	2,565E-01	2,873E-01
199,5	8,254E-03	2,738E-02	5,623E-02	9,085E-02	1,280E-01	1,655E-01	2,021E-01	2,371E-01	2,703E-01	3,014E-01
200,0	1,000E-02	3,162E-02	6,310E-02	1,000E-01	1,389E-01	1,778E-01	2,154E-01	2,512E-01	2,848E-01	3,162E-01
200,5	1,212E-02	3,652E-02	7,079E-02	1,101E-01	1,509E-01	1,911E-01	2,297E-01	2,661E-01	3,001E-01	3,318E-01
201,0	1,468E-02	4,217E-02	7,943E-02	1,212E-01	1,638E-01	2,054E-01	2,448E-01	2,818E-01	3,162E-01	3,481E-01
201,5	1,778E-02	4,870E-02	8,913E-02	1,334E-01	1,778E-01	2,207E-01	2,610E-01	2,985E-01	3,332E-01	3,652E-01
202,0	2,154E-02	5,623E-02	1,000E-01	1,468E-01	1,931E-01	2,371E-01	2,783E-01	3,162E-01	3,511E-01	3,831E-01
202,5	2,610E-02	6,494E-02	1,122E-01	1,616E-01	2,096E-01	2,548E-01	2,966E-01	3,350E-01	3,700E-01	4,019E-01
203,0	3,162E-02	7,499E-02	1,259E-01	1,778E-01	2,276E-01	2,738E-01	3,162E-01	3,548E-01	3,899E-01	4,217E-01
203,5	3,831E-02	8,660E-02	1,413E-01	1,957E-01	2,471E-01	2,943E-01	3,371E-01	3,758E-01	4,108E-01	4,424E-01
204,0	4,642E-02	1,000E-01	1,585E-01	2,154E-01	2,683E-01	3,162E-01	3,594E-01	3,981E-01	4,329E-01	4,642E-01
204,5	5,623E-02	1,155E-01	1,778E-01	2,371E-01	2,913E-01	3,398E-01	3,831E-01	4,217E-01	4,561E-01	4,870E-01
205,0	6,813E-02	1,334E-01	1,995E-01	2,610E-01	3,162E-01	3,652E-01	4,084E-01	4,467E-01	4,806E-01	5,109E-01
205,5	8,254E-02	1,540E-01	2,239E-01	2,873E-01	3,433E-01	3,924E-01	4,354E-01	4,732E-01	5,065E-01	5,360E-01
206,0	1,000E-01	1,778E-01	2,512E-01	3,162E-01	3,728E-01	4,217E-01	4,642E-01	5,012E-01	5,337E-01	5,623E-01
206,5	1,212E-01	2,054E-01	2,818E-01	3,481E-01	4,047E-01	4,532E-01	4,948E-01	5,309E-01	5,623E-01	5,900E-01
207,0	1,468E-01	2,371E-01	3,162E-01	3,831E-01	4,394E-01	4,870E-01	5,275E-01	5,623E-01	5,926E-01	6,190E-01
207,5	1,778E-01	2,738E-01	3,548E-01	4,217E-01	4,771E-01	5,233E-01	5,623E-01	5,957E-01	6,244E-01	6,494E-01
208,0	2,154E-01	3,162E-01	3,981E-01	4,642E-01	5,179E-01	5,623E-01	5,995E-01	6,310E-01	6,579E-01	6,813E-01
208,5	2,610E-01	3,652E-01	4,467E-01	5,109E-01	5,623E-01	6,043E-01	6,391E-01	6,683E-01	6,933E-01	7,148E-01
209,0	3,162E-01	4,217E-01	5,012E-01	5,623E-01	6,105E-01	6,494E-01	6,813E-01	7,079E-01	7,305E-01	7,499E-01
209,5	3,831E-01	4,870E-01	5,623E-01	6,190E-01	6,629E-01	6,978E-01	7,263E-01	7,499E-01	7,698E-01	7,867E-01
210,0	4,642E-01	5,623E-01	6,310E-01	6,813E-01	7,197E-01	7,499E-01	7,743E-01	7,943E-01	8,111E-01	8,254E-01
210,5	5,623E-01	6,494E-01	7,079E-01	7,499E-01	7,814E-01	8,058E-01	8,254E-01	8,414E-01	8,547E-01	8,660E-01
211,0	6,813E-01	7,499E-01	7,943E-01	8,254E-01	8,483E-01	8,660E-01	8,799E-01	8,913E-01	9,006E-01	9,085E-01
211,5	8,254E-01	8,660E-01	8,913E-01	9,085E-01	9,211E-01	9,306E-01	9,380E-01	9,441E-01	9,490E-01	9,532E-01
212,0	1,000E+00	1,000E+00	1,000E+00	1,000E+00	1,000E+00	1,000E+00	1,000E+00	1,000E+00	1,000E+00	1,000E+00
212,5	1,212E+00	1,155E+00	1,122E+00	1,101E+00	1,086E+00	1,075E+00	1,066E+00	1,059E+00	1,054E+00	1,049E+00
213,0	1,468E+00	1,334E+00	1,259E+00	1,212E+00	1,179E+00	1,155E+00	1,136E+00	1,122E+00	1,110E+00	1,101E+00
213,5	1,778E+00	1,540E+00	1,413E+00	1,334E+00	1,280E+00	1,241E+00	1,212E+00	1,189E+00	1,170E+00	1,155E+00
214,0	2,154E+00	1,778E+00	1,585E+00	1,468E+00	1,389E+00	1,334E+00	1,292E+00	1,259E+00	1,233E+00	1,212E+00
214,5	2,610E+00	2,054E+00	1,778E+00	1,616E+00	1,509E+00	1,433E+00	1,377E+00	1,334E+00	1,299E+00	1,271E+00
215,0	3,162E+00	2,371E+00	1,995E+00	1,778E+00	1,638E+00	1,540E+00	1,468E+00	1,413E+00	1,369E+00	1,334E+00
215,5	3,831E+00	2,738E+00	2,239E+00	1,957E+00	1,778E+00	1,655E+00	1,565E+00	1,496E+00	1,442E+00	1,399E+00
216,0	4,642E+00	3,162E+00	2,512E+00	2,154E+00	1,931E+00	1,778E+00	1,668E+00	1,585E+00	1,520E+00	1,468E+00
216,5	5,623E+00	3,652E+00	2,818E+00	2,371E+00	2,096E+00	1,911E+00	1,778E+00	1,679E+00	1,602E+00	1,540E+00
217,0	6,813E+00	4,217E+00	3,162E+00	2,610E+00	2,276E+00	2,054E+00	1,896E+00	1,778E+00	1,688E+00	1,616E+00
217,5	8,254E+00	4,870E+00	3,548E+00	2,873E+00	2,471E+00	2,207E+00	2,021E+00	1,884E+00	1,778E+00	1,695E+00
218,0	1,000E+01	5,623E+00	3,981E+00	3,162E+00	2,683E+00	2,371E+00	2,154E+00	1,995E+00	1,874E+00	1,778E+00
218,5	1,212E+01	6,494E+00	4,467E+00	3,481E+00	2,913E+00	2,548E+00	2,297E+00	2,113E+00	1,974E+00	1,866E+00
219,0	1,468E+01	7,499E+00	5,012E+00	3,831E+00	3,162E+00	2,738E+00	2,448E+00	2,239E+00	2,081E+00	1,957E+00
219,5	1,778E+01	8,660E+00	5,623E+00	4,217E+00	3,433E+00	2,943E+00	2,610E+00	2,371E+00	2,192E+00	2,054E+00
220,0	2,154E+01	1,000E+01	6,310E+00	4,642E+00	3,728E+00	3,162E+00	2,783E+00	2,512E+00	2,310E+00	2,154E+00

Table 2 (cont.)

Temp.	Z Value									
F	26 F	30 F	35 F	40 F	45 F	50 F	55 F	60 F	70 F	80 F
150.0	4.125E-03	8.577E-03	1.693E-02	2.818E-02	4.190E-02	5.754E-02	7.460E-02	9.261E-02	1.301E-01	1.679E-01
151.0	4.507E-03	9.261E-03	1.808E-02	2.985E-02	4.410E-02	6.026E-02	7.779E-02	9.624E-02	1.345E-01	1.728E-01
152.0	4.924E-03	1.000E-02	1.931E-02	3.162E-02	4.642E-02	6.310E-02	8.111E-02	1.000E-01	1.389E-01	1.778E-01
153.0	5.380E-03	1.080E-02	2.062E-02	3.350E-02	4.885E-02	6.607E-02	8.458E-02	1.039E-01	1.436E-01	1.830E-01
154.0	5.878E-03	1.166E-02	2.202E-02	3.548E-02	5.142E-02	6.918E-02	8.820E-02	1.080E-01	1.484E-01	1.884E-01
155.0	6.422E-03	1.259E-02	2.352E-02	3.758E-02	5.412E-02	7.244E-02	9.197E-02	1.122E-01	1.534E-01	1.939E-01
156.0	7.017E-03	1.359E-02	2.512E-02	3.981E-02	5.696E-02	7.586E-02	9.590E-02	1.166E-01	1.585E-01	1.995E-01
157.0	7.667E-03	1.468E-02	2.683E-02	4.217E-02	5.995E-02	7.943E-02	1.000E-01	1.212E-01	1.638E-01	2.054E-01
158.0	8.377E-03	1.585E-02	2.865E-02	4.467E-02	6.310E-02	8.318E-02	1.043E-01	1.259E-01	1.693E-01	2.113E-01
159.0	9.152E-03	1.711E-02	3.060E-02	4.732E-02	6.641E-02	8.710E-02	1.087E-01	1.308E-01	1.749E-01	2.175E-01
160.0	1.000E-02	1.848E-02	3.268E-02	5.012E-02	6.989E-02	9.120E-02	1.134E-01	1.359E-01	1.808E-01	2.239E-01
161.0	1.093E-02	1.995E-02	3.490E-02	5.309E-02	7.356E-02	9.550E-02	1.182E-01	1.413E-01	1.868E-01	2.304E-01
162.0	1.194E-02	2.154E-02	3.728E-02	5.623E-02	7.743E-02	1.000E-01	1.233E-01	1.468E-01	1.931E-01	2.371E-01
163.0	1.304E-02	2.326E-02	3.981E-02	5.957E-02	8.149E-02	1.047E-01	1.286E-01	1.525E-01	1.995E-01	2.441E-01
164.0	1.425E-02	2.512E-02	4.252E-02	6.310E-02	8.577E-02	1.096E-01	1.341E-01	1.585E-01	2.062E-01	2.512E-01
165.0	1.557E-02	2.712E-02	4.541E-02	6.683E-02	9.027E-02	1.148E-01	1.398E-01	1.647E-01	2.131E-01	2.585E-01
166.0	1.701E-02	2.929E-02	4.850E-02	7.079E-02	9.501E-02	1.202E-01	1.458E-01	1.711E-01	2.202E-01	2.661E-01
167.0	1.859E-02	3.162E-02	5.179E-02	7.499E-02	1.000E-01	1.259E-01	1.520E-01	1.778E-01	2.276E-01	2.738E-01
168.0	2.031E-02	3.415E-02	5.532E-02	7.943E-02	1.053E-01	1.318E-01	1.585E-01	1.848E-01	2.352E-01	2.818E-01
169.0	2.219E-02	3.687E-02	5.908E-02	8.414E-02	1.108E-01	1.380E-01	1.653E-01	1.920E-01	2.431E-01	2.901E-01
170.0	2.424E-02	3.981E-02	6.310E-02	8.913E-02	1.166E-01	1.445E-01	1.723E-01	1.995E-01	2.512E-01	2.985E-01
171.0	2.649E-02	4.299E-02	6.739E-02	9.441E-02	1.227E-01	1.514E-01	1.797E-01	2.073E-01	2.596E-01	3.073E-01
172.0	2.894E-02	4.642E-02	7.197E-02	1.000E-01	1.292E-01	1.585E-01	1.874E-01	2.154E-01	2.683E-01	3.162E-01
173.0	3.162E-02	5.012E-02	7.686E-02	1.059E-01	1.359E-01	1.660E-01	1.954E-01	2.239E-01	2.772E-01	3.255E-01
174.0	3.455E-02	5.412E-02	8.209E-02	1.122E-01	1.431E-01	1.738E-01	2.037E-01	2.326E-01	2.865E-01	3.350E-01
175.0	3.775E-02	5.843E-02	8.767E-02	1.189E-01	1.506E-01	1.820E-01	2.125E-01	2.417E-01	2.961E-01	3.447E-01
176.0	4.125E-02	6.310E-02	9.363E-02	1.259E-01	1.585E-01	1.905E-01	2.215E-01	2.512E-01	3.060E-01	3.548E-01
177.0	4.507E-02	6.813E-02	1.000E-01	1.334E-01	1.668E-01	1.995E-01	2.310E-01	2.610E-01	3.162E-01	3.652E-01
178.0	4.924E-02	7.356E-02	1.068E-01	1.413E-01	1.756E-01	2.089E-01	2.409E-01	2.712E-01	3.268E-01	3.758E-01
179.0	5.380E-02	7.943E-02	1.141E-01	1.496E-01	1.848E-01	2.188E-01	2.512E-01	2.818E-01	3.377E-01	3.868E-01
180.0	5.878E-02	8.577E-02	1.218E-01	1.585E-01	1.945E-01	2.291E-01	2.619E-01	2.929E-01	3.490E-01	3.981E-01
181.0	6.422E-02	9.261E-02	1.301E-01	1.679E-01	2.047E-01	2.399E-01	2.731E-01	3.043E-01	3.607E-01	4.097E-01
182.0	7.017E-02	1.000E-01	1.389E-01	1.778E-01	2.154E-01	2.512E-01	2.848E-01	3.162E-01	3.728E-01	4.217E-01
183.0	7.667E-02	1.080E-01	1.484E-01	1.884E-01	2.268E-01	2.630E-01	2.970E-01	3.286E-01	3.852E-01	4.340E-01
184.0	8.377E-02	1.166E-01	1.585E-01	1.995E-01	2.387E-01	2.754E-01	3.097E-01	3.415E-01	3.981E-01	4.467E-01
185.0	9.152E-02	1.259E-01	1.693E-01	2.113E-01	2.512E-01	2.884E-01	3.229E-01	3.548E-01	4.114E-01	4.597E-01
186.0	1.000E-01	1.359E-01	1.808E-01	2.239E-01	2.644E-01	3.020E-01	3.367E-01	3.687E-01	4.252E-01	4.732E-01
187.0	1.093E-01	1.468E-01	1.931E-01	2.371E-01	2.783E-01	3.162E-01	3.511E-01	3.831E-01	4.394E-01	4.870E-01
188.0	1.194E-01	1.585E-01	2.062E-01	2.512E-01	2.929E-01	3.311E-01	3.661E-01	3.981E-01	4.541E-01	5.012E-01
189.0	1.304E-01	1.711E-01	2.202E-01	2.661E-01	3.082E-01	3.467E-01	3.818E-01	4.137E-01	4.693E-01	5.158E-01
190.0	1.425E-01	1.848E-01	2.352E-01	2.818E-01	3.244E-01	3.631E-01	3.981E-01	4.299E-01	4.850E-01	5.309E-01
190.5	1.490E-01	1.920E-01	2.431E-01	2.901E-01	3.328E-01	3.715E-01	4.065E-01	4.382E-01	4.930E-01	5.386E-01
191.0	1.557E-01	1.995E-01	2.512E-01	2.985E-01	3.415E-01	3.802E-01	4.151E-01	4.467E-01	5.012E-01	5.464E-01
191.5	1.628E-01	2.073E-01	2.596E-01	3.073E-01	3.503E-01	3.890E-01	4.239E-01	4.553E-01	5.095E-01	5.543E-01
192.0	1.701E-01	2.154E-01	2.683E-01	3.162E-01	3.594E-01	3.981E-01	4.329E-01	4.642E-01	5.179E-01	5.623E-01
192.5	1.778E-01	2.239E-01	2.772E-01	3.255E-01	3.687E-01	4.074E-01	4.420E-01	4.732E-01	5.265E-01	5.705E-01
193.0	1.859E-01	2.326E-01	2.865E-01	3.350E-01	3.782E-01	4.169E-01	4.514E-01	4.823E-01	5.353E-01	5.788E-01
193.5	1.943E-01	2.417E-01	2.961E-01	3.447E-01	3.881E-01	4.266E-01	4.609E-01	4.917E-01	5.441E-01	5.872E-01
194.0	2.031E-01	2.512E-01	3.060E-01	3.548E-01	3.981E-01	4.365E-01	4.707E-01	5.012E-01	5.532E-01	5.957E-01
194.5	2.123E-01	2.610E-01	3.162E-01	3.652E-01	4.084E-01	4.467E-01	4.806E-01	5.109E-01	5.623E-01	6.043E-01
195.0	2.219E-01	2.712E-01	3.268E-01	3.758E-01	4.190E-01	4.571E-01	4.908E-01	5.208E-01	5.717E-01	6.131E-01
195.5	2.319E-01	2.818E-01	3.377E-01	3.868E-01	4.299E-01	4.677E-01	5.012E-01	5.309E-01	5.811E-01	6.219E-01
196.0	2.424E-01	2.929E-01	3.490E-01	3.981E-01	4.410E-01	4.786E-01	5.118E-01	5.412E-01	5.908E-01	6.310E-01
196.5	2.534E-01	3.043E-01	3.607E-01	4.097E-01	4.524E-01	4.898E-01	5.226E-01	5.517E-01	6.006E-01	6.401E-01
197.0	2.649E-01	3.162E-01	3.728E-01	4.217E-01	4.642E-01	5.012E-01	5.337E-01	5.623E-01	6.105E-01	6.494E-01
197.5	2.769E-01	3.286E-01	3.852E-01	4.340E-01	4.762E-01	5.129E-01	5.450E-01	5.732E-01	6.207E-01	6.588E-01
198.0	2.894E-01	3.415E-01	3.981E-01	4.467E-01	4.885E-01	5.248E-01	5.565E-01	5.843E-01	6.310E-01	6.683E-01
198.5	3.025E-01	3.548E-01	4.114E-01	4.597E-01	5.012E-01	5.370E-01	5.683E-01	5.957E-01	6.414E-01	6.780E-01
199.0	3.162E-01	3.687E-01	4.252E-01	4.732E-01	5.142E-01	5.495E-01	5.803E-01	6.072E-01	6.521E-01	6.879E-01
199.5	3.305E-01	3.831E-01	4.394E-01	4.870E-01	5.275E-01	5.623E-01	5.926E-01	6.190E-01	6.629E-01	6.978E-01
200.0	3.455E-01	3.981E-01	4.541E-01	5.012E-01	5.412E-01	5.754E-01	6.051E-01	6.310E-01	6.739E-01	7.079E-01
200.5	3.612E-01	4.137E-01	4.693E-01	5.158E-01	5.552E-01	5.888E-01	6.179E-01	6.432E-01	6.850E-01	7.182E-01
201.0	3.775E-01	4.299E-01	4.850E-01	5.309E-01	5.696E-01	6.026E-01	6.310E-01	6.556E-01	6.964E-01	7.286E-01
201.5	3.946E-01	4.467E-01	5.012E-01	5.464E-01	5.843E-01	6.166E-01	6.443E-01	6.683E-01	7.079E-01	7.392E-01
202.0	4.125E-01	4.642E-01	5.179E-01	5.623E-01	5.995E-01	6.310E-01	6.579E-01	6.813E-01	7.197E-01	7.499E-01
202.5	4.311E-01	4.823E-01	5.353E-01	5.788E-01	6.150E-01	6.457E-01	6.719E-01	6.945E-01	7.316E-01	7.608E-01
203.0	4.507E-01	5.012E-01	5.532E-01	5.957E-01	6.310E-01	6.607E-01	6.861E-01	7.079E-01	7.438E-01	7.718E-01
203.5	4.711E-01	5.208E-01	5.717E-01	6.131E-01	6.473E-01	6.761E-01	7.006E-01	7.217E-01	7.561E-01	7.830E-01
204.0	4.924E-01	5.412E-01	5.908E-01	6.310E-01	6.641E-01	6.918E-01	7.154E-01	7.356E-01	7.686E-01	7.943E-01
204.5	5.147E-01	5.623E-01	6.105E-01	6.494E-01	6.813E-01	7.079E-01	7.305E-01	7.499E-01	7.814E-01	8.058E-01
205.0	5.380E-01	5.843E-01	6.310E-01	6.683E-01	6.989E-01	7.244E-01	7.460E-01	7.644E-01	7.943E-01	8.175E-01
205.5	5.623E-01	6.072E-01	6.521E-01	6.879E-01	7.171E-01	7.413E-01	7.618E-01	7.792E-01	8.075E-01	8.294E-01
206.0	5.878E-01	6.310E-01	6.739E-01	7.079E-01	7.356E-01	7.586E-01	7.779E-01	7.943E-01	8.209E-01	8.414E-01
206.5	6.144E-01	6.556E-01	6.964E-01	7.286E-01	7.547E-01	7.762E-01	7.943E-01	8.097E-01	8.345E-01	8.536E-01
207.0	6.422E-01	6.813E-01	7.197E-01	7.499E-01	7.743E-01	7.943E-01	8.111E-01	8.254E-01	8.483E-01	8.660E-01
207.5	6.713E-01	7.079E-01	7.438E-01	7.718E-01	7.943E-01	8.128E-01	8.283E-01	8.414E-01	8.624E-01	8.785E-01
208.0	7.017E-01	7.356E-01	7.686E-01	7.943E-01	8.149E-01	8.318E-01	8.458E-01	8.577E-01	8.767E-01	8.913E-01
208.5	7.335E-01	7.644E-01	7.943E-01	8.175E-01	8.360E-01	8.511E-01	8.637E-01	8.743E-01	8.913E-01	9.042E-01
209.0	7.667E-01	7.943E-01	8.209E-01	8.414E-01	8.577E-01	8.710E-01	8.820E-01	8.913E-01	9.060E-01	9.173E-01
209.5	8.014E-01	8.254E-01	8.483E-01	8.660E-01	8.799E-01	8.913E-01	9.006E-01	9.085E-01	9.211E-01	9.306E-01
210.0	8.377E-01	8.577E-01	8.767E-01	8.913E-01	9.027E-01	9.120E-01	9.197E-01	9.261E-01	9.363E-01	9.441E-01
210.5	8.756E-01	8.913E-01	9.060E-01	9.173E-01	9.261E-01	9.333E-01	9.391E-01	9.441E-01	9.519E-01	9.577E-01
211.0	9.152E-01	9.261E-01	9.363E-01	9.441E-01	9.501E-01	9.550E-01	9.590E-01	9.624E-01	9.676E-01	9.716E-01
211.5	9.567E-01	9.624E-01	9.676E-01	9.716E-01	9.747E-01	9.772E-01	9.793E-01	9.810E-01	9.837E-01	9.857E-01
212.0	1.000E+00	1.000E+00	1.000E+00	1.000E+00	1.000E+00	1.000E+00	1.000E+00	1.000E+00	1.000E+00	1.000E+00
212.5	1.045E+00	1.039E+00	1.033E+00	1.029E+00	1.026E+00	1.023E+00	1.021E+00	1.019E+00	1.017E+00	1.014E+00
213.0	1.093E+00	1.080E+00	1.068E+00	1.059E+00	1.053E+00	1.047E+00	1.043E+00	1.039E+00	1.033E+00	1.029E+00
213.5	1.142E+00	1.122E+00	1.104E+00	1.090E+00	1.080E+00	1.072E+00	1.065E+00	1.059E+00	1.051E+00	1.044E+00
214.0	1.194E+00	1.166E+00	1.141E+00	1.122E+00	1.108E+00	1.096E+00	1.087E+00	1.080E+00	1.068E+00	1.059E+00
214.5	1.248E+00	1.212E+00	1.179E+00	1.155E+00	1.136E+00	1.122E+00	1.110E+00	1.101E+00	1.086E+00	1.075E+00
215.0	1.304E+00	1.259E+00	1.218E+00	1.189E+00	1.166E+00	1.148E+00	1.134E+00	1.122E+00	1.104E+00	1.090E+00
215.5	1.363E+00	1.308E+00	1.259E+00	1.223E+00	1.196E+00	1.175E+00	1.158E+00	1.144E+00	1.122E+00	1.106E+00
216.0	1.425E+00	1.359E+00	1.301E+00	1.259E+00	1.227E+00	1.202E+00	1.182E+00	1.166E+00	1.141E+00	1.122E+00
216.5	1.490E+00	1.413E+00	1.345E+00	1.296E+00	1.259E+00	1.230E+00	1.207E+00	1.189E+00	1.160E+00	1.138E+00
217.0	1.557E+00	1.468E+00	1.389E+00	1.334E+00	1.292E+00	1.259E+00	1.233E+00	1.212E+00	1.179E+00	1.155E+00
217.5	1.628E+00	1.525E+00	1.436E+00	1.372E+00	1.325E+00	1.288E+00	1.259E+00	1.235E+00	1.198E+00	1.172E+00
218.0	1.701E+00	1.585E+00	1.484E+00	1.413E+00	1.359E+00	1.318E+00	1.286E+00	1.259E+00	1.218E+00	1.189E+00
218.5	1.778E+00	1.647E+00	1.534E+00	1.454E+00	1.395E+00	1.349E+00	1.313E+00	1.283E+00	1.238E+00	1.206E+00
219.0	1.859E+00	1.711E+00	1.585E+00	1.496E+00	1.431E+00	1.380E+00	1.341E+00	1.308E+00	1.259E+00	1.223E+00
219.5	1.943E+00	1.778E+00	1.638E+00	1.540E+00	1.468E+00	1.413E+00	1.369E+00	1.334E+00	1.280E+00	1.241E+00
220.0	2.031E+00	1.848E+00	1.693E+00	1.585E+00	1.506E+00	1.445E+00	1.398E+00	1.359E+00	1.301E+00	1.259E+00

Table 3 Lethal rates, min at the 250 F reference temperature/min at *T* F

$$F^{z}_{250}/F^{z}_{T} = 10^{\frac{T-250}{z\,\mathrm{F}}}$$

Temp.	Z Value									
F	6 F	8 F	10 F	12 F	14 F	16 F	18 F	20 F	22 F	24 F
200,0	4,642E-09	5,623E-07	1,000E-05	6,813E-05	2,683E-04	7,499E-04	1,668E-03	3,162E-03	5,337E-03	8,254E-03
201,0	6,813E-09	7,499E-07	1,259E-05	8,254E-05	3,162E-04	8,660E-04	1,896E-03	3,548E-03	5,926E-03	9,085E-03
202,0	1,000E-08	1,000E-06	1,585E-05	1,000E-04	3,728E-04	1,000E-03	2,154E-03	3,981E-03	6,579E-03	1,000E-02
203,0	1,468E-08	1,334E-06	1,995E-05	1,212E-04	4,394E-04	1,155E-03	2,448E-03	4,467E-03	7,305E-03	1,101E-02
204,0	2,154E-08	1,778E-06	2,512E-05	1,468E-04	5,179E-04	1,334E-03	2,783E-03	5,012E-03	8,111E-03	1,212E-02
205,0	3,162E-08	2,371E-06	3,162E-05	1,778E-04	6,105E-04	1,540E-03	3,162E-03	5,623E-03	9,006E-03	1,334E-02
206,0	4,642E-08	3,162E-06	3,981E-05	2,154E-04	7,197E-04	1,778E-03	3,594E-03	6,310E-03	1,000E-02	1,468E-02
207,0	6,813E-08	4,217E-06	5,012E-05	2,610E-04	8,483E-04	2,054E-03	4,084E-03	7,079E-03	1,110E-02	1,616E-02
208,0	1,000E-07	5,623E-06	6,310E-05	3,162E-04	1,000E-03	2,371E-03	4,642E-03	7,943E-03	1,233E-02	1,778E-02
209,0	1,468E-07	7,499E-06	7,943E-05	3,831E-04	1,179E-03	2,738E-03	5,275E-03	8,913E-03	1,369E-02	1,957E-02
210,0	2,154E-07	1,000E-05	1,000E-04	4,642E-04	1,389E-03	3,162E-03	5,995E-03	1,000E-02	1,520E-02	2,154E-02
211,0	3,162E-07	1,334E-05	1,259E-04	5,623E-04	1,638E-03	3,652E-03	6,813E-03	1,122E-02	1,688E-02	2,371E-02
212,0	4,642E-07	1,778E-05	1,585E-04	6,813E-04	1,931E-03	4,217E-03	7,743E-03	1,259E-02	1,874E-02	2,610E-02
213,0	6,813E-07	2,371E-05	1,995E-04	8,254E-04	2,276E-03	4,870E-03	8,799E-03	1,413E-02	2,081E-02	2,873E-02
214,0	1,000E-06	3,162E-05	2,512E-04	1,000E-03	2,683E-03	5,623E-03	1,000E-02	1,585E-02	2,310E-02	3,162E-02
215,0	1,468E-06	4,217E-05	3,162E-04	1,212E-03	3,162E-03	6,494E-03	1,136E-02	1,778E-02	2,565E-02	3,481E-02
216,0	2,154E-06	5,623E-05	3,981E-04	1,468E-03	3,728E-03	7,499E-03	1,292E-02	1,995E-02	2,848E-02	3,831E-02
217,0	3,162E-06	7,499E-05	5,012E-04	1,778E-03	4,394E-03	8,660E-03	1,468E-02	2,239E-02	3,162E-02	4,217E-02
218,0	4,642E-06	1,000E-04	6,310E-04	2,154E-03	5,179E-03	1,000E-02	1,668E-02	2,512E-02	3,511E-02	4,642E-02
219,0	6,813E-06	1,334E-04	7,943E-04	2,610E-03	6,105E-03	1,155E-02	1,896E-02	2,818E-02	3,899E-02	5,109E-02
220,0	1,000E-05	1,778E-04	1,000E-03	3,162E-03	7,197E-03	1,334E-02	2,154E-02	3,162E-02	4,329E-02	5,623E-02
221,0	1,468E-05	2,371E-04	1,259E-03	3,831E-03	8,483E-03	1,540E-02	2,448E-02	3,548E-02	4,806E-02	6,190E-02
222,0	2,154E-05	3,162E-04	1,585E-03	4,642E-03	1,000E-02	1,778E-02	2,783E-02	3,981E-02	5,337E-02	6,813E-02
223,0	3,162E-05	4,217E-04	1,995E-03	5,623E-03	1,179E-02	2,054E-02	3,162E-02	4,467E-02	5,926E-02	7,499E-02
224,0	4,642E-05	5,623E-04	2,512E-03	6,813E-03	1,389E-02	2,371E-02	3,594E-02	5,012E-02	6,579E-02	8,254E-02
225,0	6,813E-05	7,499E-04	3,162E-03	8,254E-03	1,638E-02	2,738E-02	4,084E-02	5,623E-02	7,305E-02	9,085E-02
226,0	1,000E-04	1,000E-03	3,981E-03	1,000E-02	1,931E-02	3,162E-02	4,642E-02	6,310E-02	8,111E-02	1,000E-01
227,0	1,468E-04	1,334E-03	5,012E-03	1,212E-02	2,276E-02	3,652E-02	5,275E-02	7,079E-02	9,006E-02	1,101E-01
228,0	2,154E-04	1,778E-03	6,310E-03	1,468E-02	2,683E-02	4,217E-02	5,995E-02	7,943E-02	1,000E-01	1,212E-01
229,0	3,162E-04	2,371E-03	7,943E-03	1,778E-02	3,162E-02	4,870E-02	6,813E-02	8,913E-02	1,110E-01	1,334E-01
230,0	4,642E-04	3,162E-03	1,000E-02	2,154E-02	3,728E-02	5,623E-02	7,743E-02	1,000E-01	1,233E-01	1,468E-01
231,0	6,813E-04	4,217E-03	1,259E-02	2,610E-02	4,394E-02	6,494E-02	8,799E-02	1,122E-01	1,369E-01	1,616E-01
232,0	1,000E-03	5,623E-03	1,585E-02	3,162E-02	5,179E-02	7,499E-02	1,000E-01	1,259E-01	1,520E-01	1,778E-01
233,0	1,468E-03	7,499E-03	1,995E-02	3,831E-02	6,105E-02	8,660E-02	1,136E-01	1,413E-01	1,688E-01	1,957E-01
234,0	2,154E-03	1,000E-02	2,512E-02	4,642E-02	7,197E-02	1,000E-01	1,292E-01	1,585E-01	1,874E-01	2,154E-01
235,0	3,162E-03	1,334E-02	3,162E-02	5,623E-02	8,483E-02	1,155E-01	1,468E-01	1,778E-01	2,081E-01	2,371E-01
236,0	4,642E-03	1,778E-02	3,981E-02	6,813E-02	1,000E-01	1,334E-01	1,668E-01	1,995E-01	2,310E-01	2,610E-01
237,0	6,813E-03	2,371E-02	5,012E-02	8,254E-02	1,179E-01	1,540E-01	1,896E-01	2,239E-01	2,565E-01	2,873E-01
238,0	1,000E-02	3,162E-02	6,310E-02	1,000E-01	1,389E-01	1,778E-01	2,154E-01	2,512E-01	2,848E-01	3,162E-01
239,0	1,468E-02	4,217E-02	7,943E-02	1,212E-01	1,638E-01	2,054E-01	2,448E-01	2,818E-01	3,162E-01	3,481E-01
240,0	2,154E-02	5,623E-02	1,000E-01	1,468E-01	1,931E-01	2,371E-01	2,783E-01	3,162E-01	3,511E-01	3,831E-01
240,5	2,610E-02	6,494E-02	1,122E-01	1,616E-01	2,096E-01	2,548E-01	2,966E-01	3,350E-01	3,700E-01	4,019E-01
241,0	3,162E-02	7,499E-02	1,259E-01	1,778E-01	2,276E-01	2,738E-01	3,162E-01	3,548E-01	3,899E-01	4,217E-01
241,5	3,831E-02	8,660E-02	1,413E-01	1,957E-01	2,471E-01	2,943E-01	3,371E-01	3,758E-01	4,108E-01	4,424E-01
242,0	4,642E-02	1,000E-01	1,585E-01	2,154E-01	2,683E-01	3,162E-01	3,594E-01	3,981E-01	4,329E-01	4,642E-01
242,5	5,623E-02	1,155E-01	1,778E-01	2,371E-01	2,913E-01	3,398E-01	3,831E-01	4,217E-01	4,561E-01	4,870E-01
243,0	6,813E-02	1,334E-01	1,995E-01	2,610E-01	3,162E-01	3,652E-01	4,084E-01	4,467E-01	4,806E-01	5,109E-01
243,5	8,254E-02	1,540E-01	2,239E-01	2,873E-01	3,433E-01	3,924E-01	4,354E-01	4,732E-01	5,065E-01	5,360E-01
244,0	1,000E-01	1,778E-01	2,512E-01	3,162E-01	3,728E-01	4,217E-01	4,642E-01	5,012E-01	5,337E-01	5,623E-01
244,5	1,212E-01	2,054E-01	2,818E-01	3,481E-01	4,047E-01	4,532E-01	4,948E-01	5,309E-01	5,623E-01	5,900E-01
245,0	1,468E-01	2,371E-01	3,162E-01	3,831E-01	4,394E-01	4,870E-01	5,275E-01	5,623E-01	5,926E-01	6,190E-01
245,5	1,778E-01	2,738E-01	3,548E-01	4,217E-01	4,771E-01	5,233E-01	5,623E-01	5,957E-01	6,244E-01	6,494E-01
246,0	2,154E-01	3,162E-01	3,981E-01	4,642E-01	5,179E-01	5,623E-01	5,995E-01	6,310E-01	6,579E-01	6,813E-01
246,5	2,610E-01	3,652E-01	4,467E-01	5,109E-01	5,623E-01	6,043E-01	6,391E-01	6,683E-01	6,933E-01	7,148E-01
247,0	3,162E-01	4,217E-01	5,012E-01	5,623E-01	6,105E-01	6,494E-01	6,813E-01	7,079E-01	7,305E-01	7,499E-01
247,5	3,831E-01	4,870E-01	5,623E-01	6,190E-01	6,629E-01	6,978E-01	7,263E-01	7,499E-01	7,698E-01	7,867E-01
248,0	4,642E-01	5,623E-01	6,310E-01	6,813E-01	7,197E-01	7,499E-01	7,743E-01	7,943E-01	8,111E-01	8,254E-01
248,5	5,623E-01	6,494E-01	7,079E-01	7,499E-01	7,814E-01	8,058E-01	8,254E-01	8,414E-01	8,547E-01	8,660E-01
249,0	6,813E-01	7,499E-01	7,943E-01	8,254E-01	8,483E-01	8,660E-01	8,799E-01	8,913E-01	9,006E-01	9,085E-01
249,5	8,254E-01	8,660E-01	8,913E-01	9,085E-01	9,211E-01	9,306E-01	9,380E-01	9,441E-01	9,490E-01	9,532E-01
250,0	1,000E+00	1,000E+00	1,000E+00	1,000E+00	1,000E+00	1,000E+00	1,000E+00	1,000E+00	1,000E+00	1,000E+00
250,5	1,212E+00	1,155E+00	1,122E+00	1,101E+00	1,086E+00	1,075E+00	1,066E+00	1,059E+00	1,054E+00	1,049E+00
251,0	1,468E+00	1,334E+00	1,259E+00	1,212E+00	1,179E+00	1,155E+00	1,136E+00	1,122E+00	1,110E+00	1,101E+00
251,5	1,778E+00	1,540E+00	1,413E+00	1,334E+00	1,280E+00	1,241E+00	1,212E+00	1,189E+00	1,170E+00	1,155E+00
252,0	2,154E+00	1,778E+00	1,585E+00	1,468E+00	1,389E+00	1,334E+00	1,292E+00	1,259E+00	1,233E+00	1,212E+00
252,5	2,610E+00	2,054E+00	1,778E+00	1,616E+00	1,509E+00	1,433E+00	1,377E+00	1,334E+00	1,299E+00	1,271E+00
253,0	3,162E+00	2,371E+00	1,995E+00	1,778E+00	1,638E+00	1,540E+00	1,468E+00	1,413E+00	1,369E+00	1,334E+00
253,5	3,831E+00	2,738E+00	2,239E+00	1,957E+00	1,778E+00	1,655E+00	1,565E+00	1,496E+00	1,442E+00	1,399E+00
254,0	4,642E+00	3,162E+00	2,512E+00	2,154E+00	1,931E+00	1,778E+00	1,668E+00	1,585E+00	1,520E+00	1,468E+00
254,5	5,623E+00	3,652E+00	2,818E+00	2,371E+00	2,096E+00	1,911E+00	1,778E+00	1,679E+00	1,602E+00	1,540E+00
255,0	6,813E+00	4,217E+00	3,162E+00	2,610E+00	2,276E+00	2,054E+00	1,896E+00	1,778E+00	1,688E+00	1,616E+00
255,5	8,254E+00	4,870E+00	3,548E+00	2,873E+00	2,471E+00	2,207E+00	2,021E+00	1,884E+00	1,778E+00	1,695E+00
256,0	1,000E+01	5,623E+00	3,981E+00	3,162E+00	2,683E+00	2,371E+00	2,154E+00	1,995E+00	1,874E+00	1,778E+00
256,5	1,212E+01	6,494E+00	4,467E+00	3,481E+00	2,913E+00	2,548E+00	2,297E+00	2,113E+00	1,974E+00	1,866E+00
257,0	1,468E+01	7,499E+00	5,012E+00	3,831E+00	3,162E+00	2,738E+00	2,448E+00	2,239E+00	2,081E+00	1,957E+00
257,5	1,778E+01	8,660E+00	5,623E+00	4,217E+00	3,433E+00	2,943E+00	2,610E+00	2,371E+00	2,192E+00	2,054E+00
258,0	2,154E+01	1,000E+01	6,310E+00	4,642E+00	3,728E+00	3,162E+00	2,783E+00	2,512E+00	2,310E+00	2,154E+00
258,5	2,610E+01	1,155E+01	7,079E+00	5,109E+00	4,047E+00	3,398E+00	2,966E+00	2,661E+00	2,434E+00	2,260E+00
259,0	3,162E+01	1,334E+01	7,943E+00	5,623E+00	4,394E+00	3,652E+00	3,162E+00	2,818E+00	2,565E+00	2,371E+00
259,5	3,831E+01	1,540E+01	8,913E+00	6,190E+00	4,771E+00	3,924E+00	3,371E+00	2,985E+00	2,703E+00	2,488E+00
260,0	4,642E+01	1,778E+01	1,000E+01	6,813E+00	5,179E+00	4,217E+00	3,594E+00	3,162E+00	2,848E+00	2,610E+00
260,5	5,623E+01	2,054E+01	1,122E+01	7,499E+00	5,623E+00	4,532E+00	3,831E+00	3,350E+00	3,001E+00	2,738E+00
261,0	6,813E+01	2,371E+01	1,259E+01	8,254E+00	6,105E+00	4,870E+00	4,084E+00	3,548E+00	3,162E+00	2,873E+00
261,5	8,254E+01	2,738E+01	1,413E+01	9,085E+00	6,629E+00	5,233E+00	4,354E+00	3,758E+00	3,332E+00	3,014E+00
262,0	1,000E+02	3,162E+01	1,585E+01	1,000E+01	7,197E+00	5,623E+00	4,642E+00	3,981E+00	3,511E+00	3,162E+00
262,5	1,212E+02	3,652E+01	1,778E+01	1,101E+01	7,814E+00	6,043E+00	4,948E+00	4,217E+00	3,700E+00	3,318E+00
263,0	1,468E+02	4,217E+01	1,995E+01	1,212E+01	8,483E+00	6,494E+00	5,275E+00	4,467E+00	3,899E+00	3,481E+00
263,5	1,778E+02	4,870E+01	2,239E+01	1,334E+01	9,211E+00	6,978E+00	5,623E+00	4,732E+00	4,108E+00	3,652E+00
264,0	2,154E+02	5,623E+01	2,512E+01	1,468E+01	1,000E+01	7,499E+00	5,995E+00	5,012E+00	4,329E+00	3,831E+00
264,5	2,610E+02	6,494E+01	2,818E+01	1,616E+01	1,086E+01	8,058E+00	6,391E+00	5,309E+00	4,561E+00	4,019E+00
265,0	3,162E+02	7,499E+01	3,162E+01	1,778E+01	1,179E+01	8,660E+00	6,813E+00	5,623E+00	4,806E+00	4,217E+00
265,5	3,831E+02	8,660E+01	3,548E+01	1,957E+01	1,280E+01	9,306E+00	7,263E+00	5,957E+00	5,065E+00	4,424E+00
266,0	4,642E+02	1,000E+02	3,981E+01	2,154E+01	1,389E+01	1,000E+01	7,743E+00	6,310E+00	5,337E+00	4,642E+00
266,5	5,623E+02	1,155E+02	4,467E+01	2,371E+01	1,509E+01	1,075E+01	8,254E+00	6,683E+00	5,623E+00	4,870E+00
267,0	6,813E+02	1,334E+02	5,012E+01	2,610E+01	1,638E+01	1,155E+01	8,799E+00	7,079E+00	5,926E+00	5,109E+00
267,5	8,254E+02	1,540E+02	5,623E+01	2,873E+01	1,778E+01	1,241E+01	9,380E+00	7,499E+00	6,244E+00	5,360E+00
268,0	1,000E+03	1,778E+02	6,310E+01	3,162E+01	1,931E+01	1,334E+01	1,000E+01	7,943E+00	6,579E+00	5,623E+00
268,5	1,212E+03	2,054E+02	7,079E+01	3,481E+01	2,096E+01	1,433E+01	1,066E+01	8,414E+00	6,933E+00	5,900E+00
269,0	1,468E+03	2,371E+02	7,943E+01	3,831E+01	2,276E+01	1,540E+01	1,136E+01	8,913E+00	7,305E+00	6,190E+00
269,5	1,778E+03	2,738E+02	8,913E+01	4,217E+01	2,471E+01	1,655E+01	1,212E+01	9,441E+00	7,698E+00	6,494E+00
270,0	2,154E+03	3,162E+02	1,000E+02	4,642E+01	2,683E+01	1,778E+01	1,292E+01	1,000E+01	8,111E+00	6,813E+00

Table 3 (cont.)

Temp. F	Z Value 26 F	30 F	35 F	40 F	45 F	50 F	55 F	60 F	70 F	80 F
200,0	1,194E-02	2,154E-02	3,728E-02	5,623E-02	7,743E-02	1,000E-01	1,233E-01	1,468E-01	1,931E-01	2,371E-01
201,0	1,304E-02	2,326E-02	3,981E-02	5,957E-02	8,149E-02	1,047E-01	1,286E-01	1,525E-01	1,995E-01	2,441E-01
202,0	1,425E-02	2,512E-02	4,252E-02	6,310E-02	8,577E-02	1,096E-01	1,341E-01	1,585E-01	2,062E-01	2,512E-01
203,0	1,557E-02	2,712E-02	4,541E-02	6,683E-02	9,027E-02	1,148E-01	1,398E-01	1,647E-01	2,131E-01	2,585E-01
204,0	1,701E-02	2,929E-02	4,850E-02	7,079E-02	9,501E-02	1,202E-01	1,458E-01	1,711E-01	2,202E-01	2,661E-01
205,0	1,859E-02	3,162E-02	5,179E-02	7,499E-02	1,000E-01	1,259E-01	1,520E-01	1,778E-01	2,276E-01	2,738E-01
206,0	2,031E-02	3,415E-02	5,532E-02	7,943E-02	1,053E-01	1,318E-01	1,585E-01	1,848E-01	2,352E-01	2,818E-01
207,0	2,219E-02	3,687E-02	5,908E-02	8,414E-02	1,108E-01	1,380E-01	1,653E-01	1,920E-01	2,431E-01	2,901E-01
208,0	2,424E-02	3,981E-02	6,310E-02	8,913E-02	1,166E-01	1,445E-01	1,723E-01	1,995E-01	2,512E-01	2,985E-01
209,0	2,649E-02	4,299E-02	6,739E-02	9,441E-02	1,227E-01	1,514E-01	1,797E-01	2,073E-01	2,596E-01	3,073E-01
210,0	2,894E-02	4,642E-02	7,197E-02	1,000E-01	1,292E-01	1,585E-01	1,874E-01	2,154E-01	2,683E-01	3,162E-01
211,0	3,162E-02	5,012E-02	7,686E-02	1,059E-01	1,359E-01	1,660E-01	1,954E-01	2,239E-01	2,772E-01	3,255E-01
212,0	3,455E-02	5,412E-02	8,209E-02	1,122E-01	1,431E-01	1,738E-01	2,037E-01	2,326E-01	2,865E-01	3,350E-01
213,0	3,775E-02	5,843E-02	8,767E-02	1,189E-01	1,506E-01	1,820E-01	2,125E-01	2,417E-01	2,961E-01	3,447E-01
214,0	4,125E-02	6,310E-02	9,363E-02	1,259E-01	1,585E-01	1,905E-01	2,215E-01	2,512E-01	3,060E-01	3,548E-01
215,0	4,507E-02	6,813E-02	1,000E-01	1,334E-01	1,668E-01	1,995E-01	2,310E-01	2,610E-01	3,162E-01	3,652E-01
216,0	4,924E-02	7,356E-02	1,068E-01	1,413E-01	1,756E-01	2,089E-01	2,409E-01	2,712E-01	3,268E-01	3,758E-01
217,0	5,380E-02	7,943E-02	1,141E-01	1,496E-01	1,848E-01	2,188E-01	2,512E-01	2,818E-01	3,377E-01	3,868E-01
218,0	5,878E-02	8,577E-02	1,218E-01	1,585E-01	1,945E-01	2,291E-01	2,619E-01	2,929E-01	3,490E-01	3,981E-01
219,0	6,422E-02	9,261E-02	1,301E-01	1,679E-01	2,047E-01	2,399E-01	2,731E-01	3,043E-01	3,607E-01	4,097E-01
220,0	7,017E-02	1,000E-01	1,389E-01	1,778E-01	2,154E-01	2,512E-01	2,848E-01	3,162E-01	3,728E-01	4,217E-01
221,0	7,667E-02	1,080E-01	1,484E-01	1,884E-01	2,268E-01	2,630E-01	2,970E-01	3,286E-01	3,852E-01	4,340E-01
222,0	8,377E-02	1,166E-01	1,585E-01	1,995E-01	2,387E-01	2,754E-01	3,097E-01	3,415E-01	3,981E-01	4,467E-01
223,0	9,152E-02	1,259E-01	1,693E-01	2,113E-01	2,512E-01	2,884E-01	3,229E-01	3,548E-01	4,114E-01	4,597E-01
224,0	1,000E-01	1,359E-01	1,808E-01	2,239E-01	2,644E-01	3,020E-01	3,367E-01	3,687E-01	4,252E-01	4,732E-01
225,0	1,093E-01	1,468E-01	1,931E-01	2,371E-01	2,783E-01	3,162E-01	3,511E-01	3,831E-01	4,394E-01	4,870E-01
226,0	1,194E-01	1,585E-01	2,062E-01	2,512E-01	2,929E-01	3,311E-01	3,661E-01	3,981E-01	4,541E-01	5,012E-01
227,0	1,304E-01	1,711E-01	2,202E-01	2,661E-01	3,082E-01	3,467E-01	3,818E-01	4,137E-01	4,693E-01	5,158E-01
228,0	1,425E-01	1,848E-01	2,352E-01	2,818E-01	3,244E-01	3,631E-01	3,981E-01	4,299E-01	4,850E-01	5,309E-01
229,0	1,557E-01	1,995E-01	2,512E-01	2,985E-01	3,415E-01	3,802E-01	4,151E-01	4,467E-01	5,012E-01	5,464E-01
230,0	1,701E-01	2,154E-01	2,683E-01	3,162E-01	3,594E-01	3,981E-01	4,329E-01	4,642E-01	5,179E-01	5,623E-01
231,0	1,859E-01	2,326E-01	2,865E-01	3,350E-01	3,782E-01	4,169E-01	4,514E-01	4,823E-01	5,353E-01	5,788E-01
232,0	2,031E-01	2,512E-01	3,060E-01	3,548E-01	3,981E-01	4,365E-01	4,707E-01	5,012E-01	5,532E-01	5,957E-01
233,0	2,219E-01	2,712E-01	3,268E-01	3,758E-01	4,190E-01	4,571E-01	4,908E-01	5,208E-01	5,717E-01	6,131E-01
234,0	2,424E-01	2,929E-01	3,490E-01	3,981E-01	4,410E-01	4,786E-01	5,118E-01	5,412E-01	5,908E-01	6,310E-01
235,0	2,649E-01	3,162E-01	3,728E-01	4,217E-01	4,642E-01	5,012E-01	5,337E-01	5,623E-01	6,105E-01	6,494E-01
236,0	2,894E-01	3,415E-01	3,981E-01	4,467E-01	4,885E-01	5,248E-01	5,565E-01	5,843E-01	6,310E-01	6,683E-01
237,0	3,162E-01	3,687E-01	4,252E-01	4,732E-01	5,142E-01	5,495E-01	5,803E-01	6,072E-01	6,521E-01	6,879E-01
238,0	3,455E-01	3,981E-01	4,541E-01	5,012E-01	5,412E-01	5,754E-01	6,051E-01	6,310E-01	6,739E-01	7,079E-01
239,0	3,775E-01	4,299E-01	4,850E-01	5,309E-01	5,696E-01	6,026E-01	6,310E-01	6,556E-01	6,964E-01	7,286E-01
240,0	4,125E-01	4,642E-01	5,179E-01	5,623E-01	5,995E-01	6,310E-01	6,579E-01	6,813E-01	7,197E-01	7,499E-01
240,5	4,311E-01	4,823E-01	5,353E-01	5,788E-01	6,150E-01	6,457E-01	6,719E-01	6,945E-01	7,316E-01	7,608E-01
241,0	4,507E-01	5,012E-01	5,532E-01	5,957E-01	6,310E-01	6,607E-01	6,861E-01	7,079E-01	7,438E-01	7,718E-01
241,5	4,711E-01	5,208E-01	5,717E-01	6,131E-01	6,473E-01	6,761E-01	7,006E-01	7,217E-01	7,561E-01	7,830E-01
242,0	4,924E-01	5,412E-01	5,908E-01	6,310E-01	6,641E-01	6,918E-01	7,154E-01	7,356E-01	7,686E-01	7,943E-01
242,5	5,147E-01	5,623E-01	6,105E-01	6,494E-01	6,813E-01	7,079E-01	7,305E-01	7,499E-01	7,814E-01	8,058E-01
243,0	5,380E-01	5,843E-01	6,310E-01	6,683E-01	6,989E-01	7,244E-01	7,460E-01	7,644E-01	7,943E-01	8,175E-01
243,5	5,623E-01	6,072E-01	6,521E-01	6,879E-01	7,171E-01	7,413E-01	7,618E-01	7,792E-01	8,075E-01	8,294E-01
244,0	5,878E-01	6,310E-01	6,739E-01	7,079E-01	7,356E-01	7,586E-01	7,779E-01	7,943E-01	8,209E-01	8,414E-01
244,5	6,144E-01	6,556E-01	6,964E-01	7,286E-01	7,547E-01	7,762E-01	7,943E-01	8,097E-01	8,345E-01	8,536E-01
245,0	6,422E-01	6,813E-01	7,197E-01	7,499E-01	7,743E-01	7,943E-01	8,111E-01	8,254E-01	8,483E-01	8,660E-01
245,5	6,713E-01	7,079E-01	7,438E-01	7,718E-01	7,943E-01	8,128E-01	8,283E-01	8,414E-01	8,624E-01	8,785E-01
246,0	7,017E-01	7,356E-01	7,686E-01	7,943E-01	8,149E-01	8,318E-01	8,458E-01	8,577E-01	8,767E-01	8,913E-01
246,5	7,335E-01	7,644E-01	7,943E-01	8,175E-01	8,360E-01	8,511E-01	8,637E-01	8,743E-01	8,913E-01	9,042E-01
247,0	7,667E-01	7,943E-01	8,209E-01	8,414E-01	8,577E-01	8,710E-01	8,820E-01	8,913E-01	9,060E-01	9,173E-01
247,5	8,014E-01	8,254E-01	8,483E-01	8,660E-01	8,799E-01	8,913E-01	9,006E-01	9,085E-01	9,211E-01	9,306E-01
248,0	8,377E-01	8,577E-01	8,767E-01	8,913E-01	9,027E-01	9,120E-01	9,197E-01	9,261E-01	9,363E-01	9,441E-01
248,5	8,756E-01	8,913E-01	9,060E-01	9,173E-01	9,261E-01	9,333E-01	9,391E-01	9,441E-01	9,519E-01	9,577E-01
249,0	9,152E-01	9,261E-01	9,363E-01	9,441E-01	9,501E-01	9,550E-01	9,590E-01	9,624E-01	9,676E-01	9,716E-01
249,5	9,567E-01	9,624E-01	9,676E-01	9,716E-01	9,747E-01	9,772E-01	9,793E-01	9,810E-01	9,837E-01	9,857E-01
250,0	1,000E+00	1,000E+00	1,000E+00	1,000E+00	1,000E+00	1,000E+00	1,000E+00	1,000E+00	1,000E+00	1,000E+00
250,5	1,045E+00	1,039E+00	1,033E+00	1,029E+00	1,026E+00	1,023E+00	1,021E+00	1,019E+00	1,017E+00	1,014E+00
251,0	1,093E+00	1,080E+00	1,068E+00	1,059E+00	1,053E+00	1,047E+00	1,043E+00	1,039E+00	1,033E+00	1,029E+00
251,5	1,142E+00	1,122E+00	1,104E+00	1,090E+00	1,080E+00	1,072E+00	1,065E+00	1,059E+00	1,051E+00	1,044E+00
252,0	1,194E+00	1,166E+00	1,141E+00	1,122E+00	1,108E+00	1,096E+00	1,087E+00	1,080E+00	1,068E+00	1,059E+00
252,5	1,248E+00	1,212E+00	1,179E+00	1,155E+00	1,136E+00	1,122E+00	1,110E+00	1,101E+00	1,086E+00	1,075E+00
253,0	1,304E+00	1,259E+00	1,218E+00	1,189E+00	1,166E+00	1,148E+00	1,134E+00	1,122E+00	1,104E+00	1,090E+00
253,5	1,363E+00	1,308E+00	1,259E+00	1,223E+00	1,196E+00	1,175E+00	1,158E+00	1,144E+00	1,122E+00	1,106E+00
254,0	1,425E+00	1,359E+00	1,301E+00	1,259E+00	1,227E+00	1,202E+00	1,182E+00	1,166E+00	1,141E+00	1,122E+00
254,5	1,490E+00	1,413E+00	1,345E+00	1,296E+00	1,259E+00	1,230E+00	1,207E+00	1,189E+00	1,160E+00	1,138E+00
255,0	1,557E+00	1,468E+00	1,389E+00	1,334E+00	1,292E+00	1,259E+00	1,233E+00	1,212E+00	1,179E+00	1,155E+00
255,5	1,628E+00	1,525E+00	1,436E+00	1,372E+00	1,325E+00	1,288E+00	1,259E+00	1,235E+00	1,198E+00	1,172E+00
256,0	1,701E+00	1,585E+00	1,484E+00	1,413E+00	1,359E+00	1,318E+00	1,286E+00	1,259E+00	1,218E+00	1,189E+00
256,5	1,778E+00	1,647E+00	1,534E+00	1,454E+00	1,395E+00	1,349E+00	1,313E+00	1,283E+00	1,238E+00	1,206E+00
257,0	1,859E+00	1,711E+00	1,585E+00	1,496E+00	1,431E+00	1,380E+00	1,341E+00	1,308E+00	1,259E+00	1,223E+00
257,5	1,943E+00	1,778E+00	1,638E+00	1,540E+00	1,468E+00	1,413E+00	1,369E+00	1,334E+00	1,280E+00	1,241E+00
258,0	2,031E+00	1,848E+00	1,693E+00	1,585E+00	1,506E+00	1,445E+00	1,398E+00	1,359E+00	1,301E+00	1,259E+00
258,5	2,123E+00	1,920E+00	1,749E+00	1,631E+00	1,545E+00	1,479E+00	1,427E+00	1,386E+00	1,323E+00	1,277E+00
259,0	2,219E+00	1,995E+00	1,808E+00	1,679E+00	1,585E+00	1,514E+00	1,458E+00	1,413E+00	1,345E+00	1,296E+00
259,5	2,319E+00	2,073E+00	1,868E+00	1,728E+00	1,626E+00	1,549E+00	1,488E+00	1,440E+00	1,367E+00	1,314E+00
260,0	2,424E+00	2,154E+00	1,931E+00	1,778E+00	1,668E+00	1,585E+00	1,520E+00	1,468E+00	1,389E+00	1,334E+00
260,5	2,534E+00	2,239E+00	1,995E+00	1,830E+00	1,711E+00	1,622E+00	1,552E+00	1,496E+00	1,413E+00	1,353E+00
261,0	2,649E+00	2,326E+00	2,062E+00	1,884E+00	1,756E+00	1,660E+00	1,585E+00	1,525E+00	1,436E+00	1,372E+00
261,5	2,769E+00	2,417E+00	2,131E+00	1,939E+00	1,801E+00	1,698E+00	1,618E+00	1,555E+00	1,460E+00	1,392E+00
262,0	2,894E+00	2,512E+00	2,202E+00	1,995E+00	1,848E+00	1,738E+00	1,653E+00	1,585E+00	1,484E+00	1,413E+00
262,5	3,025E+00	2,610E+00	2,276E+00	2,054E+00	1,896E+00	1,778E+00	1,688E+00	1,616E+00	1,509E+00	1,433E+00
263,0	3,162E+00	2,712E+00	2,352E+00	2,113E+00	1,945E+00	1,820E+00	1,723E+00	1,647E+00	1,534E+00	1,454E+00
263,5	3,305E+00	2,818E+00	2,431E+00	2,175E+00	1,995E+00	1,862E+00	1,760E+00	1,679E+00	1,559E+00	1,475E+00
264,0	3,455E+00	2,929E+00	2,512E+00	2,239E+00	2,047E+00	1,905E+00	1,797E+00	1,711E+00	1,585E+00	1,496E+00
264,5	3,612E+00	3,043E+00	2,596E+00	2,304E+00	2,100E+00	1,950E+00	1,835E+00	1,744E+00	1,611E+00	1,518E+00
265,0	3,775E+00	3,162E+00	2,683E+00	2,371E+00	2,154E+00	1,995E+00	1,874E+00	1,778E+00	1,638E+00	1,540E+00
265,5	3,946E+00	3,286E+00	2,772E+00	2,441E+00	2,210E+00	2,042E+00	1,913E+00	1,813E+00	1,665E+00	1,562E+00
266,0	4,125E+00	3,415E+00	2,865E+00	2,512E+00	2,268E+00	2,089E+00	1,954E+00	1,848E+00	1,693E+00	1,585E+00
266,5	4,311E+00	3,548E+00	2,961E+00	2,585E+00	2,326E+00	2,138E+00	1,995E+00	1,884E+00	1,721E+00	1,608E+00
267,0	4,507E+00	3,687E+00	3,060E+00	2,661E+00	2,387E+00	2,188E+00	2,037E+00	1,920E+00	1,749E+00	1,631E+00
267,5	4,711E+00	3,831E+00	3,162E+00	2,738E+00	2,448E+00	2,239E+00	2,081E+00	1,957E+00	1,778E+00	1,655E+00
268,0	4,924E+00	3,981E+00	3,268E+00	2,818E+00	2,512E+00	2,291E+00	2,125E+00	1,995E+00	1,808E+00	1,679E+00
268,5	5,147E+00	4,137E+00	3,377E+00	2,901E+00	2,577E+00	2,344E+00	2,170E+00	2,034E+00	1,838E+00	1,703E+00
269,0	5,380E+00	4,299E+00	3,490E+00	2,985E+00	2,644E+00	2,399E+00	2,215E+00	2,073E+00	1,868E+00	1,728E+00
269,5	5,623E+00	4,467E+00	3,607E+00	3,073E+00	2,712E+00	2,455E+00	2,262E+00	2,113E+00	1,899E+00	1,753E+00
270,0	5,878E+00	4,642E+00	3,728E+00	3,162E+00	2,783E+00	2,512E+00	2,310E+00	2,154E+00	1,931E+00	1,778E+00

Table 4 Lethal rates, min at the 100 C reference temperature/min at *T* C

$$F^z_{100}/F^z_T = 10^{\frac{T-100}{z\,\mathrm{C}}}$$

Temp. C	Z Value 3 C	4 C	5 C	6 C	7 C	8 C	9 C	10 C	11 C	12 C
75,0	4,642E-09	5,623E-07	1,000E-05	6,813E-05	2,683E-04	7,499E-04	1,668E-03	3,162E-03	5,337E-03	8,254E-03
75,5	6,813E-09	7,499E-07	1,259E-05	8,254E-05	3,162E-04	8,660E-04	1,896E-03	3,548E-03	5,926E-03	9,085E-03
76,0	1,000E-08	1,000E-06	1,585E-05	1,000E-04	3,728E-04	1,000E-03	2,154E-03	3,981E-03	6,579E-03	1,000E-02
76,5	1,468E-08	1,334E-06	1,995E-05	1,212E-04	4,394E-04	1,155E-03	2,448E-03	4,467E-03	7,305E-03	1,101E-02
77,0	2,154E-08	1,778E-06	2,512E-05	1,468E-04	5,179E-04	1,334E-03	2,783E-03	5,012E-03	8,111E-03	1,212E-02
77,5	3,162E-08	2,371E-06	3,162E-05	1,778E-04	6,105E-04	1,540E-03	3,162E-03	5,623E-03	9,006E-03	1,334E-02
78,0	4,642E-08	3,162E-06	3,981E-05	2,154E-04	7,197E-04	1,778E-03	3,594E-03	6,310E-03	1,000E-02	1,468E-02
78,5	6,813E-08	4,217E-06	5,012E-05	2,610E-04	8,483E-04	2,054E-03	4,084E-03	7,079E-03	1,110E-02	1,616E-02
79,0	1,000E-07	5,623E-06	6,310E-05	3,162E-04	1,000E-03	2,371E-03	4,642E-03	7,943E-03	1,233E-02	1,778E-02
79,5	1,468E-07	7,499E-06	7,943E-05	3,831E-04	1,179E-03	2,738E-03	5,275E-03	8,913E-03	1,369E-02	1,957E-02
80,0	2,154E-07	1,000E-05	1,000E-04	4,642E-04	1,389E-03	3,162E-03	5,995E-03	1,000E-02	1,520E-02	2,154E-02
80,5	3,162E-07	1,334E-05	1,259E-04	5,623E-04	1,638E-03	3,652E-03	6,813E-03	1,122E-02	1,688E-02	2,371E-02
81,0	4,642E-07	1,778E-05	1,585E-04	6,813E-04	1,931E-03	4,217E-03	7,743E-03	1,259E-02	1,874E-02	2,610E-02
81,5	6,813E-07	2,371E-05	1,995E-04	8,254E-04	2,276E-03	4,870E-03	8,799E-03	1,413E-02	2,081E-02	2,873E-02
82,0	1,000E-06	3,162E-05	2,512E-04	1,000E-03	2,683E-03	5,623E-03	1,000E-02	1,585E-02	2,310E-02	3,162E-02
82,5	1,468E-06	4,217E-05	3,162E-04	1,212E-03	3,162E-03	6,494E-03	1,136E-02	1,778E-02	2,565E-02	3,481E-02
83,0	2,154E-06	5,623E-05	3,981E-04	1,468E-03	3,728E-03	7,499E-03	1,292E-02	1,995E-02	2,848E-02	3,831E-02
83,5	3,162E-06	7,499E-05	5,012E-04	1,778E-03	4,394E-03	8,660E-03	1,468E-02	2,239E-02	3,162E-02	4,217E-02
84,0	4,642E-06	1,000E-04	6,310E-04	2,154E-03	5,179E-03	1,000E-02	1,668E-02	2,512E-02	3,511E-02	4,642E-02
84,5	6,813E-06	1,334E-04	7,943E-04	2,610E-03	6,105E-03	1,155E-02	1,896E-02	2,818E-02	3,899E-02	5,109E-02
85,0	1,000E-05	1,778E-04	1,000E-03	3,162E-03	7,197E-03	1,334E-02	2,154E-02	3,162E-02	4,329E-02	5,623E-02
85,5	1,468E-05	2,371E-04	1,259E-03	3,831E-03	8,483E-03	1,540E-02	2,448E-02	3,548E-02	4,806E-02	6,190E-02
86,0	2,154E-05	3,162E-04	1,585E-03	4,642E-03	1,000E-02	1,778E-02	2,783E-02	3,981E-02	5,337E-02	6,813E-02
86,5	3,162E-05	4,217E-04	1,995E-03	5,623E-03	1,179E-02	2,054E-02	3,162E-02	4,467E-02	5,926E-02	7,499E-02
87,0	4,642E-05	5,623E-04	2,512E-03	6,813E-03	1,389E-02	2,371E-02	3,594E-02	5,012E-02	6,579E-02	8,254E-02
87,5	6,813E-05	7,499E-04	3,162E-03	8,254E-03	1,638E-02	2,738E-02	4,084E-02	5,623E-02	7,305E-02	9,085E-02
88,0	1,000E-04	1,000E-03	3,981E-03	1,000E-02	1,931E-02	3,162E-02	4,642E-02	6,310E-02	8,111E-02	1,000E-01
88,5	1,468E-04	1,334E-03	5,012E-03	1,212E-02	2,276E-02	3,652E-02	5,275E-02	7,079E-02	9,006E-02	1,101E-01
89,0	2,154E-04	1,778E-03	6,310E-03	1,468E-02	2,683E-02	4,217E-02	5,995E-02	7,943E-02	1,000E-01	1,212E-01
89,5	3,162E-04	2,371E-03	7,943E-03	1,778E-02	3,162E-02	4,870E-02	6,813E-02	8,913E-02	1,110E-01	1,334E-01
90,0	4,642E-04	3,162E-03	1,000E-02	2,154E-02	3,728E-02	5,623E-02	7,743E-02	1,000E-01	1,233E-01	1,468E-01
90,5	6,813E-04	4,217E-03	1,259E-02	2,610E-02	4,394E-02	6,494E-02	8,799E-02	1,122E-01	1,369E-01	1,616E-01
91,0	1,000E-03	5,623E-03	1,585E-02	3,162E-02	5,179E-02	7,499E-02	1,000E-01	1,259E-01	1,520E-01	1,778E-01
91,5	1,468E-03	7,499E-03	1,995E-02	3,831E-02	6,105E-02	8,660E-02	1,136E-01	1,413E-01	1,688E-01	1,957E-01
92,0	2,154E-03	1,000E-02	2,512E-02	4,642E-02	7,197E-02	1,000E-01	1,292E-01	1,585E-01	1,874E-01	2,154E-01
92,5	3,162E-03	1,334E-02	3,162E-02	5,623E-02	8,483E-02	1,155E-01	1,468E-01	1,778E-01	2,081E-01	2,371E-01
93,0	4,642E-03	1,778E-02	3,981E-02	6,813E-02	1,000E-01	1,334E-01	1,668E-01	1,995E-01	2,310E-01	2,610E-01
93,5	6,813E-03	2,371E-02	5,012E-02	8,254E-02	1,179E-01	1,540E-01	1,896E-01	2,239E-01	2,565E-01	2,873E-01
94,0	1,000E-02	3,162E-02	6,310E-02	1,000E-01	1,389E-01	1,778E-01	2,154E-01	2,512E-01	2,848E-01	3,162E-01
94,5	1,468E-02	4,217E-02	7,943E-02	1,212E-01	1,638E-01	2,054E-01	2,448E-01	2,818E-01	3,162E-01	3,481E-01
95,0	2,154E-02	5,623E-02	1,000E-01	1,468E-01	1,931E-01	2,371E-01	2,783E-01	3,162E-01	3,511E-01	3,831E-01
95,2	2,512E-02	6,310E-02	1,096E-01	1,585E-01	2,062E-01	2,512E-01	2,929E-01	3,311E-01	3,661E-01	3,981E-01
95,4	2,929E-02	7,079E-02	1,202E-01	1,711E-01	2,202E-01	2,661E-01	3,082E-01	3,467E-01	3,818E-01	4,137E-01
95,6	3,415E-02	7,943E-02	1,318E-01	1,848E-01	2,352E-01	2,818E-01	3,244E-01	3,631E-01	3,981E-01	4,299E-01
95,8	3,981E-02	8,913E-02	1,445E-01	1,995E-01	2,512E-01	2,985E-01	3,415E-01	3,802E-01	4,151E-01	4,467E-01
96,0	4,642E-02	1,000E-01	1,585E-01	2,154E-01	2,683E-01	3,162E-01	3,594E-01	3,981E-01	4,329E-01	4,642E-01
96,2	5,412E-02	1,122E-01	1,738E-01	2,326E-01	2,865E-01	3,350E-01	3,782E-01	4,169E-01	4,514E-01	4,823E-01
96,4	6,310E-02	1,259E-01	1,905E-01	2,512E-01	3,060E-01	3,548E-01	3,981E-01	4,365E-01	4,707E-01	5,012E-01
96,6	7,356E-02	1,413E-01	2,089E-01	2,712E-01	3,268E-01	3,758E-01	4,190E-01	4,571E-01	4,908E-01	5,208E-01
96,8	8,577E-02	1,585E-01	2,291E-01	2,929E-01	3,490E-01	3,981E-01	4,410E-01	4,786E-01	5,118E-01	5,412E-01
97,0	1,000E-01	1,778E-01	2,512E-01	3,162E-01	3,728E-01	4,217E-01	4,642E-01	5,012E-01	5,337E-01	5,623E-01
97,2	1,166E-01	1,995E-01	2,754E-01	3,415E-01	3,981E-01	4,467E-01	4,885E-01	5,248E-01	5,565E-01	5,843E-01
97,4	1,359E-01	2,239E-01	3,020E-01	3,687E-01	4,252E-01	4,732E-01	5,142E-01	5,495E-01	5,803E-01	6,072E-01
97,6	1,585E-01	2,512E-01	3,311E-01	3,981E-01	4,541E-01	5,012E-01	5,412E-01	5,754E-01	6,051E-01	6,310E-01
97,8	1,848E-01	2,818E-01	3,631E-01	4,299E-01	4,850E-01	5,309E-01	5,696E-01	6,026E-01	6,310E-01	6,556E-01
98,0	2,154E-01	3,162E-01	3,981E-01	4,642E-01	5,179E-01	5,623E-01	5,995E-01	6,310E-01	6,579E-01	6,813E-01
98,2	2,512E-01	3,548E-01	4,365E-01	5,012E-01	5,532E-01	5,957E-01	6,310E-01	6,607E-01	6,861E-01	7,079E-01
98,4	2,929E-01	3,981E-01	4,786E-01	5,412E-01	5,908E-01	6,310E-01	6,641E-01	6,918E-01	7,154E-01	7,356E-01
98,6	3,415E-01	4,467E-01	5,248E-01	5,843E-01	6,310E-01	6,683E-01	6,989E-01	7,244E-01	7,460E-01	7,644E-01
98,8	3,981E-01	5,012E-01	5,754E-01	6,310E-01	6,739E-01	7,079E-01	7,356E-01	7,586E-01	7,779E-01	7,943E-01
99,0	4,642E-01	5,623E-01	6,310E-01	6,813E-01	7,197E-01	7,499E-01	7,743E-01	7,943E-01	8,111E-01	8,254E-01
99,2	5,412E-01	6,310E-01	6,918E-01	7,356E-01	7,686E-01	7,943E-01	8,149E-01	8,318E-01	8,458E-01	8,577E-01
99,4	6,310E-01	7,079E-01	7,586E-01	7,943E-01	8,209E-01	8,414E-01	8,577E-01	8,710E-01	8,820E-01	8,913E-01
99,6	7,356E-01	7,943E-01	8,318E-01	8,577E-01	8,767E-01	8,913E-01	9,027E-01	9,120E-01	9,197E-01	9,261E-01
99,8	8,577E-01	8,913E-01	9,120E-01	9,261E-01	9,363E-01	9,441E-01	9,501E-01	9,550E-01	9,590E-01	9,624E-01
100,0	1,000E+00	1,000E+00	1,000E+00	1,000E+00	1,000E+00	1,000E+00	1,000E+00	1,000E+00	1,000E+00	1,000E+00
100,2	1,166E+00	1,122E+00	1,096E+00	1,080E+00	1,068E+00	1,059E+00	1,053E+00	1,047E+00	1,043E+00	1,039E+00
100,4	1,359E+00	1,259E+00	1,202E+00	1,166E+00	1,141E+00	1,122E+00	1,108E+00	1,096E+00	1,087E+00	1,080E+00
100,6	1,585E+00	1,413E+00	1,318E+00	1,259E+00	1,218E+00	1,189E+00	1,166E+00	1,148E+00	1,134E+00	1,122E+00
100,8	1,848E+00	1,585E+00	1,445E+00	1,359E+00	1,301E+00	1,259E+00	1,227E+00	1,202E+00	1,182E+00	1,166E+00
101,0	2,154E+00	1,778E+00	1,585E+00	1,468E+00	1,389E+00	1,334E+00	1,292E+00	1,259E+00	1,233E+00	1,212E+00
101,2	2,512E+00	1,995E+00	1,738E+00	1,585E+00	1,484E+00	1,413E+00	1,359E+00	1,318E+00	1,286E+00	1,259E+00
101,4	2,929E+00	2,239E+00	1,905E+00	1,711E+00	1,585E+00	1,496E+00	1,431E+00	1,380E+00	1,341E+00	1,308E+00
101,6	3,415E+00	2,512E+00	2,089E+00	1,848E+00	1,693E+00	1,585E+00	1,506E+00	1,445E+00	1,398E+00	1,359E+00
101,8	3,981E+00	2,818E+00	2,291E+00	1,995E+00	1,808E+00	1,679E+00	1,585E+00	1,514E+00	1,458E+00	1,413E+00
102,0	4,642E+00	3,162E+00	2,512E+00	2,154E+00	1,931E+00	1,778E+00	1,668E+00	1,585E+00	1,520E+00	1,468E+00
102,2	5,412E+00	3,548E+00	2,754E+00	2,326E+00	2,062E+00	1,884E+00	1,756E+00	1,660E+00	1,585E+00	1,525E+00
102,4	6,310E+00	3,981E+00	3,020E+00	2,512E+00	2,202E+00	1,995E+00	1,848E+00	1,738E+00	1,653E+00	1,585E+00
102,6	7,356E+00	4,467E+00	3,311E+00	2,712E+00	2,352E+00	2,113E+00	1,945E+00	1,820E+00	1,723E+00	1,647E+00
102,8	8,577E+00	5,012E+00	3,631E+00	2,929E+00	2,512E+00	2,239E+00	2,047E+00	1,905E+00	1,797E+00	1,711E+00
103,0	1,000E+01	5,623E+00	3,981E+00	3,162E+00	2,683E+00	2,371E+00	2,154E+00	1,995E+00	1,874E+00	1,778E+00
103,2	1,166E+01	6,310E+00	4,365E+00	3,415E+00	2,865E+00	2,512E+00	2,268E+00	2,089E+00	1,954E+00	1,848E+00
103,4	1,359E+01	7,079E+00	4,786E+00	3,687E+00	3,060E+00	2,661E+00	2,387E+00	2,188E+00	2,037E+00	1,920E+00
103,6	1,585E+01	7,943E+00	5,248E+00	3,981E+00	3,268E+00	2,818E+00	2,512E+00	2,291E+00	2,125E+00	1,995E+00
103,8	1,848E+01	8,913E+00	5,754E+00	4,299E+00	3,490E+00	2,985E+00	2,644E+00	2,399E+00	2,215E+00	2,073E+00
104,0	2,154E+01	1,000E+01	6,310E+00	4,642E+00	3,728E+00	3,162E+00	2,783E+00	2,512E+00	2,310E+00	2,154E+00
104,2	2,512E+01	1,122E+01	6,918E+00	5,012E+00	3,981E+00	3,350E+00	2,929E+00	2,630E+00	2,409E+00	2,239E+00
104,4	2,929E+01	1,259E+01	7,586E+00	5,412E+00	4,252E+00	3,548E+00	3,082E+00	2,754E+00	2,512E+00	2,326E+00
104,6	3,415E+01	1,413E+01	8,318E+00	5,843E+00	4,541E+00	3,758E+00	3,244E+00	2,884E+00	2,619E+00	2,417E+00
104,8	3,981E+01	1,585E+01	9,120E+00	6,310E+00	4,850E+00	3,981E+00	3,415E+00	3,020E+00	2,731E+00	2,512E+00
105,0	4,642E+01	1,778E+01	1,000E+01	6,813E+00	5,179E+00	4,217E+00	3,594E+00	3,162E+00	2,848E+00	2,610E+00
105,2	5,412E+01	1,995E+01	1,096E+01	7,356E+00	5,532E+00	4,467E+00	3,782E+00	3,311E+00	2,970E+00	2,712E+00
105,4	6,310E+01	2,239E+01	1,202E+01	7,943E+00	5,908E+00	4,732E+00	3,981E+00	3,467E+00	3,097E+00	2,818E+00
105,6	7,356E+01	2,512E+01	1,318E+01	8,577E+00	6,310E+00	5,012E+00	4,190E+00	3,631E+00	3,229E+00	2,929E+00
105,8	8,577E+01	2,818E+01	1,445E+01	9,261E+00	6,739E+00	5,309E+00	4,410E+00	3,802E+00	3,367E+00	3,043E+00
106,0	1,000E+02	3,162E+01	1,585E+01	1,000E+01	7,197E+00	5,623E+00	4,642E+00	3,981E+00	3,511E+00	3,162E+00
106,2	1,166E+02	3,548E+01	1,738E+01	1,080E+01	7,686E+00	5,957E+00	4,885E+00	4,169E+00	3,661E+00	3,286E+00
106,4	1,359E+02	3,981E+01	1,905E+01	1,166E+01	8,209E+00	6,310E+00	5,142E+00	4,365E+00	3,818E+00	3,415E+00
106,6	1,585E+02	4,467E+01	2,089E+01	1,259E+01	8,767E+00	6,683E+00	5,412E+00	4,571E+00	3,981E+00	3,548E+00
106,8	1,848E+02	5,012E+01	2,291E+01	1,359E+01	9,363E+00	7,079E+00	5,696E+00	4,786E+00	4,151E+00	3,687E+00
107,0	2,154E+02	5,623E+01	2,512E+01	1,468E+01	1,000E+01	7,499E+00	5,995E+00	5,012E+00	4,329E+00	3,831E+00

Table 4 (cont.)

Temp. C	Z Value 14 C	16 C	18 C	20 C	25 C	30 C	35 C	40 C	45 C	50 C
75,0	1,638E-02	2,738E-02	4,084E-02	5,623E-02	1,000E-01	1,468E-01	1,931E-01	2,371E-01	2,783E-01	3,162E-01
75,5	1,778E-02	2,943E-02	4,354E-02	5,957E-02	1,047E-01	1,525E-01	1,995E-01	2,441E-01	2,855E-01	3,236E-01
76,0	1,931E-02	3,162E-02	4,642E-02	6,310E-02	1,096E-01	1,585E-01	2,062E-01	2,512E-01	2,929E-01	3,311E-01
76,5	2,096E-02	3,398E-02	4,948E-02	6,683E-02	1,148E-01	1,647E-01	2,131E-01	2,585E-01	3,005E-01	3,388E-01
77,0	2,276E-02	3,652E-02	5,275E-02	7,079E-02	1,202E-01	1,711E-01	2,202E-01	2,661E-01	3,082E-01	3,467E-01
77,5	2,471E-02	3,924E-02	5,623E-02	7,499E-02	1,259E-01	1,778E-01	2,276E-01	2,738E-01	3,162E-01	3,548E-01
78,0	2,683E-02	4,217E-02	5,995E-02	7,943E-02	1,318E-01	1,848E-01	2,352E-01	2,818E-01	3,244E-01	3,631E-01
78,5	2,913E-02	4,532E-02	6,391E-02	8,414E-02	1,380E-01	1,920E-01	2,431E-01	2,901E-01	3,328E-01	3,715E-01
79,0	3,162E-02	4,870E-02	6,813E-02	8,913E-02	1,445E-01	1,995E-01	2,512E-01	2,985E-01	3,415E-01	3,802E-01
79,5	3,433E-02	5,233E-02	7,263E-02	9,441E-02	1,514E-01	2,073E-01	2,596E-01	3,073E-01	3,503E-01	3,890E-01
80,0	3,728E-02	5,623E-02	7,743E-02	1,000E-01	1,585E-01	2,154E-01	2,683E-01	3,162E-01	3,594E-01	3,981E-01
80,5	4,047E-02	6,043E-02	8,254E-02	1,059E-01	1,660E-01	2,239E-01	2,772E-01	3,255E-01	3,687E-01	4,074E-01
81,0	4,394E-02	6,494E-02	8,799E-02	1,122E-01	1,738E-01	2,326E-01	2,865E-01	3,350E-01	3,782E-01	4,169E-01
81,5	4,771E-02	6,978E-02	9,380E-02	1,189E-01	1,820E-01	2,417E-01	2,961E-01	3,447E-01	3,881E-01	4,266E-01
82,0	5,179E-02	7,499E-02	1,000E-01	1,259E-01	1,905E-01	2,512E-01	3,060E-01	3,548E-01	3,981E-01	4,365E-01
82,5	5,623E-02	8,058E-02	1,066E-01	1,334E-01	1,995E-01	2,610E-01	3,162E-01	3,652E-01	4,084E-01	4,467E-01
83,0	6,105E-02	8,660E-02	1,136E-01	1,413E-01	2,089E-01	2,712E-01	3,268E-01	3,758E-01	4,190E-01	4,571E-01
83,5	6,629E-02	9,306E-02	1,212E-01	1,496E-01	2,188E-01	2,818E-01	3,377E-01	3,868E-01	4,299E-01	4,677E-01
84,0	7,197E-02	1,000E-01	1,292E-01	1,585E-01	2,291E-01	2,929E-01	3,490E-01	3,981E-01	4,410E-01	4,786E-01
84,5	7,814E-02	1,075E-01	1,377E-01	1,679E-01	2,399E-01	3,043E-01	3,607E-01	4,097E-01	4,524E-01	4,898E-01
85,0	8,483E-02	1,155E-01	1,468E-01	1,778E-01	2,512E-01	3,162E-01	3,728E-01	4,217E-01	4,642E-01	5,012E-01
85,5	9,211E-02	1,241E-01	1,565E-01	1,884E-01	2,630E-01	3,286E-01	3,852E-01	4,340E-01	4,762E-01	5,129E-01
86,0	1,000E-01	1,334E-01	1,668E-01	1,995E-01	2,754E-01	3,415E-01	3,981E-01	4,467E-01	4,885E-01	5,248E-01
86,5	1,086E-01	1,433E-01	1,778E-01	2,113E-01	2,884E-01	3,548E-01	4,114E-01	4,597E-01	5,012E-01	5,370E-01
87,0	1,179E-01	1,540E-01	1,896E-01	2,239E-01	3,020E-01	3,687E-01	4,252E-01	4,732E-01	5,142E-01	5,495E-01
87,5	1,280E-01	1,655E-01	2,021E-01	2,371E-01	3,162E-01	3,831E-01	4,394E-01	4,870E-01	5,275E-01	5,623E-01
88,0	1,389E-01	1,778E-01	2,154E-01	2,512E-01	3,311E-01	3,981E-01	4,541E-01	5,012E-01	5,412E-01	5,754E-01
88,5	1,509E-01	1,911E-01	2,297E-01	2,661E-01	3,467E-01	4,137E-01	4,693E-01	5,158E-01	5,552E-01	5,888E-01
89,0	1,638E-01	2,054E-01	2,448E-01	2,818E-01	3,631E-01	4,299E-01	4,850E-01	5,309E-01	5,696E-01	6,026E-01
89,5	1,778E-01	2,207E-01	2,610E-01	2,985E-01	3,802E-01	4,467E-01	5,012E-01	5,464E-01	5,843E-01	6,166E-01
90,0	1,931E-01	2,371E-01	2,783E-01	3,162E-01	3,981E-01	4,642E-01	5,179E-01	5,623E-01	5,995E-01	6,310E-01
90,5	2,096E-01	2,548E-01	2,966E-01	3,350E-01	4,169E-01	4,823E-01	5,353E-01	5,788E-01	6,150E-01	6,457E-01
91,0	2,276E-01	2,738E-01	3,162E-01	3,548E-01	4,365E-01	5,012E-01	5,532E-01	5,957E-01	6,310E-01	6,607E-01
91,5	2,471E-01	2,943E-01	3,371E-01	3,758E-01	4,571E-01	5,208E-01	5,717E-01	6,131E-01	6,473E-01	6,761E-01
92,0	2,683E-01	3,162E-01	3,594E-01	3,981E-01	4,786E-01	5,412E-01	5,908E-01	6,310E-01	6,641E-01	6,918E-01
92,5	2,913E-01	3,398E-01	3,831E-01	4,217E-01	5,012E-01	5,623E-01	6,105E-01	6,494E-01	6,813E-01	7,079E-01
93,0	3,162E-01	3,652E-01	4,084E-01	4,467E-01	5,248E-01	5,843E-01	6,310E-01	6,683E-01	6,989E-01	7,244E-01
93,5	3,433E-01	3,924E-01	4,354E-01	4,732E-01	5,495E-01	6,072E-01	6,521E-01	6,879E-01	7,171E-01	7,413E-01
94,0	3,728E-01	4,217E-01	4,642E-01	5,012E-01	5,754E-01	6,310E-01	6,739E-01	7,079E-01	7,356E-01	7,586E-01
94,5	4,047E-01	4,532E-01	4,948E-01	5,309E-01	6,026E-01	6,556E-01	6,964E-01	7,286E-01	7,547E-01	7,762E-01
95,0	4,394E-01	4,870E-01	5,275E-01	5,623E-01	6,310E-01	6,813E-01	7,197E-01	7,499E-01	7,743E-01	7,943E-01
95,2	4,541E-01	5,012E-01	5,412E-01	5,754E-01	6,427E-01	6,918E-01	7,292E-01	7,586E-01	7,822E-01	8,017E-01
95,4	4,693E-01	5,158E-01	5,552E-01	5,888E-01	6,546E-01	7,025E-01	7,389E-01	7,674E-01	7,903E-01	8,091E-01
95,6	4,850E-01	5,309E-01	5,696E-01	6,026E-01	6,668E-01	7,134E-01	7,487E-01	7,762E-01	7,984E-01	8,166E-01
95,8	5,012E-01	5,464E-01	5,843E-01	6,166E-01	6,792E-01	7,244E-01	7,586E-01	7,852E-01	8,066E-01	8,241E-01
96,0	5,179E-01	5,623E-01	5,995E-01	6,310E-01	6,918E-01	7,356E-01	7,686E-01	7,943E-01	8,149E-01	8,318E-01
96,2	5,353E-01	5,788E-01	6,150E-01	6,457E-01	7,047E-01	7,470E-01	7,788E-01	8,035E-01	8,233E-01	8,395E-01
96,4	5,532E-01	5,957E-01	6,310E-01	6,607E-01	7,178E-01	7,586E-01	7,891E-01	8,128E-01	8,318E-01	8,472E-01
96,6	5,717E-01	6,131E-01	6,473E-01	6,761E-01	7,311E-01	7,703E-01	7,996E-01	8,222E-01	8,403E-01	8,551E-01
96,8	5,908E-01	6,310E-01	6,641E-01	6,918E-01	7,447E-01	7,822E-01	8,102E-01	8,318E-01	8,490E-01	8,630E-01
97,0	6,105E-01	6,494E-01	6,813E-01	7,079E-01	7,586E-01	7,943E-01	8,209E-01	8,414E-01	8,577E-01	8,710E-01
97,2	6,310E-01	6,683E-01	6,989E-01	7,244E-01	7,727E-01	8,066E-01	8,318E-01	8,511E-01	8,665E-01	8,790E-01
97,4	6,521E-01	6,879E-01	7,171E-01	7,413E-01	7,870E-01	8,191E-01	8,428E-01	8,610E-01	8,754E-01	8,872E-01
97,6	6,739E-01	7,079E-01	7,356E-01	7,586E-01	8,017E-01	8,318E-01	8,539E-01	8,710E-01	8,844E-01	8,954E-01
97,8	6,964E-01	7,286E-01	7,547E-01	7,762E-01	8,166E-01	8,446E-01	8,653E-01	8,810E-01	8,935E-01	9,036E-01
98,0	7,197E-01	7,499E-01	7,743E-01	7,943E-01	8,318E-01	8,577E-01	8,767E-01	8,913E-01	9,027E-01	9,120E-01
98,2	7,438E-01	7,718E-01	7,943E-01	8,128E-01	8,472E-01	8,710E-01	8,883E-01	9,016E-01	9,120E-01	9,204E-01
98,4	7,686E-01	7,943E-01	8,149E-01	8,318E-01	8,630E-01	8,844E-01	9,001E-01	9,120E-01	9,214E-01	9,290E-01
98,6	7,943E-01	8,175E-01	8,360E-01	8,511E-01	8,790E-01	8,981E-01	9,120E-01	9,226E-01	9,309E-01	9,376E-01
98,8	8,209E-01	8,414E-01	8,577E-01	8,710E-01	8,954E-01	9,120E-01	9,241E-01	9,333E-01	9,404E-01	9,462E-01
99,0	8,483E-01	8,660E-01	8,799E-01	8,913E-01	9,120E-01	9,261E-01	9,363E-01	9,441E-01	9,501E-01	9,550E-01
99,2	8,767E-01	8,913E-01	9,027E-01	9,120E-01	9,290E-01	9,404E-01	9,487E-01	9,550E-01	9,599E-01	9,638E-01
99,4	9,060E-01	9,173E-01	9,261E-01	9,333E-01	9,462E-01	9,550E-01	9,613E-01	9,661E-01	9,698E-01	9,727E-01
99,6	9,363E-01	9,441E-01	9,501E-01	9,550E-01	9,638E-01	9,698E-01	9,740E-01	9,772E-01	9,797E-01	9,817E-01
99,8	9,676E-01	9,716E-01	9,747E-01	9,772E-01	9,817E-01	9,848E-01	9,869E-01	9,886E-01	9,898E-01	9,908E-01
100,0	1,000E+00	1,000E+00	1,000E+00	1,000E+00	1,000E+00	1,000E+00	1,000E+00	1,000E+00	1,000E+00	1,000E+00
100,2	1,033E+00	1,029E+00	1,026E+00	1,023E+00	1,019E+00	1,015E+00	1,013E+00	1,012E+00	1,010E+00	1,009E+00
100,4	1,068E+00	1,059E+00	1,053E+00	1,047E+00	1,038E+00	1,031E+00	1,027E+00	1,023E+00	1,021E+00	1,019E+00
100,6	1,104E+00	1,090E+00	1,080E+00	1,072E+00	1,057E+00	1,047E+00	1,040E+00	1,035E+00	1,031E+00	1,028E+00
100,8	1,141E+00	1,122E+00	1,108E+00	1,096E+00	1,076E+00	1,063E+00	1,054E+00	1,047E+00	1,042E+00	1,038E+00
101,0	1,179E+00	1,155E+00	1,136E+00	1,122E+00	1,096E+00	1,080E+00	1,068E+00	1,059E+00	1,053E+00	1,047E+00
101,2	1,218E+00	1,189E+00	1,166E+00	1,148E+00	1,117E+00	1,096E+00	1,082E+00	1,072E+00	1,063E+00	1,057E+00
101,4	1,259E+00	1,223E+00	1,196E+00	1,175E+00	1,138E+00	1,113E+00	1,096E+00	1,084E+00	1,074E+00	1,067E+00
101,6	1,301E+00	1,259E+00	1,227E+00	1,202E+00	1,159E+00	1,131E+00	1,111E+00	1,096E+00	1,085E+00	1,076E+00
101,8	1,345E+00	1,296E+00	1,259E+00	1,230E+00	1,180E+00	1,148E+00	1,126E+00	1,109E+00	1,096E+00	1,086E+00
102,0	1,389E+00	1,334E+00	1,292E+00	1,259E+00	1,202E+00	1,166E+00	1,141E+00	1,122E+00	1,108E+00	1,096E+00
102,2	1,436E+00	1,372E+00	1,325E+00	1,288E+00	1,225E+00	1,184E+00	1,156E+00	1,135E+00	1,119E+00	1,107E+00
102,4	1,484E+00	1,413E+00	1,359E+00	1,318E+00	1,247E+00	1,202E+00	1,171E+00	1,148E+00	1,131E+00	1,117E+00
102,6	1,534E+00	1,454E+00	1,395E+00	1,349E+00	1,271E+00	1,221E+00	1,187E+00	1,161E+00	1,142E+00	1,127E+00
102,8	1,585E+00	1,496E+00	1,431E+00	1,380E+00	1,294E+00	1,240E+00	1,202E+00	1,175E+00	1,154E+00	1,138E+00
103,0	1,638E+00	1,540E+00	1,468E+00	1,413E+00	1,318E+00	1,259E+00	1,218E+00	1,189E+00	1,166E+00	1,148E+00
103,2	1,693E+00	1,585E+00	1,506E+00	1,445E+00	1,343E+00	1,278E+00	1,234E+00	1,202E+00	1,178E+00	1,159E+00
103,4	1,749E+00	1,631E+00	1,545E+00	1,479E+00	1,368E+00	1,298E+00	1,251E+00	1,216E+00	1,190E+00	1,169E+00
103,6	1,808E+00	1,679E+00	1,585E+00	1,514E+00	1,393E+00	1,318E+00	1,267E+00	1,230E+00	1,202E+00	1,180E+00
103,8	1,868E+00	1,728E+00	1,626E+00	1,549E+00	1,419E+00	1,339E+00	1,284E+00	1,245E+00	1,215E+00	1,191E+00
104,0	1,931E+00	1,778E+00	1,668E+00	1,585E+00	1,445E+00	1,359E+00	1,301E+00	1,259E+00	1,227E+00	1,202E+00
104,2	1,995E+00	1,830E+00	1,711E+00	1,622E+00	1,472E+00	1,380E+00	1,318E+00	1,274E+00	1,240E+00	1,213E+00
104,4	2,062E+00	1,884E+00	1,756E+00	1,660E+00	1,500E+00	1,402E+00	1,336E+00	1,288E+00	1,253E+00	1,225E+00
104,6	2,131E+00	1,939E+00	1,801E+00	1,698E+00	1,528E+00	1,423E+00	1,353E+00	1,303E+00	1,265E+00	1,236E+00
104,8	2,202E+00	1,995E+00	1,848E+00	1,738E+00	1,556E+00	1,445E+00	1,371E+00	1,318E+00	1,278E+00	1,247E+00
105,0	2,276E+00	2,054E+00	1,896E+00	1,778E+00	1,585E+00	1,468E+00	1,389E+00	1,334E+00	1,292E+00	1,259E+00
105,2	2,352E+00	2,113E+00	1,945E+00	1,820E+00	1,614E+00	1,491E+00	1,408E+00	1,349E+00	1,305E+00	1,271E+00
105,4	2,431E+00	2,175E+00	1,995E+00	1,862E+00	1,644E+00	1,514E+00	1,427E+00	1,365E+00	1,318E+00	1,282E+00
105,6	2,512E+00	2,239E+00	2,047E+00	1,905E+00	1,675E+00	1,537E+00	1,445E+00	1,380E+00	1,332E+00	1,294E+00
105,8	2,596E+00	2,304E+00	2,100E+00	1,950E+00	1,706E+00	1,561E+00	1,465E+00	1,396E+00	1,346E+00	1,306E+00
106,0	2,683E+00	2,371E+00	2,154E+00	1,995E+00	1,738E+00	1,585E+00	1,484E+00	1,413E+00	1,359E+00	1,318E+00
106,2	2,772E+00	2,441E+00	2,210E+00	2,042E+00	1,770E+00	1,609E+00	1,504E+00	1,429E+00	1,373E+00	1,330E+00
106,4	2,865E+00	2,512E+00	2,268E+00	2,089E+00	1,803E+00	1,634E+00	1,524E+00	1,445E+00	1,387E+00	1,343E+00
106,6	2,961E+00	2,585E+00	2,326E+00	2,138E+00	1,837E+00	1,660E+00	1,544E+00	1,462E+00	1,402E+00	1,355E+00
106,8	3,060E+00	2,661E+00	2,387E+00	2,188E+00	1,871E+00	1,685E+00	1,564E+00	1,479E+00	1,416E+00	1,368E+00
107,0	3,162E+00	2,738E+00	2,448E+00	2,239E+00	1,905E+00	1,711E+00	1,585E+00	1,496E+00	1,431E+00	1,380E+00

Table 5 Lethal rates, min at the 120 C reference temperature/min at *T* C

$$F^{z}_{120}\big/ F^{z}_{T} = 10^{\frac{T-120}{z\,\mathrm{C}}}$$

T C	Z 3 C	4 C	5 C	6 C	7 C	8 C	9 C	10 C	11 C	12
93.0	1.000E-09	1.778E-07	3.981E-06	3.162E-05	1.389E-04	4.217E-04	1.000E-03	1.995E-03	3.511E-03	5.623
93.5	1.468E-09	2.371E-07	5.012E-06	3.831E-05	1.638E-04	4.870E-04	1.136E-03	2.239E-03	3.899E-03	6.190
94.0	2.154E-09	3.162E-07	6.310E-06	4.642E-05	1.931E-04	5.623E-04	1.292E-03	2.512E-03	4.329E-03	6.813
94.5	3.162E-09	4.217E-07	7.943E-06	5.623E-05	2.276E-04	6.494E-04	1.468E-03	2.818E-03	4.806E-03	7.499
95.0	4.642E-09	5.623E-07	1.000E-05	6.813E-05	2.683E-04	7.499E-04	1.668E-03	3.162E-03	5.337E-03	8.254
95.5	6.813E-09	7.499E-07	1.259E-05	8.254E-05	3.162E-04	8.660E-04	1.896E-03	3.548E-03	5.926E-03	9.085
96.0	1.000E-08	1.000E-06	1.585E-05	1.000E-04	3.728E-04	1.000E-03	2.154E-03	3.981E-03	6.579E-03	1.000
96.5	1.468E-08	1.334E-06	1.995E-05	1.212E-04	4.394E-04	1.155E-03	2.448E-03	4.467E-03	7.305E-03	1.101
97.0	2.154E-08	1.778E-06	2.512E-05	1.468E-04	5.179E-04	1.334E-03	2.783E-03	5.012E-03	8.111E-03	1.212
97.5	3.162E-08	2.371E-06	3.162E-05	1.778E-04	6.105E-04	1.540E-03	3.162E-03	5.623E-03	9.006E-03	1.334
98.0	4.642E-08	3.162E-06	3.981E-05	2.154E-04	7.197E-04	1.778E-03	3.594E-03	6.310E-03	1.000E-02	1.468
98.5	6.813E-08	4.217E-06	5.012E-05	2.610E-04	8.483E-04	2.054E-03	4.084E-03	7.079E-03	1.110E-02	1.616
99.0	1.000E-07	5.623E-06	6.310E-05	3.162E-04	1.000E-03	2.371E-03	4.642E-03	7.943E-03	1.233E-02	1.778
99.5	1.468E-07	7.499E-06	7.943E-05	3.831E-04	1.179E-03	2.738E-03	5.275E-03	8.913E-03	1.369E-02	1.957
100.0	2.154E-07	1.000E-05	1.000E-04	4.642E-04	1.389E-03	3.162E-03	5.995E-03	1.000E-02	1.520E-02	2.154
100.5	3.162E-07	1.334E-05	1.259E-04	5.623E-04	1.638E-03	3.652E-03	6.813E-03	1.122E-02	1.688E-02	2.371
101.0	4.642E-07	1.778E-05	1.585E-04	6.813E-04	1.931E-03	4.217E-03	7.743E-03	1.259E-02	1.874E-02	2.610
101.5	6.813E-07	2.371E-05	1.995E-04	8.254E-04	2.276E-03	4.870E-03	8.799E-03	1.413E-02	2.081E-02	2.873
102.0	1.000E-06	3.162E-05	2.512E-04	1.000E-03	2.683E-03	5.623E-03	1.000E-02	1.585E-02	2.310E-02	3.162
102.5	1.468E-06	4.217E-05	3.162E-04	1.212E-03	3.162E-03	6.494E-03	1.136E-02	1.778E-02	2.565E-02	3.481
103.0	2.154E-06	5.623E-05	3.981E-04	1.468E-03	3.728E-03	7.499E-03	1.292E-02	1.995E-02	2.848E-02	3.831
103.5	3.162E-06	7.499E-05	5.012E-04	1.778E-03	4.394E-03	8.660E-03	1.468E-02	2.239E-02	3.162E-02	4.217
104.0	4.642E-06	1.000E-04	6.310E-04	2.154E-03	5.179E-03	1.000E-02	1.668E-02	2.512E-02	3.511E-02	4.642
104.5	6.813E-06	1.334E-04	7.943E-04	2.610E-03	6.105E-03	1.155E-02	1.896E-02	2.818E-02	3.899E-02	5.109
105.0	1.000E-05	1.778E-04	1.000E-03	3.162E-03	7.197E-03	1.334E-02	2.154E-02	3.162E-02	4.329E-02	5.623
105.5	1.468E-05	2.371E-04	1.259E-03	3.831E-03	8.483E-03	1.540E-02	2.448E-02	3.548E-02	4.806E-02	6.190
106.0	2.154E-05	3.162E-04	1.585E-03	4.642E-03	1.000E-02	1.778E-02	2.783E-02	3.981E-02	5.337E-02	6.813
106.5	3.162E-05	4.217E-04	1.995E-03	5.623E-03	1.179E-02	2.054E-02	3.162E-02	4.467E-02	5.926E-02	7.499
107.0	4.642E-05	5.623E-04	2.512E-03	6.813E-03	1.389E-02	2.371E-02	3.594E-02	5.012E-02	6.579E-02	8.254
107.5	6.813E-05	7.499E-04	3.162E-03	8.254E-03	1.638E-02	2.738E-02	4.084E-02	5.623E-02	7.305E-02	9.085
108.0	1.000E-04	1.000E-03	3.981E-03	1.000E-02	1.931E-02	3.162E-02	4.642E-02	6.310E-02	8.111E-02	1.000
108.5	1.468E-04	1.334E-03	5.012E-03	1.212E-02	2.276E-02	3.652E-02	5.275E-02	7.079E-02	9.006E-02	1.101
109.0	2.154E-04	1.778E-03	6.310E-03	1.468E-02	2.683E-02	4.217E-02	5.995E-02	7.943E-02	1.000E-01	1.212
109.5	3.162E-04	2.371E-03	7.943E-03	1.778E-02	3.162E-02	4.870E-02	6.813E-02	8.913E-02	1.110E-01	1.334
110.0	4.642E-04	3.162E-03	1.000E-02	2.154E-02	3.728E-02	5.623E-02	7.743E-02	1.000E-01	1.233E-01	1.468
110.5	6.813E-04	4.217E-03	1.259E-02	2.610E-02	4.394E-02	6.494E-02	8.799E-02	1.122E-01	1.369E-01	1.616
111.0	1.000E-03	5.623E-03	1.585E-02	3.162E-02	5.179E-02	7.499E-02	1.000E-01	1.259E-01	1.520E-01	1.778
111.5	1.468E-03	7.499E-03	1.995E-02	3.831E-02	6.105E-02	8.660E-02	1.136E-01	1.413E-01	1.688E-01	1.957
112.0	2.154E-03	1.000E-02	2.512E-02	4.642E-02	7.197E-02	1.000E-01	1.292E-01	1.585E-01	1.874E-01	2.154
112.5	3.162E-03	1.334E-02	3.162E-02	5.623E-02	8.483E-02	1.155E-01	1.468E-01	1.778E-01	2.081E-01	2.371
113.0	4.642E-03	1.778E-02	3.981E-02	6.813E-02	1.000E-01	1.334E-01	1.668E-01	1.995E-01	2.310E-01	2.610
113.5	6.813E-03	2.371E-02	5.012E-02	8.254E-02	1.179E-01	1.540E-01	1.896E-01	2.239E-01	2.565E-01	2.873
114.0	1.000E-02	3.162E-02	6.310E-02	1.000E-01	1.389E-01	1.778E-01	2.154E-01	2.512E-01	2.848E-01	3.162
114.5	1.468E-02	4.217E-02	7.943E-02	1.212E-01	1.638E-01	2.054E-01	2.448E-01	2.818E-01	3.162E-01	3.481
115.0	2.154E-02	5.623E-02	1.000E-01	1.468E-01	1.931E-01	2.371E-01	2.783E-01	3.162E-01	3.511E-01	3.831
115.2	2.512E-02	6.310E-02	1.096E-01	1.585E-01	2.062E-01	2.512E-01	2.929E-01	3.311E-01	3.661E-01	3.981
115.4	2.929E-02	7.079E-02	1.202E-01	1.711E-01	2.202E-01	2.661E-01	3.082E-01	3.467E-01	3.818E-01	4.137
115.6	3.415E-02	7.943E-02	1.318E-01	1.848E-01	2.352E-01	2.818E-01	3.244E-01	3.631E-01	3.981E-01	4.299
115.8	3.981E-02	8.913E-02	1.445E-01	1.995E-01	2.512E-01	2.985E-01	3.415E-01	3.802E-01	4.151E-01	4.467
116.0	4.642E-02	1.000E-01	1.585E-01	2.154E-01	2.683E-01	3.162E-01	3.594E-01	3.981E-01	4.329E-01	4.642
116.2	5.412E-02	1.122E-01	1.738E-01	2.326E-01	2.865E-01	3.350E-01	3.782E-01	4.169E-01	4.514E-01	4.823
116.4	6.310E-02	1.259E-01	1.905E-01	2.512E-01	3.060E-01	3.548E-01	3.981E-01	4.365E-01	4.707E-01	5.012
116.6	7.356E-02	1.413E-01	2.089E-01	2.712E-01	3.268E-01	3.758E-01	4.190E-01	4.571E-01	4.908E-01	5.208
116.8	8.577E-02	1.585E-01	2.291E-01	2.929E-01	3.490E-01	3.981E-01	4.410E-01	4.786E-01	5.118E-01	5.412
117.0	1.000E-01	1.778E-01	2.512E-01	3.162E-01	3.728E-01	4.217E-01	4.642E-01	5.012E-01	5.337E-01	5.623
117.2	1.166E-01	1.995E-01	2.754E-01	3.415E-01	3.981E-01	4.467E-01	4.885E-01	5.248E-01	5.565E-01	5.843
117.4	1.359E-01	2.239E-01	3.020E-01	3.687E-01	4.252E-01	4.732E-01	5.142E-01	5.495E-01	5.803E-01	6.072
117.6	1.585E-01	2.512E-01	3.311E-01	3.981E-01	4.541E-01	5.012E-01	5.412E-01	5.754E-01	6.051E-01	6.310
117.8	1.848E-01	2.818E-01	3.631E-01	4.299E-01	4.850E-01	5.309E-01	5.696E-01	6.026E-01	6.310E-01	6.556
118.0	2.154E-01	3.162E-01	3.981E-01	4.642E-01	5.179E-01	5.623E-01	5.995E-01	6.310E-01	6.579E-01	6.813
118.2	2.512E-01	3.548E-01	4.365E-01	5.012E-01	5.532E-01	5.957E-01	6.310E-01	6.607E-01	6.861E-01	7.079
118.4	2.929E-01	3.981E-01	4.786E-01	5.412E-01	5.908E-01	6.310E-01	6.641E-01	6.918E-01	7.154E-01	7.356
118.6	3.415E-01	4.467E-01	5.248E-01	5.843E-01	6.310E-01	6.683E-01	6.989E-01	7.244E-01	7.460E-01	7.644
118.8	3.981E-01	5.012E-01	5.754E-01	6.310E-01	6.739E-01	7.079E-01	7.356E-01	7.586E-01	7.779E-01	7.943
119.0	4.642E-01	5.623E-01	6.310E-01	6.813E-01	7.197E-01	7.499E-01	7.743E-01	7.943E-01	8.111E-01	8.254
119.2	5.412E-01	6.310E-01	6.918E-01	7.356E-01	7.686E-01	7.943E-01	8.149E-01	8.318E-01	8.458E-01	8.577
119.4	6.310E-01	7.079E-01	7.586E-01	7.943E-01	8.209E-01	8.414E-01	8.577E-01	8.710E-01	8.820E-01	8.913
119.6	7.356E-01	7.943E-01	8.318E-01	8.577E-01	8.767E-01	8.913E-01	9.027E-01	9.120E-01	9.197E-01	9.261
119.8	8.577E-01	8.913E-01	9.120E-01	9.261E-01	9.363E-01	9.441E-01	9.501E-01	9.550E-01	9.590E-01	9.624
120.0	1.000E+00	1.000E+00	1.000E+00	1.000E+00	1.000E+00	1.000E+00	1.000E+00	1.000E+00	1.000E+00	1.000
120.2	1.166E+00	1.122E+00	1.096E+00	1.080E+00	1.068E+00	1.059E+00	1.053E+00	1.047E+00	1.043E+00	1.039
120.4	1.359E+00	1.259E+00	1.202E+00	1.166E+00	1.141E+00	1.122E+00	1.108E+00	1.096E+00	1.087E+00	1.080
120.6	1.585E+00	1.413E+00	1.318E+00	1.259E+00	1.218E+00	1.189E+00	1.166E+00	1.148E+00	1.134E+00	1.122
120.8	1.848E+00	1.585E+00	1.445E+00	1.359E+00	1.301E+00	1.259E+00	1.227E+00	1.202E+00	1.182E+00	1.166
121.0	2.154E+00	1.778E+00	1.585E+00	1.468E+00	1.389E+00	1.334E+00	1.292E+00	1.259E+00	1.233E+00	1.212
121.2	2.512E+00	1.995E+00	1.738E+00	1.585E+00	1.484E+00	1.413E+00	1.359E+00	1.318E+00	1.286E+00	1.259
121.4	2.929E+00	2.239E+00	1.905E+00	1.711E+00	1.585E+00	1.496E+00	1.431E+00	1.380E+00	1.341E+00	1.308
121.6	3.415E+00	2.512E+00	2.089E+00	1.848E+00	1.693E+00	1.585E+00	1.506E+00	1.445E+00	1.398E+00	1.359
121.8	3.981E+00	2.818E+00	2.291E+00	1.995E+00	1.808E+00	1.679E+00	1.585E+00	1.514E+00	1.458E+00	1.413
122.0	4.642E+00	3.162E+00	2.512E+00	2.154E+00	1.931E+00	1.778E+00	1.668E+00	1.585E+00	1.520E+00	1.468
122.2	5.412E+00	3.548E+00	2.754E+00	2.326E+00	2.062E+00	1.884E+00	1.756E+00	1.660E+00	1.585E+00	1.525
122.4	6.310E+00	3.981E+00	3.020E+00	2.512E+00	2.202E+00	1.995E+00	1.848E+00	1.738E+00	1.653E+00	1.585
122.6	7.356E+00	4.467E+00	3.311E+00	2.712E+00	2.352E+00	2.113E+00	1.945E+00	1.820E+00	1.723E+00	1.647
122.8	8.577E+00	5.012E+00	3.631E+00	2.929E+00	2.512E+00	2.239E+00	2.047E+00	1.905E+00	1.797E+00	1.711
123.0	1.000E+01	5.623E+00	3.981E+00	3.162E+00	2.683E+00	2.371E+00	2.154E+00	1.995E+00	1.874E+00	1.778
123.2	1.166E+01	6.310E+00	4.365E+00	3.415E+00	2.865E+00	2.512E+00	2.268E+00	2.089E+00	1.954E+00	1.848
123.4	1.359E+01	7.079E+00	4.786E+00	3.687E+00	3.060E+00	2.661E+00	2.387E+00	2.188E+00	2.037E+00	1.920
123.6	1.585E+01	7.943E+00	5.248E+00	3.981E+00	3.268E+00	2.818E+00	2.512E+00	2.291E+00	2.125E+00	1.995
123.8	1.848E+01	8.913E+00	5.754E+00	4.299E+00	3.490E+00	2.985E+00	2.644E+00	2.399E+00	2.215E+00	2.073
124.0	2.154E+01	1.000E+01	6.310E+00	4.642E+00	3.728E+00	3.162E+00	2.783E+00	2.512E+00	2.310E+00	2.154
124.2	2.512E+01	1.122E+01	6.918E+00	5.012E+00	3.981E+00	3.350E+00	2.929E+00	2.630E+00	2.409E+00	2.239
124.4	2.929E+01	1.259E+01	7.586E+00	5.412E+00	4.252E+00	3.548E+00	3.082E+00	2.754E+00	2.512E+00	2.326
124.6	3.415E+01	1.413E+01	8.318E+00	5.843E+00	4.541E+00	3.758E+00	3.244E+00	2.884E+00	2.619E+00	2.417
124.8	3.981E+01	1.585E+01	9.120E+00	6.310E+00	4.850E+00	3.981E+00	3.415E+00	3.020E+00	2.731E+00	2.512
125.0	4.642E+01	1.778E+01	1.000E+01	6.813E+00	5.179E+00	4.217E+00	3.594E+00	3.162E+00	2.848E+00	2.610
125.2	5.412E+01	1.995E+01	1.096E+01	7.356E+00	5.532E+00	4.467E+00	3.782E+00	3.311E+00	2.970E+00	2.712
125.4	6.310E+01	2.239E+01	1.202E+01	7.943E+00	5.908E+00	4.732E+00	3.981E+00	3.467E+00	3.097E+00	2.818
125.6	7.356E+01	2.512E+01	1.318E+01	8.577E+00	6.310E+00	5.012E+00	4.190E+00	3.631E+00	3.229E+00	2.929
125.8	8.577E+01	2.818E+01	1.445E+01	9.261E+00	6.739E+00	5.309E+00	4.410E+00	3.802E+00	3.367E+00	3.043
126.0	1.000E+02	3.162E+01	1.585E+01	1.000E+01	7.197E+00	5.623E+00	4.642E+00	3.981E+00	3.511E+00	3.162
126.2	1.166E+02	3.548E+01	1.738E+01	1.080E+01	7.686E+00	5.957E+00	4.885E+00	4.169E+00	3.661E+00	3.286
126.4	1.359E+02	3.981E+01	1.905E+01	1.166E+01	8.209E+00	6.310E+00	5.142E+00	4.365E+00	3.818E+00	3.415
126.6	1.585E+02	4.467E+01	2.089E+01	1.259E+01	8.767E+00	6.683E+00	5.412E+00	4.571E+00	3.981E+00	3.548
126.8	1.848E+02	5.012E+01	2.291E+01	1.359E+01	9.363E+00	7.079E+00	5.694E+00	4.786E+00	4.151E+00	3.687
127.0	2.154E+02	5.623E+01	2.512E+01	1.468E+01	1.000E+01	7.499E+00	5.995E+00	5.012E+00	4.329E+00	3.831
127.2	2.512E+02	6.310E+01	2.754E+01	1.585E+01	1.068E+01	7.943E+00	6.310E+00	5.248E+00	4.514E+00	3.981
127.4	2.929E+02	7.079E+01	3.020E+01	1.711E+01	1.141E+01	8.414E+00	6.641E+00	5.495E+00	4.707E+00	4.137
127.6	3.415E+02	7.943E+01	3.311E+01	1.848E+01	1.218E+01	8.913E+00	6.989E+00	5.754E+00	4.908E+00	4.299
127.8	3.981E+02	8.913E+01	3.631E+01	1.995E+01	1.301E+01	9.441E+00	7.356E+00	6.026E+00	5.118E+00	4.467
128.0	4.642E+02	1.000E+02	3.981E+01	2.154E+01	1.389E+01	1.000E+01	7.743E+00	6.310E+00	5.337E+00	4.642
128.2	5.412E+02	1.122E+02	4.365E+01	2.326E+01	1.484E+01	1.059E+01	8.149E+00	6.607E+00	5.565E+00	4.823
128.4	6.310E+02	1.259E+02	4.786E+01	2.512E+01	1.585E+01	1.122E+01	8.577E+00	6.918E+00	5.803E+00	5.012
128.6	7.356E+02	1.413E+02	5.248E+01	2.712E+01	1.693E+01	1.189E+01	9.027E+00	7.244E+00	6.051E+00	5.208
128.8	8.577E+02	1.585E+02	5.754E+01	2.929E+01	1.808E+01	1.259E+01	9.501E+00	7.586E+00	6.310E+00	5.412
129.0	1.000E+03	1.778E+02	6.310E+01	3.162E+01	1.931E+01	1.334E+01	1.000E+01	7.943E+00	6.579E+00	5.623
129.2	1.166E+03	1.995E+02	6.918E+01	3.415E+01	2.062E+01	1.413E+01	1.053E+01	8.318E+00	6.861E+00	5.843
129.4	1.359E+03	2.239E+02	7.586E+01	3.687E+01	2.202E+01	1.496E+01	1.108E+01	8.710E+00	7.154E+00	6.072
129.6	1.585E+03	2.512E+02	8.318E+01	3.981E+01	2.352E+01	1.585E+01	1.166E+01	9.120E+00	7.460E+00	6.310
129.8	1.848E+03	2.818E+02	9.120E+01	4.299E+01	2.512E+01	1.679E+01	1.227E+01	9.550E+00	7.779E+00	6.556
130.0	2.154E+03	3.162E+02	1.000E+02	4.642E+01	2.683E+01	1.778E+01	1.292E+01	1.000E+01	8.111E+00	6.813

14 C	16 C	18 C	20 C	25 C	30 C	35 C	40 C	45 C	50 C
1.179E-02	2.054E-02	3.162E-02	4.467E-02	8.318E-02	1.259E-01	1.493E-01	2.113E-01	2.512E-01	2.884E-01
1.288E-02	2.207E-02	3.371E-02	4.732E-02	8.710E-02	1.308E-01	1.749E-01	2.175E-01	2.577E-01	2.951E-01
1.389E-02	2.371E-02	3.594E-02	5.012E-02	9.120E-02	1.359E-01	1.804E-01	2.239E-01	2.644E-01	3.020E-01
1.509E-02	2.548E-02	3.831E-02	5.309E-02	9.550E-02	1.413E-01	1.865E-01	2.304E-01	2.712E-01	3.090E-01
1.634E-02	2.738E-02	4.084E-02	5.623E-02	1.000E-01	1.468E-01	1.931E-01	2.371E-01	2.785E-01	3.162E-01
1.778E-02	2.943E-02	4.354E-02	5.957E-02	1.047E-01	1.525E-01	1.995E-01	2.441E-01	2.855E-01	3.236E-01
1.931E-02	3.162E-02	4.642E-02	6.310E-02	1.096E-01	1.585E-01	2.062E-01	2.512E-01	2.929E-01	3.311E-01
2.096E-02	3.398E-02	4.948E-02	6.683E-02	1.148E-01	1.647E-01	2.131E-01	2.585E-01	3.005E-01	3.388E-01
2.274E-02	3.652E-02	5.275E-02	7.079E-02	1.202E-01	1.711E-01	2.202E-01	2.661E-01	3.082E-01	3.467E-01
2.471E-02	3.924E-02	5.623E-02	7.499E-02	1.259E-01	1.778E-01	2.274E-01	2.738E-01	3.162E-01	3.548E-01
2.683E-02	4.217E-02	5.995E-02	7.943E-02	1.318E-01	1.848E-01	2.352E-01	2.818E-01	3.244E-01	3.631E-01
2.911E-02	4.532E-02	6.391E-02	8.414E-02	1.380E-01	1.920E-01	2.431E-01	2.901E-01	3.328E-01	3.715E-01
3.162E-02	4.870E-02	6.813E-02	8.913E-02	1.445E-01	1.995E-01	2.512E-01	2.985E-01	3.415E-01	3.802E-01
3.431E-02	5.213E-02	7.263E-02	9.441E-02	1.514E-01	2.073E-01	2.594E-01	3.073E-01	3.503E-01	3.890E-01
3.724E-02	5.623E-02	7.743E-02	1.000E-01	1.585E-01	2.154E-01	2.683E-01	3.162E-01	3.594E-01	3.981E-01
4.047E-02	6.043E-02	8.254E-02	1.059E-01	1.660E-01	2.239E-01	2.772E-01	3.255E-01	3.687E-01	4.074E-01
4.394E-02	6.494E-02	8.799E-02	1.122E-01	1.738E-01	2.326E-01	2.865E-01	3.350E-01	3.782E-01	4.169E-01
4.771E-02	6.978E-02	9.380E-02	1.189E-01	1.820E-01	2.417E-01	2.961E-01	3.447E-01	3.881E-01	4.266E-01
5.179E-02	7.499E-02	1.000E-01	1.259E-01	1.905E-01	2.512E-01	3.064E-01	3.548E-01	3.981E-01	4.365E-01
5.623E-02	8.058E-02	1.066E-01	1.334E-01	1.995E-01	2.610E-01	3.162E-01	3.652E-01	4.084E-01	4.467E-01
6.105E-02	8.660E-02	1.136E-01	1.413E-01	2.089E-01	2.712E-01	3.268E-01	3.758E-01	4.190E-01	4.571E-01
6.628E-02	9.306E-02	1.212E-01	1.496E-01	2.188E-01	2.818E-01	3.377E-01	3.868E-01	4.299E-01	4.677E-01
7.197E-02	1.000E-01	1.292E-01	1.585E-01	2.291E-01	2.929E-01	3.490E-01	3.981E-01	4.416E-01	4.786E-01
7.816E-02	1.075E-01	1.377E-01	1.679E-01	2.399E-01	3.043E-01	3.607E-01	4.097E-01	4.524E-01	4.898E-01
8.483E-02	1.155E-01	1.468E-01	1.778E-01	2.512E-01	3.162E-01	3.728E-01	4.217E-01	4.642E-01	5.012E-01
9.211E-02	1.241E-01	1.565E-01	1.884E-01	2.630E-01	3.286E-01	3.852E-01	4.340E-01	4.762E-01	5.129E-01
1.000E-01	1.334E-01	1.668E-01	1.905E-01	2.754E-01	3.415E-01	3.981E-01	4.467E-01	4.885E-01	5.248E-01
1.084E-01	1.433E-01	1.778E-01	2.113E-01	2.884E-01	3.548E-01	4.114E-01	4.597E-01	5.012E-01	5.370E-01
1.179E-01	1.540E-01	1.896E-01	2.239E-01	3.020E-01	3.687E-01	4.252E-01	4.732E-01	5.142E-01	5.495E-01
1.288E-01	1.655E-01	2.021E-01	2.371E-01	3.162E-01	3.831E-01	4.394E-01	4.870E-01	5.275E-01	5.623E-01
1.389E-01	1.778E-01	2.154E-01	2.512E-01	3.311E-01	3.981E-01	4.541E-01	5.012E-01	5.412E-01	5.754E-01
1.509E-01	1.911E-01	2.297E-01	2.661E-01	3.467E-01	4.137E-01	4.693E-01	5.158E-01	5.552E-01	5.888E-01
1.634E-01	2.054E-01	2.448E-01	2.818E-01	3.631E-01	4.299E-01	4.853E-01	5.309E-01	5.649E-01	6.026E-01
1.778E-01	2.270E-01	2.610E-01	2.985E-01	3.802E-01	4.467E-01	5.012E-01	5.464E-01	5.843E-01	6.166E-01
1.931E-01	2.371E-01	2.783E-01	3.162E-01	3.981E-01	4.642E-01	5.179E-01	5.623E-01	5.995E-01	6.310E-01
2.094E-01	2.548E-01	2.966E-01	3.350E-01	4.169E-01	4.823E-01	5.353E-01	5.788E-01	6.150E-01	6.457E-01
2.274E-01	2.738E-01	3.162E-01	3.548E-01	4.365E-01	5.012E-01	5.532E-01	5.957E-01	6.310E-01	6.607E-01
2.471E-01	2.943E-01	3.371E-01	3.758E-01	4.571E-01	5.208E-01	5.717E-01	6.131E-01	6.473E-01	6.761E-01
2.683E-01	3.162E-01	3.594E-01	3.981E-01	4.786E-01	5.412E-01	5.904E-01	6.310E-01	6.641E-01	6.918E-01
2.911E-01	3.398E-01	3.831E-01	4.217E-01	5.012E-01	5.623E-01	6.105E-01	6.494E-01	6.813E-01	7.079E-01
3.162E-01	3.652E-01	4.084E-01	4.467E-01	5.248E-01	5.843E-01	6.310E-01	6.683E-01	6.989E-01	7.244E-01
3.433E-01	3.924E-01	4.354E-01	4.732E-01	5.495E-01	6.072E-01	6.521E-01	6.879E-01	7.171E-01	7.413E-01
3.724E-01	4.217E-01	4.642E-01	5.012E-01	5.754E-01	6.310E-01	6.739E-01	7.079E-01	7.356E-01	7.586E-01
4.047E-01	4.532E-01	4.948E-01	5.309E-01	6.026E-01	6.556E-01	6.964E-01	7.286E-01	7.547E-01	7.762E-01
4.394E-01	4.870E-01	5.275E-01	5.623E-01	6.310E-01	6.813E-01	7.197E-01	7.499E-01	7.743E-01	7.943E-01
4.753E-01	5.188E-01	5.552E-01	5.888E-01	6.544E-01	7.035E-01	7.389E-01	7.674E-01	7.903E-01	8.091E-01
4.853E-01	5.395E-01	5.494E-01	6.026E-01	6.792E-01	7.244E-01	7.584E-01	7.852E-01	8.066E-01	8.241E-01
5.012E-01	5.445E-01	5.843E-01	6.166E-01	6.792E-01	7.244E-01	7.584E-01	7.852E-01	8.066E-01	8.241E-01
5.179E-01	5.623E-01	5.995E-01	6.310E-01	6.918E-01	7.447E-01	7.470E-01	7.788E-01	8.035E-01	8.318E-01
5.353E-01	5.788E-01	6.150E-01	6.457E-01	7.047E-01	7.447E-01	7.586E-01	7.891E-01	8.128E-01	8.395E-01
5.533E-01	5.957E-01	6.310E-01	6.607E-01	7.178E-01	7.563E-01	7.691E-01	7.994E-01	8.222E-01	8.472E-01
5.717E-01	6.131E-01	6.473E-01	6.761E-01	7.311E-01	7.703E-01	7.822E-01	8.102E-01	8.318E-01	8.551E-01
5.908E-01	6.310E-01	6.641E-01	6.918E-01	7.447E-01	7.822E-01	7.943E-01	8.209E-01	8.414E-01	8.630E-01
6.105E-01	6.494E-01	6.813E-01	7.079E-01	7.586E-01	7.943E-01	8.066E-01	8.318E-01	8.511E-01	8.710E-01
6.310E-01	6.683E-01	6.989E-01	7.244E-01	7.727E-01	8.066E-01	8.191E-01	8.414E-01	8.610E-01	8.790E-01
6.521E-01	6.879E-01	7.171E-01	7.413E-01	7.870E-01	8.191E-01	8.318E-01	8.511E-01	8.710E-01	8.872E-01
6.739E-01	7.079E-01	7.356E-01	7.586E-01	8.017E-01	8.318E-01	8.424E-01	8.610E-01	8.790E-01	8.954E-01
6.964E-01	7.286E-01	7.547E-01	7.762E-01	8.166E-01	8.446E-01	8.531E-01	8.710E-01	8.810E-01	9.036E-01
7.197E-01	7.499E-01	7.743E-01	7.943E-01	8.318E-01	8.577E-01	8.767E-01	8.913E-01	9.027E-01	9.120E-01
7.438E-01	7.718E-01	7.943E-01	8.128E-01	8.472E-01	8.710E-01	8.883E-01	9.016E-01	9.120E-01	9.204E-01
7.688E-01	7.943E-01	8.149E-01	8.318E-01	8.630E-01	8.844E-01	9.001E-01	9.120E-01	9.214E-01	9.290E-01
7.943E-01	8.175E-01	8.360E-01	8.511E-01	8.790E-01	8.974E-01	9.120E-01	9.226E-01	9.309E-01	9.376E-01
8.209E-01	8.414E-01	8.577E-01	8.710E-01	8.954E-01	9.120E-01	9.241E-01	9.333E-01	9.404E-01	9.462E-01
8.483E-01	8.660E-01	8.799E-01	8.913E-01	9.120E-01	9.261E-01	9.363E-01	9.441E-01	9.501E-01	9.550E-01
8.767E-01	8.913E-01	9.027E-01	9.120E-01	9.290E-01	9.404E-01	9.487E-01	9.550E-01	9.599E-01	9.638E-01
9.060E-01	9.173E-01	9.261E-01	9.333E-01	9.462E-01	9.550E-01	9.613E-01	9.661E-01	9.698E-01	9.727E-01
9.363E-01	9.441E-01	9.501E-01	9.550E-01	9.638E-01	9.698E-01	9.741E-01	9.772E-01	9.797E-01	9.817E-01
9.674E-01	9.716E-01	9.747E-01	9.772E-01	9.817E-01	9.848E-01	9.869E-01	9.886E-01	9.898E-01	9.908E-01
1.000E+00	1.000E+00	1.000E+00	1.000E+00	1.000E+00	1.000E+00	1.000E+00	1.000E+00	1.000E+00	1.000E+00
1.033E+00	1.029E+00	1.025E+00	1.023E+00	1.019E+00	1.015E+00	1.013E+00	1.012E+00	1.010E+00	1.009E+00
1.068E+00	1.059E+00	1.053E+00	1.047E+00	1.038E+00	1.031E+00	1.027E+00	1.023E+00	1.021E+00	1.019E+00
1.104E+00	1.090E+00	1.080E+00	1.072E+00	1.057E+00	1.047E+00	1.041E+00	1.035E+00	1.031E+00	1.028E+00
1.141E+00	1.122E+00	1.108E+00	1.096E+00	1.076E+00	1.063E+00	1.054E+00	1.047E+00	1.042E+00	1.038E+00
1.179E+00	1.155E+00	1.136E+00	1.122E+00	1.096E+00	1.080E+00	1.068E+00	1.059E+00	1.053E+00	1.047E+00
1.216E+00	1.189E+00	1.166E+00	1.148E+00	1.117E+00	1.096E+00	1.082E+00	1.072E+00	1.063E+00	1.057E+00
1.259E+00	1.227E+00	1.194E+00	1.175E+00	1.138E+00	1.113E+00	1.096E+00	1.084E+00	1.074E+00	1.067E+00
1.301E+00	1.259E+00	1.227E+00	1.202E+00	1.159E+00	1.131E+00	1.111E+00	1.096E+00	1.085E+00	1.076E+00
1.345E+00	1.296E+00	1.259E+00	1.230E+00	1.180E+00	1.148E+00	1.124E+00	1.109E+00	1.096E+00	1.086E+00
1.380E+00	1.334E+00	1.292E+00	1.259E+00	1.202E+00	1.166E+00	1.141E+00	1.122E+00	1.108E+00	1.096E+00
1.434E+00	1.372E+00	1.325E+00	1.288E+00	1.225E+00	1.184E+00	1.156E+00	1.135E+00	1.119E+00	1.107E+00
1.484E+00	1.413E+00	1.359E+00	1.318E+00	1.247E+00	1.202E+00	1.171E+00	1.148E+00	1.131E+00	1.117E+00
1.534E+00	1.454E+00	1.395E+00	1.349E+00	1.271E+00	1.221E+00	1.187E+00	1.161E+00	1.142E+00	1.127E+00
1.585E+00	1.496E+00	1.431E+00	1.380E+00	1.294E+00	1.239E+00	1.202E+00	1.175E+00	1.154E+00	1.138E+00
1.638E+00	1.540E+00	1.468E+00	1.413E+00	1.318E+00	1.259E+00	1.218E+00	1.189E+00	1.166E+00	1.148E+00
1.693E+00	1.585E+00	1.504E+00	1.445E+00	1.343E+00	1.278E+00	1.234E+00	1.202E+00	1.178E+00	1.159E+00
1.749E+00	1.631E+00	1.545E+00	1.479E+00	1.368E+00	1.298E+00	1.251E+00	1.216E+00	1.190E+00	1.169E+00
1.806E+00	1.679E+00	1.585E+00	1.514E+00	1.393E+00	1.318E+00	1.267E+00	1.230E+00	1.202E+00	1.180E+00
1.864E+00	1.728E+00	1.622E+00	1.549E+00	1.419E+00	1.339E+00	1.284E+00	1.245E+00	1.215E+00	1.191E+00
1.931E+00	1.778E+00	1.668E+00	1.585E+00	1.445E+00	1.359E+00	1.301E+00	1.259E+00	1.227E+00	1.202E+00
1.995E+00	1.830E+00	1.711E+00	1.622E+00	1.472E+00	1.380E+00	1.318E+00	1.274E+00	1.240E+00	1.213E+00
2.062E+00	1.884E+00	1.754E+00	1.660E+00	1.500E+00	1.402E+00	1.334E+00	1.288E+00	1.253E+00	1.225E+00
2.131E+00	1.919E+00	1.801E+00	1.698E+00	1.528E+00	1.423E+00	1.353E+00	1.303E+00	1.265E+00	1.236E+00
2.200E+00	1.995E+00	1.848E+00	1.738E+00	1.556E+00	1.445E+00	1.371E+00	1.318E+00	1.278E+00	1.247E+00
2.274E+00	2.054E+00	1.896E+00	1.778E+00	1.585E+00	1.468E+00	1.389E+00	1.334E+00	1.292E+00	1.259E+00
2.350E+00	2.133E+00	1.945E+00	1.820E+00	1.614E+00	1.491E+00	1.409E+00	1.349E+00	1.305E+00	1.271E+00
2.431E+00	2.175E+00	1.995E+00	1.862E+00	1.644E+00	1.514E+00	1.427E+00	1.365E+00	1.318E+00	1.282E+00
2.512E+00	2.218E+00	2.047E+00	1.905E+00	1.675E+00	1.537E+00	1.445E+00	1.380E+00	1.332E+00	1.294E+00
2.594E+00	2.304E+00	2.099E+00	1.950E+00	1.704E+00	1.560E+00	1.465E+00	1.396E+00	1.346E+00	1.306E+00
2.683E+00	2.371E+00	2.154E+00	1.995E+00	1.738E+00	1.585E+00	1.484E+00	1.413E+00	1.359E+00	1.318E+00
2.772E+00	2.441E+00	2.213E+00	2.042E+00	1.770E+00	1.609E+00	1.504E+00	1.429E+00	1.373E+00	1.330E+00
2.865E+00	2.512E+00	2.268E+00	2.089E+00	1.803E+00	1.634E+00	1.524E+00	1.445E+00	1.387E+00	1.343E+00
2.961E+00	2.585E+00	2.326E+00	2.138E+00	1.837E+00	1.660E+00	1.544E+00	1.462E+00	1.402E+00	1.355E+00
3.060E+00	2.641E+00	2.387E+00	2.188E+00	1.871E+00	1.685E+00	1.564E+00	1.479E+00	1.416E+00	1.368E+00
3.162E+00	2.738E+00	2.448E+00	2.239E+00	1.905E+00	1.711E+00	1.585E+00	1.496E+00	1.431E+00	1.380E+00
3.268E+00	2.818E+00	2.512E+00	2.291E+00	1.941E+00	1.738E+00	1.606E+00	1.514E+00	1.445E+00	1.393E+00
3.377E+00	2.911E+00	2.577E+00	2.344E+00	1.977E+00	1.765E+00	1.627E+00	1.531E+00	1.460E+00	1.406E+00
3.490E+00	2.985E+00	2.644E+00	2.399E+00	2.014E+00	1.792E+00	1.649E+00	1.549E+00	1.475E+00	1.419E+00
3.607E+00	3.073E+00	2.712E+00	2.455E+00	2.051E+00	1.820E+00	1.671E+00	1.567E+00	1.491E+00	1.432E+00
3.724E+00	3.162E+00	2.783E+00	2.512E+00	2.089E+00	1.848E+00	1.694E+00	1.585E+00	1.506E+00	1.445E+00
3.852E+00	3.255E+00	2.855E+00	2.570E+00	2.128E+00	1.876E+00	1.715E+00	1.603E+00	1.521E+00	1.459E+00
3.981E+00	3.350E+00	2.929E+00	2.630E+00	2.168E+00	1.905E+00	1.738E+00	1.622E+00	1.537E+00	1.472E+00
4.114E+00	3.447E+00	3.005E+00	2.692E+00	2.208E+00	1.936E+00	1.761E+00	1.641E+00	1.553E+00	1.486E+00
4.259E+00	3.548E+00	3.082E+00	2.754E+00	2.249E+00	1.966E+00	1.784E+00	1.660E+00	1.569E+00	1.500E+00
4.394E+00	3.652E+00	3.162E+00	2.818E+00	2.291E+00	1.995E+00	1.808E+00	1.679E+00	1.585E+00	1.514E+00
4.541E+00	3.758E+00	3.244E+00	2.884E+00	2.333E+00	2.026E+00	1.832E+00	1.698E+00	1.601E+00	1.528E+00
4.693E+00	3.848E+00	3.428E+00	2.951E+00	2.377E+00	2.057E+00	1.854E+00	1.718E+00	1.618E+00	1.542E+00
4.853E+00	3.981E+00	3.415E+00	3.020E+00	2.421E+00	2.089E+00	1.884E+00	1.738E+00	1.634E+00	1.556E+00
5.012E+00	4.097E+00	3.508E+00	3.090E+00	2.466E+00	2.122E+00	1.905E+00	1.758E+00	1.651E+00	1.570E+00
5.179E+00	4.217E+00	3.594E+00	3.162E+00	2.512E+00	2.154E+00	1.931E+00	1.778E+00	1.668E+00	1.585E+00

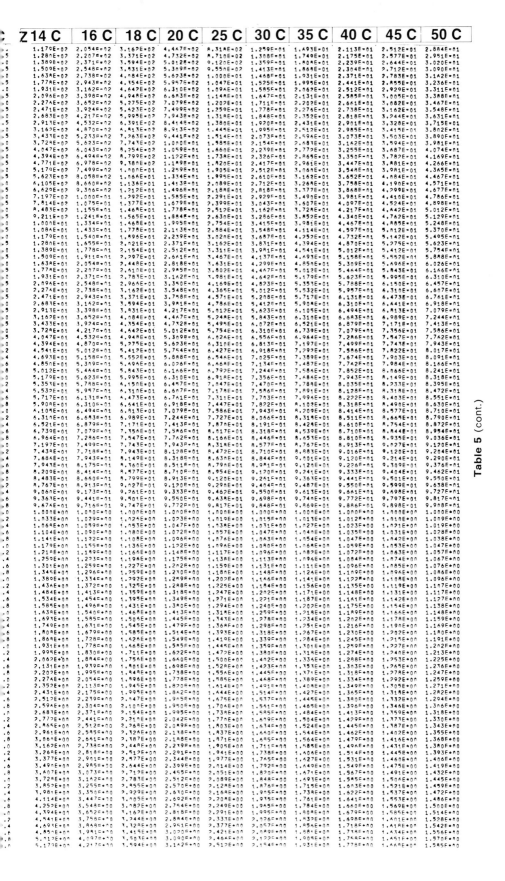

Table 5 (cont.)

Heating curve terminology The heating curve will normally be developed by plotting a function of the logarithm of the temperature difference between the temperature at any time and the heating medium temperature versus time. The log of the temperature function is plotted on the y-axis, and time on the x-axis. When either heating or cooling data for conduction heating or cooling objects are plotted in this manner, it should be possible to draw a straight line asymptote to the heating curve. The equation for this straight line asymptote is:

$$\log (T_1 - T) = \frac{-t}{f} + \log j (T_1 - T_0)$$

We have previously established that T refers to temperature and that t refers to time. The term f is a measure of the slope of the heating curve; it is the time for the temperature function to decrease by 90 %. Graphically, it is the time for the heating or cooling curve to traverse one log cycle. The value j, the lag factor in the equation, is the intercept function and we can observe that at zero time when $T = T_a$

$$j = \frac{T_1 - T_a}{T_1 - T_0}$$

The term t_B, the process time, was defined earlier as the time measured from the time the autoclave reaches sterilizing temperature to steam-off. Fully loaded commercial autoclaves or retorts usually require at least 5 min from steam-on until the processing temperature is reached. This come-up time (t_{CUT}) contributes to the sterilization cycle effectiveness; Ball (1923) determined that 42 % of the come-up time was equivalent to time at the designed heating medium temperature. The heating time t_h which is the true length of time that the container of food is subject to T_1 is equal to t_B plus $0.42\, t_{CUT}$. In making heat penetration tests under real conditions the zero time for the test is the time when the steam is turned on; $t_B = 0$ when the retort reaches T_1 and $t_h = 0$ at $0.42\, t_{CUT}$ before the sterilization time zero ($t_B - 0.42\, t_{CUT}$). The T_a used in the j value calculation is evaluated at zero heating time ($t_h = 0$).

CALCULATING THE LETHALITY VALUE OF A
HEAT STERILIZATION PROCESS

Introduction Two kinds of data must be obtained before a heat process may be evaluated: (1) a thermal death time curve or an F and z value, and (2) heating data for the product to be sterilized under realistic processing conditions either as a set of temperature versus time values or as f and j plus T_1 and T_0.

All thermal process analyses are based on the assumption that the lethal effect obtained at different temperatures is additive. In the thermal death time curve in Figure 5 it may be observed that to produce

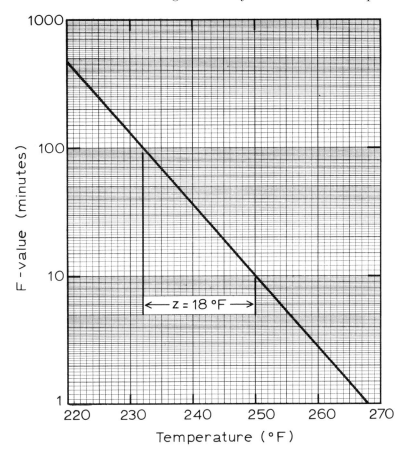

Figure 5   Thermal death time curve with an F_{250} of 10 min and a z value of 18 F.

an effect equivalent to 10 min at 250 F, 36 min at 240 F or 129 min at 230 F are required. If 10 min are required at 250 F, then in 1 min at 250 F the product will be one-tenth processed. This does not mean that one-tenth of the organisms will be destroyed; it simply means that the process is one-tenth completed in 1 min if a total of 10 min is required. At 240 F, 1/36 of the process will be completed in 1 min. As an example of how lethalities are additive, let us assume that a container of food can instantly be heated to 240 F and held at this temperature for 18 min after which time the temperature is instantly cooled to room temperature. Referring to Figure 5 we find that at 240 F, 18 min is exactly half of 36 min (the time required to sterilize at this temperature). In other words, the product was 50 % sterilized in 18 min at 240 F. The 5 min at 250 F is exactly half of the 10 min required to sterilize at 250 F; therefore, at 250 F the product received a 50 % process. If the two fractional processes are added, the result is an equivalent process of 10 min at 250 F, or 36 min at 240 F. Analytically, the calculation of the lethality of the process (F_T^z) is described by the equation:

$$F_T^z = \int L \, dt$$

where $L = 10$ and T is $f(t)$.

During the last 50 years many scientists have worked to develop improved methods of calculating the lethality of heat processes. Methods developed include: The General Method (Bigelow et al., 1920); Formula Methods (Ball, 1923, 1928; Ball and Olson, 1957); Nomogram Method (Olson and Stevens, 1939); Numerical Method (Patashnik, 1953); and Computer Method (Sasseen, 1969). In these developments accuracy of the method and ease and efficiency in application have been the objectives and it was usually not possible to satisfy both requirements. The digital computer made possible the development of a method that has great accuracy but at the same time is readily usable by the technologist.

Graphical method   The lethality or F value of the heat process is obtained using a graphical integration technique of the general equation

$$F_T^z = \int L \, dt$$

Lethal rates are listed in Tables 2–5. Tables 2 and 3 are concerned with base temperatures of 212 and 250 F for the range of z values from 6 to 80 F. Tables 4 and 5 deal with base temperatures of 100 and 120 C for the range of z values from 3 to 50 C. Both the temperature T and thermal resistance–thermal death time z must be for the same temperature scale. Conversion from one table to another can be easily done since data in the tables overlap.

Starting with the temperature-time data for the sterilization process to be evaluated ($z = 18$ F, base temperature 250 F) lethal rates are plotted on the y-axis versus time on the x-axis of rectilinear graph paper. Since the lethal rate is $10^{(T-250\,\text{F})/z}$ min at 250 F/min at T, and time is minutes at T, the area under the curve is the F_0 value in minutes at 250 F. To determine the F_0 value the area under the curve is measured using a planimeter. To convert the area under the curve to minutes at 250 F an area conversion factor is developed by determining the F_{250} of a unit area of the graph.

The lethal-rate graph illustrates at a glance the relative lethal value

Table 6   Time-temperature data and corresponding lethal rates for a thermal process, heating and cooling, where the heating curve can be represented by a single straight line
($T_1 = 250$ F, $T_2 = 70$ F, $T_0 = 120$ F, $f_h = f_c = 7.2$ min, $j = 1.92$, $z = 18$ F, $t_{CUT} = 0$)

Time (min)	Temperature (°F)	Lethal rate $\left(\dfrac{\text{min at } 250}{\text{min at } T}\right)$
0	120	
1	121	
2	133	
3	157	
4	182	
5	200	0.0017
6	214	0.0100
7	224	0.0359
8	231	0.0880
9	236	0.1668
10	239.5	0.2615
11	242.5	0.3831
12	244.5	0.4948
13	246.0	0.5995
14	247.0	0.6813
15	248.0	0.7743
16	248.5	0.8254
17	249.0	0.8799
18	249.2	0.9031
19	249.4	0.9363
20 steam off cool	249.6	0.9504
21	245.0	0.5275
22	206	0.0036
23	170	
24	144	
25	124	
26	110	
27	99	
28	91	

of the different portions of the heat process. It dramatically points out the ineffectiveness of the first few minutes after steam-on and the importance of the last few minutes of heating before cooling begins.

In Table 6 are listed the time-temperature heating data and corresponding lethal rates for a thermal process where the z value is 18 F. The heating data in Table 6 is shown graphically in Figure 6. The lethal

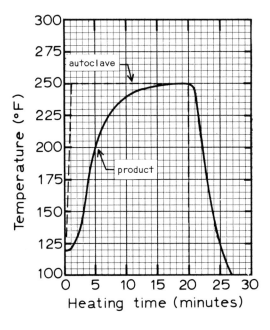

Figure 6 Time-temperature profile for sterilizer and center of object being sterilized.

rates were obtained from Table 3 under z equals 18 F. In Figure 7 the lethal-rate data in Table 6 are plotted to make a lethal-rate graph. The area measured using a planimeter is 10.6 in.^{2}; the area conversion factor is 0.80 min at 250 F per in.^{2}. Therefore, the F_{250}^{18} of the process is $10.60 \times 0.80 = 8.48$ min.

Numerical method   Numerical computation eliminates plotting the lethal-rate graph and planimetering the area substituting numerical computation for these graphical operations. Two methods that are available for finding the area of an irregular geometric figure are the Trapezoidal Rule and Simpson's Rule. In both of these procedures it is necessary to divide the area under evaluation by equally spaced parallel cords. In heat process evaluation the distance between cords will be Δt, the time interval between successive temperature measurements.

Burington (1940) states that in general, Simpson's Rule is the most accurate; however, our lethal-rate graphs are simple geometric figures since they can be made to start and end at zero and have a straight line base. Thus, the difference in the methods is not great.

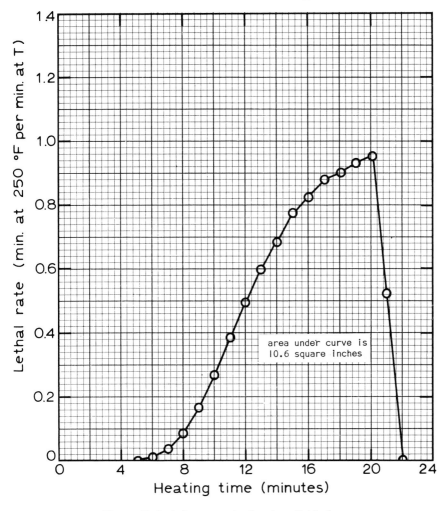

area under curve is 10.6 square inches

Figure 7 Lethal-rate graph; data from Table 6.

The Trapezoidal Rule for measuring area is written mathematically as:

$$\text{Area} = \Delta t(1/2\,(y_0 + y_n) + y_1 + y_2 + \ldots + y_{n-1})$$

The values of y in the equation above are the lethal rates $y = 10^{\frac{T-250}{z}}$ and Δt is the time interval between successive temperature measurements; therefore, the area will be F_{250}^z. Patashnik (1953) describes the evaluation of thermal processes by the Trapezoidal Rule. He points out that in the case of thermal processing calculation the data included in the analysis may be selected so y_0 and y_n are zero simplifying the above equation to:

$$\text{Area} = \Delta t(y_1 + y_2 + \ldots + y_{n-1})$$

Evaluation of the heating data in Table 6 numerically using the Trapezoidal Rule is shown in Table 7. In this example $\Delta t = 1.0$ min and the F_{250}^{18} is one times the sum of the lethal rates.

Table 7 Calculating the lethality of a heat sterilization process using the method of Patashnik

Time (min)	Temperature (°F)	Lethal rate $\left(\dfrac{\text{min at } 250}{\text{min at } T}\right)$
5	200	0.0017
6	214	0.0100
7	224	0.0359
8	231	0.0880
9	236	0.1668
10	239.5	0.2615
11	242.5	0.3831
12	244.5	0.4948
13	246.0	0.5995
14	247.0	0.6813
15	248.0	0.7743
16	249.5	0.8254
17	249.0	0.8799
18	249.2	0.9031
19	249.4	0.9363
20	249.6	0.9504
21	245.0	0.5275
22	206	0.0036

$$\Sigma \text{ of lethal rates} = 8.5231$$

$$F = \Delta t(\Sigma \text{ of lethal rates}) = 1 \times 8.5231 = 8.5 \text{ min at 250 F}$$

Digital computer method   The digital computer is ideally suited to repetitive computation problems similar to those of evaluating thermal processing data using the Trapezoidal or Simpson's Rule. The computer will carry out all manipulations and will indicate the sterilizing value F_T^z at the base temperature and for the z desired to evaluate the processing effect.

A Fortran program can be written utilizing the Trapezoidal Rule to approximate the value of the following integral:

$$F_T^z = \int_{t_1}^{t_2} L \, dt$$

where $L = 10^{\frac{T(t)-T_B}{z}}$

t = variable of integration in minutes
$T(t)$ = time-dependent temperature variable
T_B = base temperature
z = number of degrees of temperature change needed to change D value by a factor of 10.

Assume we have measured the temperature $T(t)$ every minute over the heating and cooling cycle shown in Table 6. The values have been placed on computer punch cards. The following is a standard Fortran program to approximate the lethality of the process F_T^z. Statements beginning with COMMENT are explanatory notes and are ignored by the computer.

```
    PROGRAM LETHAL (INPUT, OUTPUT)
    DIMENSION T(29)
COMMENT  −  ON THE FIRST DATA CARD WILL BE AN F OR C IN
COMMENT  −  COLUMN 1 TO INDICATE USE OF FAHRENHEIT OR
COMMENT  −  CENTIGRADE, THE BASE TEMP(TB) IN COLUMNS
COMMENT  −  2–6, AND THE VALUE OF Z IN COLUMNS 7–10
    READ 10,1S,TB,Z
10  FORMAT(A1,F5.1,F4.1)

COMMENT  −  READ THE 29 TIME-DEPENDENT TEMPERATURE
COMMENT  −  VALUES FROM DATA CARDS AND PLACE THEM
COMMENT  −  IN THE ARRAY T(1). TEMPERATURE MEASURE-
COMMENT  −  MENT INTERVALS ARE ONE MINUTE
    READ 20,(T(1),1 =1,29)
20  FORMAT (16F5.1)

COMMENT  −  APPROXIMATE THE INTEGRAL WITH THE TRAPE-
COMMENT  −  ZOIDAL RULE
    VALUE = 0.0
    Z1  =  Z*.434295
    DO 30 1 =1,28
```

```
      VALUE = VALUE+(1./2.1)*(EXP((T(1)–TB)/Z1)+
      EXP((T(1+1)–TB)/Z1))
30  CONTINUE
COMMENT – PRINT THE RESULTS
      PRINT 40,VALUE,TB,1S,Z
40  FORMAT(10/5X,*F = *,F4.1,* EQUIVALENT MINUTES AT *,
      F5.1,* DEGREES 1*,A1,*,Z = *,F4.1)
      END
F250.018.0
120.0121.0133.0157.0182.0200.0214.0224.0231.0236.0239.
5242.5244.5246.0247.0248.0
248.5249.0249.4249.6245.0206.0170.0144.0124.0110.
0099.0091.0
F = 8.5 EQUIVALENT MINUTES AT 250.0 DEGREES F, Z = 18.0
```

Since the heat process temperature-time data are used directly to calculate the lethality of the process, intermediate steps such as plotting heating curves are eliminated. Heating rate f and j value data are valuable in evaluating heat transfer to the product; computer programs have been developed that will calculate f and j as well as the lethality F_T^z of the process.

STATISTICS AND STERILIZATION PROCESSES

The sterilization process is unique among laboratory and industrial processes in that its objective is to produce items or products that contain zero microorganisms capable of growing and reproducing. This is in contrast to most industrial processes where the final product specification is a percentage composition from chemical analysis.

The zero contamination level requires a change in the method of thinking about the process. It requires a new defining of terms, and it presents a significant obstacle in the control of sterilization processes.

The problems of statistics and sterilization processes can best be discussed through the use of examples. The steps in the manufacture of sterile items are as follows:

1. The product is produced. (It may be hypodermic syringes, hypodermic syringe needles, sterile bandages, a food supplement or any of the thousands of other items that are to be marketed in a sterile condition.)

2. A number of units of the item are assembled and loaded into a sterilizer (for example, we will assume 100,000 units per sterilizer load).
3. The sterilizer is cycled through a sterilization process.
4. At the end of the cycle the product is removed and should be ready for use or consumption.

Now we will look at some observations regarding the 100,000 units that have received a sterilization treatment. The sterilization cycle will have been designed to destroy all the viable microorganisms in all 100,000 units. Ideally, the sterilization process was designed on the basis of the numbers and the heat resistance of microbial spores on the product. After these 100,000 units have been subjected to this process that was designed to make them sterile, they may all be sterile, or 0.0001 %, 0.01 %, 1 % or some other amount of the lot may not be sterile. The final result will depend on how well the actual initial conditions met the design initial conditions.

The time-temperature process designed to make each of the 100,000 units in the autoclave sterile is called the sterilization process. Since microbial spore destruction is an exponential function of time at any temperature, the number of nonsterile units in any autoclave load will be a function of the basis of the sterilization process design in relation to the actual numbers of spores on or in each unit and their resistance to the sterilizing agent.

After this lot of 100,000 units has been subjected to a sterilization treatment the following observations can be made:

1. Each one of the 100,000 units that was subjected to this sterilization process is either sterile or it is not sterile. The term *sterile* connotes an absolute condition; it has meaning in the absolute sense when used in reference to a unit or object.
2. Considering the entire sterilizer load of 100,000 units we can only describe the effectiveness of the sterilization cycle in terms of a probability level of sterility or a probability level for nonsterility. If the probability level of nonsterility is 10^{-4} then ten will be the most probable number of nonsterile units in the total lot of 100,000.

Since each item is an individual unit that may or may not be sterile, the only way we can determine if a unit is not sterile is to assay it. This brings us to the problem of assaying for sterility.

The important question facing all of us who are interested in sterile products is how to verify that a sterility specification of the order of

1 in 10^{-6} has been met. Many persons assume erroneously that it is possible to test a sample of a large lot of product and determine if all of the units in the lot are sterile. At the present time, a level of sterility of 0.999999 (1 in 10^{-6}) is used as a basis for the design of sterilization processes for drugs, objects, and devices used in the health industries. This means that the nonsterile rate is expected to be less than 1 in 1 million. If in the example the estimate of the percent nonsterile is 0.01 %, theoretically ten will be the most probable number of nonsterile units in an autoclave load of 100,000 units. Assuming there are nonsterile units in the load, how do we estimate the nonsterile rate? Can we estimate it by evaluating a sample from the lot?

The probability of finding at least one unit that is not sterile in a random sample of size N is shown in Table 8 as a function of the percentage of nonsterile units in the lot and the number of units (N) in a random sample. In the example, the percentage of nonsterile units is 0.01 or 1 unit in a lot of 10,000. The values in Table 8 indicate that if 10,000 units are tested for sterility, there will be only a 0.63 probability of finding one nonsterile unit in the sample of 10,000 units.

There is a finite probability of contamination entering the system associated with a product assay. A hypodermic syringe can be assayed for sterility by aseptically placing each needle in a tube of growth media and reading the tube for growth or no growth after a suitable incubation period at optimum growth temperature. The probability of contamination entering the tube or being deposited on the needle prior to being placed in the tube as it is removed from its sterile package and transferred into the tube is of the order of 0.1 % to 0.05 %, or one in 1000 or one in 2000 tests. Therefore, disregarding economic considerations and assuming that the contamination rate is 0.05 % we cannot verify a sterility level of 1 in 10^4.

The cost of an assay must be considered along with the value of the product used in the assay. The cost in itself for assaying 10,000 units would preclude the use of an assay procedure for determining the level of sterility in all except special cases such as calibrating a sterilization system. However, in this case, the cost is not the limiting parameter.

In producing sterile products, the sterilizing engineer or microbiologist is faced with the following constraints:

1. In the health industries, the objective is to have the nonsterile or contamination level less than 10^{-6}.
2. When 20 units per lot are assayed, the probability is 0.18, about

Table 8 Probability of finding at least one unit nonsterile in samples of size *N*

Percentage of non-sterile units in lot	Number of units in random sample						
	10	20	50	100	500	1000	10,000
0.001	0.000100	0.000200	0.000500	0.001000	0.004988	0.009950	0.095164
0.002	0.000200	0.000400	0.001000	0.001998	0.009950	0.019802	0.181271
0.005	0.000500	0.001000	0.002497	0.004988	0.024691	0.048772	0.393477
0.01	0.001000	0.001998	0.004988	0.009951	0.048773	0.095167	0.632139
0.02	0.001998	0.003992	0.009951	0.019803	0.095172	0.181286	0.864692
0.05	0.004989	0.009953	0.024696	0.048782	0.221248	0.393545	0.993270
0.1	0.009955	0.019811	0.048794	0.095208	0.393621	0.632305	0.999955
0.2	0.019821	0.039249	0.095253	0.181433	0.632489	0.864935	1.00 000
0.5	0.048890	0.095390	0.221687	0.394230	0.918428	0.993346	1.000000
1.0	0.095618	0.182093	0.394994	0.633968	0.993430	0.999957	1.000000
2.0	0.182927	0.332392	0.635830	0.867380	0.999959	1.000000	1.000000
5.0	0.401263	0.641514	0.923055	0.994079	1.000000	1.000000	1.000000
10.0	0.651322	0.878423	0.994846	0.999973	1.000000	1.000000	1.000000

1 chance in 6, that upon assay, 1 unit of the 20 will be positive if 1 % of the units in the lot are not sterile.
3. Assaying for sterility will have under the best conditions a contamination level of about 5×10^{-4} which places an upper limit on the sterility level that can be verified by assay.
4. Therefore, it is only through careful design and diligent execution of the sterilization process that a sterility probability level of the order of 1 in 10^{-6} can be achieved. The sterility level must be built into the product; it cannot be tested into the product given reasonable economic considerations.

DESIGNING AND MONITORING STERILIZATION PROCESSES

INTRODUCTION

Since we cannot test sterility into a product we must build the desired sterility level into the product. In my opinion this requires:

1. Establishing a sterilization process F value that, when delivered to the product, will produce a sterility level of 1 in 10^{-6}.
2. Monitoring each autoclave load so that we have a level of assurance (1 in 10^{-6}) that all the product received a minimum F value.
3. Having an operational system with sufficient control that will insure that:
   (a) the product to be sterilized meets the product specifications used in the sterilization process design
   (b) the probability of a product getting through the system without receiving the sterility process is $< 10^{-6}$.

DESIGN OF THE STERILIZATION CYCLE

There are three critical times associated with all wet heat sterilization processes: a minimum F value (minutes), a design F value (minutes) and the sterilization process time, t_B (minutes). The minimum F value is based only on microbial spore destruction. The design F value is a practical unit that considers the number of microbial spores in or on the product, the wet heat resistance, the nature of the process and the type of sterilization equipment. The process time is calculated using the design F value and the heating rate data for the product.

We believe that an F_{250}^{18} of 8 min is a realistic minimum F value. A sterilization process with an F_{250}^{18} of 8 min will give a 10^{16} reduction in number of spores if the $D_{250} = 0.5$ min; a 10^8 reduction if $D_{250} = 1.0$ min and a 10^4 reduction if $D_{250} = 2$ min. If we consider mesophilic sporeforming organisms, only the most resistant will have wet heat D_{250} values in the range of 0.5 to 1.0 min. The great majority will have D_{250} values less than 0.5 min.

The F value to be used in the design of the sterilization cycle may greatly exceed the minimum F_{250}^{18} value of 8 min. Perkins (1960) suggests the times and temperatures shown in Table 9 for the sterilization of a wide range of hospital and laboratory supplies. The values in Table 9 are, according to Perkins, "the minimum standards of time and temperature to be maintained throughout all portions of a load in direct contact with saturated steam...." These times are design F values; they do not provide the additional time required for steam to penetrate into bundles of fabric or into containers of product.

Table 9   Time-temperature values for the sterilization of hospital and laboratory supplies

Temperature (T)		Sterilization
(°F)	(°C)	time (min)
240	116	30
245	118	18
250	121	12
257	125	8
270	132	2
280	138	0.8

The temperature values show a 5% safety factor at 240 F, 50% at 250 F and 370% at 280 F compared to values from a thermal death time curve with an $F_{250}^{18} = 8$ min. This safety factor takes into account the fact that as we increase temperature and reduce the cycle length all factors are more critical and a larger safety margin is required.

The sterilization process time (t_B) is determined from the design F value and the product heat transfer data. In wet heat sterilization, time at a temperature produces the lethal effect on the spores. The sterilization cycle design must be based on the heating characteristics of the object or unit located in the slowest heating zone of the load. The thermocouple-potentiometer measuring system is in my opinion the most desirable method of obtaining a time-temperature profile of the sterilization process. It is necessary that the variation in the rate of heating of the slowest heating zone be known. This requires heat transfer studies with the actual process equipment under fully loaded conditions. The effect of load-to-load variation on the time-temperature profile must also be determined. The statistical worst-case conditions should be used in the final sterilization process design.

MONITORING THE STERILIZATION PROCESS

To monitor a sterilization cycle we must measure the sterilization effect delivered throughout the load of objects to be sterilized. Since the rate of heat transfer or steam penetration may not be uniform throughout the load, we will want to be sure to monitor those areas that heat the most slowly or are most remote in terms of steam penetration. Since the effectiveness of a heat sterilization process is a function of the integrated effect of time and temperature, the monitoring system must be capable of carrying out this integration or else provide the data for the integration to be done as a separate operation.

We can physically monitor a sterilization process by measuring the time and temperature variables during a process. We can measure temperature continuously or at regular time intervals simply as a function of process time. The temperature can be monitored during the heat sterilization cycle by placing a temperature sensing device, usually a thermocouple, in the slowest heating zone in the load.

The lethality of heat sterilization processes can be effectively monitored using biological indicators. The use of biological indicators is not new. The "inoculated experimental pack" procedure has been used in the food industry (Townsend et al., 1956, and Hersom and Hulland, 1963) for several decades. Spore papers for use in testing sterilizers have been reported by Kelsey (1958 and 1961). Recently Laskaris and Chaney (1969) evaluated commercially available biological indicators for monitoring autoclave sterilization.

Biological indicators fall into three general groups depending upon whether the source of the sensitive agent is (1) a natural microbial contamination of the product; (2) a material such as garden soil with its natural microbial contamination; or (3) a specific quantity of laboratory-produced microorganisms (usually bacterial spores) which have been inoculated into or on the product or onto a carrier such as a filter or chromatographic paper strip.

Biological indicators respond to the effect of time at a temperature and therefore measure the effectiveness of the sterilization process including all unknown as well as known factors influencing sterility. The temperature coefficient of the biological indicator is of the same order of magnitude as the temperature coefficient of the microbial contamination of the load being sterilized. Consequently, the biological indicator can accurately sense the effect of temperature both above and below the design temperature level. Biological indicators require no mechanical connection to the sterilizer; they can be inserted into the load prior to moving the load to the sterilizer and removed from the load after it has been removed from the sterilizer. Biological indicators are small; they can be placed directly into packages or in devices to be sterilized. A further advantage of using biological indicators is that they are relatively inexpensive.

We believe that although a biological indicator using bacterial spores can effectively monitor a sterilization process, we must keep separate the destruction of the biological indicator spores and the destruction of spores on or in the product. We must, I feel, understand the two problems we are dealing with: (1) the design of the sterilization cycle based on the nature of the product being sterilized and its microbial load, and (2) monitoring the delivery of the sterilizing effect using a biological indicator consisting of resistant spores. These two problems interface but they must be kept separate! It is wrong to try to directly relate microorganisms in the load to be sterilized to microorganisms on the biological indicator. The biological indicator can be calibrated only in terms of physical parameters, and this calibration is real, predictable, and reliable. Relating the microorganisms in the load to the microorganisms on the spore strip will, I think, obscure or cloud the fundamental relationship of the biological indicator to the design sterilization cycle.

If biological indicators are to be used officially to monitor wet heat sterilization processes, both the biological indicators themselves and their use in the sterilization process must be standardized. It is suggested that biological indicators for wet heat sterilization be standardized at the minimum F value level. One realistic specification is: A minimum of 90 % of the biological indicators must be positive (show growth) when subjected to a wet heat sterilization process at 250 F for 8 min.

SUMMARY

In monitoring a sterilization cycle I have suggested that we cannot assay a sample of the final product and validate that the sterility level is 1 in 10^{-6}. I have suggested that biological indicators can be used as monitors to insure that the product has received a prescribed minimum sterilization treatment; however, the biological indicator in itself also cannot validate that the sterility level of the product is 1 in 10^{-6}. The biological indicator can only indicate that a specified treatment has been delivered.

Validating a sterility level of the order of 1 in 10^{-6} requires that:

1. The manufacture of the product, the design criteria used in developing the sterilization process has been met.
2. The design sterilization cycle has been delivered to the product.
3. The sterilization system is safeguarded through controls and records that insure that all the product has met the design criteria and received the specified sterilization process.

The sterilization scientists and engineers have the knowledge to design, carry out, and monitor sterilization processes; however, qualified, properly trained and responsible personnel are required to carry out the operations relating to the production of sterile items if the final product is to truly have a sterility level of 1 in 10^{-6}.

References

1. Alderton, G., and Snell, N. 1963. Base exchange and heat resistance in bacterial spores. Biochem. Biophys. Res. Comm. **10**: 139–143.
2. Alderton, G., P. T. Thompson, and N. Snell. 1964. Heat adaptation and ion exchange in *Bacillus megaterium* spores. Science. **143**: 141–143.
3. Amaha, M., and K. Sakuguchi. 1957. The mode and kinetics of death of the bacterial spores by moist heat. J. Gen. Appl. Microbiol. **3**(2): 163–193.
4. Ball, C. O. 1923. Thermal process time for canned foods. Bull. Natl. Research Council **7**.
5. Ball, C. O. 1928. Mathematical solution of problems on thermal processing of canned foods. Univ. of Calif. Pub. in Public Health **1**.
6. Bigelow, W. D., and J. R. Esty. 1920. Thermal death point in relation to time of typical thermophilic organisms. J. Infect. Dis. **27**: 602.
7. Bigelow, W. D. 1921. The logarithmic nature of thermal death time curves. J. Infect. Dis. **29**: 528–536.
8. Bonestroo, B. 1970. Problems in the determination and maintenance of sterility in pre-packaged supplies used by the health industries. Master's thesis. University of Minnesota, Minneapolis, Minnesota.
9. Burington, R. S. 1940. *Handbook of mathematical tables and formula*. Handbook Publishers, Inc. Sandusky, Ohio.
10. Cavalieri, L. F., and B. H. Rosenberg. 1957. Hydrogen bond role in denaturation of nucleic acids. J. Am. Chem. Soc. **79**: 5352–5357.
11. Cox, R. A., and A. R. Peacocke. 1957. Denaturation theory: Cooperative breakage of hydrogen bonds. J. Poly. Sci. **23**: 765–779.

12. Doty, P., and S. A. Rice. 1955. Denaturation of deoxypentose nucleic acid (DNA). Biochim. et Biophys. Acta. **16**: 446.
13. Elder, R. L., and R. F. Beers, Jr. 1965. Nonphoto-reactivating repair of ultraviolet light-damaged transforming deoxyribonucleic acid by *Micrococcus lysodeikticus* extracts. J. Bact. **90**(3): 681–687.
14. Eyring, H. 1935. The activated complex and the absolute rate of chemical reactions. Chem. Rev. **17**: 65–77.
15. Glasstone, S., K. J. Laidler, and H. Eyring. 1941. *The theory of rate processes.* McGraw-Hill Book Co. New York.
16. Halvorson, H. O., and N. R. Ziegler. 1933. Application of statistics in bacteriology, I. A means of determining bacterial population by the dilution method. J. Bact. **25**: 101–121.
17. Hermans, J. 1966. Experimental free energy and enthalpy of formation of the α-helix. J. Phys. Chem. **70**(2): 510–515.
18. Hersom, A. C., and E. D. Hulland. 1963. *Canned foods: An introduction to their microbiology.* (Baumgartner) J. A. Churchill Ltd. London.
19. Johnson, F. H., H. Eyring, and M. J. Polissaro 1954. *The kinetic basis of molecular biology.* John Wiley & Sons, New York, pp. 286–368.
20. Kelsey, J. C. 1958. The testing of sterilizers. Lancet. **1**: 306–309.
21. Kelsey, J. C. 1961. The testing of sterilizers 2. Thermophilic Spore Papers, J. Clin. Path. **14**: 313–319.
22. Laskaris, T., and A. L. Chaney. 1969. Reliability of biologic autoclave sterilization indicators. Techn. Bull. Reg. Med. Techn. **39**: 201–206.
23. Mirsky, A. E., and L. Pauling. 1936. Theory: Denaturation and H bonds. Proc. Natl. Acad. Sci. U.S. **22**: 439.
24. Oginsky, E. L., and W. W. Umbreit. 1959. *An introduction to bacterial physiology,* 2nd ed. W. H. Freeman and Co., San Francisco.
25. Olson, F. C. W., and H. P. Stevens. 1939. Thermal processing of canned foods in tin containers. II. Monograms for graphic calculations of thermal processes for non-acid canned foods exhibiting straight line semi-logarithmic heating curves. Food Research. **4**: 1–10.
26. Patashnik, M. 1953. A simplified procedure for thermal process evaluation. Food Technol. **7**: 1–6.
27. Perkins, J. J. 1960. *Principles and methods of sterilization,* 2nd ed. Charles C. Thomas. Springfield, Ill.
28. Pflug, I. J., and C. F. Schmidt. 1968. Thermal destruction of microorganisms. In C. A. Lawrence and S. S. Block [Eds.], *Disinfection, sterilization and preservation.* Lea and Febiger. Philadelphia.
29. Rahn, O. 1945. *Injury and death of bacteria.* Biodynamica Monograph No. 3.
30. Sasseen, D. M. 1969. Computer program for process calculation by the simplified Ball Formula method. National Canners Association Research Laboratory, 1950 Sixth Street, Berkeley.
31. Schmidt, C. F. 1954. Thermal resistance of microorganisms. pp. 720–759. In G. F. Reddish [Ed.], *Antiseptics, disinfectants, fungicides and sterilization.* Lea and Febiger. Philadelphia.
32. Tischer, R. G., and H. Hurwicz. 1954. Thermal characteristics of bacterial population. Food Res. **19**(1): 80–91.

33. Townsend, C. T., J. R. Esty, and J. C. Baselt. 1938. Heat resistance studies on spores of putrefactive anaerobes in relation to determination of safe processes for canned foods. Food Research. **3**: 323–330.

34. Townsend, C. T., I. I. Somers, F. C. Lamb, and N. A. Olson. 1956. A Laboratory Manual for the Canning Industry. Natl. Canners Assoc. Washington, D.C.

15

Ethylene Oxide Treatment
of Naturally Contaminated
Materials

H. HESS, L. GELLER, AND
X. BÜHLMANN

Pharmaceutical Development and
Microbiological Control Departments
Ciba-Geigy Ltd, Basle

IN THE pharmaceutical industry, ethylene oxide is used for the sterilization of many plastic materials and polyethylene tubes as well as aluminum tubes with interior coatings. It is also used for the treatment of the outer surface of substances which have been precipitated or crystallized from sterile solutions. With a given material and chamber load, the efficacy of the sterilization treatment depends on a series of variables such as gas concentration, temperature, relative humidity, and the nature of the contaminants on the treated materials. The choice of a suitable biological indicator must be made in accordance with these variables.

Some authors state that microorganisms conditioned at higher relative humidities are less rapidly destroyed than at lower humidities (13, 10, 11, 9, 16). The data in the literature regarding minimal humidity requirements are contradictory (13, 10, 16). It is reasonable, however, to assume that a certain minimal humidity in the material itself is desirable for industrial sterilization operations. On the other hand, Scandinavian authors (2, 14) have advocated the use of high humidity. Such humidity is necessary to destroy the *Bacillus subtilis* sand spore preparation of the Statens Seruminstitut, Copenhagen, which is officially recognized by the Nordic Pharmacopoeia. A humidity of at least 76% at 20 C is needed for the sterilization of this indicator because some of the spores are occluded within crystals of sodium chloride. This amount of moisture, however, may be harmful to many pharmaceutical or packaging materials.

From a practical point of view, it is desirable to choose a biological indicator representative of the contaminants normally encountered on the surface of the material or objects to be sterilized. There seems to be a lack of data on the nature of the contaminants on objects, such as plastic or metal tubes, and on the contamination caused by personnel handling these objects. There is also little information on the successful sterilization of such materials. Therefore, a study was undertaken to shed more light on these topics but also with the aim of finding a suitable indicator.

Various investigations in our laboratories have shown that between 40 and 80 % of unsterilized containers (metal, glass, and plastic) were sterile before being subjected to the sterilization procedure. The rest contained at most a few microorganisms. Similar results are reported in the literature (3). The same is also generally true for synthetic active ingredients. It is therefore obvious that studies with heavily contaminated dust samples as well as with contaminants of human origin present more stringent conditions of contamination than are normally met. Hence successful sterilization of these materials offers a wide margin of safety if the same methods are applied to products.

MATERIALS AND METHODS

DUST SAMPLES

Dust samples were taken from plants manufacturing polyethylene and metal tubes, for use with eye preparations and ointments. The samples were stored in polythene bags at ambient room conditions (30 to 50 % relative humidity, RH) for later use in microbiological testing and examination with a scanning electron microscope. The air in these plants was also sampled during working hours with an Andersen sampler.

Plant A (manufacturing metal tubes for ointments) Four samples (numbered 1–4) were collected from different places in the production area. Sample 2 was taken from the air duct used for cooling the tubes. Sample 3 was taken from the floor near the machine printing the labels on the tubes at the end of the production lines.

Plant B (manufacturing polyethylene tubes and containers)   Five samples (numbered 6–10) were collected in the vicinity of the production facilities. Sample 10 was obtained from the floor at the end of the production line.

HUMAN CONTAMINATION

Dandruff was collected from a healthy person. *Sweat samples* were taken from the axilla as well as from the palm of the hand.

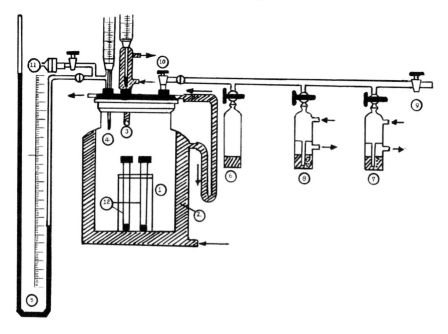

①.	Sterilizing chamber	⑦.	Wash-bottle for ethylene oxide
②.	Water jacket	⑧.	Wash-bottle for carbon dioxide
③.	Dew-point hygrometer	⑨.	Vacuum pump
④.	Thermometer	⑩.	Stop-cock for sterilizing chamber
⑤.	Mercury manometer	⑪.	Sterile filter
⑥.	Water bottle	⑫.	Test samples

Figure 1   Experimental apparatus for ethylene oxide sterilization at subatmospheric pressure.

BIOLOGICAL INDICATORS

"Hyflo spores"   *Bacillus subtilis* var. *globigii* NCTC 10073 was cultured for 8 days at 32 C on Brain Heart Infusion Agar. The organisms were harvested and washed twice in distilled water. The vegetative cells were destroyed by heating at 85 C for 15 min. Hyflo Supercel (purified Kieselguhr) was impregnated with the spore suspension and the water

was removed by lyophilization. The preparation, which contained between 10 and 20×10^6 spores per gram, was preconditioned at 35% relative humidity for 1 week before exposure to ethylene oxide treatments. The viability of such spore preparations does not decline appreciably during storage for 2 to 3 years.

"Spore sand" from Statens Seruminstitut, Copenhagen   *Bacillus subtilis* spores are dried onto quartz sand from saline solution (14). About 8×10^6 viable spores were counted in one gram of quartz sand.

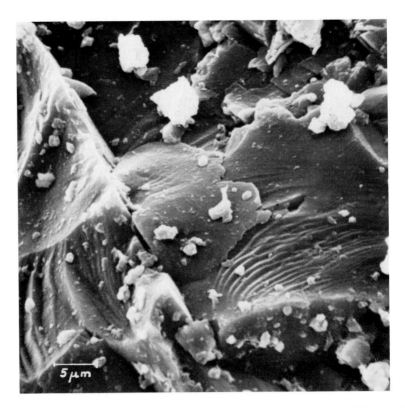

Figure 2 Scanning electron micrograph of dust sample B 10 with possible bacteria (NB round particles with a diameter of about 1 μm). $\times$ 2400.

SCANNING ELECTRON MICROGRAPHS

The dust samples and sand preparations were photographed after coating the samples with gold. No special precautions were taken to prevent shrinkage of the cells.

ETHYLENE OXIDE APPARATUS

The apparatus (Figure 1) was built in our laboratories to provide controlled conditions of temperature, relative humidity, and gas concentration. The sterilization chamber (15 cm inner diameter by 25 cm in height) consists of a glass container ① which can be closed with a metal lid. The metal lid is fastened onto the sterilization chamber with clamps to form a seal against a rubber ring located on the chamber. The

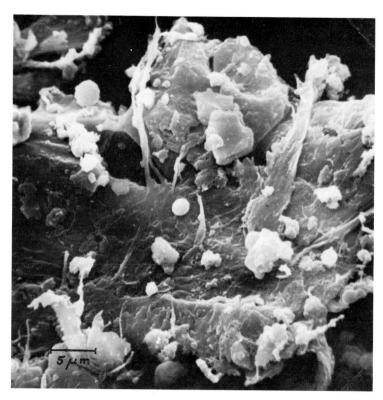

Figure 3 Scanning electron micrograph of dust sample A 2 with possible mold spores. × 2400.

sterilization chamber and lid are equipped with a water jacket surrounding the exterior walls ② through which thermostatically controlled water circulates. Entering through the lid are various control and recording instruments including a mercury manometer ⑤, a thermometer ④, a gas inlet valve with sterile filter ⑪, a dew-point hygrometer with separate water jacket for temperature regulation ③ and a control stop-cock for regulating the introduction and removal of gases ⑩. A tube from the stop-cock leads first to a water bottle ⑥, then to two wash-bottles containing a layer of liquid petroleum at the bottom as indicators for gas flow which act as inlets for ethylene oxide ⑦ and for carbon dioxide ⑧, and finally connects to another stop-cock ⑨ to a vacuum pump. The samples are contained within glass tubes loosely closed with metal caps (⑫ in Figure 1).

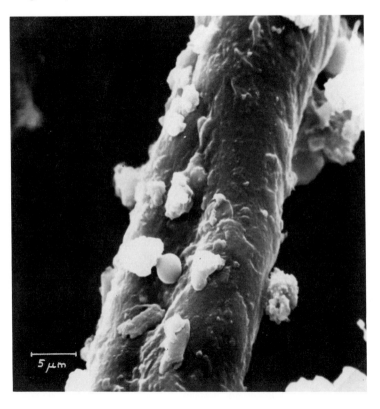

Figure 4   Scanning electron micrograph of dust sample A 2 (fiber) with possible mold spores. × 2400.

Using a standard operational protocol, test materials were exposed to ethylene oxide concentrations of 1000 or 500 mg/liter, at a controlled temperature of 35 C, and a relative humidity of $33 \pm 3\%$. A total gas pressure of 680 Torr (mm Hg) was achieved by admixture of carbon dioxide. The standard exposure time was 1 hr. Following each exposure, the samples were removed from the chamber under aseptic conditions.

MICROBIOLOGICAL TESTING

Two samples of each test material were exposed to both sterilization conditions (i.e., 1000 mg and 500 mg/liter). One sample was tested for sterility in Trypticase Soy Broth; the other was examined both quantitatively by plate count (Trypticase Soy Agar) and qualitatively in Fluid Thioglycollate Medium. The samples were incubated for 3 days at 30 C. For the air sampler, plates with Standard Methods Agar were used and then incubated aerobically for 5 days at 30 C.

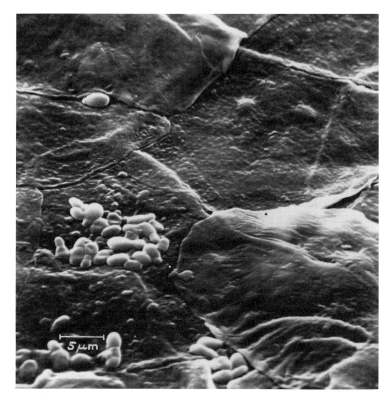

Figure 5 Microorganisms (saprophytic micrococci) on epithelial cells of dandruff. Scanning electron micrograph. × 2400.

RESULTS AND DISCUSSION

CHARACTERIZATION OF DUST SAMPLES

Because of the small amount of material in most dust samples collected near the production line, only rough estimates of total microbial count were possible. More material was available from samples 2, 3, and 10 and these results are given in Table 1 (p. 265). Samples 1 and 4 (Plant A) contained between 1000 and 3500 microorganisms per gram. At least half of them were molds (mainly *Penicillium* sp., *Scopulariopsis* sp., and *Mucor* sp.). No Enterobacteriaceae, *Staphylococcus aureus*, or *Pseudomonas aeruginosa* were detected.

Samples 6–9 (Plant B) contained up to 34,000 microorganisms per

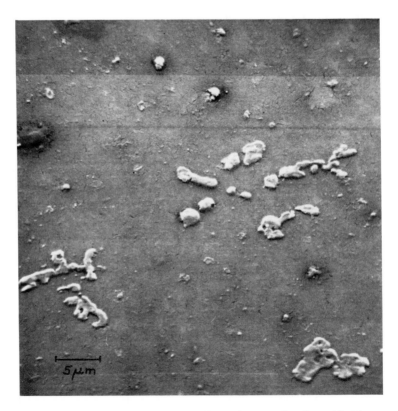

Figure 6   Sweat from axilla dried on glass. Note absence of sodium chloride crystals. Scanning electron micrograph. × 2400.

gram (mainly micrococci and short gram-negative rods, the molds being fewer in these samples). Again no Enterobacteriaceae, *Staphylococcus aureus*, or *Pseudomonas aeruginosa* were detected.

The sampling of the air in Plants A and B gave total counts of airborne microorganisms per 0.9 m³ of 179 in Plant A and 720 in Plant B. In Plant A about one-third and in Plant B about three-fourths consisted of molds (*Mucor* sp., *Penicillium* sp., *Aspergillus* sp., *Cephalosporium* sp.,

Scopulariopsis sp., *Cladosporium* sp.). The rest were bacteria, among them mainly cocci (micrococci, *Gaffkya* sp., *Sarcina* sp., *Neisseria* sp.). Aerobic sporeformers and coccoid gram-negative rods were found in low numbers only. In the scanning electron microscope, the probable presence of isolated microorganisms could be detected in several cases (Figures 2–4). In accordance with the results of the plate count, the

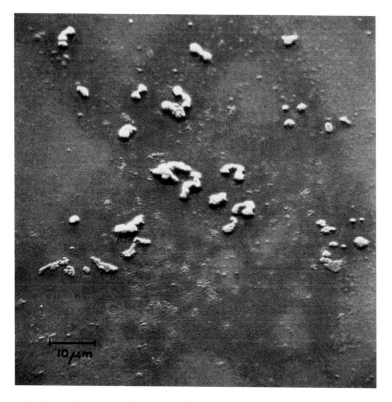

Figure 7   Sweat from palm of the hand dried on glass. No sodium chloride crystals can be detected. Scanning electron micrograph. × 1200.

organisms in sample 2 (Figures 3 and 4) appear to be mold spores and those in sample 10 (Figure 2) appear to be bacteria. No clearly defined crystals such as those in Figures 9 and 10 were detected.

CHARACTERIZATION OF DANDRUFF AND SWEAT

Dandruff was found to contain between 3 and 10×10^6 microorganisms per gram. These were mainly saprophytic micrococci (but also 3000

Serratia sp. per gram) which can be seen on the surface of epithelial cells (Figure 5).

Sweat from the axilla was collected both on glass surfaces and filter paper strips. On a surface of about 10 cm² of glass, approximately 2×10^5 microorganisms (gram-positive cocci and short rods) could be counted. The Stereoscan micrographs show only ill-defined smears with-

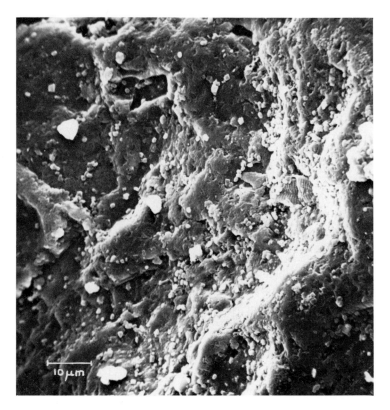

Figure 8 Quartz sand from Statens Seruminstitut, Copenhagen, with numerous spores of *B. subtilis* on surface of a grain. Scanning electron micrograph. ×1200.

out any sign of sodium chloride crystals (Figure 6). On 5 cm² of filter paper, 8500 microorganisms could be counted. All of them were gram-positive bacteria. This sample was treated with ethylene oxide.

Sweat from the palm of the hand (Figure 7) was similar in appearance to sweat from the axilla. Since the microbial count was low, such samples were therefore not subjected to ethylene oxide treatment.

CHARACTERIZATION OF "SPORE SAND" PREPARATION

The scanning electron micrographs show that most spores are on the surface of the quartz grains (Figure 8). However, a certain number of sodium chloride crystals of about 5 μm in size can be detected (Figures 9 and 10). Some spores are half-way within the crystals so that it may be assumed that spores are also completely occluded in such crystals.

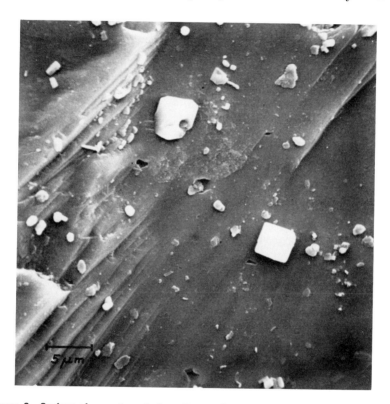

Figure 9   Surface of a quartz grain from Statens Seruminstitut with spores of *B. subtilis* and crystals of sodium chloride. Scanning electron micrograph. × 2400.

ETHYLENE OXIDE TREATMENT

The microbiological results are summarized in Table 1. Among all the samples tested, only the "spore sand" withstood a treatment of 1000 mg of ethylene oxide per liter for 1 hour at 35 C. From the results it can be seen that about 0.25 % of the spores were not killed by this exposure. The resistance to treatment is not surprising since a high humidity is necessary to dissolve the sodium chloride crystals. These results cast some doubt on the suitability of the "spore sand" as a representative biological indicator for the treatment of pharmaceutical materials with ethylene oxide. One of the arguments brought forward in favor of the "spore sand" as a suitable test object was that "a fraction of the microorganisms in ordinary airborne contaminations is extremely dry on account of environmental temperature changes" (2). No evidence in support of this statement was found, however.

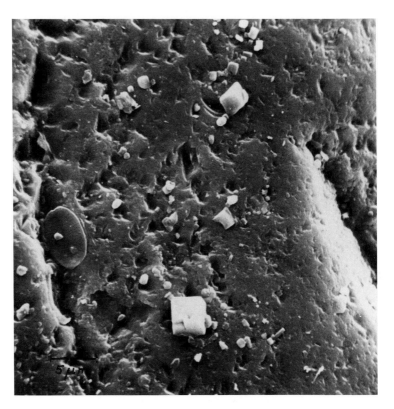

Figure 10   Surface of a quartz grain from Statens Seruminstitut with spores of *B. subtilis*; note one spore partly imbedded in sodium chloride crystal. Scanning electron micrograph. × 2400.

It has also been assumed (2) that in human environments a large percentage of the airborne microbial particles come from the skin and the respiratory and digestive organs of the human body and that some microorganisms appear together with organic material and small crystals, including sodium chloride. The results of our studies, both those obtained by scanning electron microscopy and by actual treatment with ethylene oxide, do not substantiate the presence of crystals which

Table 1   Summary of the microbiological results

Material	Treatment with ethylene oxide at 35 C and 33% RH for one hour	Sterility test in Trypticase Soy Broth	Total count (per g) in Trypticase Soy Agar	Additional qualitative test in Fluid Thioglycollate medium
Dust sample 2	1000 mg/liter	−	−	−
	500 mg/liter	−	−	−
	Control	+	10,800	+
Dust sample 3	1000 mg/liter	−	−	−
	500 mg/liter	−	−	−
	Control	+	1,600	+
Dust sample 10	1000 mg/liter	−	−	−
	500 mg/liter	+	−	−
	Control	+	39,400	+
Dandruff	1000 mg/liter	−	−	−
	500 mg/liter	−	−	−
	Control	+	9,800,000	+
Sweat (from axilla on filter paper)	1000 mg/liter	−	−	−
	500 mg/liter	−	−	−
	Control	+	8,480	−
"Hyflo spores" (spores on purified kieselguhr)	1000 mg/liter	−	−	−
	500 mg/liter	+	−	−
	Control	+	16,200,000	+
"Spore sand" Statens Seruminstitut	1000 mg/liter	+	13,300	+
	500 mg/liter	+	23,050	+
	Control	+	8,000,000	+

occlude microorganisms in such environments. This would demonstrate, further, the unnatural conditions prevailing in the "spore sand" of Statens Seruminstitut.

In conclusion, it appears that washed spores on an inert, nonhygroscopic carrier, preconditioned at 35% relative humidity and 25 C, stored in a cool place, are suitable indicators for ethylene oxide treatment of pharmaceutical materials such as plastic and metal tubes and powders. (Spores on a nonhygroscopic carrier are somewhat more resistant than those on a hygroscopic carrier (12).) Only powders which do not contain microorganisms occluded in crystals are suitable for ethylene oxide sterilization (1, 17, 8, 6, 7, 15). Washed spore preparations, also propagated by other authors (8, 12, 4, 5) have the advantage that all spores occur in a uniform state and can be used for ethylene oxide treatment under humidity conditions compatible with the products.

ACKNOWLEDGMENTS

The authors are indebted to Miss C. Brücher for the scanning electron micrographs, to Dr. Langenbucher for his help in the design of the ethylene oxide sterilization apparatus, and to Mr. W. Setz for the collection and initial testing of the dust samples.

References

1. Abbott, C. F., J. Cockton, and W. Jones. 1956. J. Pharm. Pharmacol. **8**: 709.
2. Christensen, E. A., L. O. Kallings, and D. Fystro. 1969. Läkartidningen **66**: 5117.
3. Christensen, E. A., S. Mukherji, and N. W. Holm. Aug., 1968. Microbiological control of radiation sterilization of medical supplies. I. Total count on medical products (disposable syringes and donor sets) prior to radiation sterilization. Risö Report No. 122 (Danish Atomic Energy Commission).
4. Day, L. M. 1971. Bull. Parent. Drug Assn. **25**: 73.
5. Doyle, J. E. 1971. Bull. Parent. Drug Assn. **25**: 104.
6. Doyle, J. E., and R. R. Ernst. 1967. Appl. Microbiol. **15**: 726.
7. Doyle, J. E., and R. R. Ernst. 1968. J. Pharm. Sci. **57**: 433.
8. Ernst, R. R., and J. J. Shull. 1962. Appl. Microbiol. **10**: 337.
9. Geller, L. et al. (Paper in preparation.)
10. Kaye, S., and C. R. Phillips. 1949. Amer. J. Hyg. **50**: 296.
11. Kelsey, J. C. 1967. J. Appl. Bact. **30**: 92.
12. Kereluk, K., R. A. Gammon, and R. S. Lloyd. 1970. Appl. Microbiol. **19**: 146, 152.
13. Kereluk, K., R. A. Gammon, and R. S. Lloyd. 1970. Appl. Microbiol. **19**: 157.
14. Kristensen, H. 1970. Acta. Path. Microbiol. Scan. Section B. **78**: 298.
15. Mullican, C. L., and R. K. Hoffman. 1968. Appl. Microbiol. **16**: 1110.
16. Phillips, C. R. 1961. The sterilizing properties of ethylene oxide, pp. 59–75. In the Pharmaceutical Society of Great Britain, *Recent developments in the sterilization of surgical materials*. The Pharmaceutical Press. London.
17. Royce, A., and C. Bowler. 1961. J. Pharm. Pharmacol. **13**: 87 T.

PART FOUR

Applications of Aerospace Research to Industrial Sterilization

16

Aerospace Research: Applications to Industrial Sterilization

JOHN H. BREWER
NASA Consultant

INTRODUCTION

ONE OF the principal justifications for the exploration of outer space is to determine whether life exists or has existed in the past on other planets. It may be assumed that man expects, with some finite degree of probability, that life does exist on other planets.

Mars serves as a typical example. It is the closest planet that exhibits any real similarities with Earth and, while the existence of advanced life forms is highly improbable, it is still possible that especially adapted organisms live or have lived on Mars. If man's first attempts to land life detection instruments on the red planet result in failure to detect such forms, no conclusive scientific statements regarding the overall absence of life would be possible. The question of whether or not life exists on Mars may not be answered, in reality, until many samples are returned to Earth for detailed study. Nonetheless for the foreseeable future, as experimental landings are made on planets and remote means of life detection are used, it becomes obvious that the best and most advanced techniques must be developed and used by space micro-biologists to sterilize outgoing spacecraft, to detect microbial forms in bizarre environments, and to avoid contaminating other planets with earth microbial forms.

It is in these areas then that the space microbiologist finds common ground with those also involved in industrial sterilization of medical materials. In the industrial world, the ability to provide adequate and reliable sterilization procedures and the ability to detect small numbers of microorganisms with special growth requirements are as important as in exploration of outer space. It is appropriate, then, for industrial microbiologists to follow carefully the developments being made by the NASA organization in the U.S.A. and by the Space Exploration program of the U.S.S.R.

As an introduction, we will review briefly several papers recently presented by Soviet scientists at a meeting of COSPAR-15 in Madrid, Spain. These papers bear either on sterilization procedures or on factors which limit microbiological growth.

In reviewing the period from 1969 to 1972 the representative of the International Union of Biological Sciences, A. A. Imshenetsky (2) discussed the advances made in space exploration and their effect on space biology. He pointed out: "Great strides have been made in the study of the synthesis of organic compounds from more simple chemical substances where sources of energy were physical factors found in space. These data explained the presence of organic substances of abiogenous origin in meteorites. The occurrence of new amino acids in carbonaceous chondrites were not due to the contamination." He stated that some microorganisms and enzymes were found to be very resistant to a high vacuum up to 10^{-10} Hg. Therefore, vacuum cannot kill microorganisms on the surface of a spacecraft. A very low temperature ($-196°$) also does not kill bacteria, fungi, protozoa, insects, and some higher plants.

Ultraviolet radiation is absolutely lethal for all cells and tissues, especially on those planets on which the atmosphere is devoid of dust, clouds, and a layer of ozone. However, even very large ultraviolet doses are not effective if a thin protective layer is applied on the cells.

Ionizing radiation, at doses found in space, can be a powerful factor inducing the mutation and death of the cells. However, the adaptation of terrestrial microorganisms, inhabiting water of nuclear reactors, to millions of roentgens suggests the origin of lower forms of life, extremely resistant to ionizing radiation.

The section on quarantine of the planets contains a number of statements relative to sterilization. This section reads as follows:

The sterilization of space satellites and probes stimulated the research in the field of theoretical bases of the sterilization and disinfection. The effect of various new disinfectants was studied; the mixture of ethylene oxide with methyl bromide was found to be better than the total effect of these compounds taken separately. Such synergistic effect turned out to be of a high practical value. A very high number of investigations dealt with the quarantine of the planets. Mathematical probability of the planet contamination during the starting and landing variants was established and the methods for the artificial contamination of space objects with bacterial spores, sampling, various sterilization (high temperature, ionizing radiation, gas sterilization, etc.), sterile assembling of the equipment in "clean" (devoid of microbes) rooms, etc., have been elaborated.

In several cases thermolabile materials were substituted by thermostable materials, thus permitting heating of various equipment. The best results were achieved after a short-term heating of the space object at 135 or after a long-term heating at 105. Open surfaces are sterilized with a mixture of gases. Unfortunately, some materials underwent undesirable changes during the sterilization of the equipment with ionizing radiation. As for the Earth quarantine, the Moon ground was shown to contain no microorganisms and viruses. Nevertheless, all necessary quarantine measures should be taken in the case of the ground samples from Mars.

The development of the research in the near future is closely connected with a new evidence on the planets and space. For example, a more detailed information about the conditions existing on Mars, which is to be obtained in the nearest years, would permit to revise the methods for the detection of life on this planet. At the same time these data would allow to reproduce the conditions existing on Mars more exactly in the laboratories and to elucidate their effect on terrestrial microorganisms. The investigation of prebiological systems will provide us with more insight into the pathways which were followed during this, still hardly accessible, transition from organic compounds to primary living organisms.

The investigation of the effect of weightlessness on various biological objects is of an extreme importance. Living organisms, inhabiting the lakes with a very high salt concentration, can be presumed to endure weightlessness better than animals inhabiting the earth.

The advances of organic synthesis and technology will now provide us with more new active substances with sterilizing activity and new thermostable polymers which permit to use higher temperatures for the sterilization of space probes. Spacebiology makes an extremely rapid progress, and its data contribute both to general biology and to space medicine.

From a microbiological point of view a most interesting paper presented by Imshenetsky and others (3) was "On the Xerophilic Microorganisms Multiplying Under the Simulated Martian Conditions." One is impressed by the simplicity of Soviet experimental techniques, particularly by their inexpensive method of obtaining a Martian atmosphere, moisture conditions, and temperatures. Imshenetsky et al. began their paper with the statement:

The severe conditions of the Martian climate make it unprobable to assume the existence of higher plants on Mars, but the existence of microorganisms in the planet soil is quite probable. These microorganisms could belong to anaerobic or microaerophilic xerophilic able to grow in wide temperature intervals. They supposedly should be able to assimilate mineral nitrogen, hydrocarbons and develop in presence of high salt concentrations. As the terrestrial microorganisms are characterized by high resistance towards the unfavourable environmental conditions, the possibility of their development under the simulated Martian conditions was investigated.

They found that the halotolerant forms of *B. megaterium* and *Mycococcus ruber* were able to develop in a closed system containing 3.8 % moisture, 80 % CO_2, and 20 % Ar with a barometric pressure of 7 millibars and daily temperature variation from 28° to −60° (the temperature curve on the Martian equator). The incubation time was 7 days. The culture medium was an extraction of 100 gms of felsite, limonite, lava, sulfuric ore of volcanic origin, and peat soil in weight 40:40:5:5:5:5 centrifuged at 5000 rpm for 15 min after boiling for 2 hr. This was then made into 1.5 agar and dried on glass slides after the culture was added. The slide was placed in a test tube over saturated K_2SO_4. The test tube was flushed with the gas mixture (80 % CO_2 and 20 % Ar) and evacuated to 7 millibars. The tubes were then incubated either for 3 days at 8 hr intervals reaching a maximum of 28° then to a minimum of −60°. The results indicated that xerophily and halophily may be mutually linked. Six strains were found which could grow from 6 C to 45 C and three strains at 50 C.

In other experiments additional information was obtained. Another paper "On the Mechanism of Adaptation of Microorganisms to the Extreme Low Humidity Conditions" was presented by Askenov, Babyeva, and Globubev (1). They stated that the extraction and preservation of the moisture from the air by means of the osmotic mechanism provided the existence of favorable day temperatures for living systems on Mars are possible only at temperatures about 10 degrees below zero observed at night time. Studying organisms from the high mountain deserts of the Pamirs and the Tien Shan, they concluded that capsulated forms are adapted better than noncapsulated ones to periodic oscillations of relative humidity under desert conditions. They concluded that on the basis of exposed materials lower plants and microorganisms have mechanisms of humidity regulation within the organism on the cell level. Presence of similar mechanisms allow lower forms to preserve a considerable amount of water under more favorable temperatures for development and may have an especial importance under Mars conditions.

A paper by Vaskov (4) (which was translated by Vishniac) dealt with the sterilization of many materials, particularly plastics, and the problems of absorption and release of their OB gas mixture (methyl bromide and ethylene oxide). The data and methods were the same as those given by Vaskov in another publication (5).

More interesting than the paper were the questions and answers given following the presentation. Vaskov stated that Mars 2 and 3 were sterilized in a number of ways. Individual parts were sterilized by a number of methods, radiation 2.5 Mrads and ultraviolet, also sterile assembly techniques under laminar flow, and the entire assembly was exposed to their OB gas mixture before launch (1.0 part ethylene oxide to 1.44 parts methyl bromide at 50° for 6 hr). The contamination levels on their test model were obtained by mopping and the buried contamination was determined by sterilization of the surfaces with hydrogen peroxide 6 % and then thorough flushing with sterile distilled water, then machine grinding the pieces and testing in Trypticase Soy Agar and incubating at 10–37 C. In over 200 samples none produced a positive. Vaskov stated that the lander remained enclosed in a plastic bag with a low level of sterilant gas until it left the earth's atmosphere.

References

1. Askenov, S. I., I. P. Babyeva, and V. I. Globubev. 1972. On the mechanism of adaptation of microorganisms to the extreme low humidity conditions. COSPAR, Fifteenth Plenary Meeting, May 10–24, 1972, Madrid, Spain.
2. Imshenetsky, A. A. 1972. The report of the representative of IUBS on the 15th meeting of COSPAR: Research in space biology. COSPAR, Fifteenth Plenary Meeting, May 10–24, 1972, Madrid, Spain.
3. Imshenetsky, A. A., L. A. Konzjurina, and V. M. Jakshina. 1972. On the xerophilic microorganisms multiplying under the simulated Martian conditions. COSPAR, Fifteenth Plenary Meeting, May 10–24, 1972, Madrid, Spain.
4. Vaskov, V. I. 1972. Sterilization problems of space vehicles. COSPAR, Fifteenth Plenary Meeting, May 10–24, 1972, Madrid, Spain.
5. Vaskov, V. I., N. V. Rashkova, and G. V. Scheglova. 1970. Kavantin planet: Printsipy, metody i problemy, osnovy kosmicheskoy biolgii i meditsiny. **4**(1), (**3**): 3–156.

17

The Synergistic Inactivation of Biological Systems by Thermoradiation

H. D. SIVINSKI, D. M. GARST,
M. C. REYNOLDS, C. A. TRAUTH, JR.,
R. E. TRUJILLO, W. J. WHITFIELD

Sandia Laboratories
Albuquerque, New Mexico

INTRODUCTION

THERMORADIATION is a process of sterilization in which ionizing radiation and heat are simultaneously applied. In such a process there are, accordingly, three variables: temperature, radiation dose rate, and sterilization time. Over certain ranges of temperature and dose rate, the thermoradiation process causes a much greater reduction in a given biological population than that which would be anticipated if first heat and then ionizing radiation were applied. This phenomenon is illustrated graphically in Figure 1 for dry *Bacillus subtilis* var. *niger* spores, where survival characteristics are shown first in an elevated temperature environment only, then in a γ-radiation environment at room temperature and finally in the combined environment of elevated temperature and radiation (a thermoradiation environment). The total *independent* effects of heat and gamma radiation are illustrated as a *hypothetical* curve denoted "additive". This hypothetical curve represents the sur-

The authors gratefully acknowledge the support of this work by both the United States National Aeronautics and Space Administration and the United States Atomic Energy Commission. We are also much indebted to Messrs. K. F. Kindell, T. J. David, E. C. Leonard, and Mrs. N. Laible for their exceptional technical support, and to Mrs. H. Stake and Miss C. Dutchman for their most competent efforts in preparing this manuscript.

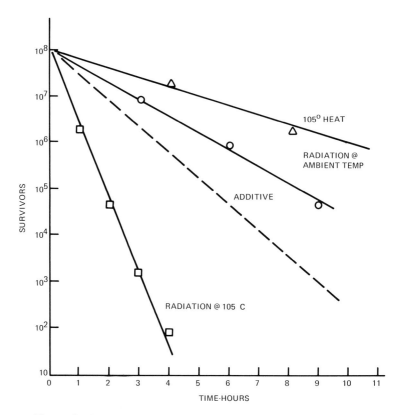

Figure 1   Synergistic inactivation of dry *B. subtilis* var. *niger* spores.

vival curve that could be anticipated if inactivation resulted only from the sum of the effects of elevated temperature and ionizing radiation acting independently. A comparison of the additive curve with the actual survivor curve experimentally obtained with thermoradiation clearly indicates that thermoradiation is a much more effective means of inactivating bacterial spores than would have been anticipated from a knowledge of spore inactivation by heat and ionizing radiation independently applied. This increased effectiveness of inactivation is termed *synergism*.

Some quantitative information about the amount of synergism in Figure 1 may be gleaned from Table 1. A *D* value is the time required to reduce a population to 10 % of its original value. Such a loss of 90 % of a population is termed a 1 *log reduction* in population. In Table 1, the time for a 1 log reduction (*D* value) in a population of dry *B. subtilis* var. *niger* spores is shown for each of the curves in Figure 1. Also shown

Table 1 Heat, radiation, and time needed for a 1 log reduction in a population of dry *B. subtilis* var. *niger* spores

Environmental conditions		D value (hours)	Radiation dose per log reduction	Degree-hours per log reduction
General	Specific			
Heat only	Temperature 105 C	4.5	0	472.5
Radiation only	27 krads/hr at 23 C	3.3	90	89.1
Additive	Hypothetical curve-sum of effects from radiation only and heat only	1.8	48.7	189.0
Thermoradiation	27 krads/hr at 105 C	0.7	18	73.5

is the total dose and the number of degree (C)-hours needed to reduce the population by 1 log.

This phenomenon of synergistic inactivation inherent in thermo-radiation can lead to considerable benefits. For example, in the above case, the time required in a heat sterilization process at 105 C can be reduced by a factor of more than six by the addition of radiation. More generally, two types of benefits that may be expected are: (1) Existing heat or radiation sterilization processes may be accelerated by the addition of the appropriate amount of the other sterilant (radiation or heat), and (2) combinations of heat and radiation will allow considerably lower doses or temperatures than either used separately, without compromising sterilizing time.

These and other benefits are assured in ranges of temperature and dose rate where thermoradiation exhibits a synergistic sterilizing effect. While the observation of a synergistic response to heat and ionizing radiation by biologically active systems is not new, a thorough experimental and analytical investigation leading to a precise definition of these ranges is. This chapter describes such experimental and analytical studies into the nature and characteristics of the thermoradiation inactivation of biological systems.

THE EXISTENCE AND NATURE OF SYNERGISM

This section is devoted first to the establishment of the proposition that *when dose rate and temperature are properly chosen, all biologically active systems so far observed are synergistically inactivated by a combination of heat and radiation.* Evidence for this hypothesis was obtained in a systematic and thorough study designed for the purpose of finding and studying this synergistic response. Following this, some of the experimentally observable properties of synergistic inactivation with combined heat and ionizing radiation are discussed.

EXISTENCE OF SYNERGISM IN MANY BIOLOGICALLY ACTIVE SYSTEMS

The initial investigation of thermoradiation was carried out with *Bacillus subtilis* var. *niger* spores treated in a dry state since most bacterial spores are exceptionally heat- and sometimes radiation-resistant. Numerous thermoradiation studies with this organism have been undertaken, with temperatures ranging from 60 to 125 C and dose rates ranging from about 2 krad/hr to near 20 krad/msec. Typical results are shown in Figures 2 through 4 at temperatures of 125 C, 105 C and 95 C and dose rates of 50, 36, and 11 krad/hr respectively. In all cases a synergism was observed. Modest experimentation was also done with spores of *B. pumilus* and a synergism was also observed. As a result of these experiments it was felt that the addition of *modest amounts* of ionizing radiation to dry heat sterilization processes designed to sterilize aerobic bacterial spores could be highly beneficial.

Because of a concern for environmental organisms, some very radiation- and heat-resistant bacterial spores from soil were studied to determine the suitability of thermoradiation for sterilization of these naturally occurring populations. The dry heat inactivation of these spores was studied at 105 C and 125 C, the radiation inactivation at dose rates of 660 and 54 krad/hr, and the thermoradiation inactivation at both 105 C and 125 C.

The dry heat destruction rate of the naturally occurring spores at 105 C was found to be extremely slow; the D value for the resistant subpopulation (neglecting N_0) was 101.54 hr. This can be compared to the D value of 4.5 hr at this temperature for *B. subtilis* var. *niger* (shown in Figure 3). The radiation-resistance experiments were conducted at dose rates of 660 and 54 krad/hr at 23 C. There was an overall high degree of

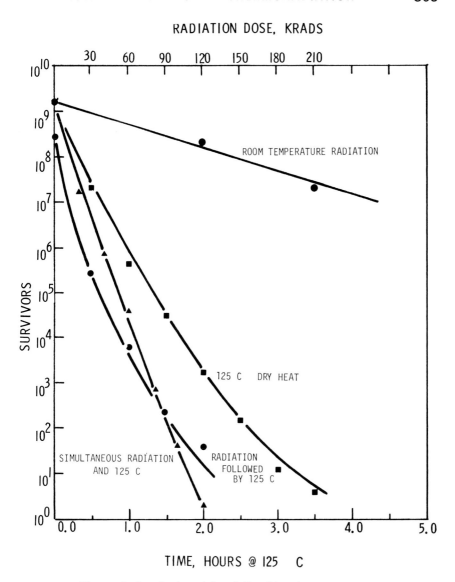

RADIATION DOSE, KRADS

TIME, HOURS @ 125 C

Figure 2 Inactivation of *B. subtilis* with various treatments.

gamma radiation resistance. The D values obtained were 222 krads at 660 krad/hr and 205 krads at 54 krad/hr. The thermoradiation resistance of these naturally occurring spores was determined by using dry heat at 105 C combined with gamma radiation at 23 krad/hr. The D value derived from these data, again neglecting N_0, was 5.36 hr or 1/20 of the dry heat D value.

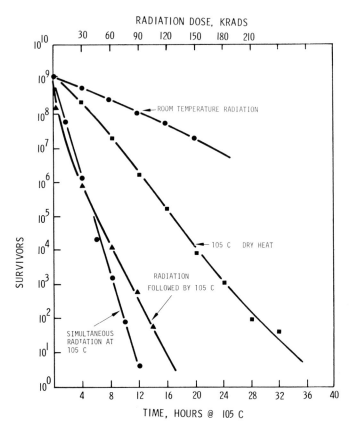

Figure 3 Comparison of radiation/dry heat sterilization of *B. subtilis*.

A number of experiments were also performed at 125 C to compare the thermoradiation resistance to the heat and radiation resistance of the naturally occurring spores. The dry heat, radiation, and thermoradiation survival curves of naturally occurring spores at 125 C are compared in Figure 5. The dry heat D value derived from a least squares fit of the resistant subpopulation was 29.45 hr. Using thermoradiation with a dose rate of 54 krad/hr and 125 C, the D value was reduced to 1.04 hr. Thus, about a 30-fold change in inactivation rate was achieved from a dry heat D value of nearly 30 hr to a thermoradiation D value of 1 hr. It was again evident from these experiments that substantial reductions in time to sterilize are available when using thermoradiation. Figure 5 shows this high degree of synergism experienced with these radiation- and heat-resistant organisms.

In an attempt to assess the generality of the thermoradiative syner-

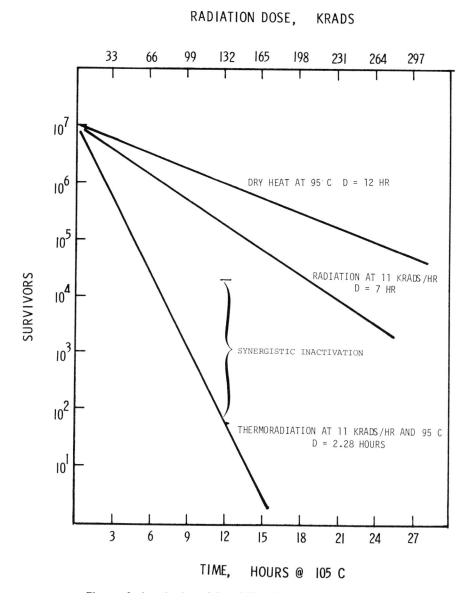

Figure 4 Inactivation of *B. subtilis* with various treatments.

gism, biologically active systems of other types have been investigated. A relatively simple biological system was studied first: the enzyme, lysozyme. The enzymatic activity of lysozyme was determined after exposure of the enzyme to heat, radiation, or thermoradiation by assaying the ability of lysozyme to lyse a suspension of *M. lysodeikticus* cell walls.

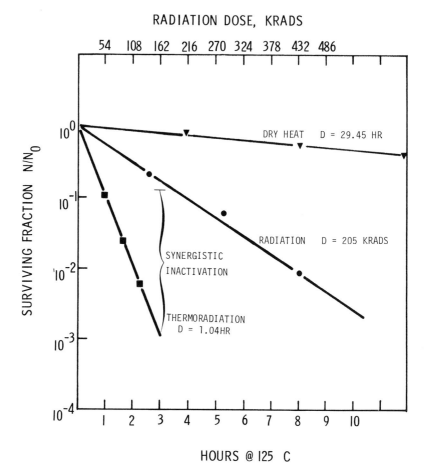

Figure 5 Comparison of thermoradiation, radiation, and dry heat inactivation of naturally occurring spores in soil.

Figure 6 shows that a combination of heat and ionizing radiation of 70 C and 27 krad/hr caused a synergistic loss of lysozyme enzymatic activity.

To investigate simple living systems, the bacteriophage T4 was selected as a test system. The viability of the phage was measured in terms of its ability to lyse *Escherichia coli* B, its host organism. Again, synergistic inactivation by thermoradiation was evidenced at 66 C and 30.6 krad/hr as shown by Figure 7.

Finally, the *E. coli* B was exposed to heat, radiation, and combinations thereof, while in an actively metabolizing state. The results at 50 C and 25 krad/hr are shown in Figure 8. From this figure, it can be

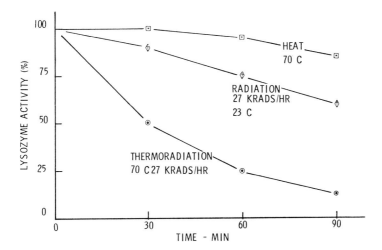

Figure 6   Thermoradiation inactivation of lysozyme.

seen that the control is undergoing division and that, once again, a synergistic inactivation is observed.

These last several experimental programs involved thermoradiation treatment of systems in aqueous solution, so it would appear that the synergistic response of biological systems to thermoradiation occurs under both wet and dry conditions. More evidence of this is given in Figure 18 of the next section.

SOME PROPERTIES OF THERMORADIATION

Investigations using *B. subtilis* var. *niger* spores in a dry state have been undertaken in an attempt to determine the effects on thermoradiation by dose rate, water activity, population density, varying substrates, nitrogen atmospheres, and encapsulation in plastic on the thermoradiation process. The results of some of these investigations are described below.

Changes in relative humidity (RH) are known to affect experimental results when organisms are subjected to both dry heat and radiation inactivation treatments. In a series of experiments designed to assess RH effects in thermoradiation, a precisely controlled humidity system was used to attain 20 %, 40 %, and 60 % RH at room temperature, which represented two extremes to the normal 35 % RH laboratory level. This air was then raised to experimental temperature. It should be understood that these extremes represent a range of only 0.5 % to 1.5 %

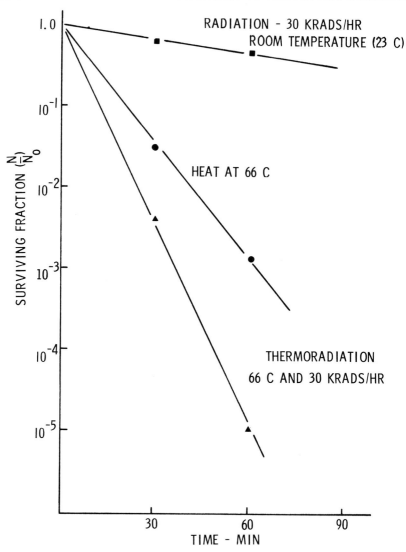

Figure 7 Thermoradiation inactivation of T4 bacteriophage.

respectively when the temperature of the air is elevated to 100 C, but it is convenient to speak of the RH at ambient temperature.

Figure 9 compares dry heat survivor curves for "dry" *B. subtilis* var. *niger* spores at 105 C under RH conditions of 20%, 40%, and 60% of the air at ambient temperature. It is readily evident that RH has a pronounced effect on inactivation by dry heat since the 105 C *D* value varied from 2.3 hr at 20% to 5.3 hr at 60% RH (ambient).

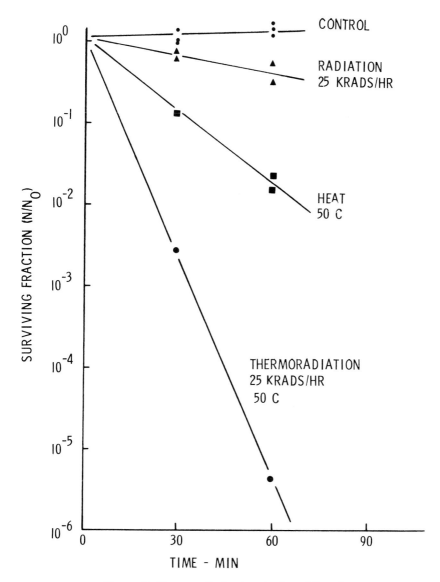

Figure 8 Thermoradiation inactivation of *E. coli*.

Experiments using the same RH levels were performed in a thermo-radiation environment (Figure 10). Using a temperature of 105 C and a radiation dose rate of 20 krad/hr, very little effect from varying RH levels was observed. This difference in RH effect for *B. subtilis* might be attributed to the combined effects of increased sensitivity to heat

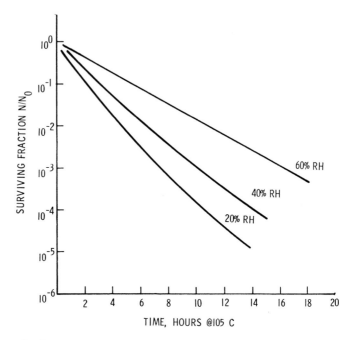

Figure 9 Comparison of dry heat with variable room ambient relative humidity.

as shown in Figure 9 and a decreased sensitivity to radiation when the normal moisture content of the organism is reduced.

The oxygen dependency of radiation inactivation has been established by a number of investigators. For example, it is known that a 33 % increase in the inactivation dose is required for *B. subtilis* spores when dry nitrogen replaces normal atmosphere in the radiation environment. Even greater reductions in radiation inactivation in nitrogen as compared to air have been found for *E. coli*. Since the so-called "oxygen enhancement ratio" plays a large role in limiting the effectiveness of radiation sterilization in some applied settings, it was felt necessary to determine the effect, if any, of a nitrogen atmosphere on thermoradiation inactivation. In order to do this, *B. subtilis* spores were subjected to both dry heat and thermoradiation treatments in nitrogen at 95 C and at dose rates of 4, 11, 38, and 85 krad/hr. The results of these studies are shown by the curves in Figure 11. The thermoradiation D values varied from about 1 hr at the 85 krad/hr dose rate to 3.4 hr at 4 krad/hr. Although the D value in N_2 for high dose rates is generally somewhat higher than in air, there is essentially no difference in D value in the region of about 10 krad/hr (at this temperature).

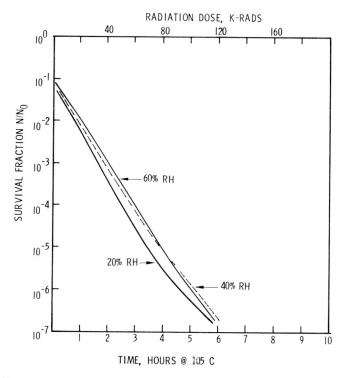

Figure 10 Comparison of simultaneous radiation/dry heat with variable room ambient relative humidity.

The most interesting and perhaps the most potentially valuable thermoradiation parameter studied was that of dose rate. Figure 12 shows the results of a series of experiments at 105 C with dose rates ranging from 2.6 to 36 krad/hr. The corresponding D values ranged from 2 hr to 40 min respectively. The significant difference, however, was the total dose required for a given reduction in population. For example, if one considers a 4 log reduction in population, the high rate (36 krad/hr) requires a total dose of 90 krads where the lowest dose rate of 2.6 krad/hr requires only a dose of 21 krads. Thus, the total dose in a thermoradiation environment required for a given reduction appears to be highly dependent upon dose rate. The difference in heating time between these two examples is not sufficient to account for any significant part of the dissimilar total dose requirements. Another implication of Figure 12 can be derived by considering a constant treatment time of 4 hr. Inactivation at 36 krad/hr would result in a total dose of 144 krads during the 4 hr period with a 6 log reduction in population. The

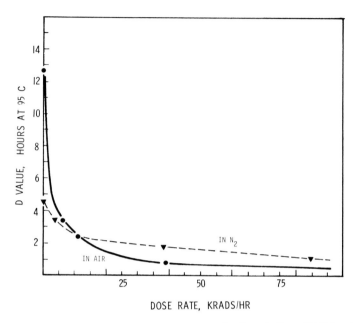

Figure 11 Thermoradiation *D* value vs. dose rate for *B. subtilis* at 95 C in air and in nitrogen.

dose required for a log reduction in population would be 24 krads. The low dose rate option of 2.6 krad/hr would result in a total dose of 10.4 krads during the same 4 hr period with a 2.5 log population reduction. In this latter case, the dose per log reduction in population would be 4.2 krads or about 1/6 the high rate requirement.

Figure 12 also illustrates the temperature/total dose combinations that may be available for a specified sterilization cycle. The *D* value at the ordinate is that of dry heat at 105 C or 4.5 hr. The *D* value drops rapidly up to 10 or 15 krad/hr as low dose rate gamma radiation is added to the dry heat. Beyond this point there is a marginal change in *D* value with increasing dose rate. There are several alternatives available, for example, if a microbial population is to be reduced by 12 logs. This could be accomplished by using heat with a total sterilization time of 54 hr. A second option would be thermoradiation at 12 krad/hr with a *D* value of 1.1 hr, or 13 hr total sterilization time and a total dose of 156 krads. Another option might be at a dose rate of 36 krad/hr. This would result in a *D* value of 0.7 hr, or 8.4 hr total sterilization time with a total dose of 302 krads. By selecting the proper combination, some undesirable side effects of sterilization can be minimized and tradeoffs between time, temperature, and radiation dose can be made to optimize the steriliza-

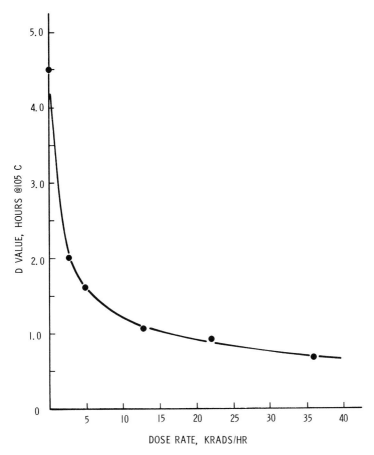

Figure 12 Thermoradiation D value for various radiation dose rates at 105 C using *B. subtilis* var. *niger* spores.

tion cycle for the material to be sterilized. How this might be done is described in the next section. It is interesting to note that the D value versus dose rate curve for treatment in air at 95 C (Figure 11) also has the same general shape as that shown in Figure 12 for 105 C.

As described previously, thermoradiation seems quite efficient when heat is combined with low dose rate gamma radiation. Very high dose rate *pulsed* 1.6 mev X-rays have also been found to be effective but to a lesser degree. The inactivation of *B. subtilis* var. *niger* using X-ray, dry heat, and then thermoradiation (X-rays at 105 C) is compared in Figure 13. As depicted by the curves in this figure, the additive inactivation of dry heat and pulsed X-radiation would be $2\frac{1}{2}$ logs after 6 hr of treatment. Using thermoradiation, the amount of inactivation is at least

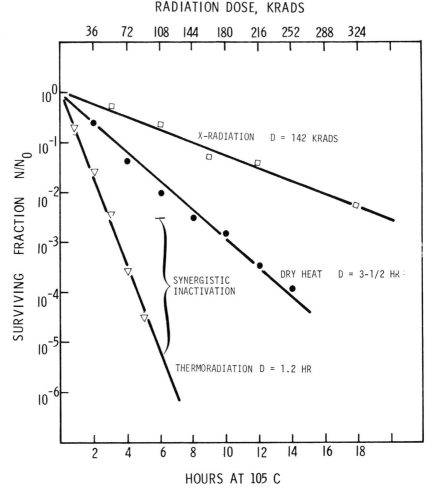

Figure 13 Dry heat thermoradiation and X-radiation inactivation of *B. subtilis*.

twice the sum of dry heat and X-ray inactivation or about 5 logs after 6 hr. The continued inverse effect of dose rate was also noted. This is portrayed in Figure 13 where the thermoradiation D value at 105° with a single 18 krad pulse (given in less than a msec, for a high dose rate) each hour was 1.2 hr. In Figure 12 the D value using steady-state 1.25 mev gamma radiation at 18 krad/hr was 1.0 hr. A very high steady-state dose rate would probably show no appreciable synergism. This is discussed in the next section.

ANALYSIS OF THERMORADIATION

It seems advisable to begin by discussing why analysis is desirable. To do this, let us consider heat sterilization and radiation sterilization separately for a moment. If one wishes to reduce a population to some small fraction of its original value using heat, there are numerous possible ways of doing this, ranging from relatively low temperatures for long periods of time to high temperatures for short periods of time. This is illustrated in Figure 14. But, there is a principle involved in this process: the higher the temperature, the shorter the time. This same principle applies to ambient temperature radiation sterilization in modified form: the higher the dose rate, the shorter the time. This principle does not, of course, tell one *how much* the sterilization time may be lessened by an increase in temperature or dose rate, but the existence of such a principle makes *experimental* determination of the temperature or radiation dose rate needed to sterilize in a given time straightforward.

The situation with thermoradiation is different in several respects. It is the case that sterilization time decreases as either the temperature or dose rate is increased. But it is also true that sterilization time may be decreased while one of the variables (temperature or dose rate) is being decreased—such a decrease being more than compensated for by an increase in the other variable. Thus there are many potential combinations of heat and radiation that may be effectively used for sterilization. The object in some rough way would be to find the "best" combination for a given application. Clearly, the "best" combination depends upon temperature or radiation dose constraints imposed by the items being sterilized. But equally important constraints on "best" arise from the existence of a synergism between heat and ionizing radiation. There is little benefit in using combined radiation and heat at dose rates and temperatures where either the "radiation at room temperature" or the "temperature" mechanism is completely dominant since, clearly, when either of these is the case, the other (radiation or heat) could be effectively dispensed with. But when neither the heat nor the "radiation at room temperature" mechanism is particularly dominant, one sees the synergistic effect described earlier. Thus, *a "best" combination of heat and radiation should be one at which synergism is evident.* Intuitively, this says that the major advantage of using combinations of heat and radiation lies with the fact that one can get more kill per unit energy expended—indeed, *much* more—by properly selecting temperatures and dose rates.

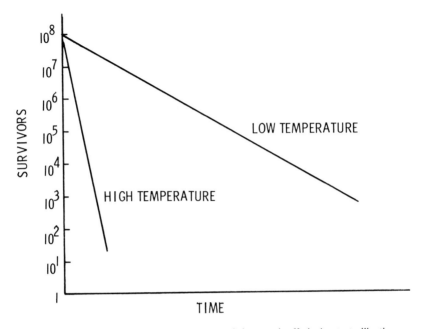

Figure 14 Illustration of temperature and time tradeoffs in heat sterilization.

The experimental determination of all possible temperature and dose rate combinations which yield a synergistic sterilization response can be a monumental task. For example, it is known that at least some synergistic inactivation of *B. subtilis* var. *niger* spores is evident in the ranges of temperature from 60 to 125 C and of dose rate from 5 krad/hr to 20 krad/msec. Under these circumstances, it is highly desirable to have an analytical expression which will predict what occurs at all intermediate temperature and dose rate combinations and to subsequently use this expression in combination with temperature and dose constraints imposed by the items being sterilized to attempt to find the "best" radiation dose rate and temperature combination for the sterilization process. The development of such a "model" and how it may be used to obtain "optimal" sterilization cycles is the subject of this section.

To begin, let us first consider heat sterilization and conventional radiation sterilization separately. In heat sterilization, one frequently encounters survival data like those of Figure 15. Sometimes survival data which are nonlinear on such a semi-logarithmic plot are encountered and theories for such data have been developed. For our purposes, it is sufficient to assume the so-called logarithmic behavior illustrated

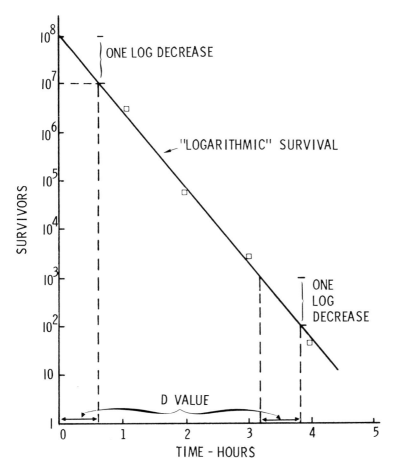

Figure 15   The nature of logarithmic survival in heat sterilization.

in Figure 15. When logarithmic behavior is seen, it is customary to represent the *expected* number of surviving organisms at time t, denoted $E(N(t))$, by an expression of the form

$$E(N(t)) = N(0)\ 10^{-t/D} \tag{1}$$

The parameter D is the D value (which, as earlier, represents that amount of time, t, needed to reduce the initial population of $N(0)$ organisms to 10% of $N(0)$). The D value is independent of time when logarithmic behavior is assumed. This is also illustrated in Figure 15.

It will be shown later that in modeling thermoradiation, it is desirable to know how $E(N(t))$ behaves as a function of temperature and to know this in some abstract sense independent of survivor data. To determine such a temperature dependence, it is necessary to ascribe some physical interpretation to D (the only parameter in Equation 1 that might be temperature dependent) from which a temperature dependence may be deduced. This can be done as follows. Suppose that the survival of an organism depends upon whether a chemical reaction of the type

$$A \xrightarrow{k_T} X \text{ (first order)} \tag{2}$$

does or does not take place. So long as A (not X) is present, the organism survives. The assumption of first order kinetics simply means that the *rate* at which A turns into X is proportional to the amount of A present —and the constant of proportionality is $-k_T$. Assuming that the concentration of A is proportional to the number of viable organisms present in a population to be sterilized yields the following expression for the expected number of survivors as a function of time.

$$E(N(t)) = N(0)\, e^{-k_T t} \tag{3}$$

For some, this expression may require some further explanation. The symbol e is a number (about 2.7) that merely "replaces" the "10" in Equation 1. Given a value for D, there is a k_T so that

$$10^{-t/D} = e^{-k_T t}$$

for all times t. (This value of k is, in fact, about $2.303/D$.) Thus Equation 3 will exhibit *exactly* the same behavior vis-à-vis survival that is exhibited by Equation 1. The advantage in the form given by Equation 3 is that k_T may be interpreted physically as a chemical rate constant because of the assumptions inherent in Equation 2. The effects of temperature on chemical rate constants have been studied, and a quite accurate representation of the dependence of k_T on temperature, T (degrees Kelvin), is

$$k_T = \frac{\kappa T}{h}\, e^{\Delta S^\ddagger/R}\, e^{-\Delta H^\ddagger/RT} \tag{4}$$

where κ is Boltzmann's constant, h is Planck's constant, R is the gas constant, and $\Delta S^\ddagger$ and $\Delta H^\ddagger$ are the activation entropy and enthalpy, respectively, of the reaction in question.

For a given species of organisms under known environmental conditions, the rate constant k_T of Equation 4 will then behave like

$$k_T = AT\, e^{-B/T} \tag{5}$$

where A and B are constants. This is in agreement with observed survival as a function of temperature (the so-called Arrhenius plot of D

value versus $1/T$ on semilogarithmic graph paper), and indeed, Equations 4 and 5 will be valid over wider ranges of temperature. Figure 16 illustrates the behavior of k_T as a function of temperature. From this figure and Equation 3 it may be deduced that sterilization times are decreased *exponentially* as the temperature is increased. In summary

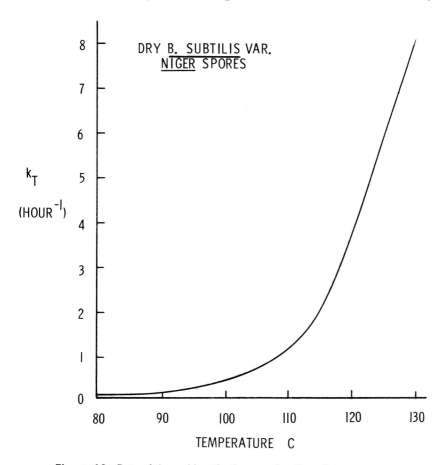

Figure 16   Rate of thermal inactivation as a function of temperature.

then, at least for our current purposes, the expected number of survivors in thermal environments may be described as a function of time, t, and temperature, T, by

$$E(N(t)) = N(0)\, e^{-k_T t} \qquad (6a)$$

with

$$k_T = \frac{\kappa T}{h}\, e^{\Delta S^{\ddagger}/R}\, e^{-\Delta H^{\ddagger}/RT} \qquad (6b)$$

Turning to classical radiation survival (radiation effects at "ambient temperature"), one may appeal to target theory to determine the dependence of survival upon radiation dose rate. Target theory holds that the deposition of sufficient energy in a critical target, which is thought to be the dominant nucleic acid of the system being irradiated, leads to the inability of the organism to reproduce. Briefly, such an assumption yields an expression for the expected number of survivors at time t, $E(N(t))$, of the form

$$E(N(t)) = N(0) \, e^{-k_R t} \tag{7a}$$

with

$$k_R = C r_d \tag{7b}$$

where r_d stands for the dose *rate* of the radiation, and C is a constant linking the energy per unit time deposited by a given dose rate and the energy absorbed by the nucleic acid. When Equation 7b is substituted into Equation 7a one obtains

$$E(N(t)) = N(0) \, e^{-C r_d \cdot t}$$

But since $r_d \cdot t$ is the total dose at time t, designated d, this is often written

$$E(N(d)) = N(0) \, e^{-Cd} \tag{8}$$

In this context, $1/C$ is a constant, denoted D_{37}, representing the dose required to reduce the population to $1/e$ or about 37 % of its original value, and Equation 8, in its most familiar form, becomes

$$E(N(d)) = N(0) \, e^{-d/D_{37}}$$

In the context of thermoradiation, the form given in Equation 7 is preferred because of its compatibility with the thermal behavior described by Equation 6. It is evident from Equation 8 that temperature independent radiation inactivation is dependent only upon total dose, so that increases in dose rate imply linearly dependent decreases in sterilization times. Thus, for example, if the dose rate is raised by a factor of two, the sterilization time is decreased by this same factor.

With this as background, let us turn to an investigation of the thermoradiation phenomenon. Figure 17 is that same figure appearing on p. 306. The rate of thermal inactivation, k_T, may be determined from the slope of the thermal survival curve, and the rate of radiation inactivation, k_R, determined similarly from the slope of the radiation survival curve. Inactivation at a *rate* $k_T + k_R$ would yield the dashed line as a survivor curve. In reality, when synergism is present, the expected number of survivors at time t in a combination heat and

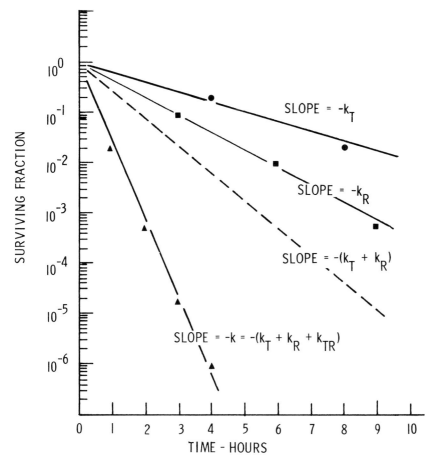

Figure 17 Relationship of symbols to survivor data.

radiation environment behaves according to

$$E(N(t)) = N(0) e^{-kt} \qquad (9)$$

where k has a value *greater* than $k_T + k_R$ (that is to say inactivation is more rapid than would be anticipated if heat and radiation effects were simply additive). Thus one may write k as

$$k = k_T + k_R + k_{TR} \qquad (10)$$

where the symbol k_{TR} represents that number which must be added to $k_T + k_R$ to obtain the actual observed inactivation rate k. Of course, one would expect the value of k_{TR} to depend upon both dose rate and temperature—with k_{TR} sometimes large and sometimes small—since k_{TR} *is a direct measure of the amount of synergism being observed.*

Ideally, knowing the forms of k_T and k_R as functions of dose rate and temperature and having sufficient thermoradiation survival data, one might deduce the *functional* dependence of k_{TR} on both temperature and dose rate. This has been done, and it turns out that k_{TR} is related to radiation dose rate, r_d, and temperature, T, by

$$k_{TR} = a r_d^{b/T} e^{-c/T} \tag{11}$$

where a, b, and c are constants depending upon other environmental conditions and the specie of organism being sterilized. The type of dose rate and temperature behavior implied for k_{TR} by Equation 11 has been directly observed in all bacterial phages, vegetative cells, and bacterial spores that have been investigated. On the other hand since thermoradiation is a relative newcomer in the field of sterilization, the broadness of the data base may leave something to be desired. Perhaps the strongest evidence for a universal behavior of k_{TR} consistent with Equation 11 comes from the observation that this particular form of behavior may be derived from the assumption that, in combination, radiation and heat act on some substrate A in cells to promote a reaction of the type

$$A + nR \xrightarrow{\;k^*\;} X$$

where R is a collection of radiation produced free radicals, some number n of which must react with A in a temperature dependent way to produce a form X which will not support replication. There is mounting evidence of the reasonableness of this approach and that A is, indeed, the dominant nucleic acid of the system. To the extent that this is correct, one would expect synergistic behavior to be similar in *form* in all systems having nucleic acid. Additionally, if the effective ultimate "target" is the nucleic acid, one might anticipate that the behavior of k_{TR} will depend in some consistent way on the content of nucleic acid of the system being sterilized. Some behavior of this type has been observed, and this is shown in Figure 18, where the temperature at which k_{TR} becomes significant increases with decreasing nucleic acid content.

In summary, then, the model currently used to represent thermoradiation effects has the form

$$E(N(t)) = N(0)\, e^{-kt}$$

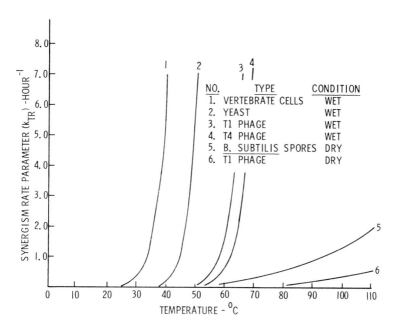

Figure 18   The behavior of synergism in different systems as a function of temperature.

with
$$k = k_T + k_R = k_{TR},$$

$$k_T = \frac{\kappa T}{h} e^{\Delta S^{\ddagger}/R} e^{-\Delta H^{\ddagger}/RT}$$

(Equation 6b)

$$k_R = C r_d \qquad (12)$$

(Equation 7b)

and
$$k_{TR} = a r_d^{b/T} e^{-c/T}$$

(Equation 11)

In theory, survival studies at two temperatures (only) are sufficient to determine the values of the two parameters $\Delta S^{\ddagger}$ and $\Delta H^{\ddagger}$ occurring in k_T. A single experiment with radiation at ambient temperature will, likewise, determine C occurring in the expression of k_R. Finally, combined experiments at two temperatures and a single-dose rate plus an

additional experiment at one of these temperatures and a different dose
rate are necessary for the determination of the values of parameters a,
b, and c occurring in k_{TR}. Note that k (Equation 10) is measured and
$k_T + k_R$ is subtracted from k to yield k_{TR}. In practice, of course, more
experiments are desirable. As an example, for *B. subtilis* var. *niger*
spores in a dry state under suitable conditions, one obtains:

$$\Delta S^{\ddagger} = 12.63 \text{ entropy units}$$
$$\Delta H^{\ddagger} = 33,590 \text{ cal/mole}$$
$$C = 0.0234 \text{ krad}^{-1}$$
$$a = e^{16.27}$$
$$b = 159.12$$
$$c = 12,944.1$$

With these parameter values, Figure 19 illustrates how well the rate, k,
predicted using Equation 12 compares with that actually obtained for
temperatures varying between 23 C and 125 C and dose rates between
0 and 65 krad/hr. Similar predictive agreement with data has been
obtained with T4 bacteriophage—the only other system investigated in
sufficient depth to permit such comparisons with any confidence. The
model is capable of *fitting* all survivor data in combined environments
obtained in our laboratory or from the literature.

Much has been said, so far, about the existence of ranges of temperature and dose rate in which a synergism will exist, but little specific
information has been given. The reason of course is precisely that given
earlier in this section—a model is necessary for a thorough treatment of
this subject. First, observe how each of the mechanisms, heat (k_T),
radiation (k_R), and synergism (k_{TR}) combine to yield an overall inactivation rate k for *B. subtilis* var. *niger* spores in a dry state based on the
above parameter values. This is shown in Figure 20 for a fixed dose rate.
Here, below about 60 C, the synergism, as evidenced by k_{TR}, begins to
become insignificant compared to k_R. Hence below this temperature at
this dose rate (about 15 krad/hr) a synergism is unlikely to be observed.
Toward the other end of the temperature scale, k_{TR} begins to become
insignificant in comparison with k_T at about 135 C (again at 15 krad/hr).
But, dose rate will have an effect upon the range of temperature in
which synergism is observed. This occurs because (Equation 12):

1. k_R increases linearly with dose rate.
2. k_{TR} depends on $r_d^{159/T}$ (T in degrees Kelvin), a fractional power of
   dose rate for T greater than 159 (for dry *B. subtilis* var. *niger*
   spores).

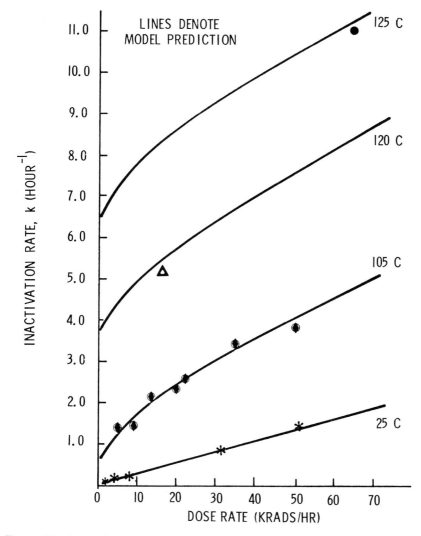

Figure 19 Comparison of model prediction with inactivation rates obtained from survivor data for *B. subtilis* var. *niger* spores in a dry state.

Thus, by decreasing the dose rate, the lowest temperature at which synergism is observed is lowered (k_R decreases more rapidly than k_{TR}) until the temperature reaches 159 K at which time both k_R and k_{TR} depend linearly on dose rate. Likewise, by increasing the dose rate, one may extend the temperature range over which synergism is observed—but only within certain limits, because eventually k_R will increase to the point that it dominates k_{TR} even beyond the point that k_T does also. Thus,

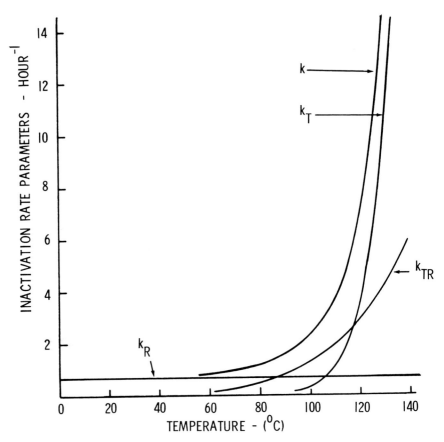

Figure 20   The contribution of the individual inactivation rate parameters to the composite inactivation parameter *k* for *B. subtilis* var. *niger* spores in a thermoradiation environment utilizing gamma radiation at 30.6 krads/hr.

for "high" constant dose rates, synergism may not be detected at any temperature. (These observations tend to explain the many contradictory reports of synergism versus no synergism appearing in the literature.)

The other side of the problem is dose rate; Figure 21 shows how dose rate influences k. This is essentially the same data as those shown in Figure 12 in the previous section. At 105 C the overall inactivation rate k increases rapidly as a function of dose rate to about 8–15 krad/hr. This is a range in which k_{TR} considerably dominates k_R. Beyond this range k_{TR} is becoming more like k_R until eventually the curve will become asymptotic with a slope indistinguishable from that of k_R. This point is not shown in the figure, but it occurs at a dose rate of several hundred krads/hr. Thus, for a good start in defining the tem-

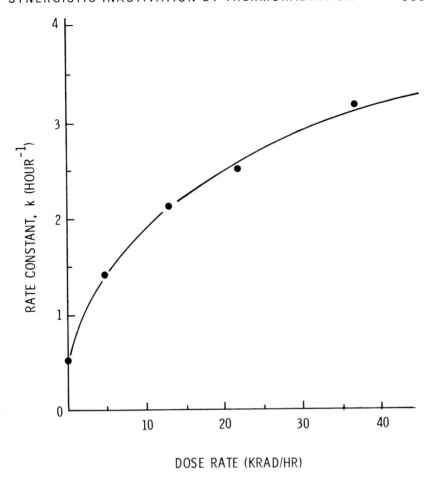

Figure 21   Rate of thermoradiation inactivation as a function of dose rate.

perature and dose rate regions where synergism is likely to be evident, one may start with relatively low dose rates (say, 10–50 krad/hr) and find a single temperature which for at least one of these dose rates shows a synergism. This temperature should be below those at which extremely rapid rates of thermal inactivation are encountered. If no synergism is obtained, the dose rate should be variously raised and lowered. When a temperature is found at which a synergism for some dose rate exists, a graph such as Figure 21 may be used to determine a good "optimal" dose rate range—that just beyond the initial "fast" rise. For this dose rate (or this range), graphs corresponding to Figure 20 may be made—and a reasonable idea of the range in which synergism is obtained may be determined.

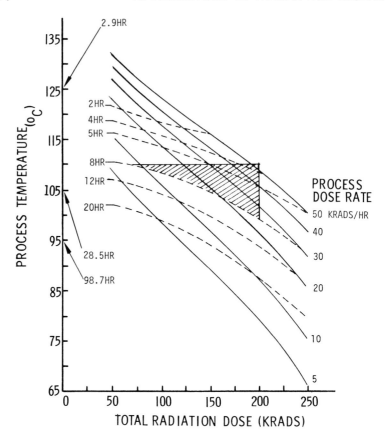

Figure 22 Planning a thermoradiation sterilization cycle.

Finally, as an overview for selection of dose rate and temperature combinations that are optimum for a given application, a plot such as that shown in Figure 22 may be made. Here, the relationship between temperature, dose rate, total dose, and sterilization time is indicated. Such a plot is obtained from Equation 12 when parameter values and a general idea of the ranges of temperature and dose rate of interest are known. The temperature and dose rate ranges shown here were chosen on the basis of considerations like those above to include much of the region where synergism was present. As an example of how Figure 22 would be used, suppose one wished to obtain an 8 log decrease in a population of dry *B. subtilis* var. *niger* spores in no more than 8 hr at a temperature no higher than 110 C and a total dose not in excess of 200 krads, he must select temperature and dose rate combinations from the shaded portion of this chart. In particular, the sterilizing dose rate may not be below ten nor above about 50 krad/hr and the sterilizing temperature must lie in the range from about 100 to 110 C. The higher temperature, higher dose rate combinations yield, of course, lower sterilization times, but with the imposed constraints, the sterilization time in this example must always exceed 3 hr.

SUMMARY

Thermoradiation is a process of sterilization that is apparently applicable to all biological systems in which ionizing radiation and heat are simultaneously applied. In certain regions of temperature and dose rate, that may be peculiar to the type of biological system being sterilized, thermoradiation exhibits a synergistic sterilizing effect. Sufficient theory of thermoradiation has been developed to allow prediction of the temperatures and radiation dose rates where this synergism is encountered. Additionally, this theory makes it possible to "tailor" sterilization cycles to the items being sterilized.

To persons or organizations currently involved with the sterilization of goods, thermoradiation offers potentially large benefits. In regions where synergism occurs, such benefits are:

1. The addition of a small dose of ionizing radiation to an existing heat sterilization process will result in much more rapid sterilization, yielding a considerably decreased process time.
2. The addition of modest heating to an existing radiation sterilization process will, in the same way, increase the processing rate.
3. With the addition of small amounts of radiation, temperatures in existing heat sterilization cycles can be lowered without affecting process time.
4. With the addition of modest amounts of heat, total radiation doses in existing radiation sterilization cycles can be appreciably lowered without affecting process time.
5. The thermoradiation process is, under many circumstances, less sensitive to environmental parameters than either heat sterilization or radiation sterilization separately.
6. It is possible to select temperatures, radiation dose rates and sterilization times in such a way that the heat and radiation separately would have little sterilizing effect, but their combination has considerable effect. This has implications for the selective sterilization of critical portions of complex, but delicate systems.

18

Sterilization Technology in the United States Space Program

LAWRENCE B. HALL

Planetary Quarantine Officer
National Aeronautics and Space Administration
Washington, D.C.

DURING the past decade the National Aeronautics and Space Administration of the United States has invested some 400 man-years in research on sterilization. The problem to be solved: how to sterilize spacecraft completely without degrading their flight and operational reliability.

Spacecraft are somewhat unique in their sterilization requirements. Seldom does industry need to sterilize objects the dimensions of which are measured in meters and the numbers of which can be counted on one hand. Moreover, there is often a need for internal sterility of the spacecraft: that is, the elimination of any life buried inside the solid materials waiting to be released on a planet's surface by high velocity impact, wind erosion, or other release phenomena.

To meet these and other problems of spacecraft sterilization the Planetary Quarantine Program has drawn from the sterilization technology of the food and medical products industries. But, where many food and medical products can be overtreated, to insure the death of the last organism, the sterilization stress applied to a spacecraft must be precise, neither so heavy that the spacecraft is damaged nor so light that a remnant of the bioload remains viable.

In order to understand and solve sterilization and other complex biological problems, NASA has developed and applied mathematical models, a technique that ought to be increasingly useful to industry.

The planetary quarantine model in its simplest form will serve to illustrate this technique. In this case, the acceptable probability that a planet will be contaminated is designated as P_c in the following equation

$$P_c = \sum_i N_{i0} \cdot P_{vt} \cdot P_{uv} \cdot P_{sa} \cdot P_r \cdot P_g$$

The value of P_c is equal to the summation, over the ith distinct sources of bioburden, of the product of the number of microorganisms in each source and the probabilities of occurrence of events which affect contamination. In this equation: N_{i0} is the number of viable terrestrial organisms (VTOs) at launch. The events of concern in this example are:

P_{vt}: probability that a randomly selected microorganism survives the vacuum-temperature conditions of interplanetary space

P_{uv}: probability that a randomly selected microorganism survives the stresses of ultraviolet radiation of space

P_{sa}: probability that a randomly selected microorganism survives the stress of entry into the atmosphere of the target planet

P_r: the probability that any single organism will be released in a viable state onto the planet's surface or into its atmosphere

P_g: the probability that any single organism will grow and proliferate on the planet.

Each of the parameters on the right side of the equation can be broken down into many subparameters. For instance, the probability of growth, P_g, can include the probabilities that the species of organism can grow on the planet, that a suitable growth environment exists on the planet, and that the organism will survive transfer from the spacecraft to a favorable environment.

When finally completed, the answer will be expressed in terms of a probability, but one that is much more valid than an educated guess. This approach of modeling and mathematical analysis defines the limits of the probability of occurrence of undesirable events—in other words, it is based upon risk management principles. In this approach a complex system can be described in terms of its related events, activities, and factors, each of which is mathematically defined and interrelated. The approach insures that attention is focused upon each factor in the system and that its evaluation is commensurate with the relative influence of that factor upon the total solution.

This simple and rudimentary illustration of systems analysis and mathematical modeling does not do justice to the value of the technique which, in skilled hands, can resolve many complex biological and physical problems that can be solved in no other way. It is particularly applicable to problems of sterilization which are basically probabilistic in nature.

In the actual practice of spacecraft sterilization it is desirable to control the bioload at the lowest practical level to minimize the stresses associated with sterilization. To keep the bioload low, clean room techniques, particularly those of downward laminar flow, were developed by the space program and applied to microbial control. An interesting finding known as the *plateau phenomenon* has shown that contamination on objects in a clean room will build up to a constant level, then hold at that level no matter how long the exposure. It has also been found that there is a marked difference in the load deposited on surfaces which are oriented in different directions. In comparison to upward-facing horizontal surfaces, vertical surfaces, such as walls, receive only one-tenth the load and downward-facing horizontal surfaces, such as ceilings, one-fiftieth to one-hundredth the load. In determining or controlling the total bioload on manufactured products, whether they be heart pacers or spacecraft, these differences can be of considerable importance.

Planetary quarantine research on methods of sterilization has centered on dry heat. The requirement for sterilization of organisms buried inside solids and between mated surfaces requires penetration that can be supplied only by heat or radiation. Of these two, the choice of heat was easy, for radiation is even more destructive than heat for many spacecraft materials.

Perhaps the greatest contribution of this research to our understanding of heat sterilization is the discovery of the important role that water plays in the lethal process. Most conventional heat sterilization has been done under conditions of water saturation. It was only when heat sterilization under dry conditions was critically examined that the process was found to be responsive not only to the two parameters of time and temperature, but also to the third parameter of water activity. Microbial resistance is at a minimum at very wet and very dry extremes and at a maximum at the midrange of water activity. Spacecraft treated by dry heat will be sterilized in the driest of atmospheres.

Of particular importance to industry is the discovery by the Sandia Laboratories, funded by NASA, that there is sterilization synergism with heat and gamma or X-irradiation. The combination of the two sterilizing agents, called *thermoradiation*, permits sterilization at astonishingly low temperatures and rates of radiation (3). The process, ready for use now, should provide industry significant benefits when it is fully utilized. Thermoradiation will be used only to a limited extent for the sterilization of spacecraft in the immediate future because of its unknown effects on spacecraft reliability, but consideration is warranted by industries sterilizing products whose operation is not sensitive or whose reliability is not critical. Full evaluation may well prove that reliability is not significantly degraded by thermoradiation.

For many years there has been recognition of the need for a residual germicide that, remaining on the treated surfaces in minute quantities, will exert a lethal effect on organisms over a period of time. Paraformaldehyde and melamine formaldehyde offer promise in the solution of this problem (1). The Becton, Dickinson Research Center and the Sandia Laboratories, funded by the NASA Planetary Quarantine Program, have evaluated and developed methods of using the compounds, including removal of the obnoxious odor. Patents are being secured by the U.S. government in order that all may use the technology. As in thermoradiation, the formaldehyde compounds are unfortunately of very limited use on spacecraft because the released gas may have unknown effects on the reliability of spacecraft materials, and the gas would certainly interfere with the extremely sensitive spectrophotometric measurements made by the spacecraft instruments in flight and on a planet's surface.

The use of ethylene oxide comes to mind, of course, in connection with the sterilization of any large object such as a spacecraft. The material was, indeed, used in attempts to sterilize the first few Ranger spacecraft in the early 1960s. Unfortunately some of those missions failed and, although there was no evidence that the ethylene oxide caused the failures, there was visual evidence of damage to some spacecraft materials. This experience, coupled with the need for undesirable humidification and a history of "skips" in some ethylene oxide operations, has resulted in the virtual abandonment of ethylene oxide by the U.S. space program.

Though not used by the United States, officials of the Union of Soviet Socialist Republics have reported on the use of a combination of ethylene oxide–methyl bromide to sterilize their Mars 1 and 2 missions (4). The mixture (1.0 part ethylene oxide to 1.44 parts of methyl bromide) was applied at the rate of 1.6 g of the mixed gas per liter of container volume at a temperature of 50 C for 6 hr. The mixture is reported to be synergistic, capable of penetrating many plastics, and is fireproof. Studies in the United States have failed to confirm that any strong synergism exists, but the work on the subject has been very limited.

Unfortunately, all of the sterilants now known, except perhaps ultraviolet radiation, cause some damage both to the extremely sensitive surfaces of spacecraft as well as to sensitive medical and surgical products. Two new, somewhat exotic, techniques offer the promise of sterilization with minimum damage. Now under investigation for NASA by the Jet Propulsion Laboratory and the Boeing Company is the use of plasma as a sterilant. Produced by a radio frequency generator in a closed container at ambient temperature, the ion stream physically removes organic contaminants from the exposed surfaces. This process has the advantage of not only killing the organism, but of also removing the "carcass" if that term may be applied to a microorganism. To date this technique has not been scaled to containers larger than about one-half cubic meter, but there do not appear to be theoretical obstacles to doing so. This process warrants and is receiving further investigation.

Even more recent than the plasma studies has been the report of the Massachusetts Institute of Technology (not supported by NASA) of the sterilant action of certain laser beams (2). *Bacillus subtilis* were rendered completely inactive in one-hundredth of a second in a 50-w, unfocused, carbon dioxide, laser beam. The cellulose acetate paper substrate was not damaged in any way. Sterility also has been obtained by others in 3 min by exposure to a laser beam passing through a beam spreader to cover an area 1 ft wide. Shading does not appear to be the problem that it is with ultraviolet light. If this should prove to be the case, laser beams may supply the solution to many problems of surface sterilization without damage to the substrate.

The research supported by NASA has often resulted in unanticipated benefits to nonspace technology. An interesting illustration is an offshoot of the development of a surface sampling technique which employs a simple, hand-held device connected to a vacuum pump which draws air and entrained contaminants from a surface through a critical orifice to a membrane filter upon which the minute contaminants are deposited. Originally intended to collect microorganisms from the surfaces of a spacecraft, the device has been in unexpected demand by law enforcement agencies who use it to gather microscopic evidence at the scene of a crime. It is reported to be so efficient that it removes microscopic, but identifiable, bits of automobile paint from the clothing of hit-and-run victims and is particularly useful in recovering the remnants of narcotics from containers, such as pockets of the suspects, despite the destruction of the main body of evidence.

The United States Planetary Quarantine Program research will continue into its second decade. For the first U.S. planetary lander, Viking '75, a final dry heat sterilization cycle is planned. The vehicle will be exposed for up to 72 hr to a temperature between 104 and 113 C at a relative humidity of less than 0.1 %.

Hopefully, as time goes on, the NASA supported research will look into new processes that will become operationally useful, not only to the space program, but to industry as a whole. All of the research reports that our centers, grantees, and contractors have generated in the past decade are made available to anyone with a legitimate interest. We began by borrowing the knowledge and skills of the pharmaceutical and medical products industries; we now have developed approaches and techniques which, we believe, can be beneficial to these industries.

References

1. Becton, Dickinson Research Center. Aug. 13, 1968–Oct. 12, 1969. *Investigation of methods for the sterilization of potting compounds and mated surfaces. Final report.* Raleigh, N.C.
2. *Reports on research.* Apr., 1962. M.I.T. Cambridge, Mass.
3. Reynolds, M. C. Dec., 1969. *The feasibility of thermoradiation for sterilization of spacecraft—A preliminary report.* 56-RR-69-857.
4. Vashkov, V. I., N. V. Rashkova, and G. V. Shcleglova. 1970. *Karantin planet: Printsipy metody i problemy, osnovy kosmicheskoy biolgii i meditsiny.* Chap. 4, Vol. 1, Pt. 3. pp. 3–156.

19

Monitoring for Microbial Flora

MARTIN S. FAVERO, PH.D.

Phoenix Laboratories
Center for Disease Control
U.S. Public Health Service
Phoenix, Arizona

INTRODUCTION

DURING the past eight years, most of the unmanned and manned spacecraft launched from the United States have been subjected to microbiological assays. The basic reason for assessing the types and levels of microbial contamination on unmanned spacecraft such as the Lunar Orbiter, the Surveyor, and the Anchored Interplanetary Monitoring Platform (AIMP), all of which were designed to impact the lunar surface or had some probability of eventual impact, was to maintain a qualitative and quantitative "inventory" of microbial populations deposited on the lunar surface. In the case of the manned Apollo spacecraft, microbiological profiles also were required because of the possibility of these organisms contaminating samples taken from the lunar surface. These samples were returned to earth and subsequently subjected to a series of microbiological assays in conjunction with the astronaut and sample quarantine program at the Lunar Receiving Laboratory (13). Although the samples themselves were processed in a sterile containment system, they were not collected aseptically from the lunar surface. Consequently, attempts were made to provide a data base upon which decisions could be made as to whether or not organisms isolated from the sample were in fact indigenous to the lunar surface or were contaminants introduced by the spacecraft or the astronauts.

A second reason for assessing the level of microbial contamination on space hardware is related to the sterilization of interplanetary spacecraft. By international agreement, the United States and its National Aeronautics and Space Administration (NASA) require that space hardware destined to impact or having a high probability of impacting planets of biological interest, for example, Mars, shall be sterilized to given probability levels (8, 9). The primary sterilization technique will be dry heat (8, 9, 12), and consequently one of the essential factors is the quantitative assessment of microbial contamination, especially bacterial spores in and on space hardware. The terminal dry heat sterilization cycle will be based in part on the number of bacterial spores present on the spacecraft as determined by microbiological assays during final assembly. Although this general approach is practiced in other fields, there is a certain degree of uniqueness in the area of spacecraft sterilization. In the food and pharmaceutical industries, sterility tests can be performed on the final product and the efficiency of the sterilization cycle can be confirmed directly. In the case of spacecraft, however, post-cycle sterility tests cannot be performed because of the destructive nature of the tests. As a result, the determination of the microbial load on a spacecraft is a significant part of the overall sterilization plan, and the techniques used in these assays must provide data from which accurate extrapolations can be made with predictable reliability (4).

The objective of this paper is to describe the general rationale and evolution of the current techniques that are used to assay spacecraft microbiologically. These techniques are of obvious interest to those concerned with industrial sterilization because of the increasing necessity to monitor for the contamination load in medical products prior to the sterilization procedure.

TYPES OF MICROORGANISMS

The types of microorganisms to which the assay procedures are directed differ depending on the general reason for performing the test. For the manned Apollo spacecraft, the basic objective was to attempt to detect and quantitate a wide variety of microorganisms including molds, vegetative bacteria, spores, and actinomycetes. However, when unmanned spacecraft that require sterilization are involved, the bacterial spore becomes the primary object of the microbiological assays.

CULTURE TECHNIQUES

It was recognized as early as 1964 that microbiological assay techniques designed for use in the food, medical, and drug fields were not completely applicable to space hardware. Problems associated with quantitatively recovering extremely low numbers of microorganisms from surfaces as well as the interior of space hardware were unique and no data were available upon which validly to base protocols. Preliminary sets of assay procedures were designed and evaluated which culminated in a set of standard procedures for the microbiological examination of space hardware published by NASA in 1967 and 1968 (18). This manual described the procedures for assaying space hardware in the intra-mural environments used for assembly and testing. The primary emphasis of these procedures was on the accurate and precise enumeration of microorganisms, especially bacterial spores in low numbers.

A general and relatively rich culture medium, Trypticase (tryptic) Soy Agar (TSA),* has been used almost exclusively. Although many other culture media have been evaluated for routine use in assaying space hardware, there has never been any positive evidence that any one culture medium was so superior to TSA that it should be considered for routine use. For example, Favero and coworkers (3) showed that some improvement in recovery might be realized when different culture media, especially those enriched with fresh meat infusions, were used for the recovery of heat injured spores. Pork infusion thioglycolate agar (PIT) was found to be three to four times more efficient than TSA for recovery of specific pure cultures of anaerobic spores injured by dry heat. However, when TSA and PIT were compared for recovery of naturally occurring microorganisms from various spacecraft assembly areas, TSA generally gave higher recoveries than PIT and in many instances, the differences were statistically significant. Because of the complexity and variation encountered in preparing fresh meat infusion media, occasional two- to threefold increases in recovery of specific organisms were not considered significant. If any medium had been found to be consistently an order of magnitude more efficient than TSA, it would then have been considered for routine use. It also was demonstrated that there was no advantage in using a liquid recovery medium (multiple tube dilution tests using trypticase soy broth or pork infusion thioglycolate broth) for enumeration of bacterial spores. While the most probable number (MPN) was higher than the viable plate count in some cases, the limits of the 95 % confidence intervals of the MPN usually encompassed the mean of the viable plate counts.

The temperature-time cycle for incubation was first set empirically at 32 C for 72 hr and experience has shown that this cycle is probably optimal for its intended purpose. Although a few microorganisms do not

* Baltimore Biological Laboratories, BioQuest, Becton, Dickinson and Co.

produce visible colonies within 72 hr, most heterotrophic, mesophilic microorganisms do. From the standpoint of quantitation, especially when extrapolations are made to estimate the level of microbial contamination on an entire spacecraft, the fact that a small portion of the microbial population had not formed visible colonies is relatively unimportant. If the tests were designed to be sterility tests, this factor obviously would be important; however, the assays being discussed within the context of spacecraft sterilization should not be thought of

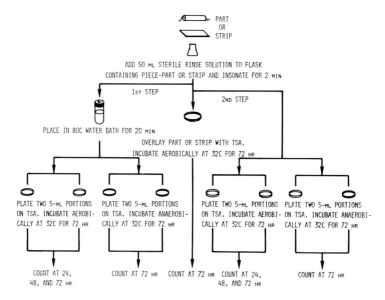

Figure 1   General assay protocol.

in any way as sterility tests. They are simply microbiological assays which are used to predict or to estimate the final level of microbial contamination on a spacecraft.

The general procedure for enumerating aerobic and anaerobic microorganisms and spores is illustrated in Figure 1. In the case of the Apollo spacecraft, although the general assay technique was the same as illustrated in Figure 1, additional selective and enriched media were employed for the purpose of detecting a wide variety of microorganisms (17).

Since the atmosphere of Mars, the first planet to be biologically examined, contains no oxygen, there has been a good deal of concern on the recovery of anaerobic microorganisms from spacecraft since these types may have a high probability of surviving or even proliferating on the planet's surface. The assay procedures that have been used for anaerobes are the same as those that were described for aerobic microorganisms except that the culture plates are incubated under strict anaerobic conditions (Figure 1). The system consists of a Brewer jar or the equivalent in which hydrogen gas is used in conjunction with an appropriate catalyst to remove oxygen. However, the main criterion to determine whether adequate anaerobiosis is achieved is demonstration that a strict aerobe, *Alcaligenes faecalis*, shows no visible growth on TSA after incubation at 32 C for 72 hr. This rationale is based on the results of several environmental studies using nitrogen gas incubators where differences in numbers were noted between aerobic and anaerobic microorganisms from the same environmental samples. This was found to be the result of very small quantities of oxygen being present in the nitrogen gas which allowed many of the aerobes to grow and produce visible colonies. The small quantities of oxygen present were not detected in most cases by chemical indicators, and most anaerobic bacteria isolated could exhibit growth even in the presence of a small amount of oxygen. Consequently, the incubation and growth environment must be free of oxygen in order to obtain true differential counts between aerobes and anaerobes.

Even though studies have shown that the level of anaerobic microbial contamination in environments associated with spacecraft is much lower than aerobic microbial contamination (16, 17), there has been much concern that the current procedures do not recover very fastidious and strictly anaerobic bacteria. In 1968, workers at the Virginia Polytechnic Institute (VPI) and our laboratories at Cape Kennedy conducted a comparative study for recovering strictly anaerobic microorganisms from space hardware. The VPI technique which is considered to be extremely efficient in recovering fastidious anaerobic microorganisms makes use of prereduced media with procedural manipulations performed in an anaerobic environment. The studies which compared the NASA and VPI techniques showed that there was no significant difference in recovery of anaerobes and anaerobic spores from spacecraft in residence at Cape Kennedy, Florida. Typical results are shown in Tables 1 and 2. The most plausible explanation of these results is that highly oxygen-sensitive anaerobes were not capable of survival on spacecraft surfaces under prolonged exposure to air in ultraclean assembly environments. Consequently, the anaerobic microbial flora present on spacecraft or in their assembly areas appears to be a select one, and it is the consensus among investigators in this field that the low levels on spacecraft are a real phenomenon and not an artifact.

Table 1   Comparison of VPI and NASA techniques for recovery of total anaerobic microorganisms from swabs

Day	No. samples assayed by each technique	Mean no. anaerobic microorganisms recovered	
		VPI technique	NASA technique
1	40	98	105
2	40	109	17
3	40	50	66

Table 2   Comparison of VPI and NASA techniques for recovery of anaerobic spores from swabs

Day	No. samples assayed by each technique	Mean no. anaerobic microorganisms recovered	
		VPI technique	NASA technique
1	40	2.5	4.7
2	40	2.3	0.8
3	40	0	0.1

As previously mentioned, when assays are directed toward spacecraft requiring dry heat sterilization, the most important part of the assay system is that which provides for enumeration of aerobic and anaerobic spores. Historically and traditionally, spore assays have involved heating of the microbial suspension prior to plating. This is referred to as "heat shock" or "heat activation," and it has been shown repeatedly that many spores require such treatment for maximal germination. Since the heat shock procedure selectively destroys vegetative bacteria, this system would seem to provide an accurate spore assay. In practice, however, this technique has limitations (2, 3, 4, 5). The need for heat shock to effect maximal germination in spores does not appear to be universal. Most investigators who study the physiological effects of heat activation use spores that require it, and since many of these studies have been reported, a casual glance at the literature might suggest to some that all spores require heat activation. However, certain spores germinate maximally without heat shock and some can be affected adversely by it. For example, viable counts of spores of *Bacillus subtilis* var. *niger* are consistently reduced two to three times after heat shocking whereas viable counts of *Bacillus subtilis* 52-30 are increased two to three times.

Consequently, in a mixed, naturally occurring spore population, which is the type of contamination with which spacecraft assays are concerned, some spores may not survive heat shock whereas others would survive and still others would be stimulated. The current procedures consist of a 15 min treatment at 80 C. This cycle is intermediate with regard to many of the cycles suggested in the literature, and since only one cycle can be used, most investigators actively engaged in microbiological assay of space hardware consider it a reasonable choice.

METHODS FOR SAMPLING SPACECRAFT

The levels of microbial contamination on the surfaces of spacecraft are usually estimated directly by one of three techniques: the swab-rinse test, the rinse test, and the vacuum probe.

The swab-rinse technique, with the exception of certain modifications, is essentially the same procedure that microbiologists have used for a number of years (5). The sample is taken from a known surface area, usually 4 in^2, and the swab is placed in a suitable rinse solution and then insonated in an ultrasonic bath (14, 15) to dislodge microorganisms. This technique is convenient, and recoveries up to 85–90% with fair precision have been reported in studies using test surfaces and artificial contamination. There is, however, always a high probability that variation in accuracy and precision can be great when actual space hardware is involved. In addition, the maximum area that can be sampled is relatively small. The majority of assays conducted on flight spacecraft have employed the swab-rinse technique and these results are discussed in a following section.

The vacuum probe was developed in order to provide a method for sampling relatively large surface areas. Petersen and Bond (11) have shown that the total recovery of surface contaminants with the vacuum probe exceeds the recovery using the swab-rinse technique. The probe is composed of a piece of Teflon tubing connected to a conical chamber (Figure 2). The tip of the tubing is shaped to form an orifice between the tip and the surface being sampled. A membrane filter is located at the end of the chamber, and under adequate vacuum (greater than 0.5 atm), critical flow occurs in the orifice created by the probe tip and the surface being sampled. Microorganisms are removed from the surface and impinged on the filter and the sides of the chamber. For microbiological assay, the filter and the chamber housing are placed in a sterile

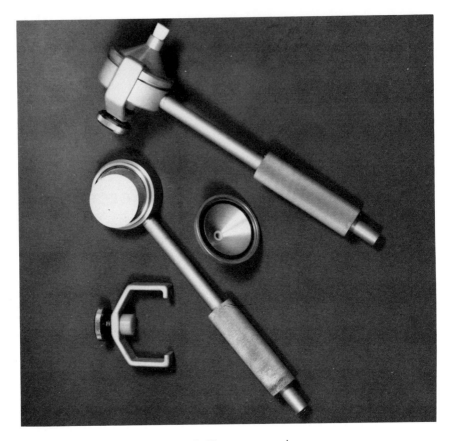

Figure 2 The vacuum probe.

rinse solution and insonated in an ultrasonic bath. Viable counts can then be done according to the basic protocol described earlier.

The assay of small piece parts is accomplished by the use of the rinse test in which the entire part is immersed in a sterile rinse fluid, insonated in an ultrasonic bath, followed by assay of the rinse fluid for one or more specific groups of microorganisms. A plastic model of the vacuum sampler was described by Farmer et al. (1).

LEVELS OF MICROBIAL CONTAMINATION DETECTED ON SPACECRAFT

Although several groups throughout the United States have been involved in the assay of flight spacecraft, most of these were conducted by our laboratories at Cape Kennedy. A total of 25 manned and unmanned spacecraft have been assayed to date. The primary difference between the unmanned spacecraft such as the Lunar Orbiters, the Surveyors, and the Anchored Interplanetary Monitoring Platforms (AIMP) and the manned Apollo spacecraft was that the unmanned spacecraft were assembled in areas that had a high degree of environmental control. It has been shown that the level of microbial contamination that collects on spacecraft surfaces is directly related to the microbiological cleanliness of the environment (3, 6, 7, 10, 16, 17). The estimated levels of microbial contamination on unmanned and manned spacecraft at the time of launch are shown in Tables 3 and 4. These data are typical and reflect the effects of environmental conditions and personnel constraints on the degree of contamination that accumulated on the spacecraft. For example, the AIMP-E was assembled and tested in a rigidly controlled environment (vertical laminar flow clean room). The contamination level was significantly lower than most other unmanned spacecraft which had been assembled in environments that were not highly controlled both from the standpoint of air ventilation and personnel density and activity.

Environmental controls in the assembly of Apollo spacecraft from a practical standpoint were almost nonexistent. Consequently, these levels were high, and as shown in Tables 5 and 6, the types of microorganisms on Apollo spacecraft were quite diversified. It has been noted repeatedly that when environmental controls are relaxed there is a marked increase in microorganisms originating from soil and dust such as bacterial sporeformers, molds, and actinomycetes. When environmental and personnel controls are relatively rigid, there is a corresponding reduction in the number of "soil" organisms and an increase in those associated with the indigenous flora of humans. Although gram-negative bacteria are detected occasionally on spacecraft, their presence is not common.

Table 3 Levels of microbial contamination on spacecraft

Spacecraft	Number of viable microorganisms per spacecraft at launch
Surveyor 2	2.9×10^5
Surveyor 3	2.0×10^6
Surveyor 4	1.4×10^5
Surveyor 5	3.4×10^5
Surveyor 6	1.8×10^4
Surveyor 7	1.2×10^5
Lunar Orbiter 3	6.0×10^5
Lunar Orbiter 4	4.4×10^4
Lunar Orbiter 5	1.1×10^5
Lunar Orbiter 6	1.8×10^5
Lunar Orbiter 7	2.9×10^5
Anchored Interplanetary Monitoring Platform A	1.5×10^5
Anchored Interplanetary Monitoring Platform D	2.7×10^4
Apollo 10[a]	8.5×10^7
Apollo 11	1.7×10^7
Apollo 12	3.3×10^8
Apollo 13	1.7×10^8
Apollo 14	5.4×10^8
Apollo 15	9.1×10^8

[a] Data are mean totals from the Command Module, Lunar Module, Spacecraft Lunar Adapter, Instrument Unit, and the S-IV-B Stage.

Table 4 Comparison of microbial contamination detected on surfaces of the Apollo command and service modules, AIMP-E and Surveyor 5, 6, and 7

Spacecraft	Microorganisms per ft^{2}[a]	Spacecraft	Microorganisms per ft^{2}[a]
Apollo		Surveyor 5	410
Command module— exterior	1,100	Surveyor 6	290
		Surveyor 7	130
Command module— interior	670	AIMP-E	62
Service module	720		

[a] Heterotrophic, mesophilic, aerobic microorganisms.

Table 5 Comparison of the numbers and types of microorganisms detected on Apollo 14 spacecraft

Microorganisms	Number	Percent
Staphylococcus spp.		
Subgroup I	11	1.0
Subgroup II	161	14.3
Subgroup III	105	9.4
Subgroup IV	85	7.6
Subgroup V	110	9.8
Subgroup VI	118	10.5
Micrococcus spp.		
Subgroup 1	28	2.5
Subgroup 2	2	0.2
Subgroup 3	11	1.0
Subgroup 4	—	—
Subgroup 5	7	0.6
Subgroup 6	—	—
Subgroup 7	121	10.8
Subgroup 8	1	0.1
Bacillus spp.		
B. alvei	1	0.1
B. badius	1	0.1
B. brevis	—	—
B. cereus	4	0.4
B. circulans	15	1.3
B. coagulans	20	1.8
B. firmus	5	0.4
B. laterosporus	—	—
B. lentus	4	0.4
B. licheniformis	2	0.2
B. macerans	2	0.2
B. megaterium	—	—
B. pantothenticus	—	—
B. polymyxa	10	0.9
B. pulvifaciens	—	—
B. pumilus	3	0.3
B. sphaericus	13	1.2
B. subtilis	3	0.3
Corynebacterium–Brevibacterium group	158	14.1
Actinomycetes	7	0.6
Streptomycetes	4	0.4
Yeasts	2	0.2
Molds	31	2.8

Table 5 (cont.)

Microorganisms	Number	Percent
Atypical *Micrococcus* spp.	36	3.2
Atypical *Bacillus* spp.	30	2.7
No growth on subculture	12	1.1
Number isolated	1123	—

Table 6 Comparison of the types of molds detected on the Apollo 11, 12, and 13 spacecrafts

Apollo 11 (34 *Isolates*)	*Apollo* 12 (36 *Isolates*)	*Apollo* 13 (14 *Isolates*)
Alternaria	Alternaria	Alternaria
Aspergillus	Aspergillus	Cephalosporium
Bipolaris	Aureobasidium	Curvularia
Curvularia	Bipolaris	Drechslera
Drechslera	Cephalosporium	Paecilomyces
Mucor	Curvularia	Penicillium
Nigrospora	Fusarium	Phoma
Penicillium	Nigrospora	Pithomyces
Pithomyces	Penicillium	Pleospora
Scopulariopsis	Phoma	Scopulariopsis
Syncephalastrum	Scopulariopsis	—

SUMMARY

Microbiological techniques for the assay of spacecraft were developed in response to international agreements concerning planetary quarantine. In general, these techniques are adequate for the quantitative recovery of heterotrophic, mesophilic microorganisms, and bacterial spores. None of the unmanned spacecraft discussed was required to be sterilized but rather had to be microbiologically clean. The data associated with their testing and assembly, however, are important because they will serve as basic guidelines for spacecraft such as the Viking which require sterilization.

References

1. Farmer, J. H., J. J. Tulis, L. A. Taylor, and V. A. Pace, Jr. 1971. Laboratory evaluation of the plastic vacuum probe surface sampler. J. Amer. Assoc. for Contamination Control **3**, No. 2: 15–18.

2. Favero, M. S. 1967. Dual meanings of activation. pp. 163–164. In G. Murrell [Ed.], *Spore newsletter*, Vol. 2. Ryde. Australia.

3. Favero, M. S. 1968. Problems associated with the recovery of bacterial spores from space hardware. pp. 88–98. In C. J. Corum [Ed.], *Developments in industrial microbiology*, Vol. 9. Washington, D.C.

4. Favero, M. S. 1971. Microbiologic assay of space hardware. Environ. Biol. & Med. **1**: 27–36.

5. Favero, M. S., J. J. McDade, J. A. Robertsen, R. K. Hoffman, and R. W. Edwards. 1968. Microbiological sampling of surfaces. J. Appl. Bacteriol. **31**: 336–343.

6. Favero, M. S., J. R. Puleo, J. H. Marshall, and G. S. Oxborrow. 1966. Comparative levels and types of microbial contamination detected in industrial clean rooms. Appl. Microbiol. **14**: 539–551.

7. Favero, M. S., J. R. Puleo, J. H. Marshall, and G. S. Oxborrow. 1968. Comparison of microbial contamination levels among hospital operating rooms and industrial clean rooms. Appl. Microbiol. **16**: 480–486.

8. Hall, L. B., and C. W. Bruch. 1965. Procedures necessary for the prevention of planetary contamination. pp. 48–62. In M. Florkin [Ed.], *Life sciences and space research*, Vol. III. North Holland Publishing Co.

9. Hall, L. B., and R. G. Lyle. 1971. Foundations of planetary quarantine. Environ. Biol. & Med. **1**: 5–8.

10. McDade, J. J., M. S. Favero, and L. B. Hall. 1967. Sterilization requirements for space exploration. J. Milk & Food Technol. **30**: 179–185.

11. Petersen, N. J., and W. W. Bond. 1969. Microbiological evaluation of the vacuum probe surface sampler. Appl. Microbiol. **18**: 1002–1006.

12. Pflug, I. J. 1971. Sterilization of space hardware. Environ. Biol. & Med. **1**: 63–81.

13. Phillips, G. B. 1971. Back contamination. Environ. Biol. & Med. **1**: 121–160.

14. Puleo, J. R., M. S. Favero, and N. J. Petersen. 1967. Use of ultrasonic energy in assessing microbial contamination on surfaces. Appl. Microbiol. **15**: 1345–1351.

15. Puleo, J. R., M. S. Favero, and G. J. Tritz. 1967. Feasibility of using ultrasonics for removing viable microorganisms from surfaces. Contamination Control **6**: 58–67.

16. Puleo, J. R., N. D. Fields, B. Moore, and R. C. Graves. 1970. Microbial contamination associated with the Apollo 6 spacecraft during final assembly and testing. Space Life Sci. **2**: 48–56.

17. Puleo, J. R., G. S. Oxborrow, N. D. Fields, and H. E. Hall. 1970. Quantitative and qualitative microbiological profiles of the Apollo 10 and 11 spacecraft. Appl. Microbiol. **20**: 384–389.

18. Standard procedures for the microbiological examination of space hardware. Oct., 1968. NHB 5340.1A. National Aeronautics and Space Administration. Washington, D.C.

PART FIVE

Use of Sterile Disposable Devices

20

Handling Sterile Products in the Hospital

BERTIL NYSTRÖM

Department of Clinical Microbiology
Karolinska Sjukhuset
Stockholm, Sweden

IT IS at the moment of use that a sterile product must be sterile. This may sound like a truism, and indeed it is one, but its implications are far from always considered by the users.

The term *sterile* means, of course, free from viable microorganisms. Such a definition is, however, no longer satisfactory. It is now generally accepted that a meaningful definition of the concept of sterility must be made in statistical terms as a defined margin of safety against nonsterility, i.e. against a product carrying at least one viable microorganism. As is implied in the Code of Practice for Radiosterilization of Medical Products recommended by the International Atomic Energy Agency (3) this margin of safety may vary depending on the intended use of the product. It also depends on the expected handling of the product. In Scandinavia it has been suggested, first by the Committee for Medical Supplies of the National Health Service in Denmark, that this margin of safety should be such that "it is possible for the manufacturer to document that there is a very low probability that the articles in question have more than one microorganism per million units" (2). This norm corresponds to the degree of safety which has been attained in hospitals for many years with proper autoclaving or dry heat sterilization (1). A similar statement on sterile drugs is found in the current edition of the *Pharmacopoea Nordica* (4).

However, a definition of the safety margin against nonsterility such as the one cited above is limited to the responsibility of the manufacturer and to his possibilities of control. The manufacturer has to produce with a good production hygiene a clean product, well packed in a suitable package, and sterilized in a good and well controlled sterilization apparatus. This is all necessary but not sufficient to guarantee a sterile product at the moment of its use.

In between come several steps. First, the product is transported from the manufacturer to the hospital, often over a considerable distance. This transportation can be and should be controlled by the manufacturer. But as soon as the product arrives at the hospital gate the responsibility for its further handling within the hospital passes from the manufacturer to the hospital, even if important steps in the handling of the product are governed by the package design, and even if the Code of Practice (3) states that instructions for storage and handling shall be furnished.

How the hospital should handle sterile products to maintain a sufficiently broad margin of safety against the product being contaminated before use, and what the responsibilities of the manufacturer and the hospital in the control of this handling are—these are the topics we shall be discussing. It seems remarkable that few textbooks on sterilization or on the control of hospital infections mention them. It also seems remarkable (and, for a manufacturer, it must be depressing—and more depressing still for a future patient) to see in many hospitals in many countries that the production hygiene in the manufacturing plant, the importance of which is so much stressed and which is surrounded by so strict official supervision and control—and rightly so—has little counterpart in the hospital.

Some definitions need to be made regarding the packaging of sterile products (Figure 1). They are packed in many layers. A sterile product has first a one- or two-layered package to be removed immediately prior to its use. This package will here be called the *product package*. A moderate quantity of product packages are normally packed together in a one- or, often, many-layered package intended for distribution to one user at one time. This package will here be called the *user package*. Again a quantity of user packages are packed together in a one- or many-layered outer package in which the products are transported from the manufacturer to the hospital. This package will here be called the *transportation package*. This outline of basically three layers of packages is of course schematic.

During handling, transportation, and storage a sterile product and its product package must be protected against five dangers to keep it sterile with a sufficient margin of safety: mechanical damage, quick temperature changes, moisture, excessive heat, and dust. Self-evidently a damaged product package does not keep its content sterile. It is the responsibility of the manufacturer to pack the product in such a way that the packages in all layers stand all reasonable handling without being damaged. It is the responsibility of the hospital to inform all staff handling sterile products as to how they should be handled and to

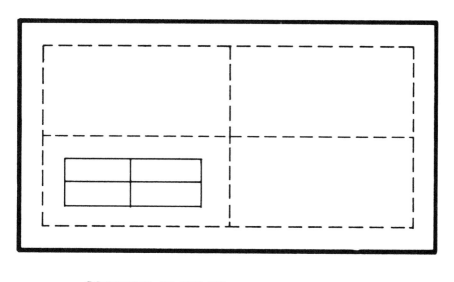

———— PRODUCT PACKAGE
– – – – USER PACKAGE
▬▬▬ TRANSPORTATION PACKAGE

Figure 1

maintain a staff discipline and a supervision of the staff such that all handling of the products is indeed "reasonable." This applies not only to the medical staff but to stores and transportation staff as well.

But the manufacturer has to realize the crude facts of everyday hospital practices and must not overestimate the care exercised in the handling of sterile products in the hospital. It is not only the carelessly handled forklift in the central store that is a danger in this connection. Look, for instance, at the handling of sterile-disposable syringes in paper product packages. It is not uncommon to see a nurse take a handful of them and plant them in a jar of some sort as flowers in a vase (Figure 2). All too easily the sharp edges of the syringe may then penetrate the

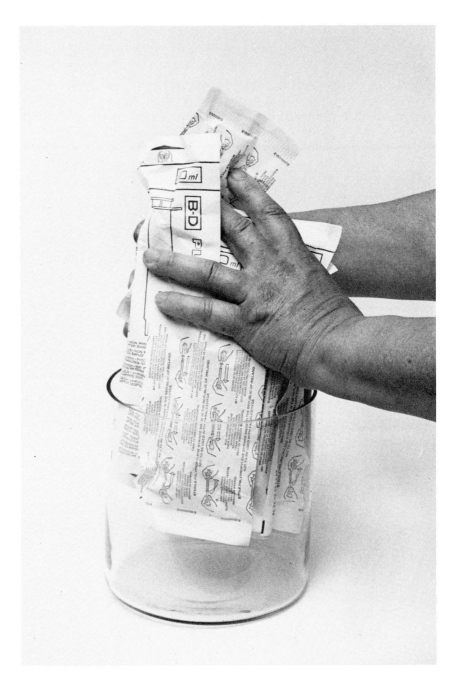

Figure 2

paper product package. It may be argued that this is a good example of bad staff discipline. It hardly seems realistic, however, to expect such an accident never to occur.

A product package made of cloth, paper, or any other porous material may let contaminated particles through if there is a pressure gradient between outside and inside. Quick temperature changes in a sterile store may build up such pressure gradients and must be avoided. It is the responsibility of the hospital to guarantee reasonably even temperatures in all sterile stores.

Product packages made of cloth, paper or any other porous material will easily let microorganisms through if they become wet. Product packages must be protected against moisture. It is the responsibility of the hospital to guarantee such protection in all sterile stores and in all transportations within the hospital.

Some types of weldings and seals in product packages may open up if exposed to excessively high temperatures. This can occur in badly ventilated sterile stores on hot summer's days when the temperature in the store has risen well above 30 C. It is of course the responsibility of the manufacturer to make seals and weldings that withstand all reasonable temperatures, but it must be the responsibility of the hospital to control the temperature in its sterile stores within reasonable limits.

A product package should of course prevent dust from penetrating if all the risks mentioned above are avoided. It must be the responsibility of the manufacturer to guarantee such a quality in his product packages. But can he do so? The package material can be controlled as to its quality. But so far as it is known no one has as yet developed a procedure for an in-line control of the quality of all seals and weldings. A double wrap, however, reduces the risk of leakages through a product package, as it is highly improbable that the two layers of the package will leak in exactly the same place. Such a double wrap is thus to be recommended for product packages where the possibility of leakages cannot be reasonably excluded.

But even if a product package does not leak, there is another important dust problem. If stored in a dusty place, or if stored for too long unprotected by a user package, the product package collects dust on its outer surface. When the package is then opened the dust whirls up and may fall onto the exposed sterile product and contaminate it before its use. It is the responsibility of the manufacturer to supply product packages with a smooth surface without pockets or other dust traps, and user packages which provide good protection for the product packages. It is the responsibility of the hospital to keep all sterile stores clean and well ventilated, to arrange proper dust protection for product packages transported without user packages, and to limit the shelf life of product packages in storage. The shelf life problem will be discussed in detail later.

We will now trace the path of the sterile product through the hospital from the hospital gate to the ward room, the dressing room, or the operating theatre where it will be used. The transportation package has passed environments with an uncontrolled and generally low hygienic level: the holds of cargo ships, railway trucks, lorries etc. To give a sufficient protection to its content it must be very solid and tight, and it should consist of several layers. When the transportation package arrives.at the hospital its surface must be presumed to be dirty, and it must not be admitted into a hygienically controlled environment. It thus must be removed, or at least its outer layer, in a reception area before its contents are allowed to enter the hospital. To avoid unnecessary transportation this reception area should be situated in connection with, but separate from, the hospital's central sterile store.

In the central store the product packages must, as mentioned, be protected against mechanical damage, quick temperature changes, moisture, excessive heat and dust. It may be argued that the user packages should offer this protection. Even if they contain only a small quantity of product packages it must, however, be presumed that some of them have to be removed in the central sterile store for products that are in little demand by some single users. It must also be presumed that not all user packages are up to standard as regards the quality and the number of product packages they contain. Thus the hygienic level of the central sterile store must be high. It must have a good artificial ventilation, be reasonably cool, with a reasonably even temperature, and preferably with a controlled relative humidity. Neither leaking pipes nor uninsulated steam or hot water pipes should be permitted in the store. It must be easy to clean, and it must be kept well cleaned. Non-sterile products should not be stored there, because such products may be a source of dust particles that unnecessarily add to the dust level in the store. This is especially the case with textiles and paper. The store staff must be trained in the proper handling of sterile products and in the importance of a high standard of personal hygiene. They should wear clean protective clothing and they should be supervised in respect to infections which may constitute a source of contamination. These demands are expensive to fulfill, and in most cases it is recommended, for purposes of economy, to have only one central sterile store in the hospital. The store should be situated in the central sterile supply department (CSSD) and contain not only industrially produced sterile disposables but also sterile products produced in the hospital's CSSD. Such a location also ensures proper training and supervision for the store staff.

Transportation from the central to the decentralized sterile store in wards and departments through ducts, lifts, and corridors must also be hygienically controlled and offer the same protection as the central store. Special attention must be paid to protection against mechanical damage and dust. Product packages not protected by a user package of good quality should be transported in closed boxes or trolleys in which other than sterile products, e.g. return goods to the CSSD, are not transported simultaneously. These boxes or trolleys must be easy to clean and disinfect and should be regularly cleaned and disinfected. If, in between transportation of sterile products, they are used for other transportations, they should always be cleaned and disinfected before transportation of sterile products.

The decentralized sterile stores in wards and departments must fulfill the same demands as the central store and offer the same protection to the product packages. The ward sterile store can be located in a room, but a cupboard is often sufficient. This cupboard should have closely fitting doors, preferably with the sort of packings used in refrigerators. That closed cabinets offer more protection than open shelves was demonstrated by Standard, Mackel, and Mallison (5). The shelves must be easy to clean and must be regularly cleaned. All sterile products in the ward or department should be stored here. Not more than a day's need —of course still protected by product packages—should be taken out and stored openly in, for instance, the dressing room. Nothing but sterile products should be stored in the sterile store.

The staff in wards and departments must be trained in the proper handling of sterile products and in proper principles for their storage, and their handling of the products as well as the stores should be properly supervised.

Products sterilized by steam or gas have a product package, and often a user package, that can be penetrated by air and by the sterilization medium at the sterilization temperature. In the long run such packages may be penetrated by microorganisms. It is common practice to give such packages a limited shelf life from the sterilization date. Exceptions to this rule can be made only if the user package is airtight. If so the limitation on the shelf life may start when the product package is removed from the user package.

It is the responsibility of the manufacturer to indicate the sterilization date on the product package. If its shelf life must be limited as from the sterilization date it is an advantage if instead of the sterilization date a last date for use is stated on the product package. It is the responsibility of the hospital to issue local regulations concerning the shelf life of such products for which the manufacturer has not stated a last date for use. Such local regulations must be made with due regard to the quality of product package and user package and to the local sterile stores and internal transportation systems. It should again be stressed that user packages should contain only a small quantity of product packages, so that the user package can be broken as near to the use of the product as possible.

Products sterilized by irradiation can be given a totally airtight product package—a substantial advantage that must be taken into consideration when choosing between products sterilized by various methods. Such a package would have an eternal shelf life from the microbiological point of view if it were not for the problem of dust collecting on its outer surface. In view of the risk of thus contaminating the product when opening the product package, the shelf life should be limited also for such product packages from the moment when they are taken out of their user packages and directly exposed to the dust in the stores. This is beyond the manufacturer's control; it must be arranged by the hospital. If a quick turnover rate could be guaranteed in all sterile stores by a well-planned and functioning distribution system this problem would be under control. However, in my experience such a guarantee can never be given, not least because of the squirrel instincts inborn in most nurses, who feel safe against shortages only with stores filled to overflowing and, as an extra security, some hidden reserves.

Of all procedures carried out during the handling of a product package in the hospital, the act of opening carries by far the highest risk of contaminating its content. It is the duty of the manufacturer to minimize this risk by proper design of the product package. It is not within the scope of this paper to discuss these aspects on package design. It should be pointed out, however, that the package design must depend upon the intended use of the product. In the case of a product to be handled in the operating theatre by a scrub nurse, it must be possible either to present it to her (Figure 3) or to slide it out of the package down upon a sterile table (Figure 4). In both cases the package must be double. The outer layer could be a parcel folded "corner-to-corner," which is easy to open and gives an excellent protection for the arm of the unscrubbed nurse when serving the product in its inner wrap (Figure 5 and Figure 3). It could also be a peel-open package, the outer wrap of which is peeled back on presentation, so that microorganisms on the outer surface of the outer wrap do not fall down upon the sterile table

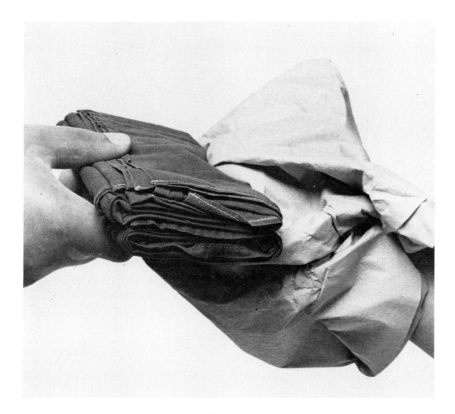

Figure 3

(Figure 6). Protection against this risk is not offered by product packages of which the outer layer is only cut or torn off.

Products to be aseptically handled in the ward or dressing room do not have to be presented in this way. Generally, however, the hygienic level of the ward is lower than that of the theatre. Thus the design of the product package for this use also must be of a high quality. Double wrappings always offer the safest protection and good peel-packs are always possible to open reasonably safely and easily.

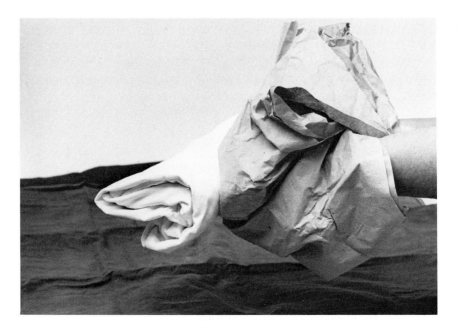

Figure 4

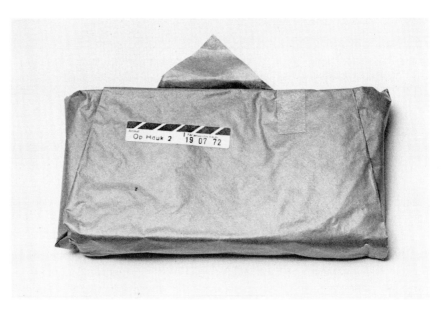

Figure 5

The package design is the responsibility of the manufacturer. It is the responsibility of the hospital to educate its staff as to how a product package should be used and a sterile product handled, and to supervise opening and handling procedures. This is not to say that manufacturers can not, and should not, cooperate in this education.

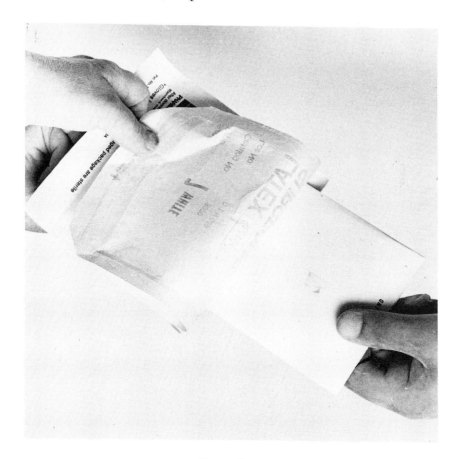

Figure 6

Finally, a malpractice seen in some hospitals should be briefly mentioned: that of resterilizing and reusing products intended for single use. Many products can not be resterilized without the hazard of deterioration of the material, e.g., balloons in balloon catheters. Many products, such as heart catheters, cannot be cleaned after use without the risk that traces of protein are left within their lumen. This can create unwanted reactions in the next patient.

To sum up, the hospital must assume responsibility for the handling of sterile products to ensure their sterility at the moment of use:

1. Transportation packages must not be allowed into hygienically controlled environments.
2. There must be central and decentralized sterile stores, where all sterile products are stored and no other products. These stores must be clean, well ventilated and reasonably dust-free.
3. The internal transportation of sterile products must offer proper protection against contamination of sterile products, and expecially against mechanical damage and dust.
4. The shelf life of all sterile products must be limited with due consideration to local storage and transportation conditions.
5. All staff handling sterile products, whether medically trained or not, must be properly trained and properly supervised.
6. If these hospital responsibilities are neglected the sterility of products can be at risk even if the manufacturers fulfill all demands that can and must be imposed upon them.

References

1. Christensen, E. A. 1964. Bakteriologisk vurdering af sterilisationsmetoders effekt. Ugeskr. Laeg. **126**: 339. In Danish.
2. Cited in Christensen, E. A., L. O. Kallings, and D. Fystro. 1969. Microbiological control of sterilization procedures and standards for the sterilization of medical equipment. Translation of a paper published simultaneously in Ugeskr. Laeg. **131**: 2123. Läkartidningen **66**: 5117, T. Norske Laegeforen. **89**: 1806.
3. International Atomic Energy Agency. 1967. Recommended Code of Practice for Radiosterilization of Medical Products. In *Radiosterilization of medical products. Proceedings of a symposium. Budapest, 5–9 June 1967.* International Atomic Energy Agency. Vienna.
4. *Pharmacopoea Nordica.* 1971. Ed. Suecica. 1964. Addendum 603, 1.4.
5. Standard, P. G., D. C. Mackel, and G. F. Mallison. 1971. Microbial penetration of muslin- and paper-wrapped sterile packs stored on open shelves and in closed cabinets. Appl. Microbiol. **22**: 432.

21

Sterilization Experience in the University Hospital of Geneva

G. DUCEL, CL. SCHEIDEGGER, AND
G. BANDERET

Canton Hospital
Geneva, Switzerland

THE Hôpital Cantonal de Genève, located in the heart of town, is a university institution attached to the University of Geneva School of Medicine. It is the only general hospital in the *canton*, an administrative entity with a population of 350,000. Its functions are threefold:

1. Patient care in all disciplines, excepting psychiatry.
2. Teaching: professional training of physicians, nurses, hospital assistants, physiotherapists, laboratory personnel, X-ray specialists, dieteticians, midwives, etc.
3. Applied research (clinical investigation).

The hospital includes all departments normal to a modern university hospital. These departments are either care units or institutes and paramedical units. With 1960 beds in 1970, it was the first university hospital in Switzerland. Below is a comparison with other hospitals

Geneva	1960 beds	Lausanne	1301 beds
Zurich	1570 beds	Berne	1101 beds
Basel	1463 beds		

The breakdown of these 1960 beds into inpatient units is:

| Medical department I | 210 |
| Medical department II | 204 |

371

Neurology	45
Surgery (including 33 beds for cardio- vascular surgery)	207
Neurosurgery	50
Orthopedics	145
Dermatology	65
ENT	70
Reanimation and intensive care units (37 for surgery, 16 for medical care)	53
Prisoners	12
Multipurpose wards	19
"Beau-Séjour" Hospital	352
Maternity ⎰ Gynecology	138
⎱ Obstetrics	117
⎱ Newborn care	32
Ophthalmology	63
Pediatrics	178
Total	1960

This hospital complex operates with a total staff of about 4000 people whose special features are a high turnover rate and a great diversity. Turnover is a yearly 40 % for the whole staff: 40 nationalities are employed in the hospital from all over Europe, Africa, the Americas and Asia. This involves major problems which have an impact on the design and implementing of sterilization processes.

In 1971, entries totaled 31,460 adding up to 562,537 hospitalization days, with the following history since 1965:

Year	Entries	Hospitalization days
1965	24,300	506,000
1966	26,200	543,000
1967	27,500	547,000
1968	29,000	558,000
1969	30,300	580,000
1970	29,233	570,507
1971	31,460	562,537

The increase in the number of hospitalization days over the past two years, as related to the larger number of inpatient entries, is the result of an effort to optimize hospital productivity by decreasing the average length of stay. The 600,000 day milestone should not be reached until a decade from now in spite of a rising population figure and a larger number of entries.

The hospital, founded in 1865, has undergone constant changes to meet new requirements. The maternity unit was opened in 1907, surgery in 1913 and ophthalmology in 1921. In 1943, it was decided to reconstruct on site and gradually to extend the hospital complex. In 1953 the initial stage was completed and the range of available facilities covered the medical and surgical *policliniques* (municipal outpatient clinics), the central pharmacy and laboratory, the blood transfusion center and the in- and outpatient ENT units.

Two new facilities became available in 1961: the Children's Hospital and the Beau-Séjour Hospital caring for rehabilitation and chronic cases. The second stage ended in 1966 with the opening of the main building which replaced century-old premises. The new structure is 590 ft long, 164 ft high and houses 10 stories of wards accommodating 1078 inpatients. Consolidated units are: medical care, surgery, orthopedics, neurology, neurosurgery, dermatology, and ENT.

Each level is broken down into 6 wards of 20 beds distributed in 2 rooms with 7 beds, 2 twins, and 1 single. The layout of professional space includes one office for medical personnel, one workroom for nurses (office and treatment preparation), one drug preparation room, one supply and material storeroom, one soiled utility room (disposal), as well as sanitary installations for patients and staff. Half of the ground-floor level, i.e., three wards, is used for the medical and surgical intensive care units. The lower levels group a 6-room operating suite, a bed disinfection area and a sterilization center which essentially serves the main building, one exception being ETO sterilization. Severe architectural constraints were imposed on these utilities since basic modules (available length, width, height) remain the same as in upper stories.

The third reconstruction stage is currently in progress. It will provide housing for medical services: X-ray unit, emergency center, various laboratories, administrative services and all activities relating to the logistic support of patient care. This stage should be completed by 1975 (Figure 1). The late 1970s should bring an additional 12-room operating suite, a new sterilization center and the design of the new maternity hospital.

The Hôpital Cantonal de Genève therefore represents an important hospital complex housed in 5 buildings of various ages built between 1907 and 1966. Such accommodation compelled us to approach sterili-

Buildings in white, on the top of the picture represent from left to right: Hôpital Beau-Séjour, Ophthalmology, Pediatry and Maternity buildings.

Bâtiment des lits: main building
Services médicaux: medical services
   building
Policliniques: outpatient clinics

Enseignement: clinical teaching building
Entrée patients: patients' entrance
Entrée des visiteurs: visitors' entrance

Figure 1   Model of the third stage of reconstruction of the Hospital.

zation from a particular angle. This is why, beside the sterilization center in the main building and operating suite sterilization facilities, satellite sterilization units had to be located in certain buildings, although they do not satisfy current hospital sanitation requirements. In some of these buildings, it was not possible to center appropriately all utilities related to sterilization (decontamination, cleaning up, packing, sterilization and storage), e.g., in the maternity, pediatrics, and outpatient care units.

There are four satellite sterilization units (Table 1), three for the maternity hospital and one for Beau-Séjour. Each one is centered around a steam sterilizer with a capacity from 3 to 19 cu. ft. Their design and operation are also dissimilar according to years of manufacture. The oldest is a manual type 1954 model. The most recent operates on automatic and graphic control and is a 1972 model.

Table 1   Satellite sterilization units

Location	Year of manufacture	Number of programs	Chamber capacity (ft^3)	Control
Beau-Séjour	1972	4	19	Automatic
Maternity 34	1954	2	3	Manual
Maternity 38	1971	4	4	Automatic + manual
Maternity (annex)	1965	4	13	Automatic + manual

Operating suites (Table 2) are fully equipped with 18 steam sterilizers of various types. Capacities range from 1 to 27 cu. ft. The oldest models purchased from 1949 to 1953 are operated manually. More recent ones, the latest installed in 1971, have manual and automatic control. In some clinics they are not entirely reserved for surgical needs. In pediatrics, for example, all sterile equipment needs are satisfied by the sterilizers in the operating suite. This is an inadequate solution. It is nevertheless dictated by architectural constraints intrinsic to the building, although it was erected in 1961. However, in all these sterilization areas, the same processing techniques and the same final inspection have been instituted as in Central Sterilization. This is why we shall limit discussion to the recent experience, since 1966, of the main building Central Sterilization.

Central Sterilization is located in the basement of the main building. It occupies an area of about one acre and is divided into four units of unequal importance: cloakrooms, decontamination, clean work, and sterile storage. An office for the responsible registered nurse is at one end, past the sterile storage area.

Table 2   Sterilization units for the operating suites

Location	Year of manufacture	Number of programs	Chamber capacity (ft^3)	Control
Pediatrics	1960	7	10	Automatic
	1960	7	3	Automatic
Main operating suite (6 sterilizers)	1965	3	3	Automatic + manual
Maternity (2 sterilizers)	1953	2	28	Manual
Emergency	1967	4	6	Automatic + manual
	1967	1 (quick)	1	Automatic + manual
	1967	1 (washer-sterilizer)	2	Automatic + manual
Outpatient surgery	1971	4	6	Automatic + manual
Ophthalmology	1957	3	6	Manual
	1949	2	4	Manual
ENT (2 sterilizers)	1952	2	3	Manual

On initial opening in 1966, the layout was as follows (see Figure 2):

1. *Cloakroom area,* including
   (a) men's cloakroom
   (b) women's cloakroom
   (c) corridor used as visitors' cloakroom
   (d) two toilets
   (e) a small storeroom.

2. *Decontamination area,* grouping four separate rooms:
   (a) one room for the reception and decontamination of septic equipment
   (b) one room for the reception and cleaning up of instruments and syringes
   (c) one room for the reception and cleaning up of flasks and stoppers and a side-area for bottling and sterilizing solutions. This is where the gas autoclave sterilizer was located
   (d) one room for the reception and preparation of gloves.

3. *Clean work area,* including a large room for the inspection of supplies and the preparation of packs to be sterilized, plus two adjoining

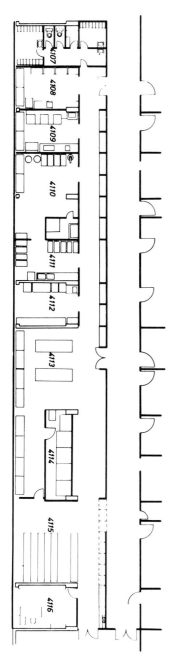

Figure 2 Layout of Central Sterilization (1965).

4107 Cloakroom
4108 Reception and dispatching;
          decontamination
4109 Cleaning
4110–4111   Sterile solutions
4112 Preparation of gloves
4113 Packaging (standard packs)
4114 Autoclaves
4115 Sterile storage
4116 R.N. office
4108–4112   Soiled area
4113–4114   Clean work area

rooms, one of which contains the array of three steam sterilizers, the other for packing up gas-sterilized supplies.

4. *Sterile storage area,* rigged as a "Compactus."

All the foregoing areas are connected by a 6 ft wide corridor running to one side, with a door between the decontamination and clean work areas. One wall of the corridor is lined with cupboards where clean unsterile items are kept (Figure 3). The sterilization area has three doors giving access to the cloakrooms, the clean work area and the sterile stores, close to the head nurse office. Initially, sterilization was performed in three steam sterilizers with 39 ft³ chambers operating on three automatic programs:

1. Linen   134 C $28\frac{1}{2}$ psi   10 min
2. Instruments   134 C $28\frac{1}{2}$ psi   10 min
3. Gloves   120 C $14\frac{1}{4}$ psi   15 min

and in a $2\frac{1}{2}$ ft³ program controlled gas sterilizer operating on a mixture of 15 % ethylene oxide and 85 % carbon dioxide, at a pressure of $82\frac{1}{2}$ psi and a temperature of 58 C for 1 hr.

This sterilization setup, although short of present central sterilization standards, proved satisfactory in the first years of operation. A transformation of the central pharmacy, in 1968, made way for the removal of solution preparation and sterilization, as dictated by mere logic. This

shift also enabled the unit to cope with the increased volume of steam
sterilization and, to a higher degree, of ETO sterilization which followed
the rapid development of yearly entries and of medical and surgical
sophistication: hemodyalizis, cardiovascular surgery, kidney transplan-
tation. It proved necessary to double the ETO sterilization capacity, an
improvement achieved in 1969 by the installation, in the former solution
sterilization room, of a 9 ft³ program controlled sterilizer operating on a

Figure 3 Corridor of Central Sterilization. One wall is lined with cupboards where clean
unsterile items are kept.

mixture of 15 % ethylene oxide and 85 % carbon dioxide at 43 psi and
48 C for 2 hr. This piece of equipment installed close to the existing
sterilizer provided a room reserved for ETO sterilization, but still in the
inappropriate environment of the decontamination area.

The adoption of disposable surgical gloves sterilized in the hospital
and of some disposable catheters as well as disposable syringes, excepting those used for arterial and sternal puncture, gradually brought
about the present situation in which some rooms in the decontamination
area are no longer or only partially in use, such as the reception, cleaning
and preparation areas for gloves, instruments and syringes.

Five years' experience in the sterilization section led to a reappraisal of sterilization functions and to the development of a new layout in keeping with new working conditions and with current hospital sanitation criteria. Pending transformations, existing facilities are exploited as most commensurate with demand. Routine daily volumes processed by Central Sterilization amount to an average of 10 steam sterilizer runs with occasional peaks to 15.5 runs in the small ETO unit and 2 in the large ETO unit.

Central Sterilization employs 28 people: 1 registered nurse, in charge; 1 technician, assistant to the head nurse, more especially entrusted with equipment operation; 24 full time employees (9 men, 15 women); and 2 part time employees. Men employees receive used items, process orders, distribute packs, load the sterilizers; execute the decontamination, cleaning up, and preparation of bulky pieces of equipment; and keep the area clean. Women employees are in charge of packing, housekeeping and light cleaning work.

Central Sterilization was initially built to meet the requirements of the main inpatient building. Its tasks multiplied and diversified with time. Steamsterilized supplies are delivered not only to every service housed in the main inpatient building but also to various external units: X-ray unit, neuroradiology, ENT, urology and ophthalmology. ETO sterilized supplies used throughout the hospital are processed by Central Sterilization. In addition, the anesthetic department send part of its equipment—mostly catheters of all types, which cannot be sterilized in their own formaldehyde chamber—to Central Sterilization. Between the main building operating suite and Central Sterilization, the workload has been split as follows: surgical instruments are sterilized within the operating suite; linen and dressing material are processed by Central Sterilization and supplied in 12 standard packs (Table 3).

This inventory, in view of the number of advantages as opposed to few shortcomings, may be considered as especially satisfactory. In fact,

Table 3   Standard packs supplied by Central Sterilization for main operating suite

Basic operating room linen	Thoracic Guersouni pack
Handy table operating room linen	Digestive tract Guersouni pack
Standard neurosurgery linen	Minor disinfection
Head surgery linen	Major disinfection
Back surgery linen	Minor intervention dressing pack
Surgeon's gowns and linen	Major intervention dressing pack

instruments can be resterilized directly in the operating suite on very short notice, within about one hour. It is even possible to resterilize an instrument inadvertently soiled within the shortest possible time in quick sterilizers. In addition, the required number of instrument sets can be strongly reduced, and related uniformization problems may be solved directly by the persons involved. Finally, the responsibility of nurses in charge of instruments is fully maintained so far as the preservation of instruments in good condition and the preparation of trays are concerned. The only drawback, beside some space occupied in the operating suite, might be the introduction of a contaminated focus in a highly sterile area. It is efficiently minimized if not completely eliminated by strict discipline and by the immediate decontamination of instruments in a 1 % phenol base solution of germicidal detergent. Central Sterilization supplies wards with 22 standard procedure packs (Table 4).

Table 4   Standard procedure packs supplied by Central Sterilization for wards

Dressing pack type 1	Sternal punction (supplementary)
Dressing pack type 2	Suboccipital punction (supplementary)
Preoperative disinfection pack	Liver needle biopsy (supplementary)
Tracheostomy dressing pack	Bone biopsy (supplementary)
Urinary catheterization pack	Punction (base)
Urine culture pack	Surgical pleural punction (supplementary)
Denudation	Medical pleural punction (supplementary)
Tracheostomy	Kidney punction (supplementary)
Biopsy (basic)	Ascites punction (supplementary)
Pleural biopsy (supplementary)	Minor intervention
Pneumothorax (supplementary)	Major intervention

A major standardization effort has been necessary. It amounted to actual reduction, normalization and noticeable savings on a number of items. One feature of this move towards standardization has been the introduction of basic assortments which can be supplemented on request by supplementary packs. In this way the basic biopsy pack can be supplemented by a special pack for, say, joint or bone biopsy. A whole range of supplies are thus issued separately and make the system as flexible as possible. Experience has supported the soundness of this procedure in the fields of treatment quality and managerial economy.

Used supplies must be submitted to various operations before they can be reused. Linen is sent to be washed, then returned to Central Sterilization ready to be sterilized. Consequently, Central Sterilization is concerned only in the ultimate stage of operations. The same does not apply to a whole range of equipments Central Sterilization has to recover in care units and process before it can reintegrate the circuit (Table 5).

Table 5 Central Sterilization: present processing of reusables

Processing station	Operation
Care unit	Recovery of reusable supplies
Central Sterilization Soiled area	Decontamination of used supplies Cleaning up of used supplies
Central Sterilization Clean work area	Inspection of used supplies Storage of unpacked supplies Packaging Storage of nonsterile packs Sterilization
Central Sterilization Sterile storage	Storage of sterile supplies
Care units Operating suite	Distribution of sterile supplies

If collection of soiled supply takes place in the hospital units, all succeeding operations are performed in Central Sterilization. Used supplies are deposited in air- and watertight paper bags. They are then stored in ward soiled utility rooms or in reserved areas. They are collected between 7 and 9 am by three men workers. Each one has a special trolley used only for collection. The first one collects supplies in septic areas; the second collects supplies in nonseptic areas; and the third collects supplies in emergency and intensive care units. In addition, some peripheral services which have used special supplies or small quantities of standard equipment return them through assistants to Central Sterilization in the same regular paper bags.

Septic supplies, upon reception in Central Sterilization, are dipped for one hour in a detergent solution containing 1 % phenol base disinfectant. They are then rinsed in warm water and washed. Bulky items (flasks, cups, bedpans, etc.) are hand washed in stainless steel sinks, while instruments and syringes are washed in automatic machines. The reason why some utensils, e.g., bedpans and cups, are hand washed is that machine washing appeared comparatively slower. Supplies from other units considered as nonseptic are washed without previous decontamination.

After this preparation, supplies are stored in the cupboards of the Central Sterilization corridor, sheltered from dust and possible recontamination which might occur because of the area's layout. They are only taken out to enter the packing line. Packs are processed on a large stainless steel table. Those to be steam sterilized are simply wrapped in paper, except for some special needles packaged in nylon bags. We apply two systems: bags for small and medium size packs and conventional wrapping for large packs. We have standardized packaging material which is limited to two grades of 40 g/m² paper, the more resilient being used exclusively for supplies destined for the operating suite. Mill delivered bags are 60 g/m² paper, bonded, thus providing thorough sterile preservation. Still, for medium size packs, we experienced various kinds of trouble for a fairly long period of time: the bonding of bags came apart in sterilizers. This was due to a change of paper grade, as the manufacturer had unnoticeably shifted to 70 g paper. The loss in paper permeability explains bonding failures in the final vacuum phase. Apart from this isolated inconvenience, we consider our packaging method as fully satisfactory. This also applies to gas sterilization for which we only use welded polyethylene sheathing.

Packs are then piled up in bins, in a predesigned array affording the free circulation of steam or gas. These baskets are loaded onto a trolley and introduced into the sterilizer chambers. Sterilization follows. When this operation and an inspection are completed, packs are unloaded on their way to the sterile supply storage. They enter (Figure 4) the "Compactus" which provides maximum pack storage in the smallest possible space. An additional advantage of the "Compactus" is to protect all stored items from dust, moisture and unwanted handling. Contents are specified on every pack, except for those in transparent wrapping, and a control tape or "sterile" stamp which become legible after sterilization only indicate without possible ambiguity whether the pack has been sterilized. Another stamp gives the extent of validity; maximum pack validity has been stated as four weeks for paper wrapped supplies, bonded or not, for safety reasons and to avoid excessive unit storage. Preservation is considered as practically unlimited for welded polythene packaging.

Requests for supplies are submitted every other day, excepting holidays, to Central Sterilization on a special form stating the needs of the unit as well as its present inventory for the requested items. They reach Central Sterilization at 9 a.m. They are processed between 9 and 10:30 a.m. on four special stainless steel closed trolleys (Figure 5). Distribution keeps four people busy, one per trolley, from 10:30 to 11:30. Deliveries to the operating suite are made during the early afternoon. The operating suite places their orders on a special form. As a rule, the single item inventory should not exceed 48 hr needs; however, routine checks have shown that storage was normally overplentiful due to the "ant-like" concerns of the head nurse who is always afraid to run short, although urgent requests are processed by Central Sterilization, except on holidays. For the operating suite, a buffer stock enables them to meet any requirement at any time.

Figure 4 "Compactus" provides maximum pack storage in the smallest possible space.

In Central Sterilization, various inspections are performed on a regular routine basis. A machine load is released only after the graphic recording of the complete sterilization cycle has been checked and ATI Steril Indicator has been introduced in the center of the load, exclusively for alarm purposes. Both data are carefully kept on file one year for medico-legal purposes. The same applies to the Bowie and Dick test performed monthly on every steam sterilizer. Every other month, com-

Figure 5 Special stainless steel closed trolley for the distribution of items.

prehensive tests are carried out with packs containing *B. stearothermophilus* spores in a commercial preparation. Technical inspections are made daily by the assistant to the head nurse. Sterilizers are overhauled once a year by the technical department (Table 6).

Table 6 Regular inspections of steam sterilizers in Central Sterilization

Periodicity	Inspection	Inspector in charge
Per load	Graphic recording	Nurse in charge
	ATI Steril Indicator	or her assistant
Per day	Technical check	Assistant to head nurse
Per month	Bowie and Dick test	Nurse in charge
		or her assistant
Every other month	*B. stearothermophilus*	Nurse in charge
		or her assistant
Per year	Technical overhaul	Technical department

Identical tests and inspections apply to gas sterilization: graphic recording checks and introduction in one pack per load of an ATI Ethylene Oxide Indicator, and technical inspections.

However, for housekeeping reasons, it has not been possible to perform regular tests with spores of *B. subtilis* v. *globigii*. We regret that no biological indicator to be introduced in packs, as they exist for steam sterilizers, is available on the market. This is one reason why we had to consider gas sterilization as an ancillary and not as a choice process.

We have given up, for steam and gas alike, the bacteriological examination of random samples taken from a batch, without previous contamination, as bacterial nongrowth might barely testify that cleaning and preparation were appropriate, but not necessarily that sterilization was correct.

As a counterpart to the shortcomings of Central Sterilization layout, we paid special attention to the maintenance and cleanliness of the premises, equipment and furniture as entrusted to the sterilization staff. Every day, floors are dusted with disposable adsorptive nonwoven material. Floors in the soiled utility area are scrubbed three times a day or as often as needed with 1 % phenol base germicidal detergent. Twice a week, the whole sterilization area is flooded with the same product by special machines with vacuum suction water recovery. Distribution trolleys are washed with the same product every other day, and collection trolleys every single day. Pieces of furniture are made of stainless steel and sprayed daily with a phenol-alcohol product.

The Hôpital Cantonal de Genève Central Sterilization supplies its clients with sterile items in directly usable form. Its efficiency cannot be denied. However, it is not immune to criticism in the fields of supply collection, decontamination and even processing in the sterilization area, a fact we are fully aware of. Its layout is obsolete, it obviously lacks the strict partitioning into soiled and clean work areas and sterile storage. We were not in a position to impose one-way circulation excluding reverse moves. This is mainly due to the location of cloakrooms and to the transverse partition into work units opening on a single longitudinal corridor, which prevent continuity in the progress of work and compel to share the path followed by soiled supplies. Consequences are a recontamination risk, but mostly possible confusion between clean and soiled supplies. Moreover, gas sterilization is located in the decontamination area, which is perfectly inappropriate. Although the introduction of disposable items (gloves, syringes and packaging material) brought some extent of relief, a restructuration of sterilization is mandatory.

The sorting out of supplies, on collection, according to their origin, septic or nonseptic units, seems well advised at first sight. We think however that, with the increased population of healthy germ-bearers and the unwanted but unavoidable scattering throughout the hospital of infected patients, this method is not the correct one, especially as long as supplies can stagnate for 24 hr in a paper bag before collection.

Every article used by a patient should be considered as contaminated. An adequate processing method is required. We believe that, for the sake of maximum safety, and to avoid germ dissemination along the collection path as well as hospital staff contamination, decontamination should occur immediately after use and in the ward itself (Table 7).

Table 7   Central Sterilization: planned processing of reusables

Processing station	Operation
Care unit	Decontamination of reusables
	Recovery of reusable supplies
Central Sterilization Soiled area	Cleaning up of used supplies
Central Sterilization Clean work area	Inspection of used supplies
	Storage of unpacked supplies
	Packaging
	Storage of nonsterile packs
	Sterilization
Central Sterilization Sterile storage	Storage of sterile storage
Care units Operating suite	Distribution of sterile supplies

This method brings unquestionable advantages: it prevents any inadvertent reuse, for medical or other purposes, of a soiled instrument; it eliminates the risk to disseminate germs which necessarily desiccate during their present long term storage; it maintains instruments in better condition by freeing them from dried pus or blood; it facilitates final cleaning up. In addition, it paves the way to a rationalization of collection which could be performed by one person as opposed to the present three.

Table 8   Utensils that should be decontaminated

Washbasins	Urinals
Emesis basins	Urine bottles
Tumblers	Gastric suction bottles
Chamber pots	Aerosol cups

Should we take stock of equipments used within the unit, we could only assess that quite a few are just not thoroughly decontaminated (Table 8). This type of equipment does not need to be sterile (12). Simple decontamination followed by cleaning up is enough. The introduction of systematic decontamination within the ward would provide for such decontamination operations which cannot be performed elsewhere for lack of elevators, as they are put to all possible uses and carry soiled as well as clean supplies and hospital staff as well as patients.

Another major criticism refers to personnel working in Central Sterilization. No one is attached to a particular area. There should logically be three teams: the first in charge of receiving, washing and sorting out supplies, the second dealing with packaging and sterilization proper, the third with order processing and distribution. This is presently not permitted by the very layout of sterilization. This would also support additional staffing which would be denied in the present juncture. Piecemeal equipment decontamination which would avoid declaring the soiled area "off limits," and a scaling of operations no longer in space but in time, with changes of clothes for the staff (a different color for each task), seem to be the only short-term solution. In addition we put particular emphasis on repeated hand washings with a multiple action disinfecting solution carefully tested on the hospital's germs.

The architectural design of the main ward building, as already mentioned, imposes on Central Sterilization rather burdening fixed constraints. Whatever they may be, the improvement of work, qualitatively as well as quantitatively, presupposes the internal reconstruction of Sterilization. Studies are in progress. In an initial stage (these coming months), the soiled area will be separated from the clean work area by an extended cloakroom. The soiled area will be reduced, since decontamination is to be performed in the care units and many presently introduced items of supply are disposable. Washing by hand will disappear, with few exceptions, and be replaced by automatic washing in special machines or, preferably, in a washing tunnel. Automation is not always faster than washing by hand, as mentioned for bedpans and cups. However, some disposable utensils come to eliminate this drawback. To compensate, machine washing offers definite advantages in hospital sanitation by eliminating bacterial aerosols. Premises, and mostly the staff, are protected, which strongly reduces the risk of recontamination and of professional diseases.

In a second stage, the clean work area should be completely modified to make room for parallel production lines (linen packs, procedure packs, etc.) feeding into dual access automatic sterilizers. However, this very costly and time-consuming conversion might never be implemented, as a new Central Sterilization for the whole hospital is contemplated. It would also necessitate the transformation of the sterile storage area, which would interfere with distribution in a way that might be difficult to accept.

As mentioned, the major criticism bears on supply decontamination in care units. Two solutions might enable us to remedy this situation: decontamination by chemical disinfecting agents or hot water decontamination (3, 5, 8, 9). With chemical decontamination, utensils are sunk immediately after use in a detergent-diluted disinfecting agent and left to soak for the prescribed period (1 % phenol solution for 1 hr). However, such a solution could not be envisaged for the bulk of articles to be decontaminated in the care unit (Table 9).

Table 9   Orthopedics Inpatient Unit: utensils to be decontaminated

Description	Consumption per day per ward
Toilet articles	
Stainless steel washbasins	27
Stainless steel chamber pots and covers	$17 \times 5 = 85$
Urinals	$10 \times 5 = 50$
Emesis basins	$17 \times 2 = 34$
Stainless steel tumblers	$17 \times 2 = 34$
Prosthesis containers	12
Thermometers	$26 \times 2 = 52$
Medical articles	
Suction bottles	4
Urine bottles	6
Redon flasks	4–8
	(aseptic units)
Redon flasks	10–15
	(septic units)
Aerosol cups	$5 \times 2 = 10$

Space is presently lacking. The soiled utility is too small to accommodate the soaking troughs we would need. It is practically impossible to locate them elsewhere. Not counting other drawbacks: poor wetting of items which, more often than not, float because of their specific gravity or air content (flasks); frequent changes of disinfecting solutions (renewal after 2 or 3 days); disinfecting power monitoring; degradation of metal or plastic objects; personnel hand skin intolerance, compelling the wearing of gloves which may be a source of hospital infection since, as we have demonstrated, the inside can be contaminated by pure cultures of *P. aeruginosa*; pollution of residual water by disinfecting agents which are not always biodegradable; all these features led us to turn away from chemical decontamination and prefer hot water decontamination as applied in many Swedish hospitals. This operation is performed in an automatic machine with the following sequence: 5 sec cold water rinsing; 70 sec tepid water cleaning; 40 sec hot water decontamination (85 C); 5 sec tepid water cooling. Bacteriological studies of this decontamination process have shown its value against hospital germs (4, 13).

Before this process is generalized in the Hôpital Cantonal de Genève, prolonged tests will be run in a surgery unit (septic orthopedics) and a medical care unit. The decision, financially a heavy one, will be made only upon appraisal of practical, economic, and bacteriological results. Among evaluation factors, water consumption may be a determining element. It is already quite high for the hospital (some 35 million $ft^3/$ year). Wastewater recycling will undoubtedly become unavoidable in coming years. Moreover, it would be a good thing to assess the degree of bacteriological pollution of residual water by hospital germs to make sure wastewater treatment and recycling plants can function without any possible doubt.

As can be seen, the problems a hospital of the size of the Geneva Hospital has to face by way of decontamination and sterilization are well known. Their resolution is nonetheless difficult due to established structures, architectural constraints, and mostly staffing and financing implications. One question then becomes pertinent: are disposables going to solve part or all of these problems?

The inception of disposables for various uses, supplied by industry, brought Central Sterilization to reconsider part of its operation, and for some articles a choice had to be made between reusable and disposable goods: surgical gloves, some catheters, syringes, and injection needles. The adoption of disposables is based on various criteria, the main ones being: quality of article; quality of packaging; storage space; sterility control; disposal of the article; and finally cost. Disposables should provide equal, if not better, working conditions as reusable items. This is not always the case. For example, some disposable syringes do not permit accurate volume measurements. It is therefore difficult to put them to any use requiring a syringe. This is one reason we discarded them for sternal or arterial punctures. Supplied items should also have successfully undergone biological tests giving information on their toxicity, tissue response, pyrogenicity, and compatibilities. Packaging should preserve sterility from production to utilization at care unit level. This is often the weak point of disposables. We assessed a number of times weld failures or the presence of holes which may be microscopic and therefore not discernible to nursing personnel (1, 6).

Storage space had to be closely calculated. As the hospital uses imported goods, and in order to cope with market disturbances or just shipment delays which might bring about a storage, inventories should cover 3 to 6 months' needs. This explains stored quantities of 350,000 to 700,000 syringes and of 50,000 to 100,000 glove packs, whether we rely on 3 or 6 months. Incidentally, this does not relieve us from maintaining production equipment for conventional reusable supplies in order to bridge immediately any supply gap, which has its own impact on storage areas (preservation of a given quantity of conventional items) and results in poor utilization of frozen shelf space in Central Sterilization.

If systematic routine inspections enable us to guarantee the sterility of packs processed in Central Sterilization, the same does not apply to disposables. The routine monitoring of the sterility of purchased equipment is mandatory. Unfortunately, under normal working conditions, aseptic random samplings are not always practicable, even when using a "steril-bench," and it is nearly impossible to perform the random checks required to make an inspection valid. This is why we prefer to judge from the sterilization test reports we request from our vendors. They should correspond to delivered batches. This is not always possible, so that we make a written guarantee of equipment sterility mandatory. In any case, any time this is deemed necessary the hospital epidemiologist visits suppliers to assess sterilization procedures and testing.

The disposal of disposables has not yet raised insuperable problems. For the time being, at care unit level, we ask the staff to throw away disposables in a special container for glass, metal, and plastic ware. These containers are lined with a thick plastic bag which, after being sealed, is picked up during a special round to be burned by the Geneva municipal garbage incineration plant. However, with constantly increasing volumes, we have three alternate solutions: incineration at care unit level, as practiced in England, that we refuse on account of installation complications and cost and of the involved air pollution; crushers in every soiled area, but we lack at the same time available space and any experience on this mode of destruction; or the installation of a stainless steel compactor, one per half story, namely for three units. The

latter solution will probably be chosen. But the destruction of disposables remains a problem because of air pollution and the related
drastic laws currently passed in Switzerland on environment protection.

Finally, what will motivate the choice of disposable types, beside hospital sanitation conditions, are economic considerations (10). By way of
determination factors guiding the choice of reusable versus disposables,
at our hospital, we retained the following:

For reusable equipment:

pa (Amortized cost of item) = Price/Number of utilizations
MC (Maintenance cost)   = Labor cost
                             + Machine depreciation
                             + Maintenance products
                             + Fluids + Energy.

For disposable equipment:

PA = Acquisition price of item
     + Storage cost (ground area, building, personnel, + interest on
       capital)
     + Cost of destruction after use.

One tends to forget this last item as it is handled by another hospital
department. Such an omission is no longer possible with the generalized
use of plastic or paper disposables requiring special incineration facilities
and because of the consequences involved for the sanitary environment
of the whole population. The economic comparison is drawn up as
follows:

pa + maintenance cost = PA + Storage cost
                           + Destruction cost.
whence:
Maintenance cost $\geq$ (PA − pa) + Storage cost
                           + Destruction cost.

If the maintenance cost is higher than the second term of the equation,
a gain is obvious and disposables should be adopted. If the maintenance cost is lesser than or equal to the second term in the equation, the
choice to be made depends either on particular constraints (labor shortage, lack of space, given sanitation conditions), or on sanitation considerations only.

One may, for example, adopt disposables for injection needles and
syringes. As a matter of fact, cleaning problems raised by such articles
make perfect preparation that would bring absolute protection against

pathogenic germ transmission an illusion. The positive aspects of the adoption of disposables should also be expressed in monetary value. Coming back to the above example, the generalized introduction of disposable needles and syringes may reduce by a few percent the risk of hospital infections, and thereby the length of stay in hospital. Our comparison then becomes:

Maintenance cost $\geq$ (PA – pa) + Storage cost
+ Destruction cost
+ Cost of shortened hospitalization
(negative algebraic value).

This expression is more complete and gives a truer picture of the actual situation, although the factor of "shortened hospitalization" is difficult to measure.

Such comparisons remain, however, dynamic, and the trend is in favor of disposables whose prices tend to decrease while labor costs keep increasing. Moreover, the difficulty of finding qualified labor also acts in favor of disposables. In view of all this, as already mentioned, we have adopted a number of disposable supplies. Although such changes should be total, for efficiency's sake and for hospital sanitation safety, full conversion is seldom possible. The adoption of standard syringes and needles proved immediately profitable, but it was not so for gloves, purchased in packs ready for use but sterilized by Central Sterilization, and for catheters which remain more expensive than those we supply.

Other disposables were introduced: they are elements for our basic packs like aluminum cups, cardboard trays, swabs, etc. However, our packs cannot consist of only disposables. They can bring confusion for our staff who do not quite know, in spite of clear guidance, which items should be discarded or reused.

There still is a whole range of disposables for which no substitute is acceptable in our hospital, whatever their price, because of quality and safety considerations—e.g., the material used in hemodialysis, transplantations, protheses, and open heart surgery. In addition, a whole new era is beginning with nonwoven textiles for operating personnel uniforms and operating linens. Prices are still far too high for our use. Nevertheless, nonwoven textiles gradually are being used for drapes in septic operations. They should be used in all types of isolation units for safety reasons and to control cross-infection more efficiently.

In spite of disposables, the need for hospital processed reusable sterile supplies gradually increases. The admitted rate of increase is a yearly

10–15 %. If we consider all our hospital's sterilization facilities except those strictly devoted to surgery, daily sterilized volumes were the following in 1970: Central Sterilization, 530 ft³; peripheral inpatient wards, 408 ft³; outpatient units, 90 ft³. Therefore, an average 1030 ft³ are sterilized daily at the Hôpital Cantonal de Genève for wards. Central Sterilization itself covers 50 % of the needs. Its capacity, like other sterilization units, is used almost fully. If the gradual increase in the overall consumption of sterile supplies is considered, it appears reasonable, in spite of the share taken by disposables, to rely on a production of some 2100 ft³/day in the 1980s. This is why we plan to build a new central service department. It should not only replace the present Central Sterilization but absorb the total workload of satellite sterilization units.

The future central service department will be located at the center of the hospital complex, in the new building accommodating the additional operating suite and all intensive care units. It will be connected to the main building and to peripheral inpatient units by underground passages. It will cover 11,000 to 13,000 ft². The internal layout will meet the most drastic requirements of hospital sanitation. There will be a decontamination area, a clean work area and a sterile area. A strict one-way circulation will be established so that neither processed supplies nor personnel attached to the separate work areas can move against the flow. Automation will be maximized to compensate for labor and qualification shortages and to yield optimal quality (2, 7). The principle of parallel production lines will be adopted, their origin being the soiled area. Supplies will reach the central service department from every source in the hospital in a decontaminated condition as previously explained. They will be cleaned in automatic washing tunnels (Figure 6). Conveyors will move them to a buffer area operated as reserve storage before packaging. Packs made up of both reusable and disposable items will be line processed, deposited in bins, and stored in an automatic multilevel system feeding into the sterilizers. These sterilizers, with fully automatic operation and monitoring, will provide quick sterilization, probably according to a single program at 137 C. Such units will remain in operation day and night, on holidays as well as on workdays, without human intervention, and will provide top quality sterilization at the lowest cost. In the sterile area, packs will be initially stored in their bins, in an automatic system which is a replica of the system in the clean work area, then in a sterile storage "Compactus". Inventory management and order processing will be computer controlled. Deliveries will still be performed with trolleys, since the layout of the hospital buildings cannot be changed.

The central service department will therefore provide individual packs, treatment trays, sterile linen, etc., to all nursing, medical and para-medical units which use sterile supplies and all outpatient units and operating suites. Operating suites will only sterilize operating instru-

Figure 6 Automatic washing tunnel Hildebrand (Central Sterilization of the Hôpital Cantonal de Lausanne).

ments. We believe that the central service department should be run by a head nurse and not by a pharmacist or a technician (7). A nurse is closer to the problems of the users and therefore in a better position to understand and solve them.

As can be predicted, industry will move ahead in the field of sterile supply offering more disposables on the market. This trend is favorable to the hospital inasmuch as it brings relief from ancillary chores, and it is undoubtedly irreversible. We still do not know what its scope will be in coming years. This is why we have annexed to our projected central service department a medical store as roomy as the sterilization area itself. The medical store will be located immediately below the central service department and will house:

1. Disposable care supplies shipped by industry as sterile or nonsterile.
2. Textiles shipped by industry as sterile or nonsterile (swabs, compresses, nonwoven disposable linen, etc.).
3. Reusable care supplies (turnover inventory, wartime reserve).
4. Sanitation and miscellaneous items.
5. Packaging supplies for the sterilization unit (paper, bags, plastic sheathing).

This store will provision the central service department with pack contents and wrapping as needed. In addition, all sterile supplies coming from the medical store will be distributed under the exclusive care and responsibility of the central service department. This is another reason we insist on its management by a head nurse directly responsible to the nursing care department (11).

As there is presently no way to predict with sufficient accuracy the future extent of sterile or nonsterile disposables that industry can provide, we have assumed a close interdependence between the Central Service and the medical store in order to obtain the flexibility required to accommodate future needs. Moreover, we shall provide sufficient capacity to process enough reusables to supply the whole hospital in the event of a severe crisis.

With this functional setup we hope to meet present and future hospital sanitation requirements. The introduction of disposables enabled us to compensate for certain shortcomings of our present Central or satellite sterilization. Such relief was brought by surgical gloves, syringes and needles with their advantages of care technology, safety, and price. In the meantime, as the range of industrial disposables broadens, we must keep under constant review the whole matter of medical disposable procurement. The economic calculation shown previously is no longer sufficient upon which to base all possible decisions and moves. Under these conditions, industry appears as a subcontractor whose potential is hardly exploited. It brings hospitals the advantage of its production methods and means, thereby freeing hospital personnel badly needed for tasks more closely related to patient care. The dialogue initiated between hospitals and industry should be intensified. A rich potential market is open to industry. Hospitals, however, will require at the lowest price a high level of service and safety which will reflect their own vital requisites. Industry, influenced by economic efficiency, can be interested only in large orders and big production batches. The normalization of patient care technology and the consequent standardization of equipments will be the only way to broaden the market and to get industry sufficiently interested in producing high quality goods at prices commensurate with hospital budgets. This financial aspect, with environment concerns, will be the deciding factors in the reusable versus disposable issue.

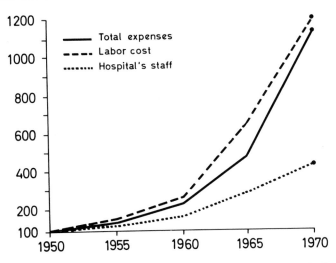

Figure 7   Hospital's operating expenses index (period 1950–1970).

If we look at hospital expenditures in Switzerland over the past 20 years, we see they are constantly rising: 1950, 250 million francs; 1960, 545 million francs; 1970, 2000 million francs. From 1950 to 1970 hospital expenditures multiplied by a factor of 8, in absolute figures, for the whole of Switzerland. For the Hôpital Cantonal de Genève this factor was not 8 but 10.4 (Figure 7). Labor ranks first, taking three-quarters of the hospital budget. Disposables may partly solve the problem of manpower shortage as well as rocketing expenditures if we consider the Central Service Department as an autarchic production unit.

The cost of health care in Switzerland is estimated as twice the amount of hospital expenditures. In 1970 it reached the 4 billion francs mark. Statisticians believe that the average annual increase over the past two decades will be maintained, if not accelerated, in the 1970s. Consequently, in 1980, the cost of health will be about 16 billion francs.

In parallel, the gross national product rises, but at a slower pace. In 1970 in Switzerland, 4 % of GNP was devoted to public health. Calculations show that in 1980 this percentage should rise to about 8 %. A desirable ceiling is some 10–12 % of GNP. It might well be reached as early as 1985. This probability underlines the significance of decisions to be made in coming years. They will affect, at large, all care techniques and related equipments. The degree of freedom for hospital executives will keep shrinking, especially with added environmental problems. The destruction of disposables is becoming a problem as it contributes, to a certain extent, to air and water pollution. New techniques, and mostly new raw materials, will have to be developed to remedy this drawback and to avoid substituting chemical pollution to hospital bacterial pollution.

References

1. Bassen, J. L. 1970. Quality control and sterile products. Hospitals J.A.H.A. **44**: 81–82.

2. Benedickter, Helen. 1969. Central service modernized. Hospitals J.A.H.A. **43**: 99–101.

3. Daley, D., K. Kereluk, and R. S. Lloyd. 1971. Microbiological aspects of the hospital environment: Bacteriological effectiveness of a utensil washer-sanitizer. Health Lab. Sci. **8**(1): 21–28.

4. Ducel, G., E. Snincak-Knudtzon, and D. Roussianos. 1972. Efficacité de la décontamination obtenue dans un lave-vases. VESKA. No. 3, pp. 145–147.

5. Francis, A. E. 1961. The use of a pasteurizing water bath for disinfection of cystoscopes. The Journal of Urology. **86**(5): 679–682.

6. Greif, E. E., H. L. Flack, and G. E. Downs. 1969. Quality control procedures for packaging sterile supplies. Hospital Pharmacy. **4**(1): 4–8.

7. Harrison, W. L., and C. C. Pulliam. 1969. Central service supply: A management survey. Hospitals J.A.H.A. **43**: 85–92.

8. Jenkins, J. R. E., and W. M. Edgar. 1964. Sterilization of anaesthetic equipment. Anaesthesia. **9**(2): 177–190.

9. Roberts, F. J., W. H. Cockcroft, and H. E. Johnson. 1969. A hot water disinfection method of inhalation therapy equipment. Can. Med. Ass. J. **101**(7): 30–32.

10. Scheidegger, C. 1970. Organisation et fonctionnement d'une Stérilisation Centrale. VESKA. No. 7, pp. 380–384.

11. Smith, Phyllis. 1969. Training of C.S. technicians. Hospital Topics. Feb.: 95–97.

12. Spaulding, E. H. 1968. Chemical disinfection of medical and surgical materials. pp. 517–531. In C. A. Laurence and S. S. Block [Eds.], *Disinfection, sterilisation and preservation*. Lea and Febiger. Philadelphia.

13. Vahlne, G. Report on the Bacterio-Hygienic Testing of the Bedpan Washer Minispolo.

22

The Hospital (Disposable) Environment

WILLSON J. FAHLBERG, PH.D.

Memorial Hospital System
Houston, Texas

> *Change is inevitable. In a progressive country,*
> *change is constant.* (B. DISRAELI, 1867)

INTRODUCTION

THE FIRST hospital in the Americas was established by Hernando Cortés in Mexico City only 32 years after Columbus discovered America. Founded as the Immaculate Conception Hospital, it is still operating as the Hospital of Jesus of Nazareth. Early hospitals were dirty, dark, dank, and crowded. Diseases were readily transmissible from one patient to another, and because of lack of knowledge about contagious illnesses they were known as charnel, or death, houses.

The understanding of the infectious nature of many diseases in the nineteenth century brought about a revolution in institutional care. Cleanliness and sterility were related to antisepsis, and hospitals instituted appropriate measures to restrict the spread of diseases. Public confidence in organized health care was increased because of the significant decrease in institutional deaths and the availability of suitably trained hospital personnel and physicians. The evolution from wards to private rooms and from charity to fee-for-service concepts resulted in society's acceptance of standardized methods of patient management. Thus, in the twentieth century with its focus upon rights of the individual, including recently equal access to health care, the role of health care institutions has been emphasized. The public today demands that hospitals furnish the best possible environment for their care. The rising bed costs reflect demands for better equipment, more sophistication in health delivery, ideal surroundings, and adequate remumeration for personnel. These factors have required the health industry to reexamine its operations and to reevaluate its methods. New concepts beyond traditional principles have emerged.

Western society has been a productive materialistic society. We have long regarded the fruits of our industry as solid, substantial, and enduring. However, the availability of vast resources, modern chemistry, automation, and industrial knowledge have advanced the principle that the replacement of certain items after a single usage might be more economical than their reclamation (5). The "Kleenex" principle introduced in the 1930s is still evolving, and hospitals have become fully aware of it for less than a score of years. Health expenditures in the United States for disposables have risen from less than $20 million in 1955 to more than $300 million for 1971. During the same period of time, the total sales of all medical supplies and equipment rose from $980 million to $3.1 billion with projections of $5.1 billion by 1973 and $8.4 billion by 1978 (Figure 1). It is estimated that by 1973 single-use items will represent 9.3 % of this total with a value of $500 million and by 1978, 10.5 % or almost $900 million (2).

There are presently in excess of 400 different single-use items available for the average hospital. Figure 2 illustrates the broad range of products. This disposable environment will be examined critically from the standpoint of medical advances, patient protection and safety, convenience, economics, and other important facets. The classes of plastics and the current sterilization procedures will be discussed. The different products —their appropriateness and suitability as related to hospitals—will be presented. Criteria for selection and recommendations for institutional standardization will be outlined. Finally, the factors involved in disposal of the plastics will be considered.

PROPERTIES

The properties of plastics are dependent upon their chemical compositions, molecular size, and physical structure. The principal plastics employed in the manufacture of disposable items for hospital use are polyolefins, polystyrenes, and polyvinylchloride. Minor chemical substitutions in their basic structures may bring about significant variations in the physical characteristics of the final product. Their most important features include inertness, relative cheapness due to inexpensive raw materials, low cost production, and finally the ease with which they can be molded into quality reproducible articles. Their variety of physical

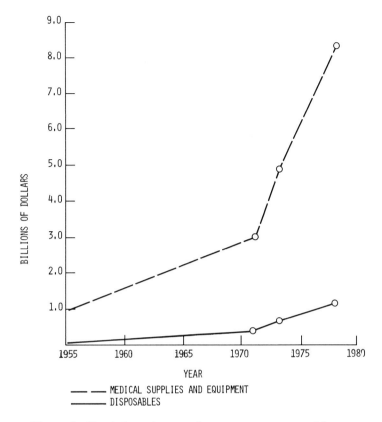

Figure 1 Hospital supply expenditures: past, present, and future.

and chemical properties has enabled them successfully to compete with stone, wood, glass, paper, etc. It also has posed problems relative to their ultimate disposal that will be discussed later.

PACKAGING AND STERILIZATION

Many prepackaged sterile items are sold to hospitals on the basis of the integrity of the manufacturer. Present federal legislation fails to provide a standardized code to guide the producers of disposable items. The Food and Drug Administration (FDA) has the responsibility for assuring consumers that the product is safe and will remain so if stored under clearly defined conditions and used in an appropriate fashion. Presently, the major burden rests with the manufacturer to develop new and better devices and to make certain that they are safe for the patient

402

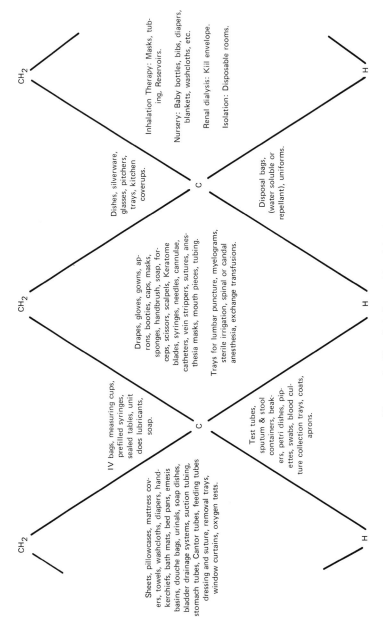

CH$_2$

CH$_2$

CH$_2$

C

C

H

H

H

Sheets, pillowcases, mattress covers, towels, washcloths, diapers, handkerchiefs, bath mats, bed pans, emesis basins, douche bags, urinals, soap dishes, bladder drainage systems, suction tubing, stomach tubes, Cantor tubes, feeding tubes dressing and suture, removal trays, window curtains, oxygen tests.

IV bags, measuring cups, prefilled syringes, sealed tables, unit does lubricants, soap.

Dishes, silverware, glasses, pitchers, trays, kitchen coverups.

Inhalation Therapy: Masks, tubing. Reservoirs.

Nursery: Baby bottles, bibs, diapers, blankets, washcloths, etc.

Renal dialysis: Kiil envelope.

Isolation: Disposable rooms.

Drapes, gloves, gowns, aprons, booties, caps, masks, sponges, handbrush, soap, forceps, scissors, scalpels, Keratome blades, syringes, needles, cannulae, catheters, vein strippers, sutures, anesthesia masks, mouth pieces, tubing.

Trays for lumbar puncture, myelograms, sterile irrigation, spinal or candal anesthesia, exchange transfusions.

Test tubes, sputum & stool containers, beakers, petri dishes, pipettes, swabs, blood culture collection trays, coats, aprons.

Disposal bags, (water soluble or repellant), uniforms.

Figure 2 Hospital disposables (plastic).

and that they are produced, packaged, and sterilized under optimum conditions with suitable quality control measures. If meaningful standards are to become a reality, the consumer, hospital, physician, manufacturer, and FDA must work together.

The producer must determine first the need for a particular item based upon a survey of the field and a careful examination of present devices to have assurance that the new product is desirable and that it will provide sufficient benefits to warrant its use. He must consider which of the different plastics available is best suited from both a health and economic standpoint. Although no specific guidelines are presently available, he should establish acceptable limits of particulate and microbial contaminants in the production areas and on the finished products prior to sterilization and sale.

All disposables must be packaged, and the package is an integral part of the disposable concept. The prime factors in determining the type of packaging are performance and cost (10). The manufacturer must select material with sufficient strength so that it will not tear too readily. Its porosity, pH, lift (surface strength), water repellance or resistance, and esthetics require attention. The sealant for disposables should be peelable but nonresealable. It may be applied cold or be a thermoplastic heat seal. The packaging machines are generally wheel, rotary action, or a combination of both. Certain items such as surgical gloves, catheter, and spinal anesthesis trays should have a double barrier in order to accommodate the procedures commonly employed in using them.

Sterility test procedures should be established for specific categories of disposables rather than relying on conventional drug sterility tests outlined in the *U.S. Pharmacopeia* (15, 34). Sterilization today has become a complex science. Personnel need to know:

1. What is the material?
2. What method of sterilization is compatible with it?
3. Are there alternative sterilizing methods?
4. Can the material withstand heat?
5. Has it been previously sterilized by irradiation?
6. What is the correct exposure time?
7. Is the package compatible with the method of sterilizing?
8. Must the item be aerated and, if so, under what conditions?
9. If the device is hollow, must this portion be moist or dry?

There are five common methods for sterilizing medical supplies: dry heat, moist heat, ionizing radiation, gases, and liquids with "cidal" activity toward microbial life and filtration. Plastic disposables are most commonly sterilized by gamma radiation, autoclaving, and ethylene oxide. The individuals responsible for sterilizing the plastics should have available microbial death rate curves which describe the D value concept and the probabilities for survivors in the sterilizing process. Unfortunately, adequate data are available only for ionizing radiation and moist and dry heat, but not for gaseous chemicals (7).

Each manufacturer should establish an ongoing quality control program. The usual procedure has been to determine the sterility of a representative sample of each lot. This technique has been adequate for steam sterilizing because it is efficient and is probably acceptable for gamma radiation. However, in dealing with ethylene oxide and other—either liquid or gaseous—agents, a low level of survivors may exist. Valid testing methods involve the use of probability tables. It is necessary to know the level at which the material may be contaminated in order properly to determine the number of samples required to give assurance of sterility. Indeed, it may become desirable to introduce biological indicators into the products prior to sterilizing in order to give the probability tables more statistical significance. The importance of the original bacterial burden introduced during manufacture and the type of packaging assume a major role in quality control (27).

HOSPITAL REQUIREMENTS

The decision to purchase disposable products for hospital use should be vested in a product standardization committee. This advisory body would include members of the medical and nursing staff, purchasing or materials management (20), central service (6, 34), pharmacy, housekeeping, and other appropriate departments (14). Their guide lines for the approval of any product should include the following criteria:

1. Will the product perform its function as well or better than the present one?
2. Will it cause new complications?
3. Will it be acceptable to the patient?
4. Will it reduce cross infection rates?
5. Will its employment permit improvements in existing techniques?
6. Can it be stored or handled more readily?
7. Will it permit standardization of acceptable procedures?
8. Is its sterility assured?

9. Does a careful comprehensive cost accounting give assurance of a greater economy (35)?

It is not practical for hospitals to run sterility controls on commercially purchased disposable products but they must remember that they share equal liability with the supplier (14, 7). Hospitals should deal only with ethical manufacturers of known integrity. Their quality control program must include careful examination of all new shipments to guarantee that they have been handled properly and stored according to the manufacturers' recommendations and that careful instruction has been given to the personnel using the product to insure that proper procedure is employed (4).

A few producers of disposable materials proclaim that their products are of such high quality that they can be reused. This is a fallacy since the item is then no longer a disposable one. Generally speaking, reprocessing disposables may create a major liability for the institution. Many of the thermoplastics originally sterilized by gamma irradiation become softened by boiling or autoclaving. Similarly, if they are irradiated a second time, many plastics are mechanically degraded and become brittle. Resterilization by ethylene oxide of some gamma-ray sterilized plastics leads to the formation of ethylene chlorohydrin which can give rise to inflammation, tissue necrosis, burns, or hemolysis of red blood cells (17, 19, 14). Litigation involving patients with hospital-acquired infections in which reprocessed disposables become a part of the issue can result in the hospital finding itself in an indefensible position. The FDA is expected to take a strong stand on this issue shortly.

DISPOSABLE PRODUCTS

Plastic disposables may be divided into two general classes: nonwoven fabrics and cast or molded articles. Disposable fabrics, according to Dr R. E. Stanley of the University of South Carolina, pose a greater threat to the textile industry than do low cost imports (15). In 1958 the health care services accounted for less than $4 million in expenditures for disposable soft goods. Last year the total was $75 million. One important reason for growth is the broad range of products available and the general public acceptance. Articles in common use today include surgical drapes, gowns, gloves, shoe coverings, caps, aprons, smocks, lab coats, patient gowns, incontinent pads, drapes, laundry bags, towels, wash cloths, bath mats, diapers, etc. While single-use sheets, pillow cases, blankets, mattress covers, and bed spreads are available, most hospitals still use conventional woven textiles (30, 8, 22).

Disposable soft goods are textile-like products intended for either one-time or limited use. Most are made from nonwoven fabrics that are sturdier than paper but less costly than cloth. Some are combinations of materials such as papers, pulps, fibers, films, foams, and woven fabrics. Because they are engineered, they can be made in many textures and forms that cannot be duplicated in woven materials. Among the types available today are:

1. Drylaid rayon staple which is viscose bonded.
2. Wet-laid rayon staple and wood pulp blend that may be either all cellulosic or print-bonded with a synthetic resin.
3. Drylaid staple rayon staple with nylon or polyester fibers bonded with synthetic resin.
4. Any of the preceding three which is laminated with a polythene film for extra protection and to achieve waterproofing.
5. Polythene films are impervious to air and water and are used largely for surgical gloves.

The bonded-fiber fabrics of rayon staple are ideal for surgeon, patient, and infant gowns. Because they can absorb moisture and have good electric conductivity, they rarely develop electrostatic charges. Protection from staining may be achieved by bonding with a polythene film (33).

Certain primary considerations must be understood by hospitals prior to a general introduction of nonwoven fabrics (3). Hospitals should determine, first, if the article satisfies the specific need; second, if it is acceptable to the users; and third, if it is cheaper than the cost of laundering the corresponding durable (1). If the cost is not lower, does it have enough other significant advantages to warrant its introduction? Institutions should be aware of certain disadvantages in that the disposable fabrics tend to tear more easily. Nurses and service personnel will have to handle them more carefully. The incorporation of a polythene film may restrict normal heat exchange between the patient and his environment.

Laundering is a labor-intensive activity and, thus, rising payroll costs are an important consideration (18). Hospitals with existing laundry facilities must determine to what degree a change to nonwoven soft goods will affect the cost of their present operation (29). A partial switch, which may appear the most logical, can result in an increase in the cost of washing the cotton or other reusables that the institution elects to retain. This would arise because the marginal costs of laundering increase faster than the marginal savings in using disposables.

Molded or injected disposable articles may be hard or soft, depending upon their individual requirements. A general idea of the wide variety available is outlined in Figure 2. Some institutions, such as the Macon (Georgia) Hospital, have instituted a total system of disposables. They claim to have achieved cost control of patient supplies, thus recovering about $84,000 per year (26). However, most hospitals have selectively changed over to disposables. Certain items such as syringes, catheters, dressing trays, OR packs (31), specimen bottles, stomach and oxygen catheters, oxygen masks, etc., are in common usage in many hospitals. Other products like disposable thermometers, Kiil envelopes for artificial kidneys, vein strippers, myelogram, caudal anesthesia and exchange transfusion tray kits, forceps and anesthesia tubing and bags have a more limited appeal (11, 28). A survey in Canada of 260 hospitals revealed that there were no major differences in usage per bed of disposables among large, medium, and small institutions. Chief considerations in selecting disposables were their cost, storage space needed, and disposal (23). The Action survey in London disclosed that a substantial amount of nursing time was saved each week by the use of disposables. The survey's figures suggested savings of approximately 50 hr of nursing time per year per bed. Disposable linens, dishes, and cutlery were included in the initial study, but because they were uneconomical in this trial, the data were not included in the conclusions (12).

Factors of economics as well as public and hospital personnel acceptance of disposable plastic dinnerware have not been resolved. Four choices in the selection of dinnerware are currently available to dietary personnel: paper goods, plastics, china, and a combination of the preceding three. Paper plates and cups have primarily been used for patients in isolation or in cases of emergency. They are available in a limited range of sizes and designs. With the advent of plastics, disposable wares are now made of paper and plastic-coated, plasticized, or plastic-laminated materials. They may be composed entirely of plastic foam, polystyrene, high impact polystyrene, polyethylene, or polypropylene. This type of dinnerware may withstand temperature ranges of 40–180 F, it is not affected by the acid or base content of food or by fatty foods. Disposable dishes may save money through the reduced expense of cleaning, dishwashing, and transportation. They can be stored without danger of bacterial contamination for prolonged periods of time and they reduce the possibility of cross infection. A wide selection of sizes and shapes is available, and the noise of handling them is sharply reduced when compared with chinaware (25). Disadvantages include the need for greater storage space, disposal problems, and lack of general patient acceptance of certain items. It has been difficult to obtain comparative cost figures, but there is some suggestion that disposable dinnerware is more economical (32, 24). Combinations of disposable and permanent dinnerware appear to offer dietary departments the greatest opportunity to meet the wide variety of demands required of them.

DISPOSAL

Disposables may be a boon to the patient, the physician, the nursing staff, central supply, and administration, but they are a bane to purchasing because of logistics and to building services who have the responsibility for disposing of them. The latter must arrange for their safe collection and transportation and then decide upon the best acceptable method for disposal processing.

Theoretically, there are many methods of disposing of plastics. Recycling might be an ideal procedure, but the present abundance of raw materials and the cheapness of the finished product must be weighed against the economics of collection, decontamination, and resterilization. Water-soluble plastics, such as the present laundry bags, might have limited value. However, much of the current usage of plastics is related to water vehicle contact, and large volume disposal of such materials would raise the question of water pollution (29). Destruction or degradation by irradiation is possible, but no large-scale operations have demonstrated its effectiveness. Present means of chemical destruction require sophisticated techniques and result in undesirable end products.

Currently, the three most acceptable methods of disposal are pulping, compacting, and incineration. The use of wet grinding and disposal into the sanitary sewer system are presently being conducted by a number of institutions. Water must be continuously fed with the plastics, and the range of disposable materials include syringes, needles, medicine cups, disposable razors and blades, cannulas, vials, and similar products. There are, however, severe limitations with the system:

1. In operation it generates an aerosol which excludes grinding infected materials.
2. It requires frequent maintenance in sharpening the cutting surfaces.

3. The grinders are noisy and vibrate.
4. The additional amount of inert material added to the sewage poses a problem for the processing plant.
5. Many urban communities recycle their water, and contamination by infectious waste or chemicals may pose a problem.
6. In many communities, pulping and disposing of large amounts of inorganics are against the law (36).

Closed-system pulping is a procedure where the waste is first ground to a pulp with water and then transferred to a chamber for water extraction, with the latter being returned to the grinding section of the unit. This process has several drawbacks in that the grinders and extractors are usually distal to each other, requiring some method of transporting liquid pulp and returning water and, further, they cannot handle many materials (13).

Compactors represent an inexpensive, single method of waste processing. They will accept any material, and the volume reduction is dependent upon the materials being compacted, but it generally ranges between a 4:1 to 6:1 ratio. The machines require little maintenance and have a reasonably long life expectancy. The wired, plastic encapsulated bales should be placed in a controlled landfill operation. Although some biodegradation has been observed, it has generally been related to an antioxidant, a stabilizer, or a plasticizer incorporated in the plastic. (The author is not aware of any published articles demonstrating the importance of biological factors in the ultimate degradation of plastics in common usage today.) Certain problems are also associated with this method:

1. Material must be collected and stored in an area adjacent to the compactor.
2. Because a portion of the material to be compacted may be infected, the institutional engineers must consider methods of odor control and sanitation of area (13).
3. Needles, syringes, disposable surgical instruments, and other items perforate the plastic envelope enclosing the bale and become infectious hazards to the personnel handling them.
4. Some county codes in the United States would not permit the transport of this potentially infectious material through city streets or dumping it at a municipal landfill operation (29).
5. Most bales contain plastics plus other hospital refuse, a portion of which may be biodegradable. Thus, the bale does not represent a

stable inert block, and its volume may shrink in time. There have been suggestions that chemicals could be added to the bale to inhibit bacterial decomposition, but presently no practical solution has been advanced (16).

Incineration probably represents the best current method for destroying waste plastic articles (9). Some plastics ignite explosively and burn intensely, others burn very slowly, some will not support combustion, and still others have been specially treated to resist heat and flame (13). This procedure provides for the greatest reduction in volume and weight. Most hospital administrators and engineers are familiar with incinerator operations. If properly managed, they eliminate the need for concern for environmental contamination by infectious agents. With the present technology they appear to offer the best solution for coping with ever-increasing volumes of plastic waste.

Present hospital incinerators generally will not meet federal pollution standards because of the volumes of plastic they are required to process and the temperatures at which they normally operate. Present waste levels for a small hospital (40–60 beds) require an incinerator capable of processing 500 lb of waste per hr; a medium hospital (100–200 beds) would need a unit able to handle 1000 lb/hr; and a large hospital (200 beds +) would require a plant able to handle amounts of 3000 lb/hr or more, depending upon size and the degree of commitment to disposables (13). The burning of plastics in the average incinerator at 2000 F results in the liberation of large amounts of hydrocarbons. Polyvinylchloride will further corrode the stack because when it is burned hydrochloric acid is formed. A similar problem is encountered with the fluorine-containing polymers (polytetrafluoroethylene) which liberate hydrogen fluoride (9). If plastics are incinerated at 2800 F with presence of excess oxygen, carbon dioxide and water are the chief end products. Further, if the stack is tall enough, the amount of air pollution is not significant. It has been suggested that the residue from incineration could be incorporated into an aggregate for concrete, but with the exception of a few, large urban medical centers, the costs for transporting, grinding, and mixing such materials would be prohibitive.

Each institution must address itself to the problem of solid waste disposal. Older hospitals may be forced to rely upon a single disposal system, while newer ones may take advantage of a combination. Hospitals in the planning state should consider a systems approach based upon the diversity of materials to be collected, stored, handled and disposed of. They must recognize the present state of the art, but build in the potential to respond to tomorrow's needs.

SUMMARY

The role of plastics in the modern hospital has been examined. Advantages and disadvantages of the three major chemical types available have been considered. Methods of packaging and sterilizing have been discussed. The problems inherent in determining whether complete sterilization with gases and liquids has been achieved and also in determining certain recommended testing procedures have been described. A description of the wide variety of plastic articles available for hospital use and the different services involved has been outlined. An acceptable procedure for informed decision making in the selection and standardization of disposables has been presented. Comparisons of woven and nonwoven fabrics and disposable and permanent dinnerware have been made. The different methods of safe disposal of used plastics have been discussed and related to institutional size and federal, state, or local codes.

References

1. Armstrong, K. N. 1971. Long-range planning. Brit. Hosp. J. Soc. Serv. Rev. Nov. 20: 2428–2429.
2. Automated equipment holds spotlight at British show. 1970. Mod. Hos. **115**: 52.
3. Baron, H. von. 1970. Soziale Medizin und Hygiene. Munch. Med. Wochenschr. **36**: 1619–1622.
4. Bassen, Jonas, L. 1970. Quality control and sterile products. Hospitals. **44**: 81–82.
5. Bayer, L. W. 1971. The quality of cleanness. Br. Med. J. Nov. 20: 2425.
6. Brown, Marjorie. 1969. Economy and efficiency—the service component of CSR. Canad. Hosp. **46**: 57.
7. Bruch, Carl W. 1971. Are your disposables safe? Hospitals. **45**: 138–146.
8. Buston, Mona N. 1971. The world of disposables. Exec. Housekeeper. **18**: 20–21.
9. Callely, A. G., and C. F. Forster. 1971. Plastic waste and its disposal. Brit. Hosp. J. Soc. Serv. Rev. Nov. 20: 2434.
10. Cramer, W. M. 1970. Packaging characteristics of disposables. Hosp. Progr. **51**: 32–48.
11. Dickinson, K. M. 1971. Disposable vein strippers. Brit. Med. J. ii: 524.
12. Disposables. 1969. Editorial in New Zeal. Med. J. **69**: 162–163.
13. Disposing of Disposables. 1970. Hospitals. **43**: 78–82.
14. Donn, Richard. 1972. Responsibility for sterility isn't disposable. Hospitals. **46**: 122–124.

15. Edwards, Charles C. 1971. Position of medical devices in the health field. Med. Res. Engin. Oct.–Nov.: 5–7.
16. First international disposables show. 1971. Hospitals. **45**: 107–111.
17. Ginsberg, Frances, and Barbara Clarke. 1971. Errors in handling can make sterile disposables unsafe. Mod. Hosp. Oct.: 156–158.
18. Greene, V. W. 1970. Microbiological contamination control in hospitals. Hospitals. **44**: 98–103.
19. Hastings, G. W. 1970. Disposable syringes: The dangers of reuse. Med. J. Aust. **1**: 1126.
20. Herrmann, Frederick N. 1970. Materials management. Hospitals. **44**: 117–120.
21. Hilborn, James. 1970. Throwing it away. Canad. Hosp. **47**: 78–83.
22. Hospital housekeepers discuss disposables. Symposium. Exec. Housekeeper. **18**: 56–58.
23. How do hospitals like disposables? 1971. Hosp. Adm. Can. Feb.: 51–52.
24. Isaacman, Ted. 1968. Wesley saves money by "throwing away meals." Mod. Hosp. **110**: 106–107.
25. Jernigan, Anna Katherine. 1970. Disposables in food service. Hospitals. **44**: 80–81.
26. King, Damon D. 1971. A total system of disposables. Hospitals. **45**: 84–89.
27. Leininger, Harold V. 1970. Sterility testing of sterile disposable devices and drugs at the National Center for Microbiological Analysis. Hospital Care. **2**: 20–33.
28. Mrava, Gene L., David C. Weber, Tadamasa Kon, Paul Lips, Yukihiko Nose. 1970. The disposable Kiil Envelope. Med. Res. Engin. **9**: 23–26.
29. See new solutions to disposal problem. 1970. Mod. Hosp. **115**: 148–152.
30. Small, R. E. 1971. Nonwoven disposables . . . Past, present and future. Exec. Housekeeper. **18**: 31–39.
31. Spivack, Julius, and David S. Watt. 1970. Disposable OR Packs. Hospitals. **44**: 105–114.
32. Staniland, G. A. B. 1970. Hospital milk kitchen. Lancet. **1**: 194.
33. Thomas, H. A. 1970. Disposable protective garments. Soc. Med. **63**: 60–62.
34. Toward better disposables. 1972. Hospitals. **46**: 92–93.
35. Vallas, Alex J. 1970. Standards for judging disposables include labor savings, improved care. Mod. Hosp. **114**: 74.
36. Wet grinding of disposables. 1970. Hospitals. **44**: 7–75.

INDEX